LIFE OF FREDERICK
COURTENAY SELOUS, D.S.O.

FREDERICK COURTENAY SELOUS, D.S.O.,

Captain 25th ROYAL FUSILIERS.

Killed in Action, January 4th, 1917.

LIFE OF FREDERICK COURTENAY SELOUS, D.S.O.

CAPT. 25TH ROYAL FUSILIERS

BY

J. G. MILLAIS, F.Z.S.

Author of
"Rhododendrons," "The Mammals of Great Britain and Ireland,"
"The Wild Fowler in Scotland," "Newfoundland and its Untrodden Ways,"
"The Natural History of the British Surface-Feeding Ducks,"
"British Diving Ducks," etc.

WITH 14 FULL-PAGE ILLUSTRATIONS BY THE AUTHOR
AND 2 PORTRAITS

❧Juniper Grove❧

All images and text within this book have been
faithfully reproduced from those of the 1919
Longmans, Green and Co. edition.

Though Millais used the spelling *Courtenay*,
the more common spelling of Selous'
middle name was *Courteney*.

❧Juniper Grove❧
ISBN 978-1-60355-066-6
©2007 Juniper Grove

PREFACE

IN preparing the life of my friend, Fred Selous, I have to thank his brother Edmund, and his sister Mrs. Jones (Ann Selous) for contributions regarding his parents and early life. I am also indebted to his friends, Sir Alfred Pease, Captain P. B. Vanderbyl and Mr. Heatley Noble for certain notes with regard to short expeditions made in his company. Mr. Abel Chapman, a life-long friend, has also assisted me with numerous letters which are of interest. But most of all have I to thank Mrs. Selous, who from the first has given me every assistance in furnishing details of her husband's adventurous life, and allowed me to read and extract from the numerous letters he wrote to different members of his family during a considerable part of his life. Selous had many friends, but none evinced a more keen understanding of his life and work than Colonel Theodore Roosevelt, Ex-President of the United States, and I feel grateful to him for the attention he has given to the following pages and the use he has allowed me to make of his numerous letters.

The Author has also to thank Messrs. Macmillan and Co. and Messrs. Rowland Ward and Co. for the use they allowed him to make of two of Selous' works, namely, *A Hunter's Wanderings* and *Travel and Adventure in S.E. Africa*. He is much indebted to their kindness in this matter, since they give in the hunter's own words accurate details of his life.

J. G. MILLAIS,

COMPTON'S BROW, HORSHAM.

CONTENTS

LIST OF ILLUSTRATIONS

THE LIFE OF
FREDERICK COURTENAY
SELOUS, D.S.O.

CHAPTER I

1851–1865

MEN of all ages are apt to set up for themselves heroes. It is their instinct to worship exceptional force of character and to follow a leader ; but as we survey the tempest of human suffering we are now more apt to wonder if there are any great men left in the world and think that perhaps, after all, we have made a mistake in putting on pedestals the heroes of the past; for tried in the light of the present day they would, perchance, not have proved heroes at all. The cynic may even sneer at this lovable trait in human nature and affect to place all men in a commonplace ratio, but then it is easier to be a cynic than a man of faith. Nevertheless, Humanity must have something to trust, to acclaim and admire, and so millions of all ages cling to their worship of the hero, even though he may wear top hat and trousers. There will always be great men amongst the mass of pygmies, though many say the age of hero-worship has gone—doubtless swamped in the scale of colossal events. Still, if the great men of the past were not as large as they seemed, the little men of to-day may be greater, in spite of the fact that the chief actors in the modern drama of life are nations and not individuals.

But what constitutes a great man will ever be the result

B

of individual opinion. In Russia to-day millions, perhaps, think Lenin and Trotsky are demi-gods, whilst an equal number call them traitors and would prefer to see them hanged. To us, perhaps, the belief that Right will triumph over wrong, and the man who in simple faith gives up all that is sweet and pleasant to serve his country in the most fearful strife the world has ever seen, is the embodiment of heroism. There are tens of thousands of men who have done the same as Frederick Selous and none are less heroes than he ; each and all of them are as much entitled to their pedestal of fame, although they may not have exhibited the mind that influences for years in many lands. They have all counted the cost and endured the sacrifice, and they do not talk about their inner thoughts. This, to our minds, is true heroism.

So in studying the life of one Englishman, great in the sense that everything he did was big, honourable, clever, and brave, we shall realize how character is formed in the iron mill of experience, how a man unhelped by wealth or social advantages and gifted only with exceptional talents in a line, mainly unprofitable in a worldly sense, came to win through the difficulties and dangers of a more than usually strenuous life and reach the haven of completed work. Selous was a type of Englishman of which we are justly proud. His very independence of character and impatience of restraint when once he knew a thing was right was perhaps his greatest asset. He knew what he wanted to do and did it even if it resulted, as it did on one occasion, in his personal unpopularity. It was this fearless striving towards the Light and constant love of what was beautiful in Nature, that forced him into Literature, so that others might see with his eyes the things that he thought were best. And thus he rose and became a type and an influence in our national life, and in time swayed the lives of others.

The Selous family were originally French Huguenots, who settled in Jersey after the revocation of the Edict of Nantes. Annoyance at being turned out of France caused Gideon Slous to omit the " e " from the surname, but later this was re-adopted by his son Frederick Lokes Selous, father of Frederick Courtenay. Of the character of his parents and uncles Edmund Selous kindly sends me the following notes :—

" . . . I can only say generally, that my father was a man of high and varied talents and very high character, of French, or at any rate, Jersey descent, and that he started with nothing in life, and with only such education (beyond what he owed to his mother, an uncommon woman, who probably did better for him) as an ordinary private school had afforded, equipped himself with French and Italian in perfection, entered the Stock Exchange at an early age, had a successful career there, and rose to be Chairman of its Committee. He was a fine whist and chess player (more especially, or more notedly, the latter) and was reputed, I believe, at one time, to be the best amateur player of the clarionet. Music was his constant and greatest delight, but his pen was also an instrument which (though he sought no public beyond his friends) he often used very entertainingly. He was a brilliant—often a witty—talker, with a distinction of manner, more French- than English-seeming in its light debonairness, and his individualities, traits, foibles, etc., were so many and vivid, that to write either of him or of Dr. Johnson with scanted pen, would be much the same thing. My two uncles, the artist and dramatist, who lived next door, on each side of us, would also require portraiture for anything beyond this bare statement. Both were out-of-the-canvas-stepping personalities, carrying with them atmosphere and aroma.

" My mother was an exceptionally thoughtful and broad-minded woman—more advanced, on most subjects, than where they stand now—a vivid and vital being, of great vivacity, gladness (that never was levity) and conversational powers, with a gift for the interchange of ideas (which is not, by any means, always the same thing). She was also a poet, as her little volume of collected pieces, ' Words without Music ' (a modest title) testifies, at least to myself. She had joyous ' L'Allegro '-like country instincts, a deep inborn love of the beauties of nature (which she sketched charmingly), and great feeling for, and interest in both plant and animal *life*. I underline that word, in its last connection, because killing was quite another thing for her, and her whole soul shrank away from it. But of course, as you know, what, in root and origin, may be the same, is often differentiated in the sexes, and so inherited by each. It was, I think, undoubtedly through our mother (though he did not, personally, much resemble either parent) that my brother inherited everything that made him distinctively himself. By this I mean that though much and that the best—as, for instance, his patriotism and love of truth—may have come to him from both sides, and some from the other only, it was that one that gave to it, and the whole, its original life-shaping turn. The whole was included in the blood of the Bruces of Clackmannan, representative, I believe, of the elder branch of the family that gave Robert Bruce to the throne of Scotland, but what exact position, in our family tree, is occupied by Bruce, the Abyssinian explorer, I do not quite know. However, he must have been some sort of ancestor of my brother, and Bruce, since the intermingling, has been a family name, though not given to any of us surviving infancy, owing to an idea which had arisen, through several instances of such association, that it had become unlucky. In this regard, it has been rather the patronymic, which, from one war to another, has borne the malevolent influence. None have come back, either wounded, invalided or at all. All killed outright—but this by the way. Had it not been for my mother, therefore, my brother, in all probability, would either never, or not in any preponderating degree, have felt the ' call of the wild,' for my father not only never felt it, but never was able to comprehend the feeling. There was, in fact, nothing at all in him of what was my brother's life and being. He was, in the proper evolutionary sense of the word, essentially a civilized man and a Londoner. Sport was, for him, an unknown (and much disliked) quantity, and though taking, in an air-tight-compartment sort of way, some interest in insects, he had not much about him of the real naturalist. Those feelings (imperishably summed up by Jack London in the title of his masterpiece) which, coming out of a remote past, beckon back the only supposedly or but half-made-up civilized amongst us, from late into early conditions, were not, as I say, his heritage ; and this was equally (or even more) the case with his brothers—my two uncles—and as far as I know or have ever heard, all the precedent members of the family. I believe, therefore, that by the intervention—merciful or otherwise—of the Bruce, Sherborn, and Holgate families, between them, my brother was saved, or debarred, from going either into the Stock Exchange or one of the settled professions. Which kind of phraseology best suits the conjuncture I know not, but I think I know what my brother's own opinion would be, since it put the particular circumstances of that event of his life, in which, of all others, he would esteem himself most happy and fortunate—I mean his death—upon a footing of certainty.

" I have alluded to my brother's independence of home (or, I think, of any) influence. I look upon him as a salient illustration of Darwin's finding that the force of heredity is stronger, in the individual, than that of education and surroundings. So far back as I can remember—at least with any distinctness—he was always just himself, with a settled determination that, in its calm, unobtrusive force (giving the idea of inevitability) had in it something elemental. He may not have lisped Africa (which was far from the family thoughts) but, if not, he, at least, came so near to it, as to have made us all almost remember that he did. He seems to have brought with him into this world ' from afar,' a mind long made up as to the part he should play in it, and his career was more than half run before any circumstance admitted by him as deflective from its true course, arose. . . ."

Mrs. Jones (Ann Selous) also paints a pleasing picture of the early life of the family in their London house :—

" We lived in Gloucester Road, Regent's Park, in a house my father built for himself. At that time there were no other houses near, but all fields between his home and Primrose Hill, some way off; but this superior state of things his children never knew. Our uncles, my father's brothers, lived on either side of us. My father was vice-Chairman of the Stock Exchange for five years, and Chairman for three, until a very serious illness obliged him to resign and give up everything in the way of work. He was a fine chess player, his name is to be seen in the games amongst those of the great players of the day. He was also a very fine clarionet player, which instrument he taught himself when very young, and I well remember his beautiful tone, far beyond that of Lazarus, the chief professional player of the day, who no doubt sacrificed tone to technique. Whenever there was a speech to be made my father was equal to the occasion, having great fluency and humour and real wit. He was a delightful talker and his memory was a store-house of knowledge and recollections that he could draw upon whenever required. He was a very genial and admirable host, very high-spirited and excitable. He could never forget the Revocation of the Edict of Nantes, when the Huguenots, his forebears, were driven from France. ' They turned us out ! They turned us out ! ' he used to say to my mother, a real thought of bitterness to him. His greatest pleasure and relaxation was a walking-tour in Switzerland, a land he specially loved. He had often been there with one or other of his brothers, or with his great friend Baron Bramwell, the famous judge. These trips must have been ideal, my father and his brothers having in themselves everything that was necessary to make them gifted in all the arts, and so appreciative of nature and everything else, and with their lively sense of humour and wide interests they were able to extract the most from all they might chance upon in their travels, those being the days before tourists flooded the country and huge hotels swamped the more interesting inns. My father loved the busy life of the City, and had no country tastes such as farming or hunting, but he delighted in the life by the river—in canoeing, specially—and in a farmer's country home in the Isle of Wight, where, when we were children, we spent the summers. He was a fine swimmer and would swim out with one or other of us on his back. I well remember his energy, mental and physical, were remarkable. The loss of sight seemed only to affect his later years. His mind was clear and equal to dealing with his affairs to the last. At a very advanced age he had started tricycling and delighted in it. I think my father and my brother Fred were very dissimilar in character, interests and tastes. There was no ' call of the wild ' in my father—nor, I think, in my mother, except through her imagination. My father left a few reminiscences which were never finished, as dictation tired him—he was then over eighty and blind. They are full of interesting memories which end unfortunately when he was still very young."

" I was born," writes my father, "on the 9th of March, 1802. . . . I was a precocious child, for I was told that I knew my letters at about two years of age, and could read at three and a half and recite on a table at about four. I perfectly recollect declaiming the quarrel between Brutus and Cassius in Shakespeare's ' Julius Cæsar.' Also I remember the announcement of the death of Nelson in October, 1805, and witnessing his funeral procession in January, 1806.[1] I was perched on the shoulders of a journeyman baker named Guesnel at the corner of Poland Street, from whence I beheld the catafalque containing the remains of the illustrious Nelson, the whole affair resembling much the interment of the Duke of Wellington, which I witnessed in 1852 —forty-six years later. My brother Harry (the artist, H. C. Selous), who was thirteen months younger than I, remembers witnessing this spectacle too. . . . I can recollect weeping bitterly at hearing the first news of our great admiral's death, and the awe and wonder with which I looked upon the ceremony of his interment. . . . I was sent to school at Islington at the age of seven, and upon the master desiring me to read from a book which he gave to me he expressed himself so surprised at my reading that he told my mother he would not put me into any of the reading classes of the upper boys, as I should put them to shame.

[1] The body was sent home in a cask of brandy which was said to have been partially drunk by the sailors. This gruesome theft was known as " tapping the admiral."

I was at that time so strong and so hungry that I frequently carried some of the biggest boys round the playground (which was a large one) for an extra slice of bread and butter with which they repaid me. I was at school about a twelve-month and then came under my mother's care for instruction, and to her I owe more than I can possibly express with regard to my early education. She taught me the French language, Greek and Roman history, and the three R's—reading, writing, and arithmetic. When I was ten years, I was sent to a school called the Burlington school, where I improved my French, became a tolerable Latin scholar, and gained a smattering of mathematics. After being for two years at this academy, I was recalled to home rule and education and never had any further instruction from master or professor. At this time my brother and myself were allowed to wander about the streets uncontrolled and might have been considered as a sort of street Arabs, though we always selected our associates carefully." (Later on my father had to work very hard, very long hours, up till midnight four days in the week, but it did him no harm, and he was very strong and active. A great part of his time was occupied in reading every variety of book he could get hold of, from which he gained much general information, having an unusually good memory. Plutarch's lives were his first admired works. Pope, Addison and Johnson came next. He made the acquaintance of some of the celebrated Italian singers and learnt to speak their language fluently. All this part about the Italian singers is very interesting, and many things connected with the theatre likewise.)

" I also witnessed another performance which shocked me more than anything I ever beheld, for I was then very young. It was in 1815 or 16, I think, I happened to be rather early one day in my long walk to Great St. Helen's, which took me past St. Sepulchre's and the broad opening to the narrow streets of the Old Bailey. The sun was shining brightly across Newgate, and on chancing to look towards Ludgate Hill I saw dangling to a beam at the west side of Newgate five human beings suspended by the neck. One of them was a woman, who with a feeling for symmetry had been hung in the centre. All five had white night-caps drawn over their faces to conceal the horrible convulsions of the features. I don't know what their crimes had been, people were hanged in those savage days for stealing a shilling, or even cutting a stick from a plantation. The time appointed for cutting down the bodies had nearly arrived, and the crowd had diminished to an apathetic group principally engaged in cracking nuts and jokes, and eating brandy balls all hot ; but horror gave speed to my steps and I soon left hideous Newgate behind me. I recollect a great sensation caused by the execution of Fauntleroy for forgery." Here end these notes by my father.

" I think I remember rightly that at fourteen my father was not only making a livelihood for himself, but supporting his father and mother. He was most charitable and had the kindest heart in the world, and that high sense of honour which so distinguished his son. I think that though these few extracts from his reminiscences are not, perhaps, of importance, yet they throw some light on my father's character, and indirectly it may be on my brother's also, for certainly in strength of purpose, energy, and will to succeed, also in vigorous health and constitution, they were alike. They also had both a great facility for learning languages. We were amused to read in a book on African travel by, I think, a Portuguese, whose name for the moment I forget, that he came across the great hunter (I forget if he put it like that) Selous, ' somewhere ' in Africa, who addressed him in the French of the ' Boulevard des Italiens !' As I think this traveller was supposed to have a lively imagination, we accepted Fred's superior accent (after so many years of never speaking or hearing French) with some grains of salt. But not very many years ago at some international meeting to do with sport, at Turin or Paris, Fred representing England, he made a speech in French, on which he was much complimented, for accent, wit, and fluency alike.[1]

[1] The occasion of this speech was when the society of St. Hubert presented Selous with the medal of the " Académie des Sports," " pour services rendus à la Chasse aux grandes fauves " on July 15th, 1911.

" My mother, like my father, had a wonderful memory, and was a great reader, from childhood, her home possessing a big library. Scott was her great delight then, and indeed always, and poetry was as nectar and ambrosia to her. She had great facility in writing herself, very charmingly, both poetry and prose, all of the fantastic and imaginative order, and she had quite a gift for painting. Considering all the calls made on her time, of home and family (social, likewise), which were never neglected, it was wonderful that she could yet find time for all her writing and painting. Her perseverance and industry in the arts that she loved were really remarkable. We children greatly benefited by her love of poetry and story, for she was a true ' raconteuse ' and we drank in with delight the tales from the old mythologies of romance and adventure. She would tell us of deeds of ' derring-do ' and all that was inspiring in the way of freedom and love of country. Certainly with her, as with Sir Edward Clarke, poetry was ' a never failing source of pleasure and comfort ' to the last. (As it was also with me.) In the last year of her long life she could still repeat her poetic treasures with the greatest fire and spirit. She had a vigorous and original personality, with strong and decided views which she would express with energy. Her hands were full of character, strong yet most delicate, and much character in her features, with a smile that lit up her face like a ray of sunshine. Her maiden name was Sherborn—Ann Sherborn—(her mother's maiden name, Holgate). . . . Her relations and ancestors were county folk— gentlemen farmers some of them. The Sherborns of Bedfont near Staines, held the great tythe, and her uncle was the squire. None of the last generation married, the name has died with them and may be seen only in the little Bedfont churchyard.

" My mother's uncle (her mother's brother), William Holgate, was fond of searching out genealogies and he managed to trace the Abyssinian Bruces until it joined our Bruce family tree. There were many original—and it may be eccentric—characters amongst my mother's relations and forebears, and many interesting stories that we loved to hear, about them. Her genealogical tree interested us greatly, partly because the names were so curious, as it went back to the early days of history, and because of the stories connected with them, and also because if not Bruce himself, his elder brother, David King of Scotland, figured in it. Then there was Archbishop Holgate of York, who was a great rogue (I looked up his life in the Minster precincts when I was there) and hand and glove with Henry VIII in the spoliation of the monasteries, yet he redeemed himself by the establishment of Free Schools, which flourish in York to this day.

" It may be that this spirit of romance and adventure that we breathed in from our earliest years, had some influence on my brother Fred, and fired his imagination ; but why from the very first there should have been the persistent desire like an ' idée fixe ' for Africa, I cannot tell, unless, indeed, it might be something of ' Abyssinian ' Bruce cropping up again. But as a child he would have a waggon for a toy, to load and unload, and for his school prize books he would always choose one on Africa. This desire for the dark continent remained constant in him till satisfied, and indeed to the last.

" My mother had quite an unusual interest in, and know-ledge of, natural history, and my father also made some fine collections of butterflies, etc., which are still to be seen in my brother's museum. My father's youngest brother, Angiolo—a man of the most polished and courtly manners —was as dark as my father was fair. Entirely educated by his mother, there was little in which he did not excel. He had a beautiful voice and was a charming singer, often to his own accompaniment on the guitar, and was a well-known dramatist in his time, some of his plays being most successful. How well I remember the first night of his ' True to the Core,' when we all went across the river to the Surrey Theatre and helped with our feet and umbrellas in the general enthusiasm. He was a fine actor and dramatic reader, and a charming artist. We have a perfect gem of his—Don Quixote, sitting in his study—the colouring, the face and expression, the painting, are perfect, and one feels

that Don Quixote must have looked just so. The haggard
face and the wild look in the eyes that are seeing visions.
But it was unfortunate that my uncle neglected this talent
altogether. My uncle, Harry Selous, was of course the
artist, excelling chiefly, I think, in his beautiful outlines of
the ' Pilgrim's Progress,' and his ' Metamorphoses of Ovid,'
on which subjects he could draw on his imagination for
ever, it seemed. It is a thousand pities they have never
been produced. His illustrations of the Life of Bruce and
Hereward the Wake are fine, and The Prisoners of Calais
and Boadicea are well known. The latter *most* fine, I think.
He would paint the most charming landscapes with great
rapidity, and his chalk (coloured) and pencil sketches from
his travels in Switzerland are charming too, and endless
numbers of them. He painted some of the famous Coliseum
panoramas, each in turn being painted out by the next one,
which always seemed very dreadful. His original illustrations drawn on wood, were exquisite, and it was cruel to
see how they were spoilt in the wood-cutting, but he valued
his work so lightly that he did not seem to mind much
about it. My grandfather, Gideon Slous, had a very great
talent for painting, and was a fine colourist, quite like an
old master, and he painted some beautiful miniatures also.
He was a man of violent temper."

Frederick Courtenay Selous was born in the house in
Regent's Park on December 31st, 1851. The other children
of his parents were : Florence, " Locky," now Mrs. Hodges ;
Annie, married to Mr. R. F. Jones ; Sybil, " Dei," married
to Mr. C. A. Jones ; Edmund, married to Fanny, daughter
of Mrs. Maxwell (Miss Braddon). He is a well-known student
of British bird-life and has published many interesting
books on British Natural History.

Of the childhood of Frederick little more need be said.
He was an active little fellow, never more happy than when
playing with his wooden waggon and oxen or listening to his
mother's stories of romance and adventure. At the age of
nine he went to school at Bruce Castle, Tottenham, of which
Arthur Hill was the headmaster, and there chiefly dis-

tinguished himself by being constantly in trouble. Later he went for a short time to a small school in Northamptonshire, kept by the Revd. Charles Darnell, whose daughter (Mrs. Frank Juckes) recalls one characteristic incident.

" One night my father on going round the dormitories to see that all was in order, discovered Freddy Selous, lying flat on the bare floor clothed only in his nightshirt. On being asked the cause of this curious behaviour he replied, ' Well, you see, one day I am going to be a hunter in Africa and I am just hardening myself to sleep on the ground.' "

One day in 1914, I found Selous busy at his desk at Worplesdon. On being asked what was the nature of his work, he said he was writing an account of his school days for a boys' magazine. He did not seem to think it would be of wide interest, and so had written his early adventures in simple form merely for the perusal of boys and had changed his own name to that of " John Leroux."

" It was a damp and dismal winter's day towards the end of January, 1861, on which the boys reassembled after their Christmas holidays at a well-known school not far from London. Nevertheless, despite the gloom and the chilliness of the weather conditions outside the fine old mansion which had but lately been converted into a school, there was plenty of life and animation in the handsome oak-panelled banqueting hall within, at one end of which a great log fire blazed cheerfully. Generally speaking the boys seemed in excellent spirits, or at any rate they made a brave show of being so to keep up appearances, and the music of their laughter and of their fresh young voices was good to hear. Here and there, however, a poor little fellow stood apart, alone and friendless, and with eyes full of tears. Such unfortunates were the new boys, all of them youngsters of nine or ten, who had left their homes for the first time, and whose souls were full of an unutterable misery, after their recent partings from fond mothers and gentle sisters. The youngest, and possibly the most homesick of all the new boys was standing by himself at some distance from the fire, entirely oblivious of all that was going on around him, for he was too miserable to be able to think of anything but the home in which he had grown to boyhood and all the happiness, which it seemed to his young soul, he could never know again amidst his new surroundings.

" Now as it is this miserable little boy who is to be the hero of this story, he merits, I think, some description. Though only just nine years old he looked considerably more, for he was tall for his age, and strongly built. He was very fair with a delicate pink and white complexion, which many a lady might have envied, whilst his eyes sometimes appeared to be grey and sometimes blue. His features, if not very handsome or regular, were good enough and never failed to give the impression of an open and honest nature. Altogether he would have been considered by most people a typical specimen of an English boy of Anglo-Saxon blood. Yet, as a matter of fact, as in the case of so many Englishmen, there was but little of the Saxon element in his composition, for whilst his father came from the Isle of Jersey, and was therefore of pure Norman descent, his forebears on his mother's side were some of them Scotch and others from a district in the north of England in which the Scandinavian element is supposed to preponderate over the Saxon. But though our hero bore a Norman-French name the idea that he was not a pure-blooded Englishman had never occurred to him, for he knew that his Jersey ancestors had been loyal subjects of the English crown ever since, as a result of the battle of Hastings, Duke William of Normandy became King of England.

" It was not long before the new boy's melancholy meditations were rudely broken in upon by a handsome lad of about his own size, though he was his senior by more than a year. ' Hullo,' said young Jim Kennedy, looking roguishly into the sad, almost tearful, eyes of the young Jerseyman, ' who gave you that collar ? Why, you look like Queen Elizabeth.'

" A fond mother had indeed bedecked her darling boy with a beautiful collar of lace work several inches in breadth which spread over his shoulders, but which he soon found it advisable to discard as it made him the butt of every wit in the school. But though the collar was suppressed, the name of Queen Elizabeth, that august lady to whom Kennedy when first addressing him had declared that his mother's fond gift had given him a resemblance, stuck to him for many a long day.

" The laughing, jeering interrogatory, acted like a tonic on the new boy, who though of a gentle, kindly disposition, possessed a very hot temper. His soft grey eyes instantly grew dark with anger as looking his questioner squarely in the face he answered slowly, ' What is that to you, who gave me my collar ? '

" ' Hullo ! ' again said Jim Kennedy, ' you're a cocky new boy. What's your name ? '

" ' My name is John Leroux,' said the young Jerseyman quietly and proudly, for his father had taught him to be proud of his Norman ancestry, and had instilled into his son his own firm belief that the Normans were a superior people to the Saxons, than whom he averred they had done more for the advancement of England to its present great position, and for the spread of the empire of Britain over half the world.

" Kennedy repeated the unfamiliar name two or three times, and then with a derisive laugh said, ' Why, you're a Frenchy.' Now although it was quite true that on his father's side John Leroux was of Norman-French descent, for some reason difficult to analyse, the suggestion that he was a Frenchman filled his young heart with fury. His face grew scarlet and his fists clenched involuntarily as he answered fiercely, ' How dare you call me a Frenchy ! I'm not a Frenchman, I'm an Englishman.'

" ' No, you're not,' said Kennedy, ' you're a Frenchy, a frog-eating Frenchy.' Without another word young Leroux, from whose face all the colour had now gone, sprang at his tormentor, and taking him unawares, struck him as hard a blow as he was capable of inflicting full in the mouth. And then the fight commenced.

" Fifty years ago manners were rougher and ruder in these islands than they are to-day. Prize-fighting was a respected and popular calling, and set fights between boys at school of all ages were of constant occurrence.

" A ring was soon formed around the combatants and though the majority of the onlookers resented what they called the ' coxiness ' of the new boy and wanted to see him get a licking, there were quite a number of young barbarians whose sympathies were entirely with Leroux, for his pluck in engaging in a fight on his first day at school made a strong appeal to them. The boys were evenly matched, for though Kennedy was more than a year older, he was no taller, and little if any stronger than his opponent, who, moreover, had had a certain amount of instruction from his father in the use of his fists. The battle had lasted for some minutes, and had been waged with the greatest determination on both sides, and no very severe damage to either participant, when the door at the end of the room opened and Mr. Mann, the tall young Scotch mathematical master, strode into the room. Taking in the position at a glance, he elbowed his way through the crowd of boys, who were watching the fight, and seizing the combatants simultaneously, each in one of his strong large hands, he whirled them apart, and held them out of reach of one another, though they both strained hard to resume the fray.

" ' You young rascals,' he said, ' why what on earth are you fighting about, and on the first day of the term too ! Now tell me what on earth it was all about and make it up.'

" ' He called me a Frenchman, and I'm not,' said young Leroux, and the stress of battle over, the poor boy commenced to sob.

" A more generous lad than Jim Kennedy never stepped, and at the sight of his adversary's distress, his dark eyes filled with tears, and as Mr. Mann relaxed his grasp on his shoulder, he at once came forward with outstretched hand to Leroux and said, ' I'll never call you a Frenchy again ; shake hands and let us be friends.' And so the two tearful young Britons, each of whose faces bore some traces of the recent battle, shook hands and from that time forth, as long as they were at school together, became the most devoted of friends.

" This was John Leroux's first introduction to school life. Like any other healthy vigorous boy, he soon shook off the despondency of homesickness, and became perfectly happy in his new surroundings. He worked well and conscientiously at his lessons, and played hard at all games, and was not only a general favourite with all his schoolfellows, but was also beloved by all the masters in spite of the fact that his adventurous disposition was constantly leading him to transgress all the rules of the school. With young Leroux the love of nature and the desire for the acquisition of objects of natural history of all kinds was an inborn and absorbing passion. Before leaving home he had already commenced to make collections of birds' eggs and butterflies, and throughout his school-days his interest in these and kindred subjects constantly grew. During the spring and summer months all his time that was not occupied in lessons or games was spent in birds'-nesting and collecting butterflies, whilst in the winter he trapped and skinned water rats and other small animals, and sometimes caught a stoat or a weasel. He soon became by far the best and most venturesome climber in the whole school, and there was not a rook's nest in any one of the fine old elms or oak-trees in which these birds built in the park in which the schoolhouse stood, from which he was not able to get the eggs, which for the most part he gave away to less athletic or adventurous collectors. After he had been espied on one occasion high up amongst the nests in one of the tallest elm-trees by the headmaster himself, who was genuinely alarmed for his safety, all tree-climbing in the park was forbidden. This rule was, of course, constantly broken, and by no one more frequently than by Leroux. However, as it takes some time to climb to a rook's nest, and as a boy is a conspicuous object amongst the topmost branches of a tree in the early spring before the leaves are out, our young friend was constantly being detected either by one of the undermasters or one of the men working in the grounds, who had all had strict orders to be on the watch. It was owing to this persecution, as he considered it, that Leroux conceived the idea of taking the rooks' eggs he wanted

c

at night, and with the help of Kennedy and another kindred spirit he made several raids on the rookery with perfect success when all the masters were in bed. The dormitories were on the first story and therefore not very high above the ground, and as the walls of the house were covered with ivy, it was not very difficult for an active boy to get out of the window and down or up the ivy-covered wall, with the help of the rope which Leroux brought from home in his portmanteau after one Christmas holiday. Having allowed sufficient time to pass after Mons. Delmar, the French master, had made his nightly rounds to see that all the boys were snug in bed, and all lights out, Leroux and Kennedy, who were in the same dormitory, and who had both apparently been fast asleep when the French master passed through the room, suddenly woke up and producing a candle and a box of matches from beneath their respective pillows, kindled a light and hastily made their preparations. The window having been softly opened, one end of the rope was fastened to one of the legs of the nearest bed, whilst the free end was lowered down the wall to the ground. This having been accomplished the candle was blown out, and then Leroux and Kennedy climbed down the ivy with the help of the rope. Although all the boys in the dormitory took the greatest interest in these proceedings and were ready to render any assistance necessary, a boy named Barnett always hauled up the rope as soon as the adventurers were on the ground, and hid it under the bed near the window in case of accidents until their return, for which he kept a sharp look-out. Once on the ground Leroux and his companion made their way to one or other of several large oak-trees in the park in which there were a number of rooks' nests; for these oaks were not only not as lofty as the elms, but were, moreover, much easier to climb. Kennedy, though a fairly good climber, was not the equal of Leroux in this respect, and after assisting the latter to reach the lowest branches, he always waited for his return at the foot of the tree. When the rooks were thus rudely disturbed at night, they always made what seemed to the two boys a most appalling noise, but if anyone ever heard it he never guessed the true cause, or took any steps to investigate its meaning, and although during three successive years the two boys raided the rookery on several different occasions, their escapades were never discovered or even suspected. Once, however, they only just got back into their dormitory before the policeman made his nightly round. As a rule he did not make his circuit of the house flashing his lantern on all the windows until after midnight, but on the occasion in question he came much earlier than usual, and Leroux and Kennedy had only just scrambled up the ivy-covered wall, and reached their room with the assistance of the rope which the watchful Barnett had let down for them, when they saw the policeman's lantern flash round the end of the house, through their still open window, which they then closed very cautiously without making any noise. It was the policeman's nightly round of the house, which was thus so forcibly brought to his notice, that gave Leroux an idea, which he and Kennedy and Barnett, together with some other boys, subsequently acted upon with great success. This was nothing more nor less than to play a practical joke on the policeman by hanging a dummy figure out of the window one night, on which he would be sure to flash his lantern when he made his round of the house. In each dormitory there was a huge clothes-basket, not very high but very capacious, and choosing an evening when their basket was very full of clothes for the wash, Leroux and his friends, with the help of a bolster, a coat, shirt, and pair of trousers, and some of the contents of the clothes-basket, made a very good imitation of the figure of a boy. The top end of the bolster which was pinched in a little lower down by the shirt collar, made a nice round ball for the head, and on this a mask and a tow wig, which had been bought just before Guy Fawkes day, were fixed. Then the rope which had done such good service on the occasions of the raids on the rookery, was fastened round the dummy figure's neck, and the really meritorious imitation of a dead boy lowered out of the window and allowed to dangle some six feet beneath it. The head, which with its mask and wig of tow now hung over to one side, gave the somewhat podgy and certainly very inanimate looking figure quite a realistic appearance. The work of preparing this figure after the French master had been round the dormitories, occupied the boys some time, and when at last, after the rope had been fastened round its neck, it was lowered out of the window, it was past eleven o'clock. The boys then took it in turns to watch for the coming of the policeman, each watcher kneeling at the window well wrapped in his bedclothes. It was Barnett who was on duty when at last the policeman came. ' Cavy,' he whispered, ' here he comes,' and all the boys, whose excitement had kept them awake, made their way to the window, across which the light of the lantern soon flashed. The result was immediate and exceeded the utmost expectations of Leroux and his companions. The policeman—a young man but lately enrolled in the force—was seen to be gesticulating and shouting at the top of his voice, evidently trying to attract the attention of those in the room above him, from which the boy figure, with its ghastly pale cardboard face, hung dangling at the end of a rope. There was, however, no response from the listening boys. Suddenly the policeman ceased his outcries, and running down the footpath turned the corner of the house. Immediately after there was a terrific banging at the front door, accompanied by loud shouting. ' Quick,' said Leroux, ' up with the window, and let's get the dummy in.' At the same time Kennedy ran to the further door of the dormitory and holding it slightly ajar, peered out on the landing, which overlooked the large hall at the end of which was the main entrance of the house from whence all the noise proceeded. And now anxious voices were heard, and lights appeared from all directions. ' Old Rex '—the headmaster—' has opened the hall door,' said Kennedy, ' and is talking to the policeman. My eye,' he continued, ' Old Cockeye's there too, she's crying out and snuffling like a good 'un.' I grieve to say that ' Old Cockeye ' was the disrespectful nickname which had been given by the boys to the matron —a most exemplary lady with an unfortunate squint in the left eye. And now there was a babble of approaching voices as the party in the hall rapidly ascended the staircase leading to the dormitories. Kennedy softly closed the door at which he had been listening, and already Leroux and Barnett had shut the window after having pulled up the rope with the dummy figure attached to the end of it, which was hastily thrust under the nearest bed. ' Mind we're all asleep ; we don't know anything about it,' said Kennedy in a loud whisper as he jumped into his bed and composed his features into an appearance of placid innocence, which indeed was the attitude adopted by all the other boys in the room. Then the dormitory door was thrown wide open and the headmaster rushed in, candle in hand, closely followed by the policeman, the matron and two of the undermasters. At the same time the door of the other end of the room was flung open, and a strange half-clad figure, with wild eyes and candle in hand, came forward amongst the sleeping boys not one of whom, strange to say, showed the slightest sign of having been in any way disturbed by all the hubbub. ' Mon Dieu,' said Mons. Delmar, ' qu'est-ce qu'il y a donc ? ' as he ran to meet the headmaster. The latter was indeed a pathetic figure as he stood half-dressed looking round the room with wild eyes, his long grey hair falling over his shoulders. In his right hand he held a candle-stick, whilst his left was clasped over his forehead. ' Great God,' he said, ' no—no—impossible,' as if talking to himself, and then suddenly turning to the policeman, ' Why, officer, you must be mistaken, every boy is here in his bed.'

" ' I seed him, sir ; I seed him with my own eyes, indeed I did,' answered the policeman.

" ' Oh, deary, deary, deary me,' wailed the matron, whose unfortunate obliquity of vision had gained her so irreverent a nickname.

" ' Which window was it, officer ? ' asked the headmaster.

" ' The one near the end of the room,' replied the police-man. In another moment the window in question was thrown wide open and several heads were protruded into the cold night air.

" ' There's nothing here,' said the headmaster.

" ' Well, I'm——' said the policeman, leaving it to his

audience to finish the sentence according to their several inclinations. At this moment an exclamation from the French master caused everyone to turn round. In his anxiety to get to the window, one of the undermasters had pushed the end of Leroux's bed sharply to one side—without however awakening its occupant—and exposed to the Frenchman's sharp eyes a portion of the rope which had been attached to the dummy figure which was the cause of all the excitement. Stooping down to catch hold of it, he at once saw the dummy under the bed, and pulled it out with an exclamation which Leroux afterwards affirmed was certainly ' sacré.'

" ' Well, I'm——' again said the policeman, without going any further, and so again leaving his hearers in doubt as to what he was. Old Rex, the headmaster, then seized Leroux by the shoulder, and shook him violently, but for some time without any other effect than to cause him to snore loudly ; otherwise he appeared not only to be fast asleep, but to have sunk into a kind of comatose condition. At last, however, he could stand the shaking no longer, and so opened his eyes.

" ' Do you know anything about this, Leroux ? ' said old Rex sternly.

" ' Yes, sir,' said Leroux.

" ' It was a cruel hoax,' said the headmaster.

" ' I wanted to play a joke on the Bobby,' said Leroux.

" ' Well, I'm——' murmured that functionary, once more discreetly veiling any further information which might otherwise have been forthcoming by covering his mouth with his left hand.

" ' Officer, these boys have played a shameful trick on you, but you did your duty. I'm sorry that you should have been disturbed in this way. Boys, I know you are all awake, I shall inquire into this matter to-morrow.' So saying, but looking very much relieved, the headmaster turned on his heel and left the room, followed by all those who had entered it with him after having been roused from their sleep by the policeman.

" Now ' old Rex,' the headmaster of the fine school at

which our hero acquired the rudiments of learning, was a reformer and an idealist, and corporal chastisement was never inflicted on the boys on any consideration whatever. The punishments for minor offences were various tasks during play hours, or compulsory walks conducted by old Rex himself, and which most of the boys rather enjoyed. For more serious misdemeanours the offending scholars were separated from their fellows, and placed in solitary confinement in a distant part of the house for periods ranging from a day to a week, during which they got nothing to eat or drink but dry bread with a mere trace of butter on it, and weak tea. As a sequel to the great dummy joke, the fame of which by some means was spread through all the neighbouring parishes, Leroux and Kennedy, who acknowledged that they were the ringleaders in the matter, were condemned to three days' solitary confinement, to be followed by various tasks and compulsory walks during the play hours of the following week, whilst the rest of the boys in the dormitory got off with some extra lessons to be learnt whilst their school-fellows were enjoying themselves in the playground during the next two half-holidays, and a long lecture on the heinousness of the crime, to which old Rex said with perfect truth he believed they had been willing accessories.

"After the perpetration of the dummy joke, however, the French master, whether on his own initiative or at the instigation of the headmaster, commenced to make himself a great nuisance, not only coming round the dormitories with a lighted candle as usual soon after the boys had gone to bed, but often returning later on without a candle and wearing carpet slippers. The single combats and inter-dormitory bolster-fights which were a feature of the school-life were constantly being interfered with. The door of the dormitory in which our hero slept had always to be kept ajar and a boy placed there to watch for the coming of Mons. Delmar when any fun was going on, and the suddenness with which at the single word 'cavy,' the confused noise of an animated bolster-fight was succeeded by the most deathlike stillness was truly astonishing. Before

Mons. Delmar could strike a light, every boy was not only in bed, but sleeping so soundly that nothing the puzzled French master could say or do could arouse them to consciousness. Various plans were discussed by the most enterprising boys in the different dormitories, with a view to discouraging these informal visits after the lights had been put out. One night a piece of cord was tied by Leroux across the gangway at about a foot from the ground between the two beds nearest the door of the room in which he slept, over which it was hoped Mons. Delmar would trip on entering. On this occasion, however, he did not enter the room at all, but after opening the door, lighted the candle he held in his hand and merely looked round, turning on his heels again without speaking a word. It was hoped that he had not noticed the string, and another opportunity might be given him of falling over it. On the next night, however, the boys in the adjoining dormitory set a trap for him by placing the large inverted clothes-basket over the half open door of the room, in such a way that it would, with reasonable good luck, be very likely to fall like an extinguisher over the head and shoulders of anyone entering the dormitory, and when Mons. Delmar presently pushed the door open, down came the large wicker basket. As it was dark it was impossible to determine exactly whether it came down over his head and shoulders or only fell on his head, but his candlestick was certainly knocked out of his hand and he swore most volubly in his own language. After having found and lighted his candle he first harangued his young tormentors, all of whom were apparently overcome by a deathlike sleep, and then went straight off to the headmaster's study. The result of his complaint was the infliction of certain tasks and compulsory walks on all the occupants of the offending dormitory, but after this there was no further spying on the boys. Poor Mons. Delmar ! no doubt he had only been acting under instructions, though perhaps he entered on his detective duties a little too zealously.

" Altogether John Leroux spent four very happy years at his first school, and besides making good progress with his lessons, showed great aptitude for all games and athletic exercises, especially football and swimming. Ever since the fight on the evening of the day of his first entrance to the school he and Kennedy had been the closest of friends. The two boys had paid several visits to one another's homes during the holidays, and it was chiefly because Kennedy's parents had decided to send their son to a great public school in the Midlands, for the entrance examination for which he had been undergoing a special preparation, that it was finally decided that Leroux should be sent to the same seat of learning. Up till then, however, Leroux, though well advanced for his age in all other subjects, had been spared the study of Greek, at the particular request of his father, who as a practical business man, looked upon the time spent by a schoolboy in acquiring a very imperfect knowledge of any dead language, save Latin, as entirely wasted. But to pass the entrance examination for any of our great public schools fifty years ago some knowledge of Greek was absolutely necessary, and so when Kennedy at the age of fourteen, passed into the great school, his friend Leroux who hoped to rejoin him there as soon as he had reached the same age, was in the meantime sent to the establishment of a clergyman living in a remote village in Northamptonshire to be specially coached in Greek.

" The Rev. Charles Darnell, Rector of the parish of Belton, was a short stout elderly man of a very easy-going disposition, who exercised but little supervision over the dozen pupils he was able to find accommodation for in his rambling old Rectory. But he employed a couple of good tutors well up to their work, and his son, who was a curate in a neighbouring parish and just as irascible as his father was placid in temperament, also helped to coach the boys in his charge.

" At the time of our story Belton was a small village of stonebuilt cottages, all the windows in which were of the old diamond-paned pattern. The village was dominated by an ancient and picturesque church, surrounded by yew-trees, amongst which were scattered the moss-grown tombstones of many generations of Beltonians. A feature of the churchyard was the family vault of a large landowner in the neighbourhood. The present representative of this ancient family, locally known as ' old squire,' was an eccentric bachelor, who lived in a picturesque old Manor House with only two or three servants. It was said in the village that he had never been seen outside the boundaries of his estate for many years, and that he seldom walked abroad even in his own grounds till after dark.

" It was during his first term, in very early spring, that Leroux, accompanied by a fellow-pupil, took a wood-owl's eggs from a hollow ash-tree in the deserted park, and he subsequently spent many of his half-holidays birds'-nesting all over the neglected estate. He never met a keeper, nor, indeed, anyone else to question his right to be there, not even in the empty stables or in the thick shrubberies and weed-grown plots of ground near the great house which had once been gardens. There were two small lakes in the park, and in one of them during the autumn and winter months Leroux and one or two of his more adventurous fellow-students used to set ' trimmers,' on which they caught a good many pike, some of quite a good size, and now and again they shot a moorhen with a saloon pistol which belonged to a boy named Short.

" Whatever the boys caught or shot was taken to a certain cottage in the village, the residence of an old woman who was a very clever cook, and at this cottage Leroux and his friends enjoyed many a good meal of baked pike stuffed with the orthodox ' pudding,' and even found the moorhens, which the old woman skinned before cooking, very palatable.

" Belton being in the centre of a noted hunting-country, the hounds sometimes passed in full cry within sight of the Rectory, and whenever this happened the Rector's pupils were allowed by an old-established custom, even if they were in the middle of a lesson, to throw down their books and join in the run.

" During the year he spent at the Rectory Leroux worked hard at his lessons, and made good progress in Greek as well as in all other subjects which he had to get up, in view of the approaching entrance examination to the great

Midland school. Games were neglected at this period, as there were not enough pupils at the Rectory to make up two sides either at football or cricket, but for Leroux and his fellow-pupils of similar tastes, the old squire's deserted estate formed a most glorious playground in which they found a fine field for the exercise and development of the primitive instincts which had come down to them from their distant ancestors of palaeolithic times. The only pranks that Leroux indulged in during his year at Belton were all connected with the old church of which Mr. Darnell was the incumbent, and at which his pupils were obliged to attend the two services held every Sunday. As in many of the old churches in the remote districts of Northampton-shire at that time, there was no organ, but the hymns were sung to an accompaniment of flute, violin and 'cello, the performers on these instruments being seated in a kind of minstrels' gallery at the end of the church facing the pulpit.

" After the service on Sunday evening the musical instruments were taken by the musicians to their own homes, but one Sunday afternoon Leroux and Short—the owner of the saloon pistol—surreptitiously entered the church and thoroughly soaped the bows of the violin- and violoncello-players, and introduced several peas into the flute. That evening the music was very defective, but although the musicians knew that their instruments had been tampered with there is no reason to believe that they ever suspected that any of the Rector's ' young gentlemen ' had had any-thing to do with the trick which had been played upon them. In future, however, the bows and the flute were removed between the services, as Leroux discovered about a month later, when he thought it was time to repeat his first success-ful experiment. An aged parishioner, who was always dressed in a smock-frock and grey woollen stockings, had his seat on a bench just in front of the pews where Mr. Darnell's pupils sat. This old man invariably removed his shoes on sitting down, and placed them carefully under his seat, and on several occasions during the sermon, Leroux managed to remove them with the help of a stick to the end of which a piece of wire in the shape of a hook had been attached.

Once the shoes had been drawn to Leroux's seat they were passed down by the other boys from pew to pew, and finally left at a considerable distance from their original place of deposition. The old fellow always made a great fuss about the removal of his shoes, which not only amused the Rector's pupils and all the younger members of the congregation, but must also have had an exhilarating influence on the spirits of their elders, upon whom the effect of the usual dull sermon always appeared to be very sedative to say the least of it. However, no public complaint was ever made, and when the old man at length took the precaution to keep his shoes on his feet during service, all temptation to meddle with them was removed."

CHAPTER II

1865-1870

WHEN the time came for Fred to go to Rugby both Mr. Darnell and Mr. Hill advised Mr. Wilson, to whose house it was proposed to send him, not on any account to have a boy whose escapades would be a constant source of trouble, but fortunately Mr. Wilson liked ' naughty ' boys and disregarded their warnings.

Selous entered Rugby in January, 1866, and was a pupil in Mr. Wilson's house for two years. His letters to his mother at this period are of the usual schoolboy type, mostly requests for money, books or additions to the commissariat. He was always reading when he got the chance, the choice invariably tending towards travel and adventure. He writes :—

" *January*, 1866.

" I am reading a new book by Mr. Livingstone. It is called ' The Zambesi and its Tributaries,' from 1858-1864. It is very interesting and is about the discovery of two large lakes. Send me two catapults." And " I am sorry to hear the rat skins are eaten, but very glad that the stoat's has not met with the same fate." Another letter shows his consideration for his parents in the matter of money and is somewhat characteristic.

" MY DEAR MAMA,

" I hope you are quite well, I am now at Rugby and very comfortable. I have a study with another boy, and we have an allowance of candles and tea and sugar, etc., given out every week, and we make our own tea and breakfast in our studies and it is very nice indeed. I have passed into Upper Middle two when Lower Middle two would have done. I have to pay over some subscriptions.

" £1 subscription to the racket court.

" 10s. to football club, 10s. to cricket club, 10s. for our own house subscription, all of which I am forced to pay. I have to buy a great many things which I could not help and I have spent a lot of my money on them. I will write them down to show you that not one of them was extravagance but quite the opposite.

" 7s. 6d. to have my watch mended, 1s. to go to Harbro' to get my watch and come back. 1s. to have my dirty clothes washed. 2s. for a book I have to use at Rugby which I had not got. 3s. to come from Welton to Rugby after coming back to get my boxes. All these were necessary, weren't they ?

" It is not my fault that there are such a lot of expenses at a public school, but it is only the first half. Please send in a registered letter, I have seen a great many boys receive them. I have passed very high, 10th out of 75, and that will partly make up to you for some of the subscriptions Give my best love to Papa and brothers and sisters.

" I remain your affectionate son,

" FREDDY."

From this time his life at Rugby is thus given in his own words :—

" In January, 1866, when John Leroux was just fourteen years of age, he easily passed the entrance examination to the great school in the Midlands and became a member of the house which his old friend Jim Kennedy had entered just a year earlier. Here he spent two and a half very happy years, and as at the end of that time he was only sixteen, he would in the ordinary course have continued his studies for at least another two years before leaving school, had it not been his father's wish that he should go abroad to learn French and German before reaching an age at which it would be necessary to settle down to the real business of life and make his own living. At the great school there were three half-holidays weekly, but the boys were expected to do a good deal of preparation for the next day's lessons during their leisure time. Some boys shirked these out-of-class studies, but Leroux always did whatever was expected of him most conscientiously and often very slowly and with much labour, as he never used a crib to assist him with his Latin and Greek translations. He was not at all brilliant, but was well up in the school for his age, and had he stayed another term would have been in the sixth—the highest form in the school. However famous the great Midland school may have been fifty years ago, as a seat of learning, it was certainly not less famous for the great game of football, the playing of which was as compulsory on the scholars as the study of Greek. Primitive Rugby football was a very different affair to the highly scientific game of the present day. There was more running with the ball, far less kicking into touch, and no heeling out behind the scrimmage. Hacking was not only permissible but was one of the main features of the game, and when the ball was put down in the scrimmage the object of each side was to ' hack it through,' that is, to clear a path for the ball by kicking the skins of every one in the way as hard as possible. There were twenty boys on each side in the old Rugby game of whom the backs and half-backs only numbered five altogether—such a thing as a three-quarter back was un-dreamt of—so that there were fifteen forwards on each side. When anyone ran with the ball, the cry was ' hack him over,' and as often as not the runner was brought down with a neat kick on the shin. It was altogether a rough, possibly a rather brutal game ; but it made the boys strong and hardy, and with the exception of badly bruised shins there were very few accidents. A young boy, on his first entrance to the big school, could only wear duck trousers at football, but if he played up, and did not flinch from the hacking, the Captain of his twenty gave him his ' flannels ' and then exchanged his duck for flannel trousers. There was no school twenty, and therefore no school cap, and all the most hotly contested matches were between the different houses for the honour of being ' cock house.' Every house had its own cap, but in each house, except in the case of the school house, where there was a large number of pupils, there were only a few caps in each football twenty. For instance, in Leroux's house, where there were fifty-two pupils, there were only four who had got their caps. Though one of the youngest boys in the house Leroux threw himself into the game with a zest and enthusiasm which at once compelled attention, and won him his ' flannels ' in his first term, and after playing up well in the first great match in the autumn term of the same year he was given his cap. He thus got his cap whilst still in his fourteenth year, and was the youngest boy in the whole school who possessed that much-coveted prize. The only other sport besides football indulged in by the boys at the great school during the term between Christmas and Easter was that known as ' house washing.' Led by one of the oldest and strongest boys, the whole house were accustomed to spend one half-holiday every week, during the cold, damp, dreary months of February and March, in jumping backwards and forwards over a small brook or river, which at that time of the year was usually swollen by recent rain. The first jumps were taken across the narrowest parts of the stream, and here only the youngest and weakest boys got into the water. But it was a point of honour to go on taking bigger and bigger jumps, until every boy in the house had failed to reach the opposite bank and all had got thoroughly soused. The last jump was known as ' Butler's Leap.' Here the stream ran through a tunnel beneath one of the high roads traversing the district, but before doing so it ran for a short distance parallel with the road, which had been built up to the height of the bridge above it. From the brick wall on either side of the bridge low wooden barriers, perhaps two and a half feet high, had been placed on the slope of the road on either side to the level of the fields below, and it was thus possible to get a run across the whole width of the road and leap the low barrier in an attempt to reach the opposite bank of the stream, which was here over twenty feet wide, and some twenty feet below the level of the top of the bridge. A hero named Butler had either been the first boy to attempt this desperate leap, or he had actually cleared the stream and landed on the opposite bank. Tradition concerning the details of the exploit varied, but whether Butler had made the great jump or only attempted it, he had immortalised his name by his daring. Now, only the biggest and most venturesome boys in each house were expected to attempt Butler's Leap, but nevertheless some of the younger ones always had a try at it, and amongst these were Kennedy and Leroux. They cleared the wooden barrier at the side of the road, and fell through the air into the stream below, but far short of the further bank, which they had to reach by swimming.

" From a perusal of the letters which Leroux faithfully wrote every week to his mother, it would seem that with the exception of the fierce football contests for ' cock ' house, and occasional snowball encounters with the town ' louts '—the contemptuous appellation given by the boys at the school to all their fellow-citizens—all his most interesting experiences were connected with his passion for birds'-nesting, and the pursuit of sport, at first with a saloon pistol and subsequently with a pea-rifle, on the domains of neighbouring landowners. The master of Leroux's house was a man of very fine character and most kindly disposition, and was much beloved by all his pupils. He was always a most kind friend to Leroux, and being a teacher of natural science—it was certain experiments in chemistry which had earned for him amongst the boys the sobriquet of ' Jim Stinks '—was much drawn to him by his very pronounced taste for the study of natural history, and his practical knowledge of English birds and beasts. In his second year at the school, Leroux got into the first mathematical set in the upper school, and on Tuesdays, Thursdays, and Saturdays, and on every third week on Mondays as well, had no lessons in school, after 10.15 in the morning. But on these half-holidays, or almost whole holidays, all the boys in the school had to attend and answer to their names at a ' call over ' which was held at the big school during the afternoon, and from which no boy could escape except with the written permission of his house-master.

D

During the summer Leroux's kindly house-master often allowed his favourite pupil to be absent from ' call over,' and he was thus able, by taking the train, to visit districts and pursue his ornithological rambles at quite a long distance from the school. On these distant excursions, however, although he paid no attention whatever to the numerous notice-boards intimating that trespassers would be prosecuted, he was never caught by a gamekeeper, though he had some good runs to escape their attentions. In the more immediate vicinity of the school, possibly the keepers were more on the look-out for birds'-nesting boys, who were often brought up by their captors before the head-master, the great Dr. Temple, familiarly known in the school as ' Old Froddy.' This great and good man, however, always let the young trespassers off very lightly.

" One Sunday afternoon Leroux was pursued by a game-keeper to the very doors of the chapel, and indeed it was only under the stimulus of this pursuit that he could possibly have got in in time for the service, and ' cutting chapel ' meant having to write out the whole of the fourth Georgic of Virgil, which was just over 500 lines. When the bell ceased tolling, Leroux was still some distance from the chapel door, and handicapped besides with the top-hat, which all the boys always had to wear on Sunday, and a clutch of sparrowhawk's eggs twisted up in his handker-chief, on which he had to hold his hand in his coat-pocket, to prevent them from shaking together. But old Patey, who always checked off the boys at ' call over ' and on their entrance to the chapel, took in the situation at a glance and held the door ajar till Leroux got inside, and then slammed it to in the gamekeeper's face. Leroux fully ex-pected that his pursuer would wait outside till chapel was over and try and identify him as he came out, but he prob-ably got tired of waiting or else thought it impossible to pick out the boy he had chased and of whom he had only had a back view, amongst over five hundred other boys.

" About three miles from the big school in the midst of a wide expanse of undulating meadow-land, interspersed with small woods, stood the fine old manor house of Pilton

Range. As there was no game preservation on this estate, there were no keepers to shoot down magpies, carrion crows, kestrels and sparrowhawks, and Leroux consequently found it a very fine hunting ground for the nests of these birds. One day soon after the Easter holidays, and during his second year at the big school, Leroux paid a visit to the Pilton Range grounds, to look at a magpie's nest which he had found building a fortnight before. He was walking along a high hedge bordering a field, about a mile away from the house, when a man dressed as a labourer climbed over a gate at the other end of the field and came walking towards him. Now Leroux had often met labouring men on the Pilton Range estate before, but had never been interfered with in any way by them, so he paid no attention to the man who was now coming towards him, but walked quietly to meet him. The heavily built labourer came slouching along, apparently without taking the slightest interest in the approaching boy, but just as he was passing him, and without having previously spoken a word, he shot out his right hand, and caught Leroux by the waistcoat just beneath the collar. 'Well, what do you want?' said Leroux.

" ' You come along o' me to Mr. Blackstone '—the bailiff of the Pilton Range estate—said the labourer. Now Leroux had set his heart on visiting the magpie's nest, which he thought would be sure to contain eggs by now, and he was very averse to having his plans deranged by a visit to Mr. Blackstone. He first therefore offered to give his name to his captor to be reported to the headmaster, and when this proposition was received with a derisive laugh he pulled a letter from his coat pocket, and offered the envelope as a proof of his veracity. Possibly the heavy-looking lout who had taken him prisoner could not read. At any rate he never even glanced at the envelope which Leroux held out for his inspection, but merely repeating his invitation to ' come along o' me to Mr. Blackstone,' proceeded to walk towards the gate in the corner of the field at which he had made his first appearance. Leroux felt that he was very firmly held, for the labourer's fingers had passed through the armhole of his waistcoat, so he at first pretended to be resigned to his fate, and walked quietly along beside his obdurate captor. Just before reaching the gate, however, he gave a sudden wrench, and almost got free, but on his waistcoat beginning to tear, desisted. In the struggle, however, boy and man had swung face to face, as the labourer held Leroux with his right hand clenched on the left side of the boy's waistcoat near the collar. After this Leroux refused to walk beside his captor any further, but forced him to walk backwards and pull him every step of the way, and as he was then fifteen years old and a strong heavy boy for his age, their progress was slow. Fortunately for the labourer he was able to open the gate in the corner of the field in which he had made his capture, as well as two others which had to be passed before reaching the Hall, with his left hand, for he would never have been able to have got Leroux over these gates. Leroux would have attacked the man with his fists and hacked him on the shins, but he knew that that would have put him in the wrong with the headmaster, so he just leaned back, and made his captor walk backwards and pull him along every step of the way up to the Hall. He also made a point of bringing his heels down heavily on the labourer's feet at every step. At last, however, Leroux was dragged through the open gates of the great archway leading into the courtyard of Pilton Range, where at that moment Mr. Blackstone the bailiff happened to be standing just outside his office door. He was a tall, grim-looking old man with iron-grey hair, and seemed to be leaning heavily on a thick stick he held in his right hand as if he was slightly lame.

" ' I've brought un to see Mr. Blackstone,' said the perspiring labourer, still holding Leroux in his grasp.

" ' You young rascal, I'd like to lay this stick about your back,' said Mr. Blackstone, brandishing that formidable weapon in front of the captive. Then putting his left hand in his waistcoat pocket, he extracted a coin with his finger and thumb which Leroux thought was a two-shilling piece and offered it to his employee, remarking, ' Here's something for you, John ; I see you've had some trouble with this young rascal.'

" Then addressing Leroux he said, ' Now, boy, I want your name.' The labourer received the proffered piece of silver in his left hand, but force of habit caused him, no doubt quite unconsciously, to release his hold of Leroux with his right hand at the same time in order to touch his cap to Mr. Blackstone in acknowledgment of his employer's generosity. On the instant that Leroux felt himself free he was round and through the great archway almost at a bound.

" ' After him, John,' he heard the irate bailiff shout, and the discomfited labourer at once gave chase, but he stood no chance whatever of overtaking the active, well-trained boy, and when Leroux half broke, half jumped through the hedge at the bottom of the field below the Hall, he was pursued no further. After scrambling through the hedge and running in its shelter to the corner of the field he was then in, Leroux stood on the watch for some little time, and then feeling very elated at the way in which he had given the bailiff the slip, without letting him know his name, determined not to leave the Pilton Range ground without looking at the magpie's nest, he had been on his way to examine when first seized by the labourer. As he had expected he found that the nest contained a full complement of eggs, which were that evening carefully blown and added to his collection, which was even then quite the best made by any boy in the whole school. On his many subsequent visits to the Pilton Range estate, Leroux took good care never to allow any labouring man he happened to see to get anywhere near him, nor did he ever renew his acquaintance with Mr. Blackstone.

" Of all his birds'-nesting exploits, the one which Leroux himself always considered the greatest achievement was his raid on the Heronry at Tombe Abbey. Tombe Abbey was about fifteen miles distant from the big school, and it was during his second year of study there, that whilst rambling in that neighbourhood on a day when he had been excused from attending all ' callings over ' by his house-master, Leroux had noticed a number of herons flying over the park in the midst of which the Abbey stood. He at once entered the sacred

precincts to investigate, and soon discovered the Heronry
situated on an island in the middle of a large sheet of ornamental water. The twenty or thirty large nests of sticks
were built as is always the case in England, high up in a
grove of large trees growing on the island. Leroux watched
the herons from amongst some bushes on the edge of the
lake for some time and assured himself that there were
young birds in most if not in all of the nests, as he could see
their parents feeding them. To have swum across the
lake to the island and then climb up to one or more of the
nests in the hope of finding some eggs would therefore
probably have been a bootless quest, and at that time
perhaps Leroux would hardly have been able to have summoned up sufficient courage for such an undertaking, but
all through the following months the idea of one day swimming to the island in the park at Tombe Abbey and taking
some herons' eggs, grew in his mind, and when he returned
to school after the following Christmas holidays, he had
fully determined to make the attempt. Through reference
to an ornithological work in his house-library Leroux had
learned that herons are very early breeders, so he made his
plans accordingly, and obtained leave from his house-master
to be absent from all ' callings over ' on March 7th, and
hurrying to the station as soon as his mathematical lesson
was over at a quarter past ten in the morning, he took the
first train to the nearest station to Tombe Abbey. It was a
bitterly cold day with a dull sky and the wind in the east,
and when, after making his way cautiously across the park,
Leroux reached the shelter of the bushes on the edge of the
lake, he found that there was a fringe of thin ice all round
the water's edge. In one way, however, the cold dreary
day was favourable to the boy's enterprise, as no one was
likely to be out walking in the park. Under cover of the
bushes Leroux stripped himself to the skin, and without
any hesitation waded into the ice-cold water, until it became
deep enough to allow him to swim. At this time he was
probably the best swimmer in the whole school, for during
his first year and when only fourteen years of age he had won
the second prize in the annual swimming-match, and would

certainly have taken the first prize the following year, but for some reason or other there was no competition. In his third year and a few months after his visit to Tombe Abbey when the competition was again revived, he met with an accident at cricket on the very morning of the race, which destroyed his chances of winning it. Once in the deep water of the lake, Leroux, swimming with a strong side-stroke, soon reached the island in the centre, and selecting the easiest tree to climb in which some of the herons' nests were built, naked as he was, he lost no time in getting up to them. There were four eggs in each of the two nests he actually inspected, and transferring these to an empty sponge-bag which he had brought with him, and which he now held in his mouth, he soon reached the ground again at the foot of the tree without having broken or even cracked a single egg. A hasty look round assured him that no one was in sight anywhere in the park, so still holding the sponge-bag containing the eight large blue eggs in his teeth, he soon recrossed the lake to the mainland, and then lost no time in pulling his clothes over his wet and shivering limbs. But though his teeth were chattering, Leroux's young heart was full of joy and exultation at the successful accomplishment of his enterprise, and he thought but little of his personal discomfort. Once dressed he soon reached the boundary of the park, and early in the afternoon was able to report himself to his house-master, though he did not think it necessary to enter into any details as to his day's ramble, and probably had it not been for the fact that the great Midland school at this time boasted a natural history society, of which Leroux was a prominent member as well as keeper of the ornithological note-book, the incident of the taking of the herons' eggs at Tombe Abbey might never have been known to anyone but a few of Leroux's most intimate friends. However, at the next evening meeting of the society, in the innocence of his heart Leroux exhibited the great blue eggs, the contemplation of which was still his chief joy. One of the undermasters, Mr. Kitchener, was that night in the chair, and this unprincipled pedagogue, after having obtained the admission from Leroux

that he had taken the herons' eggs himself, required him in
the most unsportsmanlike manner to state exactly when
and where he had become possessed of them. All prevarica-
tion was foreign to Leroux's nature, and when thus chal-
lenged he did not hesitate to tell the story of his visit to
Tombe Abbey, and how he had swum across the lake and
climbed to the herons' nests stark naked on a cold day in
early March. The hardihood of the exploit, however, made
no appeal to the mean soul of Mr. Kitchener, who not only
confiscated the herons' eggs on the spot, but ordered Leroux
to write out the fourth Georgic of Virgil, a very common
punishment at public schools in those days, as it runs to
almost exactly 500 lines. Through the good offices of his
own house-master the herons' eggs were given back to Leroux,
but the story of his adventure became noised abroad, even
beyond the confines of the school, as he was to discover a
few months later.

" Although Leroux had become the happy possessor of a
saloon pistol, soon after his entrance to the school, he had
never found this a very satisfactory weapon, and had determined to possess himself of something better as soon as
possible. He practised rifle-shooting regularly at the butts,
and in his third year shot in most of the matches for the
school eleven, always doing very well at the longer ranges
at which the boys were allowed to kneel or lie down, but
failing rather at the 200 yards, at which range in those days
even the youngest members of the rifle-corps were required
to shoot standing with heavy Enfield rifles with a very hard
pull. It was this excessively hard pull, combined with the
weight of the long Enfield rifle, which made it so difficult
for a young boy to shoot steadily standing at the 200
yards' range. During the Easter holidays before his last
term at the great school, Leroux bought with his savings,
augmented by a liberal present from his mother, a good
pea-rifle with a detachable barrel, which could be concealed
up the coat-sleeve of the right arm, whilst the stock was
hidden under the coat on the other side of the body. But
Leroux never used this rifle on private ground unless he
was accompanied by a friend, so that in case of pursuit one

boy could run with the barrel and the other with the stock. There was an old disused canal not far away from the school, on the property of a local landowner named Lowden Beigh, which was a favourite resort of Leroux and his friends on Sunday afternoons between dinner-time and afternoon chapel. In the still waters of this old canal bordered with beds of reeds and rushes, and in many places overspread with waterlilies, pike were always to be found on a hot summer's day, not exactly basking in the sun, but lying motionless in the water, not more than a few inches from the surface, and Leroux had discovered that the concussion caused by a bullet fired into the water in the immediate vicinity of these fish, even though it did not touch them, was sufficient to stun them and cause them to float helpless for a short time belly upwards on the top of the water, from which they could be retrieved with a long stick. The pike which were obtained in this way were, however, be it said, always of small size. This old canal too swarmed with moorhens which afforded excellent practice with the little rifle. It was on a hot Sunday afternoon in late June, that Leroux and a great friend of his, a very tall boy who had somewhat outgrown his strength, paid what proved to be their last visit to the canal. As it so happened, where they first struck the canal they had only seen some very small pike not worth shooting at and only one shot had been fired at a moorhen, which had missed its mark. However, there was a better hunting ground beyond the bridge where the high road crossed the old canal, and this they proceeded to make for. Before entering the last field which lay between them and the high road, the little rifle was taken to pieces, and Leroux then hid the stock under the left side of his coat, his companion, whose arms were longer than his, concealing the barrel up his right coat-sleeve. The two boys then strolled leisurely along the bank of the canal, towards the gate which opened into the high road just below the bridge. They were close to this gate, in fact almost touching it, when a gamekeeper, in velveteen coat and gaiters, suddenly appeared from behind the hedge on the other side of it and stood confronting them.

" ' Well, young gents,' he said, ' what have you been doing along the canal ? '

" ' We've been looking for cuckoos' eggs in the reed warblers' nests,' said Leroux readily, and it was indeed a perfectly true answer, though it did not cover the whole scope of their operations.

" ' Well, I must have your names. Mr. Lowden Beigh[1] means to put a stop to you young gents trespassing on his ground every Sunday,' said the gamekeeper, pulling out a pocket-book and pencil to take them down in. Leroux and his friend at once gave their names, and told the keeper how to spell them, for they knew that even if they were reported to the headmaster, that good old sportsman would not be likely to inflict any punishment on them for merely strolling quietly along the bank of the old canal on a Sunday afternoon, even though they had been trespassing on the property of Mr. Lowden Beigh.

" Having given up their names to the keeper the two boys proceeded to climb over the gate into the high road, and considering what they carried hidden under their coats, this was a somewhat ticklish operation.

" Leroux was nearest to the keeper, and having his right arm free probably got over the gate without arousing any suspicion in the man's mind, but the latter probably noticed the unusual stiffness of the tall boy's right arm when he was getting over the gate, though he did not immediately grasp the cause of it. However, the probable meaning of it must soon have flashed across his mind, for the boys had not walked twenty yards down the road when they heard him say, ' Darned if ye ain't got one o' they little guns with ye.' They heard no more. ' Come on,' said Leroux, and the two boys dashed off down the road at their best pace, closely pursued by the keeper, who though middle-aged was a spare-made, active-looking fellow. It was a very hot day and the two boys were in their Sunday clothes and wearing top-hats, and handicapped with the rifle, the barrel of which was rather heavy. Still at first they gained on the keeper, and at the end of a quarter of a mile had

[1] Mr. Boughton Leigh.

increased the distance between him and them to quite
fifty yards, when suddenly they came almost face to face
with old ' Froddy,' the great headmaster himself, who had
just emerged from a lane into the high road. With his
head held high in the air and his hat on the back of his
head, he came striding along all alone, at a pace of at least
four miles an hour. His thoughts were evidently far from
the earth he trod, and probably he never saw the boys at
all, but they instantly recognized him.

" ' Old Froddy, by Jove ! ' ejaculated Leroux ; ' come on
through the hedge,' and without an instant's hesitation he
dashed at and broke his way into the field to the right of
the road, his friend scrambling through the gap he had
made in the hedge close behind him. The boys were now
in a large grass field across which they started to run
diagonally, the keeper following doggedly behind them,
though when they gained the further corner of the field he
was nearly a hundred yards behind them. As they climbed
the gate into the next field Leroux's tall young friend was
panting painfully, and before they were half-way across it
he said he would not be able to run much further with the
rifle-barrel. There was a large hayrick in the far corner of
this field, so Leroux urged his companion to try and carry
the rifle-barrel as far as there and then throw it down
behind the rick, just as they passed it, and were for the
moment hidden from the keeper. Leroux who was comparatively fresh and whom the keeper would never have
caught, still stuck to the stock of his rifle, and intended to
return for the barrel the next day, which happened to be
one of the three-weekly Monday half-holidays. He did not
think there would be much chance of its discovery before
then. However, as bad luck would have it, and by an
extraordinary chance, the gamekeeper saw it as he passed
the rick. He had probably turned to look behind him,
thinking that possibly the boys had run round the rick, and
must have seen the glint of the sun on the barrel. The boys
had not got very far over the next field before they heard
the gamekeeper shouting, and on turning his head Leroux
saw that he was standing near the gate waving something

over his head, which as it glinted and flashed in the sun he knew was the barrel of his rifle. It was no good running any further, the keeper had their names and half the rifle, so they walked back to him and Leroux had to surrender the other half.

Now Leroux had great affection for this, his first rifle, and hated the idea of having it confiscated, so he tried to make terms with the keeper, and offered to give him all the money he could afford, if he would return him the rifle, and be content to report him and his friend for trespassing. The keeper refused this bribe with much apparent indignation, saying that no amount of money that might be offered to him would tempt him to swerve from his duty, which was to take the rifle straight to his master, Mr. Lowden Beigh. So the two boys walked slowly and sadly back to the school, arriving there just in time for the afternoon service in the chapel, which, however, did nothing to cheer them.

" Every day during the following week Leroux expected to be summoned to the headmaster's study and taxed with trespassing with a rifle on Mr. Lowden Beigh's land. But at the end of this time, as nothing happened, he felt convinced that the keeper had never given up the little rifle to his master at all, but had kept it himself, in the hope of being able to dispose of it for more money than had been offered him for its return. At any rate Leroux determined to write to Mr. Lowden Beigh, tell him exactly what had happened, and ask him to let him have the rifle back again at the end of the term. This he did, and the following day received an answer requesting him to call at the Hall with the friend who was with him when the rifle was taken, on the following Sunday afternoon. The two boys complied with this request and they were very kindly entertained and treated to wine and cake by Mr. Lowden Beigh. He asked Leroux if it was he who had taken the herons' eggs at Tombe Abbey, and when he admitted that it was, said, ' Why, you're the biggest poacher in the school.' He then told the boys that the keeper had never said a word to him about the rifle, but that he had demanded it from him immediately on reading Leroux's letter, and then dismissed the man from his service. Finally, Mr. Lowden Beigh told Leroux that if he would again come to the Hall, the day before the big school broke up at the end of the term, he would return him his rifle, and this promise he faithfully kept.

" It was whilst he was at home during the Christmas holidays immediately preceding the commencement of his second year at the great Midland school, that John Leroux, then just fifteen years of age, was an eye-witness of, and indeed, a participant in, the terrible disaster on the ice in Regent's Park, which took place on January 15th, 1867.

" At that time he was living with his parents at no great distance from the scene of the accident, of which he wrote an account to a school friend whilst the events related were still fresh in his memory.

" As a result of a long-continued frost, the ice on the ornamental water in the park had become excessively thick, and during the early part of January, 1867, thousands of people might have been seen skating there daily. At length, however, a thaw set in, and as the ice became gradually more rotten in appearance, the skaters rapidly decreased in numbers.

" On the day of the accident Leroux went to the park alone after lunch, and on his arrival at the ornamental water, found that the ice had been broken all round the shore of the lake by the men employed by the Royal Humane Society, with the object of preventing people from getting on to the ice. At the same time several servants of the Society were doing their best to persuade the more adventurous spirits who had got on to the ice by means of planks, to leave it. At that time there were probably not more than three or four hundred people on the whole expanse of the ornamental water. At least they appeared to be very thinly scattered over it, compared with the crowds of a few days before, when the ice was sound and strong, before the thaw had set in.

" Having come to the park to skate, and being perhaps of a somewhat self-willed and adventurous disposition,

Leroux put on his skates, and watching his opportunity, got on to the ice, which though quite three inches in thickness, was seamed in every direction with a multiplicity of cracks, through which the water constantly welled up and ran over the surface. It was indeed evident that the solid ice-slab with which the lake had been originally covered was now formed of innumerable small pieces, really independent one of another, but still fitting closely together like the sections of a child's puzzle after they have been put in their places. Leroux himself never doubted that it was the breaking of the ice for the space of three or four feet all round the shores of the lake, which allowed room for the cracks in the unbroken ice gradually to widen until at last the whole sheet broke into separate pieces. As the skaters passed to and fro upon it, the whole surface of the ice-sheet seemed to rise and sink in response to their passage, and every moment the gaps gaped wider.

" It was getting on towards four o'clock in the afternoon, and Leroux was just then right in the middle of the lake, midway between the largest island and the bridge leading towards the Park Road, when he heard a cry behind him, and looking round saw that the ice was breaking in the direction of the bridge. It was a sight which he never forgot. Right across the whole breadth of the lake the sections into which the ice-sheet had been divided by the cracks were disengaging themselves one from another. The line of breaking advanced steadily towards where the boy was standing, each separate section of ice as the pressure was removed from behind, first breaking loose, and after being tilted into the air, again falling flat into its place. As no one fell into the water when the ice first broke up, the pressure which was the immediate cause of the catastrophe must have been exerted from a distance, and it was probably the weight of the people on the ice some way off which caused it to bulge where it first broke to such an extent as to detach some of the smaller sections which were already really separated one from another by the ever-widening cracks.

" There was a regular panic amongst the comparatively

small number of people between Leroux and the point near the bridge where the ice first commenced to break up, and they all went flying along as fast as their skates would carry them, straight down the centre of the lake towards the narrow channel between the two islands in front of them. At the same time there was a stampede for the shore from every part of the lake, and as the great bulk of the people then on the ice were near the edge when it so suddenly commenced to break up, most of them either got to land without assistance, or being caught in the breaking ice when within a rope's throw of the shore, were subsequently rescued ; but every one who got into the water amongst the thick heavy ice-slabs at any distance from the shore was drowned, and most of these unfortunate people disappeared immediately beneath the heavy slabs of ice, between which they fell into the water, and which closed over them at once.

" When the ice first began to break up, Leroux could not help standing still for a few moments, and watching the rapidly advancing line of breakage, and then when he turned to run for it or rather skate for it, he was quite alone, and at some little distance behind the crowd of people who had first taken the alarm. Suddenly there was a wild, despairing cry ahead, and Leroux saw that the ice was breaking up in the narrow channel between the two islands. At this juncture many people undoubtedly lost their heads as they skated right into the broken ice and almost all of them at once disappeared. It was between the two islands that the greatest loss of life occurred, as of the forty-nine bodies subsequently recovered in different parts of the lake, twenty-four were found in close proximity to one another at this spot, and yet there was scarcely a head to be seen at the time of the accident above the broken ice, as the weight of the heavy slabs forced those who fell in between them under water almost immediately. Although he was only a boy of fifteen at this time, he had never missed a chance of falling through weak or rotten ice every winter since he first went to school, and these various experiences had no doubt given him a good deal of self-confidence. At

any rate he felt neither frightened nor flurried by the somewhat alarming circumstances of the position in which he
now found himself, but quickly made up his mind as to the
best course to adopt to save his life. As the ice had already
broken up both before and behind him, but was still solid
immediately behind him he stopped short where he was,
and lay down at full length on the longest piece of ice he
could see which was free from widely open cracks. He had
scarcely done so, when the wave of breakage which had
commenced near the bridge passed him, all the great cracks
with which the ice-sheet was seamed opening to such an
extent that every separate slab became detached. Many
of these slabs were first tilted a little into the air, as had
happened when the ice first broke up near the bridge,
but they immediately fell flat again into their places, so
that the whole of the ice-sheet in the central part of the
ornamental water seemed to be in one piece, though in
reality the cracks which divided it into innumerable small
slabs were now so wide that each piece was independent
the one of the other, and most of them would not have been
large enough to support the weight of a man standing near
their edge, without heeling over and precipitating him into
the water.

" Fortunately for Leroux the ice had not been broken
round the edge of the largest island in the lake to his left,
and although the cracks had opened all round where he lay,
as the wave of breakage passed, to such an extent as to have
made it impossible to have walked or skated across the dis-
integrated slabs, without tilting one or other of them,
and so falling into the water, yet he was only a short distance
from the unbroken ice-sheet which rested on the island.
The slab on which he was lying was quite large enough to
bear his weight easily, and as he was out of all danger for
the time being, he was able to look around and note what
was going on. Directly the ice broke up there was, of course,
tremendous excitement on the shore of the lake nearest the
Zoological Gardens, where great crowds of people had been
congregated the whole afternoon. Many gallant and successful attempts were made to rescue those who were fighting

for life amongst the ice-slabs ; but Leroux's impression was that no one was saved who had got into the water at any considerable distance from the shore. At the spot where the largest number of people were drowned, almost every-one who fell into the water disappeared immediately. Still here and there men kept their heads above water for a long time, and all these poor fellows might have been rescued, had it not been for the breaking of a rope. It was soon realized that it would be quite impossible to save the people who were so far out amongst the ice that a rope could not be thrown to them from the shore except by some special means, and someone hit upon the idea of dragging a boat to them over the ice. Leroux saw the boat pulled up over the still unbroken ice beyond the bridge, and long ropes were then made fast to its bow and carried over the bridge to each side of the lake, where willing hands enough were ready to work them. Had the ropes only held, the boat might have been pulled from one side or the other of the lake to all those who were in the water amongst the ice-slabs at a distance from the shore ; but unfortunately before the boat had been pulled far beyond the bridge one of the ropes broke, and as it was then apparently recognized that they were not strong enough to stand the strain required, the experiment was not tried again. There were only two men in the water anywhere near Leroux, and they were about half-way between where he lay and the shore of the lake. He had seen them at first trying to force their way through the ice, but the slabs were so thick and heavy that they threatened at every moment to turn over on them, and they soon became exhausted and remained quiet. At last one of them disappeared and not long afterwards only a hat on the ice remained to mark the spot where his com-panion in misfortune had also sunk. Leroux soon realized that there was no hope of rescue from the shore, and indeed amidst all the excitement of saving or attempting to save the lives of those who had got into the water within reach he had probably been overlooked or possibly his position had been considered hopeless.

" At length when the light was commencing to fade

E

Leroux made up his mind to try and reach the island on his left by crawling from one slab of ice to another. He fully realized that if he once got into the water he would never get out, but not being very heavy in those days, and by moving only very slowly and cautiously, and carefully selecting his route he succeeded at last in reaching the unbroken ice near the island. He had one very narrow escape, as a table of ice very nearly turned over on him before he had got sufficiently far on it to keep it flat. Luckily there was a much larger slab just beyond it, on to which he crawled without much difficulty. After crossing the island he again got on to unbroken ice and skated across it, to the shore near the lower bridge.

" By that time it was rapidly growing dusk, everybody whom it had been possible to reach with a rope from the shore had been rescued, and all the rest were still and cold beneath the ice. But although Leroux knew that a considerable number of people must have been drowned, until he saw the long list of those who had lost their lives in the next morning's ' Times ' he had no idea that the disaster was so serious as it really was."

The following reminiscences of Selous as a schoolboy at Rugby were contributed to the ' Meteor,' the Rugby school paper (February 7th, 1917), by Canon Wilson, D.D. :—

" I first heard of Selous some time in 1863, soon after I became a house-master. The master of his preparatory school at Tottenham told me that a Mr. Slous—for so the name was then spelt—was going to enter his son at my house. ' Take my advice,' was the gist of the letter, ' and say your house is full ; the boy will plague the life out of you.' I wrote to enquire the nature of the plague. ' He breaks every rule ; he lets himself down out of a dormitory window to go birds'-nesting ; he is constantly complained of by neighbours for trespassing ; he fastened up an assistant master in a cowshed into which he had chased the young villain early one summer morning ; somehow the youngster scrambled out, and fastened the door on the outside, so that the master missed morning school.'

" Such were his crimes ; so, of course, I wrote back and said that he was the boy for me.

" His father brought him down from town, a bright-eyed, fair-haired boy of twelve or thirteen, who had no suspicion that I knew all about his iniquities. When his father departed, I had a little of the usual talk with a new boy, about work and games and so on ; and then I asked him what he meant to be. ' I mean to be like Livingstone,' he replied. I had seen Livingstone when he came to Cambridge, in 1857, I think, and spoke in the Senate House, appealing for a Universities Mission to Central Africa ; so we talked Livingstone and Africa, and Natural History. I soon saw that he had the fire and the modesty of genius and was a delightful creature.

" He was quite exemplary as a young member of the House and School, so far as I knew. He was ' late ' for chapel sometimes in long summer afternoons ; how much late I did not inquire. I guessed what he was about and he did his lines like a man.

" He was extraordinarily acute in all his senses—sight, hearing, smell, taste. He asked me, for example, one day to some brook a few miles away to watch kingfishers. We crawled up warily when we got near the spot. He could see exactly what they were catching and carrying, from a distance at which I could only see a bird flying. His power of hearing was also more than acute. One day at our table in hall I told a lady who sat next me that a nightingale had been heard singing in somebody's spinney. We decided to drive down to it after dinner, and on reaching the spot, we found Selous already there, roaming about in the spinney. I called to him, and he came to the edge of the wood. ' What are you doing there ? ' ' Looking for a nightingale's nest, sir.' ' But why here ? ' ' I heard you say at dinner that one was singing here.' Now he was sixteen or eighteen feet away, at a different table, and we were fifty in hall, talking and clattering with knives and forks. And yet he heard me distinctly. He could disentangle the voices, and listen to one, as a dog can follow one scent among many. Then as to smell and taste. He told me that when he shot a new bird with his ' tweaker '—you will learn presently what the ' tweaker ' was in his case—he always *tasted* its flesh.

" He was extremely accurate in his observation, and in his estimates of distance, size, number, etc.; in fact, he was the most truthful observer I can imagine ; free from all exaggeration and egotism, and he retained this simplicity and accuracy and modesty all his life. He was a beautiful runner, a football-player with singular dash and a first-rate swimmer ; but he left Rugby at seventeen, I think, so that he did not win any great athletic distinctions at school.

" But I must tell you some stories about him.

" On some great public occasion of rejoicing the streets of Rugby were decorated with flags. When my man called me at 7.0 a.m., he said, ' I think I ought to tell you, sir, that there is a broomstick and duster showing in every chimney in the house.' ' Very well,' I replied, ' go and tell Mr. Selous that they must be taken down by 12 o'clock.' He had let himself down at night out of the dormitory window that looks into the study quadrangle and had collected brooms and dusters from the studies. He had somehow clambered up waterpipes and gutters and roofs, broomsticks and all ; and when I went out people in the road were admiring our extemporized decorations—duster flags and broom-handles sticking out of the chimney pots at all angles. There was another flag, of the same nature, perilously near the top of the taller of two poplars that stood close to the boys' entrance. They were all taken down by dinner-time ; I never enquired how, or by whom.

" There used to be a vine, trained up the south face of the house, and one year, I think in 1868, it bore an extraordinary crop of grapes which ripened beautifully. One day at dinner I told the head of the dormitory on the second floor, over the drawing-room, that they might gather all that they could reach from the window. *I forgot Selous* as this was not his bedroom, but the dormitory did not forget him. An aunt of mine was sleeping in the bedroom below, and she remarked next morning at breakfast that she heard, or thought she heard, voices at night quite close to her windows. Had anything happened ? I went out into the garden to look, the vine was stripped more than half-way down the windows of the first floor. It was Selous, of course ; they let him down somehow. I was told that he filled a pillow-case with grape-bunches, and feasted the House. Mr. C. K. Francis, the well-known Metropolitan Police Magistrate, his contemporary in my house, has told this story of Selous to the readers of the ' Daily Telegraph ' (January 15th), and says that they let Selous down in a blanket.

" Of course Selous was an active member of the School Natural History Society. I must tell you about a meeting of that Society. Dr. Walter Flight, who was in charge of the minerals of the British Museum, was staying with me, and I asked him whether he would like to come as a visitor to an ordinary meeting of our Society. I knew it would be an interesting one. Selous had shortly before raided the heronry on the island at Coombe Abbey. He swam the pond from the end distant from the house, climbed several trees, took one egg from each nest, swam back and was chased, but escaped by sheer speed. Lord Craven complained to the H.M. The H.M. warned our Society pretty plainly, and our committee censured Selous. At the meeting we were going to attend, Selous, as was widely known, was going to make his defence. The room, the old Fifth Form Room, next to the School House Dining Hall, was crowded. Flight and I squeezed in. ' Are your meetings always like this ? ' he asked. ' You will see,' I replied, ' that the school takes a great interest in natural history.' ' I am very glad to see this,' he said.

" Exhibits were made, a paper read, and then began the real business of the evening—the official condemnation by our president, Mr. Kitchener, and Selous' spirited defence.

" Selous presented the eggs to the Natural History Society, and they were safe in the collection twenty years ago, I am told. I hope they are there still.

" He also climbed the great elm trees, which then stood in the close, for rooks' eggs. This feat was also performed at night, and the cawing of the rooks roused Dr. Temple, but Selous was not detected in the darkness.

" Selous' special contribution to our Society was on birds. If I remember right his first list of birds noted at Rugby exceeded ninety. I will tell the story how one very rare bird was added to our list. It was in the very hard winter of 1867 ; snow was lying on the ground. In the evening, some hours after lock-up a ring at the front door came at the moment I was going to my study, the door of which is close to the front door. I opened the front door and there stood Selous, with a bird dangling from his hand. I don't know which of us was most surprised. ' Come in to the study ; what have you got there ? ' ' Oh, sir, it's William-son's duck ; it's very rare.' (I invent the name Williamson, I know it was somebody's duck.) ' Go and fetch the bird-book from the House Library.' (I had put an excellent bird-book in several volumes into the Library for his use.) ' Leave the bird.' I examined the bird, neatly shot through the neck. He was quite right, a note in the book said that it had been occasionally seen at certain places on the East coast ; only once, I think, inland as far as Northampton-shire. ' How did you get it ? ' ' I saw it at Swift's and followed it to Lilbourne and got it there.' ' How ? ' ' With my tweaker,' was the reply. ' It must be a very powerful tweaker ? ' I said. ' Yes, sir, it's a very strong one ; I thought you would not mind my being late for once, as it's very rare.'

" Some six years later, when he came back from a four years' solitary travel and exploration in what is now called Rhodesia, or even further inland, this incident of the tweaker turned up. ' I did wonder,' he said, ' whether you were such an innocent as really to believe it was a tweaker.' ' My dear Selous,' I said, ' I knew the bird was shot, and I knew you had a gun, and the farmhouse where you kept it, but you kept it so dark and made such excellent use of it that I said nothing about it.'

" One of the most difficult problems presented to all who are in authority is : how much ought I *not* to know and see ?

" I think it was on this occasion that he came down to a house-supper. He had told me lots of stories about his adventures in Africa during those four years. They are told in his books, every one of which is, I hope, in the School Library and well read   I asked him to tell some of them to the house. No he would not ; so finally at the supper, I said that if he would not, I would, and I began with the story of his going to ask Lobengula, King of the Matabele, for leave to shoot elephants. ' You are only a boy,' the King said. ' You must shoot birds. The first elephant you hunt will kill you.' Selous jumped up. ' Oh, sir, let me tell it,' and we had a never-to-be-forgotten evening.

" But it is time to stop. One of his friends, Sir Ralph Williams, well said of him in a letter in ' The Times,' of January 10th, ' The name of Fred Selous stands for all that is straightest and best in South African story,' and I will venture to say that it stands for the same in Rugby annals.   " J. M. WILSON.

"Worcester, 22 *January*, 1917."

In August, 1868, at the age of seventeen, Selous left Rugby and went to Neuchâtel, in Switzerland, where he lived at the " Institution Roulet." He spent his time learning French and the violin and commenced his studies to be a doctor, for which profession he evinced no enthusiasm. Writing to his mother in November, he says :—

" As for my future medical examinations I don't know how I shall come off ; I do not want particularly to be a doctor, but I shall go in for that as I can't see anything else that I should like better, except sheep-farming or something of that sort in one of the colonies, but I suppose I must give up that idea ; however, if I become a surgeon I do not intend to try and get a practice in England, but I should try and get a post as ship's surgeon, or army surgeon in India, if I could get any leave of absence which would give me a little time to myself, but anyhow I am certain I shall never be able to settle down quietly in England. You talked about me being at an age of irresponsibility, but I don't see that I am, as supposing I don't manage to learn these infernal languages (why was anyone fool enough to build the tower of Babel ?) everyone will be disgusted with me."

In December there was more talk of his going to Dresden to learn German, but he himself voted for Wiesbaden as being more of a country district where he would have more opportunities for shooting and fishing. After a short visit home his father took him to Wiesbaden in the spring of 1869, when he wrote to his sister " Locky " :—

" Many thanks for your spiritual letter which almost tempts me to commit suicide ; if I can't get good shooting and fishing in this world I'll have it in the next, if what the Chinaman says is true ; but by hook or by crook I will have some in this world too, and make some rare natural history collections into the bargain. But first I must make a little money, but how ? not by scribbling away on a three-legged stool in a dingy office in London. I am becoming more and more convinced every day that I should never be able to stand that and everybody I know or have ever had anything to do with says the same thing. I have a great many qualifications for getting on in one of our colonies, viz. perseverance, energy, and a wonderfully good constitution. What makes me recur to the old subject is this : I have made the acquaintance of a family here of the name of K——. I always forget their name although I know them intimately. This gentleman, a German from Brunswick, has been twenty years in Natal (where he made his fortune) and since then eight years in England, and now has become regularly English (speaking English, indeed, without the slightest accent). His wife is an Englishwoman who was born in the Cape Colony, but has always lived with him in Natal ; and then he has a very large family. These people give the most splendid accounts of Natal. Firstly, they say that the climate is superb, there being no winter and it not being so hot in summer as in Germany. Then they say that the country is lovely beyond description. They do not praise Cape Colony, only Natal, which they describe as a perfect paradise. They say, too, that Natal itself is a wonderfully gay place and that the society there is very good. The wife says she can't stand Europe at all, the climate is so detestable compared with that of Natal. She says that she often used to go for weeks and weeks up country with her husband and children on shooting excursions, sleeping out in tents all the time, and that taking into consideration the beautiful climate and country there is no enjoyment equal to it, and I am fully of her opinion. They travelled once three days with Dr. Livingstone, but you will hear all about it from them when you come over here."

He arrived at Wiesbaden in September and took up his residence with Herr Knoch, who lived in the Roderallee. In December he met the Colchester family, with whom he became great friends.

At this time he enjoyed the music every afternoon at the Kursaal, and was amused in the evening to see the gambling that went on. One night a Russian lost 100,000 francs. "What an April fool!" is Selous' only comment. He had at this time a nice dog named Bell, to whom he was much attached. He is always writing for trout-flies, or books on sport or natural history. " I wouldn't care to go to Rome and see the Holy Week, but I should like to go to Russia, Sweden, or some other country where some shooting or fishing is to be had, but I must be patient and make some money, though I don't know how. Yesterday I went down to the Rhine, after my German and music lessons, but only brought back three small fish. A few days ago an officer was shot dead in a duel at Mayence. Verdict, ' Serve him right.' "

Miss Colchester thus recalls certain incidents of Selous' life at Wiesbaden. " As showing his sporting nature, I may mention that he swam the Rhine near Biebrich to retrieve a wild duck he had shot for us. It was blocked with ice at the time, but that did not daunt him. One day we were all skating on the frozen waters of the Kursaal Gardens when the ice suddenly broke up and I was thrown into the deep water. Without a moment's hesitation Fred jumped in and supported me under the arms until help came. He was a dear boy and we all loved him."

Selous set himself to learn the language as thoroughly as he could in the time at his disposal, but the cold study of German verbs was hard for a boy of seventeen with the spring in his bones and the sun glinting on the forest oaks.

When summer came young Selous spent all his spare time chiefly with his friend Colchester, roving the woods and opens in search of birds'-nests and butterflies. The woods in the neighbourhood of Wiesbaden were, as is usual in Germany, strictly preserved and, therefore, being forbidden ground, offered an especial attraction to the young naturalist. On two of these forays he had been stopped and warned by a forester named Keppel, who though an oldish man was immensely active and powerful. From him Selous had several narrow escapes, but the day of reckoning was at hand. In the heart of the forest Selous had one day observed a pair of honey-buzzards, which being frequently seen afterwards about the same spot, he concluded must have a nest somewhere. These birds are somewhat uncommon even in Germany, and Selous naturally longed to find the nest and take the eggs. At last one day he and Colchester found the nest on the top of a high fir tree, but on climbing up to it Selous observed that there were no eggs. A few days later the two marauders set off at dawn and again approached the nest, Colchester being left at the foot of the tree to keep watch. Selous was in the act of descending the tree when Keppel suddenly appeared and by his words and actions showed that he was in a furious rage.

" Now I shall take you to prison," he roared, as he seized hold of the coat in which Selous had hidden the two eggs he had taken.

By this time, however, the fighting spirit was aroused on both sides, for Selous had no intention either of being captured or resigning his treasures quietly. A fierce struggle ensued in which the coat was torn in half, when at last Selous, losing his temper, gave the old forester a right-hander on the jaw which dropped him like a felled ox.

The boys were now alarmed and for a moment Selous thought he must have killed the man, but as he showed

signs of recovering they took to their heels and ran home
with all possible speed. Since complications were bound to
follow Selous at once consulted a lawyer, who advised him
to pack up his traps and leave Prussia. Accordingly he
took the train and went to Salzburg in Austria, where he
knew he would be beyond the power of German courts.
Selous' chief sorrow over the unfortunate affair seems to be
that he lost his rare eggs.

Soon after he arrived at Salzburg Selous heard that his
friend, Charley Colchester, who had escaped to Kronberg,
but was followed and arrested, had been condemned to a
week's imprisonment (without the option of a fine) for
taking eggs on two occasions.

" If I had been caught," writes Selous, " I should have got
two or three months instead of a week's imprisonment, for
both the lawyer and the Burgomaster to whom I spoke,
said that the taking of eggs was but a small matter in the
eyes of Prussian law compared with resisting an official."

The Austrian with whom he lived at Salzburg seems to
have been a pleasant fellow named Rochhart, who had
travelled much in Greece and America. Selous seems to
have liked the genial Austrians far better than the Prussians
and especially enjoyed the Tyrolese music and the butterfly
hunting in the woods when the weather was fine. Writing
to his mother (July 5th, 1870), he speaks of his enthusiasm
as a collector :—

" Why I feel the absence of the sun so very acutely is
because, when the sun is not shining no butterflies, or none
worth having, are to be got. Now this is just the time for
the Purple Emperors, some specimens of which I want very
much to get, and so I have been exceedingly provoked. I
found out the place where the P.E.'s were to be found and
for the last seven days I have been every day to that place
(which is from five to six miles from Salzburg) and there I
have waited from twelve to three, through rain and everything else, hoping and hoping for a passing sunbeam, as I
could see them every now and then at the tops of the trees,
and if the sun had but come out for a few minutes some of
them would have been sure to have come down and settled in

the road. Well during all the hours of watching in those
seven days the sun never, never, never broke through the
clouds for one instant, and each day I returned home more
disappointed and more indignant against providence than
the day before. I think that if this sort of thing had continued for another week I should have gone into a chronic
state of melancholy and moroseness for the rest of my life,
and people would have said, ' Ah, he must have had some
great disappointment in early life.' These are the sort of
things that rile me more than anything else, for you can't
think how I put my whole soul into egg and butterfly collecting when I'm at it, and how I boil up and over with
impotent rage at not being able to attain the object of my
desires on account of the weather over which I have no
control. However, perseverance can struggle against anything. This afternoon the sun shone out and I immediately
caught two Purple Emperors (*Apatura Iris*), and two very
similar butterflies unknown in England (*Apatura Ilia*), also
a great many White Admirals (*Limenitis Camilla*), not quite
the same as the English White Admiral (*Limenitis Sybilla*),
but very like ; all butterflies well worth having. If the
weather will but continue fine for a few days I will soon
make some good additions to my collection, but it is hopeless
work collecting butterflies in bad weather. I think I must
be set down as a harmless lunatic by the peasants in the
neighbourhood already."

Selous was not long at Salzburg before he found an old
chamois hunter and poacher, with whom he made frequent
excursions into the neighbouring mountains. On one of
these trips he killed two chamois, and the head of one of
these is still in the museum at Worplesdon.

The Franco-German war now began and Selous was greatly
incensed that the general feeling in England was in favour
of Prussia.

" Vive la France, à bas la Prusse," he writes to his
mother (July 22nd, 1870), " your saying the war is ' likely
to become a bloody butchery through all the Christian
nations of civilized Europe,' is rather a startler. Since this
morning I have read all the Cologne and Vienna papers for

the last week and you are most certainly several miles ahead of the most far-seeing and sanguinary politician, in either Austria or Prussia. You say that Bavaria has joined Prussia and Austria is likely to do so too. Bavaria cannot help itself or would not have joined Prussia. The Crown Prince of Prussia is in Munich with 15,000 Prussian troops, and the Bavarians are forced by treaty to aid Prussia or they would not do so. Prussia is the only power that is likely to take any part in the war at present. Austria most certainly will not interfere unless she is forced into it. And England and America are less likely still to do so. The post now goes to England by Trieste, by sea, of course, and supposing the war does become a bloody butchery through all the Christian nations of civilized Europe, an Italian passenger steamer would surely not be meddled with. Whatever happens, the war cannot come here, for there is nothing to be fought for in the Tyrol and no room to fight for it in the mountain valleys if there was. So that the route to Trieste and from thence to England will always be open. The people say that in 1866, when the war between Austria and Prussia was going on, they never knew anything about it here. As for the money, you can easily send a letter of credit to a bank in Salzburg or Munich and that difficulty would be got over. For several months at least it is not at all likely that any other nation will join either party, England least of all ; and supposing that England were drawn into it eventually, you would surely be able to tell long before war was declared if such was likely to be the case, and send me word, for the postal communications will not be stopped until then via Trieste. It seems to me most ridiculous to predict so much when so little is known. Unless you really think in your heart of hearts that it is necessary for me to come, please let me remain here a few months longer ; England taking part in the war is the only thing that can stop either letters or myself from reaching you, and surely you cannot tell me in cold blood that England is likely to be drawn into the war for months and months to come, at least all the Prussian papers declare most positively that it is not likely that either America or England will take any part in the war, and surely they as a party most intensely interested would say something about it if they thought that there was the slightest chance of England assisting. Gladstone, you know, will do his utmost to keep England neutral. Austria was almost ruined by the last war, but is now rapidly increasing in wealth and if drawn into the war would be utterly ruined, so that she will do her utmost to keep out of it. Why I so particularly wish to remain here a few months longer is because if I return to England all the money and time that has been wasted in zither at any rate, if not violin lessons, will have been utterly thrown away and I shall lose a pleasure and a pastime that would have lasted me my whole life. In three or four months more, as I am working very hard at it, I shall know enough of the zither to do without a master. The violin is all very well, but it is not an instrument that one derives much pleasure from playing unaccompanied, unless one plays extremely well, whereas the zither, like the piano, needs no accompaniment. The zither I have now is not the little one you saw at Wiesbaden, but an Austrian zither which is much larger and tuned lower, and altogether a finer instrument."

He seems to have formed a very accurate estimate of the German character in war. Writing to his mother, October 20th, 1870, he says :—

" I have seen and spoken to several Bavarian soldiers in a village just beyond the Bavarian frontier, who were at Wörth and Sedan, and who have been sent back on the sick list ; they say there is a great deal of sickness among the German troops, out of the 1000 men from the two villages of Schellenberg and Berchtesgaden who were all in the actions at Wörth and Sedan, not a single one has as yet been killed, so I was told, though a great many have been wounded. I see a great deal said in the English papers about the ' Francs tireurs ' being little better than murderers. I think that the French ought to consider all the soldiers composing the German armies as so many burglars, and shoot them down like rabbits in every possible manner ; and, moreover, as the Germans are murdering the peasants, men, women, and children, for such offences as being in possession of an old sword, in every direction, I think the French would be perfectly justified in shooting every German soldier they take prisoner. After the affair at Bazeilles, I don't believe any more in the humanity of the Germans."

At this time Selous met an old Hungarian gentleman, who had large farms in Hungary, and offered to take him for two years to learn the business. But his father threw cold water on this project and told his son to remain at Salzburg until he had completed his German education. Accordingly he continued to reside there until June, 1871, when he went on a short visit to Vienna, of which he writes (June 17th, 1871) :—

" I think I have seen everything that is to be seen in Vienna. The crown jewels, which I daresay you have seen, were very interesting and very magnificent. The Emperor's stables, too, I thought very interesting ; he has an immense number of horses, some of them very beautiful indeed. We found an English groom there who had almost forgotten his own language ; he had been away from England nine years, and so it is not to be wondered at, as I daresay he rarely speaks anything but German and never reads anything at all. The theatre in Vienna (I mean the new opera house) is most magnificent. It was only completed in 1868, so I don't suppose you have ever seen it. I believe it is acknowledged to be at present the finest theatre in the world. It is an immense size, almost as large as Covent Garden, and the decorations inside and out, and the galleries and everything appertaining to it are most beautiful and tasteful. We saw ' Martha,' ' Tannhäuser,' and ' Faust ' there, and a little sort of pantomime entitled ' Flick and Flock.' I liked ' Martha ' very much. They have a splendid tenor named Walter, who took the part of Lionel. I daresay you will hear him in London some day. I didn't like ' Tannhäuser ' very much ; I couldn't understand the story at all and there were no pretty airs in it. ' Faust ' was splendid, Marguerite and Faust were, I should think, as near perfection as possible, and Mephistopheles was very good, though at first he gave me the impression of looking more like a clown than the devil. The scenery in all these pieces was splendid. ' Flick and Flock ' was exactly like an English pantomime with dumb show. The scenery was really wonderful ; there were about half a dozen transformation scenes, none of which would have disgraced a London stage on Boxing Night."

In August he arrived home in England, and during the next three months he attended classes at the University College Hospital (London) to gain some knowledge of medical science preparatory to going to Africa.

THE PLAINS OF THE ORANGE FREE STATE IN 1871.

CHAPTER III

1871–1875

THERE are few of us whose early aspirations and subsequent acts are not influenced by literature. Some book comes just at the time of our life when we are most impressionable and seems exactly to fit in with our ideas and temperament. To this rule Selous was no exception, for he often admitted in after-life that the one book which definitely sent him to Africa and made him a pioneer and a hunter of Big Game, was Baldwin's " African Hunting from Natal to the Zambesi," published in 1864. Example in any line of adventure is recurrent, and especially so if the field of adventure is not spoilt by what we may call excessive " civilization." There have been, as it were, landmarks in the literature of African sport and travel, each book being more or less cumulative in its effect. Amongst books that mattered, perhaps the first was Burchell's fully-illustrated folio and the lesser writings of an English officer who hunted in the Orange Free State late in the eighteenth and early in the nineteenth century. The works of these men incited Captain Cornwallis Harris to undertake an extensive trip as far as the Limpopo. He was a capable artist and an excellent writer, and published a magnificent folio describing his adventures and the natural history of the large mammals, which still commands a high price. He at once inspired many hunters to follow in his footsteps, and several of these, such as Roualeyn Gordon Cumming, William Cotton Oswell, Sir Francis Galton, and C. J. Anderson, wrote either books of great value or portions of standard works. Gordon Cumming did an immense amount of shooting—far too much most people now think— but his volume, written in the romantic British style, is one that will always remain a classic in the world of sporting literature. His tales of the game he saw or what he killed were not always accepted as true facts, but from all accounts, gathered from independent sources, it is now admitted that Gordon Cumming was a fearless hunter and did in the main accomplish all the principal exploits to which he laid claim.

" Lake Ngami, or Explorations in South-Western Africa," by Charles John Anderson, published in 1856, with some admirable early illustrations by Wolf, gives an account of the author's four years' wanderings (partly with Francis Galton) in the Western Wilderness, and is a truthful and excellent record of the Great Game in these districts at that time. Galton also published " Tropical Africa," but did not give much space to sport or natural history. Oswell, a great hunter and companion of Livingstone in many of his travels, also wrote in the last days of his life an admirable contribution to the " Badminton Library," which embodied an account of his life and adventures amongst the Great Game of South Africa in the forties. It is well illustrated by Wolf, the greatest painter of birds and mammals who ever lived. Other men of his date who were excellent hunters, who left no records of their lives, were Vardon, General Sir Thomas Steele, and Thomas Baines, who, without prejudice, did perhaps as much exploration, geographical work, painting, and hunting as any Afrikander of his time. Baines, I believe, really discovered the Falls of the Zambesi before Livingstone visited them, and no adequate tribute to the work of this remarkable man has ever appeared. The amount of maps he prepared of out-of-the-way corners of South Africa from the Zambesi northwards, was very great and his work was only known to the pioneers like Livingstone, Oswell, Selous and others who followed after him and made use of his industry. Baines, too, though almost uneducated, was a very capable artist and I think I must have seen at least two hundred of his paintings in oil. He liked to depict landscapes and wild animals. Whilst those of the latter were not above criticism, his views of the rivers, lakes, forests, mountains, and plains of the Free State, swarming with game, are a truthful record of the days that are no more, and will doubtless live in South African history when more ambitious, technically correct works are forgotten.[1]

After these sportsmen and writers came William Charles Baldwin, who wandered, primarily with the object of hunting elephants, from Zululand to the Zambesi and west to Lake Ngami between the years 1852 and 1860. His book " African Hunting and Adventure " was published in 1863, and was beautifully illustrated by Wolf and Zwecker. It was an immediate success and caused many, like Selous, to leave the ways of civilization and seek adventure in the wilds. Baldwin was an excellent and fearless rider (he rode in a steeplechase when he was seventy) and a good shot, and the accounts of his adventures could hardly have failed to make their impress on the minds of young men of the right kind, but, as he admits, the elephants were on the wane even in his day (he never succeeded in hunting in the main haunts in Matabeleland), so future travellers had to exploit new fields.

On the 4th of September, 1871, Selous landed at Algoa Bay with £400 in his pocket. He went there determined to make his way into the interior and to lead the free life of the hunter as described by Gordon Cumming, Baldwin, and others. First he decided to go to the Diamond Fields, and left Port Elizabeth on September 6th with a young transport rider named Reuben Thomas, who conveyed him and his baggage for the sum of eight pounds. After a slow journey of nearly two months he reached his destination. On the road by hunting hard he had managed to kill " one bushbuck ram, one duiker, one springbuck, one klipspringer, and eight grey and red roebucks, all of which I carried on my own shoulders to the waggons."

Most unfortunately, however, a valuable double breech-loading rifle with which he had been shooting was stolen on the day he reached Kimberley. Next day he bought a horse and rode over to Pniel. There he met Mr. Arthur

---

[1] There was an exhibition of Baines' collected works at the Crystal Palace some years ago, but few people took any notice of them. Baines published an excellent book " The Gold Regions of South-Eastern Africa " in 1877.

Lang, and on October 31st went with him on a trading trip through Griqualand, passing down the Vaal and Orange rivers. He found the Bechuanas an industrious race, " but they are the stingiest, most begging, grasping, and disagreeable set of people that it is possible to imagine." He was much disappointed to find the country so bare of game. " The great drawback was that there was no game whatever, not even springbucks, the Kafirs having hunted everything into the far interior, so that now there is more game within five miles of Cape Town than here, where we were more than 600 miles up country." The party returned to the Diamond Fields at the end of March and sold off their produce—cattle, goats, and ostrich feathers at a profit of about £100.

Selous then set about his preparations for a journey into the far interior. From a trader he purchased a waggon, a span of young oxen, and five horses. A young fellow named Dorehill and a Mr. Sadlier then agreed to accompany him. The whole party seems to have been very badly armed with indifferent weapons. At the end of April, 1872, Selous and his two friends trekked north and only got as far as Kuruman, a delay of a fortnight being caused through the horses running away. Here Selous met Mr. William Williams, an experienced trader and hunter, from whom he purchased two unprepossessing-looking large-bore elephant guns as used by the Boer native hunters. Cheap as these guns were, about six pounds a-piece and using only common trade gunpowder, they were most effective weapons, for in three seasons with them (1872–1874) Selous killed seventy-eight elephants, all but one of which he shot whilst hunting on foot. He used to load them whilst running at full speed by simply diving his hand into a leather bag of powder slung at his side. " They kicked most frightfully, and in my case the punishment I received from these guns has affected my nerves to such an extent as to have materially influenced my shooting ever since, and I am heartily sorry I ever had anything to do with them."

After a trying trek the party arrived at Secheli's in twenty days through more or less waterless country, but just before reaching these kraals an accident happened which might easily have cost Selous and Dorehill their lives. Selous was taking some cartridges from a box on the side of the waggon, in which was about a pound of loose gunpowder, when Dorehill came up and dropped some ashes from his pipe into the box. An immediate explosion followed and both were badly burnt. Sadlier, however, rose to the emergency and " at once rubbed a mixture of oil and salt into our skinless faces ; it was not a pleasant process." After a visit to Secheli, who was a most completely civilized Kafir, Selous and his friends moved northward on the 28th June, with Frank Mandy, who was about to trade in the Matabele country. On the road to Boatlanarma they experienced great difficulties and were once three days and three nights without water. About the middle of August they left Bamangwato, where Selous purchased a salted horse. By exchanging his new waggon for a smaller second-hand one, a trade rifle and the horse itself valued at £75, he made a deal with a shrewd but uneducated Scotchman named Peter Skinner. Of course the new purchase ran away at the first opportunity, which delayed the party for another week. Near Pelatsi Selous had his first experience of real African hardship, and his subsequent account of being lost in the bush for four days and three nights, without covering except his shirt and breeches and without food or drink, is one of the most thrilling he ever wrote.[1]

Selous and his comrades here met their first giraffes and proceeded to give chase.

" After a time the giraffes separated, and suffice it to say that, at the end of an hour or so, I found myself lying on my back, with my right leg nearly broken, by coming violently into contact with the trunk of a tree ; and, on getting up and remounting my horse, not only were the giraffes out of sight, but nowhere could I see either of my two companions. Though, of course, my inexperience contributed much to the unsuccessful issue of this, my first giraffe hunt, yet I cannot help thinking that my horse also had a good deal to do with it, for, having been bred in the

[1] " A Hunter's Wanderings," pp. 15-23.

open plains of the Transvaal Republic, he was quite at sea
in the thick forests of the interior ; and if, when going at
full gallop through a thick wood, you intend to pass on one
side of a tree, but your horse, being of a different opinion,
swerves suddenly and goes to the other, it is awkward, to
say the least of it.

" My first object was to rejoin my companions ; so, not
having heard a shot, and imagining they must by this
time have given up chasing the giraffes, I fired as a signal,
and at once heard a shot in answer far to my right, and rode
in that direction. After riding some distance I again pulled
up, and shouted with all my might, and then, not hearing
anything, fired another signal shot, but without effect. As
my horse was very tired, I now off-saddled for a short time
and then fired a third shot, and listened intently for an
answer, but all was silent as the grave ; so, as the sun was
now low, I saddled up again and struck a line for the waggon
road, thinking my friends had already done the same thing.
In this way I rode on at a slow pace, for my horse was tired
and thirsty, keeping steadily in one direction till the sun,
sinking lower and lower, at last disappeared altogether.
I expected I should have reached the road before this, and,
attributing my not doing so to the fact of the path having
taken a turn to the right, still kept on till twilight had given
place to moonlight—a fine bright moonlight, indeed, for it
wanted but two nights to the full, but, under the circumstances, perhaps a trifle cold and cheerless. Still, thinking
I must be close to the road, I kept on for another couple
of hours or so, when, it being intensely cold, I resolved to
try and light a fire, and pass the night where I was and ride
on again early the following morning. Having no matches,
I had to make use of my cartridges, of which I had only three
remaining, in endeavouring to get a light. Breaking one
of these open, I rubbed some of the powder well into a bit
of linen torn from my shirt, slightly wetted, and, putting
it into the muzzle of the rifle, ignited it with the cap and a
little powder left in the bottom of the cartridge. So far
well and good, but this was, unfortunately, almost as far
as I could get ; for, though I managed to induce some grass

to smoulder, I couldn't for the life of me make it flare, and soon had the mortification of finding myself, after two more unsuccessful attempts, just as cold and hungry as before, and minus my three cartridges to boot. Were the same circumstances to occur again, no doubt everything would be very different ; but at that time I was quite a tyro in all forest lore. It was now piercingly cold, though during the day the sun had been as hot as at midsummer in England—regular South African fashion. Still, I thought it better to pass the night where I was ; so, tying my horse to a tree, I cut a little grass with my pocket knife to lie upon, and turned in. My entire clothing consisted of a hat, shirt, pair of trousers, and veldt shoes, as I had ridden away from the waggon without my coat. However, lying on my back, with my felt hat for a pillow, I put the saddle over my chest and closed my eyes in the vain hope that I should soon fall asleep and forget my cares ; vain indeed, for the bitter cold crept in gradually and stealthily from my feet upwards, till I was soon shivering from head to foot as if my very life depended on it. After having worked hard at this unpleasant exercise for a couple of hours or more, watching the moon all the time, and cursing its tardy pace, I could stand it no longer ; so, getting up with difficulty—for I was regularly stiffened by the cold—I ran backwards and forwards to a tree at a short distance until I was again warm, when I once more lay down ; and in this manner the weary hours wore away till day dawned. During the night a couple of hyenas passed close to me, enlivening the silence with their dismal howlings. I have often thought since that they must have been on their way to drink, perhaps at some pit or spring not far off ; how I wished that I had known where ! I will take this opportunity of saying that the howl of the African hyena is about the most mournful and weird-like sound in nature, being a sort of prolonged groan, rising in cadence till it ends in a shriek ; they only laugh when enjoying a good feed.

" At first dawn of day I once more saddled up and rode in the same direction as before. My poor horse was so tired and thirsty that he would only go at a very slow

pace ; so I didn't make much progress. On coming to a
high tree I stopped and climbed up it, and looked about
me to try and recognize some landmark. On every side
the country was covered with forest, and in the distance
were several low ranges of hills, yet nothing seemed familiar
to my eye. Right ahead, in the direction in which I had
been riding, appeared a line of densely wooded hills, with one
single kopje standing alone just in front of them, and thither
I determined to ride. On the way I passed three beautiful
gemsbuck, which allowed me to come quite close to them,
though they are usually very wild ; but they had nothing to
fear from me, as I had no cartridges, and so could do nothing
more than admire them. Thus I rode on and on, until the
idea occurred to me that I must have ridden across the road
(a mere narrow track) without noticing it in the moonlight,
as I had constantly been star-gazing after the sun went
down, so as to guide my course by the position of the
Southern Cross. After a time, I at last felt so sure that this
was the case, that I turned my horse's head to the right-
about, and rode back again in the direction from which I
had just come."

He was now hopelessly lost but did not give way to
despair, as so many in a similar position have done. Nothing
but a level sea of forest surrounded him, so he turned his
jaded horse to the setting sun in the west in the hope of
again striking the road. After another night in the wilderness he awoke to find his horse gone. Far to the south-west
was a line of hills and after walking without food or water
till the moon rose, he reached the mountains. At sunrise
he topped the crest of the range, hoping to see the maize
fields of Bamangwato, but saw nothing. Worn out with
thirst, fatigue, and hunger he started again at sunrise and
at last at sundown he met two Kafirs who eventually took
him to their kraal and gave him water and milk.

" The next morning, as soon as it was light, accompanied
by the Kafir who carried my rifle, I made a start, and,
though very tired and worn out from privation, managed
to reach the waggons late in the afternoon, after an absence
of five days and four nights. How I enjoyed the meal that

was hastily prepared for me, and how delightful it was to keep out the bitter cold with a couple of good blankets, I will leave the reader to conjecture."

Of course, he lost his valuable salted horse, which although hobbled, found its way back to Bamangwato. But Selous could never claim it as he had sold his right to it to a Mr. Elstob at Tati. At Goqui he saw his first lions. Unfortunately he had fired a shot at two lionesses running away, when a fine lion with dark coloured mane stood up and offered him a splendid shot at 80 yards, but his rifle was empty, and as he had no dogs to follow the lions when they had vanished, his first encounter with lions gave him much disappointment. At the end of August they reached Tati, and on leaving this place and passing the Ramaqueban river the following day, Selous says : " Here I first saw a sable antelope, one of the handsomest animals in the world," and anyone, indeed, who sees this magnificent creature for the first time never forgets it.

Next day he reached Minyama's kraal, the frontier outpost of the Matabele country, where most of the inhabitants were Makalakas in native dress. The country now became beautiful and park-like in character, and this extends to Bulawayo, the town founded by Lobengula in 1870, and where the sable king dwelt. On receipt of messages announcing their arrival, the king arrived, dressed in a greasy shirt, a costume which shortly afterwards he discarded for native dress. " He asked me what I had come to do," writes Selous. " I said I had come to hunt elephants, upon which he burst out laughing, and said, ' Was it not steinbucks ' (a diminutive species of antelope) ' that you came to hunt ? Why, you're only a boy.' I replied that, although a boy, I nevertheless wished to hunt elephants and asked his permission to do so, upon which he made some further disparaging remarks regarding my youthful appearance, and then rose to go without giving me any answer."

But Selous was persistent and again begged for permission. " This time he asked me whether I had ever seen an elephant, and upon my saying no, answered, ' Oh, they will soon drive you out of the country, but you may go and see what you can do ! ' " When Selous asked him where he might go, Lobengula replied impatiently, " Oh, you may go wherever you like, you are only a boy."

It was about this time that the famous Boer elephant hunter, Jan Viljoen, arrived at Bulawayo and offered to take Sadlier and Selous to his waggons on the River Gwenia to join his hunting party. This was an opportunity not to be lost. In eight days the party, after crossing the Longwe, Sangwe, Shangani, and Gwelo, reached the Gwenia and found the patriarchal encampment of the Boer elephant hunters. The Boers then, as now, travelled even into the far interior with wives, children, cows, sheep, goats, and fowls, and established a " stand-place " whilst the men hunted in all directions, being absent for a week to a month at a time. A slight accident now prevented Selous from going in on foot with the Viljoens to hunt in the " fly." He went off at the Boer's request to buy some corn and on the way back, in passing some Griqua waggons at Jomani, he saw for the first time a Hottentot named Cigar, with whom later he became better acquainted.

Cigar was an experienced hunter and as it seemed now hopeless to follow Viljoen he decided to go in and hunt with the Hottentot. It may be gathered how roughly they lived from Selous' own words : " Having now run through all my supplies of coffee, tea, sugar, and meal, we had nothing in the provision line but Kafir corn and meat of the animals we shot, washed down by cold water."

Cigar—besides two Kafirs who were shooting for him, and carried their own guns and a supply of ammunition— had only three spare boys who carried his blankets, powder, Kafir corn, and a supply of fresh meat. He himself carried his own rifle, a heavy old four-bore muzzle-loader. " As for me," says Selous, " having had to leave two of my Kafirs to look after my horses and oxen, I had but one youngster with me, who carried my blanket and spare ammunition, whilst I shouldered my own old four-bore muzzle-loader, and carried besides a leather bag filled with powder, and a pouch containing twenty four-ounce round bullets. Though this was hardly doing the thing *en grand seigneur*, I was young and enthusiastic in those days and trudged along under the now intense heat with a light heart."

It must be remembered that at this time nearly all the old Boer and English elephant-hunters, such as men like Piet Schwarz, William Finaughty, Hartley, the Jennings family, J. Giffard, T. Leask, and H. Biles, had given up the game of elephant-hunting when horses could be no longer used and the elephants themselves must be pursued on foot in the " fly." Only George Wood, Jan Viljoen,[1] and the greatest hunter of all in South Africa, Petrus Jacobs, still pursued the elephant, but the difficulty, danger, distance, and scarcity of elephant haunts were now so defined and the results so small that none save the very hardiest were able to follow them.

At this time (1873) Piet Jacobs was undoubtedly the most famous hunter in South Africa. During a long life, most of which was spent in the Mashuna and Matabele country, he is supposed to have shot between 400 and 500 bull elephants, mostly killed by hunting them from horseback, but even after as an old man he killed many on foot in the " fly " country. Unlike most Boers, he constantly attacked lions whenever he had the opportunity, and Selous considers that he shot " more lions than any man that ever lived." His usual method in hunting these animals was, if the first shot missed, to loose three or four strong " Boer " dogs, which quickly ran the lion to bay. Then, as a rule, it was easily killed. One day, however, in 1873, on the Umniati river he was terribly mauled by a lion that charged after being bayed by his three dogs. His shot at the charging lion missed, and he was thrown to the ground and severely bitten on the thigh, left arm, and hand. The dogs, however, now came up and saved his life, but it was a long time before he recovered. He said that, unlike the experience of Dr. Livingstone, the bites of the lion were extremely pain-

---

[1] Finaughty states that in 1867 Jan Viljoen and his party killed 210 elephants in one trip. This is probably the largest bag of elephants ever made in one season.

ful, at which Selous humorously remarks that the absence of suffering in such a case is an especial mercy " which Providence does not extend beyond ministers of the Gospel."

Of William Finaughty, the greatest of the English elephant - hunters, neither Selous nor any contemporary writer gives any particulars, so I am indebted to Mr. G. L. Harrison, an American gentleman, for his " Recollections of William Finaughty," which was privately printed in 1916. He met Finaughty, who was then a very slight old man, with a wonderful memory and much weakened by attacks of fever, in 1913. Finaughty was one of the first white men to hunt elephants in Matabeleland, and his activities extended from 1864 to 1875, when he gave up serious hunting because he could no longer pursue them on horseback.

Finaughty describes himself as a harum-scarum youth who left Grahamstown at the age of twenty-one early in 1864. He passed north through the Free State, then swarming with tens of thousands of black wildebeest, blesbok, springbok, quagga, blue wildebeest, and ostrich, and made his way to Matabeleland, then ruled by Mzilikatse, a brother of the Zulu king Chaka. After sport with lion and buffalo on the road, for all game, including elephants, were abundant at this time, he reached Tati. Old Mzilikatse was then a physical wreck but treated the Englishman well, although at times he had violent outbursts of passion. Finaughty was witness of a great dance in which 2500 warriors took part, and on which occasion 540 oxen were slaughtered. Horse-sickness was then rife in the country and the party lost fourteen horses out of seventeen within thirty hours. In this, his first trip, Finaughty only killed three elephants, which he attributed to lack of experience. On his second trip in 1865 he did better, whilst a third in 1866 was made purely for trading, yet he shot eight elephants and then decided to become a hunter only.

On the fourth trip he shot nineteen elephants, but in 1868, on the Umbila, he states that he had " the two finest months of my life. In all I shot 95 elephants, the ivory weighing 5000 lbs."

One day he had a narrow escape in the sandy bed of the Sweswe river. He had wounded an old bull when he fired at it again as it was on the point of charging. His boy had put in two charges and the hunter was nearly knocked out of the saddle by the recoil. The elephant then charged and got right on the top of him, but, at the moment when death seemed imminent, the elephant's shoulder-bone broke and he was helpless—thus Finaughty escaped. In those days the elephants did not know the meaning of gunfire. Finaughty one day bagged six bulls in a river bed, as they did not run on the shots being fired.

In 1869 he went into the elephant country one hundred miles beyond the Tuli and remained there three years, sending out his ivory and receiving fresh provisions and ammunition on the return of his waggons. In five months he killed fifty-three elephants yielding 3000 lbs. of ivory. In one day he killed five bulls and five cows, which was his " record " bag for one day. In the two following years he killed a large number of elephants, but does not state the precise number. In 1870 he again hunted elephants without giving particulars.

From 1870 to 1874 Finaughty remained at Shoshong as a trader and prospered.

It is interesting to note that Finaughty, like many experienced hunters, does not agree with Selous in considering the lion the most dangerous of all African game. He repeatedly says that buffalo-hunting is the most risky of all forms of hunting.[1] " Far better," he says, " follow up a wounded lion than a wounded buffalo, for the latter is the fiercest and most cunning animal to be found in Africa." He himself had many narrow escapes from buffaloes and

[1] In this matter Finaughty received powerful support in the evidence of William Judd, possibly the most experienced African hunter now living ; he writes : " As for buffalo I consider them far and away the most dangerous game. The difficulty of stopping a direct charge, as they very rarely swerve even to the heaviest bullet—the way they can force themselves through bush absolutely impenetrable to man and the nasty habit they have, when wounded (and sometimes when not wounded) of breaking away, making a detour and charging up again from behind, make them an adversary worthy of the greatest respect. I personally have had more close shaves from these brutes than I have had from all other big game put together—lions and elephants included."

only one or two unpleasant incidents with lions. " No,"
he remarks again, " a man who is out after buffalo must
shoot to kill and not to wound, and if he fails to bring his
quarry down he should on no account venture to follow up
unless in open country. He should never follow a buffalo
into cover, unless he is accompanied by a number of good
dogs. Many a good man has lost his life through neglect
of this precaution." Finaughty lived in the Transvaal
from 1883 to 1887, and then moved to Johannesburg in the
early days of the " boom." In the nineties he returned to
Matabeleland to spend the rest of his days on his farm
near Bulawayo. He was still alive in 1914.

What would, however, have been only toil and hardship
to older men was small discomfort to a tough young fellow
like Selous, who was now in his natural element. Almost at
once he and Cigar tracked and killed a grand old bull which
carried tusks of 61 and 58 lbs. On the following days they
killed six elephants, Cigar accounting for four. Selous here
pays a high tribute to the good qualities of his dusky companion. " Cigar was a slight-built, active Hottentot,
possessed of wonderful powers of endurance, and a very
good game shot, though a bad marksman at a target. These
qualities, added to lots of pluck, made him a most successful
elephant-hunter ; and for foot hunting in the ' fly ' country
I do not think I could have had a more skilful preceptor ;
for although only an uneducated Hottentot—once a jockey
at Grahamstown—he continually allowed me to have the
first shot, whilst the elephants were still standing—a great
advantage to give me—and never tried in any way to over-
reach me or claim animals that I had shot, as is so often
done by Boer hunters. Strangely enough, Cigar told me,
when the celebrated hunter, Mr. William Finaughty, first
took him after elephants on horseback, he had such dreadful
fear of the huge beasts that, after getting nearly caught by
one, and never being able to kill any, he begged his master
to let him remain at the waggons. When I knew him this
fear must have worn off, and I have never since seen his
equal as a foot hunter." Selous did very well with Cigar,
getting 450 lbs. of ivory which he had shot himself, and

another 1200 lbs. which he had traded with the natives, thus making a clear profit of £300. When he saw the king, he told him that the elephants had not driven him out of the country, but that he had killed several, to which Lobengula replied, " Why, you're a man ; when are you going to take a wife ? " and suggested that he should court one at once.

Selous' friends had now all left the country, but he himself decided to remain in Matabeleland to be ready to hunt in the following year with George Wood. As usual, however, Lobengula took months to give his permission, so that it was not until the 15th June, 1873, that he gave permission to the two hunters to make a start. Even then he would not allow them to go to the Mashuna country and stated that they must hunt to the westward of the river Gwai.

A fortnight after leaving Bulawayo Selous and Wood reached Linquasi, where they began to hunt, and two days later they killed two fine bull elephants. Here they established their main hunting-camp and made raids into the " fly." During this season of four months Selous killed forty-two elephants and George Wood fifty. They also accounted for a good many rhinoceros and buffalo. Their main hunting veldt was the " fly " region between the rivers Zambesi and Gwai. It was a broken country full of hills, " kloofs," dense bush and park-like opens. This area was formerly inhabited by the Makalakas, but these had been driven across the Zambesi by raiding Matabele. These regions were consequently a great game preserve and full of elephant, black and white rhinoceros, buffalo, zebra, sable, roan, koodoo, impala, reedbuck, klipspringer, grysbok, bushbuck, waterbuck, and other antelopes. In " A Hunter's Wanderings " Selous gives many interesting accounts of his hunts after elephants, but perhaps his best is the splendid narrative of his great day, of which I am permitted to give his own description.[1]

" As soon as the day dawned, we sent a couple of Kafirs down to the water to see if any elephants had been there, and on their return in a quarter of an hour with the joyful

---

[1] " A Hunter's Wanderings," pp. 84–88.

tidings that a fine troop of bulls had drunk during the night, we at once started in pursuit. We found they had come down from the right-hand side, and returned on their own spoor, feeding along nicely as they went, so that we were in great hopes of overtaking them without much difficulty. Our confidence, however, we soon found was misplaced, for after a time they had ceased to feed, and, turning back towards the N.E., had taken to a path, along which they had walked in single file and at a quick pace, as if making for some stronghold in the hills. Hour after hour we trudged on, over rugged stony hills, and across open grassy valleys, scattered over which grew clumps of the soft-leaved machabel trees, or rather bushes ; but, though the leaves and bark of this tree form a favourite food of elephants, those we were pursuing had turned neither to the right nor to the left to pluck a single frond.

" After midday, the aspect of the country changed, and we entered upon a series of ravines covered with dense, scrubby bush. Unfortunately the grass here had been burnt off, but for which circumstance the elephants, I feel sure, would have halted for their midday sleep. In one of these thickets we ran on to three black rhinoceroses (*R. bicornis*) lying asleep. When we were abreast of them they got our wind, and, jumping up, rushed close past the head of our line, snorting vigorously. It was a family party, consisting of a bull, a cow, and a full-grown calf ; they passed so near that I threw at them the thick stick which I used for a ramrod, and overshot the mark, it falling beyond them.

" Shortly after this incident, we lost the spoor in some very hard, stony ground, and had some trouble in recovering it, as the Kafirs, being exhausted with the intense heat, and thinking we should not catch the elephants, had lost heart and would not exert themselves, hoping that we would give up the pursuit. By dint of a little care and perseverance, however, we succeeded, and after a time again entered upon a more open country. To cut a long story short, I suppose it must have been about two hours before sundown when we came to a large tree, from which

SELOUS AS A YOUNG MAN, IN HUNTING COSTUME

the elephants had only just moved on. At first we thought they must have got our wind and run, but on examination we found they had only walked quietly on. We put down the water-calabashes and axes, and the Kafirs took off their raw-hide sandals, and then we again, quickly but cautiously, followed on the spoor. It was perhaps five minutes later when we at last sighted them, seven in number, and all large, full-grown bulls. W. and I walked up to within thirty yards or so, and fired almost simultaneously ; he at one standing broadside, and I at another facing me. Our Hottentot boy also fired, and, as the animals turned, a volley was given by our Kafirs, about ten of whom carried guns. Not an elephant, however, seemed any the worse, and they went away at a great pace. Judging from the lie of the land ahead that they would turn to the right, I made a cut with my two gun-bearers, whilst W. kept in their wake. Fortune favoured me, for they turned just as I had expected, and I got a splendid broadside shot as they passed along the farther side of a little gully not forty yards off. The Kafir having, as he ran, reloaded the gun which I had already discharged and on which I placed most dependence, I fired with it at the foremost elephant, an enormous animal with long white tusks, when he was exactly opposite to me. My boy had put in the powder with his hand, and must have overloaded it, for the recoil knocked me down, and the gun itself flew out of my hands. Owing to this, I lost a little time, for, when I got hold of my second gun, the elephants had turned back again (excepting the one just hit) towards W. and the Kafirs. However, I gave another a bullet behind the big ribs as he was running obliquely away from me. The first, which I had hit right in the middle of the shoulder, was now walking very slowly up a steep hill, looking as though he were going to fall every instant ; but, nevertheless (as until an elephant is actually dead, there is no knowing how far he may go), I determined to finish him before returning to the others. On reaching the top of the hill, and hearing me coming on not a dozen yards behind him, the huge beast wheeled round, and, raising his gigantic ears, looked rue-

G

fully towards me. Poor beast, he was doubtless too far gone to charge, and, on receiving another ball in the chest, he stepped slowly backwards, and then sinking on to his haunches, threw his trunk high into the air and rolled over on his side, dead.

" During this time, the remainder of the elephants, harried and bewildered by the continuous firing of W. and our little army of native hunters, had come round in a circle, and I saw the four that still remained (for, besides the one I had killed, two more were down) coming along in single file, at the long, quick half run, half walk, into which these animals settle after their first rush. I at once ran obliquely towards them ; but, before I could get near, one more first lagged behind, and then fell heavily to the ground, so that there were but three remaining. W., being blown, had been left behind ; but most of the Kafirs were still to the fore, firing away as fast as they could load, from both sides. It was astonishing what bad shooting they made ; their bullets kept continually striking up the ground all round the elephants, sometimes in front of their trunks, sometimes behind them, and ever and anon one would come whistling high overhead. It was in vain that I shouted to them to leave off firing and let me shoot ; their blood was up, and blaze away they would.

" Just as I was getting well up alongside, the elephants crossed a little gully, and entered a small patch of scrubby bush, on the slope of the hill beyond, in the shelter of which they at once stopped and faced about, giving me a splendid chance. I had just emptied both my guns, hitting one animal full in the chest, and another, that was standing broadside to me, in the shoulder, when loud lamentations and cries of ' Mai-ai ! ' ' Mai mamo ! ' burst from my Kafir followers close behind. At the same time my two gun-carriers, throwing down their guns, ran backwards, clapping their hands, and shouting like the rest. Turning hastily round, I saw a Kafir stretched upon the earth, his companions sitting round him, wailing and clapping their hands, and at once comprehended what had occurred. The poor fellow who lay upon the ground had fired at the elephants, from about thirty yards behind myself, and then ran up an ant-hill, just as another Kafir, who preferred to keep at a safer distance, discharged a random shot, which struck poor Mendose just between the shoulder-blades, the bullet coming out on the right breast. I ran up at once to see what could be done, but all human aid was vain—the poor fellow was dead. At this moment two more shots fell close behind, and a minute or two afterwards W. and our Hottentot boy John came up. One of the three elephants had fallen after my last shot, close at hand, and a second, sorely wounded, had walked back right on to W. and John, who were following on the spoor ; and the two shots I had just heard had sealed his fate. The third, however, and only surviving one out of the original seven, had made good his escape during the confusion, which he never would have done had it not been for the untimely death of Mendose.

" The sun was now close down upon the western sky-line, and little time was to be lost. The Kafirs still continued to shout and cry, seeming utterly paralysed, and I began to think that they were possessed of more sympathetic feelings than I had ever given them credit for. However, on being asked whether they wished to leave the body for the hyenas, they roused themselves. As luck would have it, on the side of the very ant-hill on which the poor fellow had met his death was a large deep hole, excavated probably by an ant-eater, but now untenanted. Into this rude grave, with a Kafir needle to pick the thorns out of his feet, and his assegais with which to defend himself on his journey to the next world, we put the body, and then firmly blocked up the entrance with large stones, to keep the prowling hyenas from exhuming it. Poor Mendose ! he was an obedient, willing servant, and by far the best shot of all our native hunters.

" The first thing to be done now was to cut some meat from one of the elephants, and then get down to a pool of water which we had passed during the hunt, and make a ' skerm ' for the night. On reaching the nearest carcase, which proved to be in fair condition, I was much surprised to see my Kafirs throw aside every semblance of grief, and fight and quarrel over pieces of fat and other titbits in their usual manner. Even the fellow who had had the misfortune to shoot his comrade, though he kept asserting that ' his heart was dead,' was quite as eager as the rest. In the evening they laughed and chatted and sang as usual, ate most hearty suppers, and indeed seemed as if all memory of the tragedy which had occurred but a few hours before, and which at the time had seemed to affect them so deeply, had passed from their minds.

" Thus ended the best day's hunting, as regards weight of ivory, at which I had ever assisted. The next day we set the Kafirs to work with three American axes, and before nightfall the twelve tusks (not one of which was broken) were lying side by side, forming one of the finest trophies a sportsman's heart could desire to look upon. The largest pair of tusks weighed 57 lbs. apiece, and the smallest 29 lbs. and 31 lbs. respectively—a very fair lot of bull ivory."

A few days later he had an interesting day in the valley of the Dett and experienced something of the difficulties and dangers of the hunter's life.[1]

" About an hour later, we came up with them, standing some fifty yards away, on our right, under a clump of camel-thorn trees, and in a rather open place compared with the general density of the surrounding jungle. Besides the small troop of bulls we had followed, and which were nearest to us, there was a very large herd of cows standing just beyond, which, as we had not crossed their spoor, had probably drunk at Sikumi—a water-hole not many miles distant—and come to this rendezvous from the other side.

" Taking a hasty gulp of water, we at once walked towards them. As we advanced, the slight rustling of the bushes must have attracted the attention of one of the bulls, for he raised his trunk high in the air, and made a few steps forward. ' I'll take him, and do you fire at the one with the long white tusks on the left,' whispered W. ' Right you are ! ' was the reply, and the next moment we fired. I just had time to see my elephant fall on his knees, when he was hidden by the troop of cows that, awakened from

[1] " A Hunter's Wanderings," pp. 89–99.

their sleep by the shots, and not knowing exactly where the danger lay, came rushing towards us in a mass, one or two of them trumpeting, and others making a sort of rumbling noise. Seizing our second guns and shouting lustily, we again pulled trigger. Our Hottentot boy John, and five of our Kafirs, who still carried guns, also fired ; on which the herd turned and went off at right angles, enveloped in a cloud of dust. My gun had only snapped the cap, but my Kafir, to whom I threw it back, thinking in the noise and hurry that it was discharged, reloaded it on the top of the old charge—a fact which I only found out, to my sorrow, later on. The cloud of sand and dust raised by the panic-stricken elephants was at first so thick that we could distinguish nothing ; but, running behind them, I soon made out the bull I had wounded, which I recognized by the length and shape of his tusks. He was evidently hard hit, and, being unable to keep up with the herd, he turned out, and went off alone ; but he was joined almost immediately by four old cows, all with small, insignificant tusks, and, instead of running away, they walked along quite slowly, first in front of and then behind him, as if to encourage him. Seeing how severely he was wounded, I at once went after him, accompanied only by my two gun-carriers, Nuta and Balamoya, W. and the rest of the Kafirs going on after the troop. My bull was going so slowly that I had no difficulty in threading my way through the bushes and getting in front of him, which I did in order to get a broadside shot as he passed me. One of the four cows that still accompanied him walked along, carrying her head high and her tail straight in the air, and kept constantly turning from side to side. ' That cow will bother us ; shoot her,' said Nuta, and I wish I had taken his advice ; but her tusks were so small, and the bull seemed so very far gone, that I thought it would be a waste of ammunition. I therefore waited till he was a little in front of where I stood, and then gave him a bullet at very close quarters, just behind the shoulder, and, as I thought, exactly in the right place ; but he nevertheless continued his walk as if he had not felt it. Reloading the same gun, I ran behind him, holding it before me in both hands, ready to raise at a moment's notice, and, the four cows being some twenty yards in advance, I shouted, hoping he would turn. The sound of my voice had the desired effect ; for he at once raised his ears and swung himself round, or rather was in the act of doing so, for immediately his ears went up my gun was at my shoulder, and as soon as he presented his broadside I fired, on which he turned again, and went crashing through the bushes at a trot. I thought that it was a last spasmodic rush and that he would fall before going very far ; so, giving the gun back to Nuta to reload, I was running after him, with my eyes fixed on the quivering bushes as they closed behind him, when suddenly the trunk of another elephant was whirled round, almost literally above my head, and a short, sharp scream of rage thrilled through me, making the blood tingle down to the very tips of my fingers. It was one of the wretched old cows, that had thus lain in wait for me behind a dense patch of bush.

" Even had my gun been in my hands, I should scarcely have had time to fire, so close was she upon me ; but, as it was, both my Kafirs were some fifteen yards behind, and the only thing I could do was to run. How I got away I scarcely know. I bounded over and through thorn-bushes which, in cold blood, I should have judged impenetrable ; but I was urged on by the short piercing screams which, repeated in quick succession, seemed to make the whole air vibrate, and by the fear of finding myself encircled by the trunk or transfixed by the tusk of the enraged animal. After a few seconds (for I don't think she pursued me a hundred yards, though it seemed an age), the screaming ceased. During the chase, the elephant was so close behind me, that looking over my shoulder was impossible, and all that I did was to dash forward, springing from side to side so as to hinder her from getting hold of me, and it was only when the trumpeting suddenly stopped that I knew I was out of her reach. I was barelegged—as I always am when hunting on foot—and my only garment before the beast charged was a flannel shirt ; but I now stood almost *in puris naturalibus*, for my hat, the leather belt that I wore round my waist, and about three parts of my shirt, had been torn off by the bushes, and I doubt if there was a square inch of skin left uninjured anywhere on the front of my body."

Soon after another old bull charged him.

" Taking a good sight for the middle of his shoulder, I pulled the trigger. This time the gun went off—it was a four-bore elephant gun, loaded twice over, and the powder thrown in each time by a Kafir with his hands—and I went off too ! I was lifted clean from the ground, and turning round in the air, fell with my face in the sand, whilst the gun was carried yards away over my shoulder. At first I was almost stunned with the shock, and I soon found that I could not lift my right arm. Besides this, I was covered with blood, which spurted from a deep wound under the right cheek-bone, caused by the stock of the gun as it flew upwards from the violence of the recoil. The stock itself— though it had been bound round, as are all elephant-guns, with the inside skin of an elephant's ear put on green, which when dry holds it as firmly as iron—was shattered to pieces, and the only wonder was that the barrel did not burst. Whether the two bullets hit the elephant or not I cannot say ; but I think they must have done so, for he only went a few yards after I fired, and then stood still, raising his trunk every now and then, and dashing water tinged with blood over his chest. I went cautiously up to within forty yards or so of him, and sat down. Though I could not hold my arm out, I could raise my forearm, so as to get hold of the trigger ; but the shock had so told on me, that I found I could not keep the sight within a yard of the right place. The elephant remained perfectly still ; so I got Nuta to work my arm about gently, in order to restore its power, and hoped that in the meantime the Kafir, whose shouting had originally brought the elephant to me, would come up and be able to go and fetch W. No doubt, if I had shouted he would have come at once, for he could not have been very far off ; but had I done so the elephant might either have charged, or else continued his flight, neither of which alternatives did I desire. After a short time, seeing

no chance of aid arriving, and my nerves having got a little
steadier, I took my favourite gun from Nuta, and, resting
my elbow on my knee, took a quiet pot shot. I was, however,
still very unsteady even in this position, but I do not think
the bullet could have struck very far from the right place.
The elephant on receiving the shot made a rush forwards,
crashing through the bushes at a quick walk, so that we
had to run at a hard trot to keep him in sight. He now
seemed very vicious, for, hearing a dry branch snap, he
turned and ran towards us, and then stood with his ears
up, feeling about in all directions with his trunk to try and
get our wind.

" Nuta, who up to this day had always been a most staunch
and plucky gun-bearer, now seemed seized with a panic,
and refused to bring me the gun any more, calling out,
' Leave the elephant, sir ; this day you're bewitched, and
will surely be killed.' However, as the elephant was evidently very severely wounded, I had no idea of giving over
the chase as long as I could keep up, and, after bestowing a
few Anglo-Saxon idioms upon Nuta, I again ran on. The
bush now became very thick, and, as the elephant was going
straight away, I could not get a chance of a shot. About
a mile farther on, however, we came to one of those large
open turf flats which occur here and there in the midst of
the sinangas. It was quite a mile square, and perfectly
bare, with the exception of a few large camel-thorn trees,
which were scattered about in clumps. On reaching this
opening, the elephant, instead of turning back into the bush,
as I should have expected, kept his course, making straight
for the farther side, and going at that long, swinging walk,
to keep up with which a man on foot must run at a fair
pace. I had now been a long time bare-headed, exposed
to the heat of the fierce tropical sun, and the kick I had
received from the gun had so much shaken me, that I felt
dead-beat, and could scarcely drag one leg after the other.
I saw that I should never be able to run up to within shot
of the elephant, which was now about 150 yards ahead ;
so, taking the gun from Nuta, I told him to try and run
right round him, and by shouting turn him back towards

me. Relieved of the weight of the gun, and being a splendid runner, he soon accomplished this, and standing behind the stem of a camel-thorn tree a long way in advance, holloed loudly. Accordingly, I had the satisfaction of seeing the elephant stop, raise his ears, look steadily in the direction of the noise, and then wheel round, and come walking straight back towards the jungle he had just left, taking a line which would bring him past me, at a distance of about fifty or sixty yards. I stood perfectly still, with Balamoya kneeling close behind me ; for, though elephants can see very well in the open, I have always found that if they do not get your wind, and you remain motionless, they seem to take you for a tree or a stump. To this I now trusted, and as the elephant came on I had full leisure to examine him. The ground between us was as bare as a board, except that it was covered with coarse grass about a foot high, and he looked truly a gigantic and formidable beast ; his tusks were small for his size, one of them being broken at the point, and I do not think they could have weighed much over 30 lbs. apiece. He came steadily on, swinging his trunk backwards and forwards, until he was about seventy yards from where I stood, when suddenly I was dismayed to see his trunk sharply raised, as if to catch a stray whiff of wind, and the next instant he stopped and faced full towards us, with his head raised, and his enormous ears spread like two sails. He took a few steps towards us, raising his feet very slowly, and bringing them down as if afraid of treading on a thorn. It was an anxious moment ; he was evidently very suspicious, but did not know what to make of us, and had we remained motionless I believe he would still have turned and walked on again. ' Stand still ! ' I whispered between my teeth to Balamoya ; but the sight of the advancing monster was too much for him— he jumped up and bolted. The instant he moved, on came the elephant, without trumpeting, and with his trunk straight down. Though very shaky just before, the imminence of the danger braced up my nerves, and I think I never held a gun steadier than upon this occasion. As he was coming direct at me, and as he did not raise his trunk, his chest was quite covered ; there was therefore nothing left but to fire at his head. He came on at an astonishing pace, and I heard only the ' whish, whish ' of the grass as his great feet swept through it. He was perhaps twenty yards off when I pulled the trigger. I aimed a little above the root of the trunk and just between the eyes, and directly I fired I ran out sideways as fast as I could, though I had not much running left in me. Looking over my shoulder, I saw him standing with his ears still up and his head slightly turned, looking towards me ; the blood was pouring down his trunk from a wound exactly where I had aimed, and, as it was inflicted by a four-ounce ball, backed by a heavy charge of powder, I cannot understand why it did not penetrate to his brain ; it had half-stunned him, however, and saved my life, for, had he come on again, it would have been utterly impossible for me, fatigued as I was, to have avoided him. After standing still for a short time, swaying himself gently from side to side, he again turned and took across the flat. Nuta, seeing what had happened, instead of trying to turn him again, cleared out of his road, and, making a large circle, came back to me. Perhaps it was as well he did so."

Selous now gave up the pursuit without having killed a single elephant, and it was ten days before he could use his arm again.

In November, the rainy season having set in, Selous and Wood returned to Bulawayo carrying 5000 lbs. weight of ivory. Selous bears testimony to the extraordinary abundance of game at this time in South Africa, and gives a wonderful word-picture of the extraordinary collection of animals he saw one evening in October, 1873, in the valley of the Dett.

" First, a few hundred yards higher up this valley than where we were working, a herd of nine giraffes stalked slowly and majestically from the forest, and, making their way to a pool of water, commenced to drink. These giraffes remained in the open valley until dark, one or other of them, from time to time, straddling out his forelegs in a most extraordinary manner in order to get its mouth down to the water. No other animals came to drink in the pools between us and the giraffes. Possibly some got our wind before leaving the shelter of the forest, though the evening was very still. But below us, as far as one could see down the valley, the open ground was presently alive with game. One after another, great herds of buffaloes emerged from the forest on either side of the valley and fed slowly down to the water. One of these herds was preceded by about fifty zebras and another by a large herd of sable antelopes. Presently two other herds of sable antelopes appeared upon the scene, and a second herd of zebras, and five magnificently horned old koodoo bulls, whilst rhinoceroses both of the black and white species (the latter predominating in numbers) were scattered amongst the other game, singly or in twos and threes all down the valley. Of course all this great concourse of wild animals had been collected together in the neighbourhood of the valley of the Dett owing to the drying up of all the valleys in the surrounding country, and during the rainy season would have been scattered over a wide area."[1]

In 1874, Wood, Selous, Mr. and Lieutenant Garden trekked north, intending to hunt on the Zambesi and Chobe rivers. They left Tati on May 6th and approached the Victoria Falls on June 10th, stopping on the way at Daka, where Wood and Selous killed some elephants, and the latter had a somewhat narrow escape from a charging bull which he managed to kill just at the right moment. On June 27th they viewed the wonderful Falls of Zambesi, and Selous, like all other travellers, goes into ecstasies at their beauty and grandeur. Here they encountered for the first time a rare antelope, the pookoo, which gave Selous much pleasure, for it may be said that from this date he commenced his wonderful collection of African mammals. During, and after, 1874, he never failed to preserve and keep for his own collection all the best specimens of big game he shot, then having unrivalled opportunities for getting the finest trophies. This can, of course, only be achieved when animals are abundant. He often lamented afterwards that he did not take more care to get some buffalo bulls of the first

[1] " African Nature Notes and Reminiscences," p. 134.

quality, for he certainly saw and killed great numbers in those early years, yet he only kept three or four heads of bulls that were in no way remarkable, when he could have possessed the best specimens in existence. When he wanted them it was too late.

At the Zambesi, Wood decided to go eastward to the Gwai, so Selous and the Gardens travelled west into the unknown country of the Chobe. On the first day Selous killed a splendid koodoo bull which he preserved, and shortly afterwards encountered numerous herds of pookoo and other antelopes. The country about the Chobe was in fact about the best for mixed game at this period, and Selous revelled in the wealth of animal life, though he devoted most of his energies to looking for elephants, which were here difficult to kill owing to shifting winds. One day he had quite a little battle with the fierce buffalo cow.[1]

" On again arriving at the open valley mentioned above, I found it occupied by a large herd of two or three hundred buffaloes, that had emerged from the surrounding jungle during my absence, and were now feeding quietly down towards the river for their evening drink. Though I hardly liked to fire, for fear of disturbing elephants, some of which might, for all I knew, be within hearing, yet, on the other hand, I had a strong desire to secure a nice fat buffalo steak for supper, and at last forgetting all more prudent resolves, and sympathising with the feelings of my Kafirs who kept entreating me to shoot them a fat cow, I took my four-bore elephant-gun and advanced towards the still unconscious herd, resolved to kill one if possible. Those that were nearest were about one hundred and twenty yards from the edge of the bush, beyond which there was no shelter, save that afforded by a few large scattered goussy trees. However, by creeping cautiously forward on my hands and knees, I managed to get within eighty yards or so, when an old cow observing me, raised her head and gazed steadily towards where I crouched. There was no time to be lost, as I saw she was thoroughly alarmed, so, singling out a fine fat cow, that stood broadside on close beside her, I raised

[1] " A Hunter's Wanderings," pp. 120-123.

my heavy gun, and taking a quick aim behind her shoulder, fired. The loud bellow that followed the shot told me she was hard hit, but I could see nothing, for the whole herd, startled by the report of the gun, rushed together in wild affright, and now stood in a dense mass, facing towards their hidden foe, effectually screening the wounded cow from my view. In another instant, seemingly satisfied that something dangerous was near, they turned about and galloped away across the valley, making for the bush on the opposite side, and on the dust raised by their many feet subsiding, I beheld the one I had wounded still standing where she had been shot, and thought she was about done for ; but on seeing me step from behind a tree, she immediately wheeled round and made for the jungle.

" When the herd ran together, after I had fired, with several nasty-looking old bulls in their front, my native attendants had all retreated precipitately to the edge of the bush (with the exception of one of the Masaras, who was carrying a small gourd of water slung on an assegai over his shoulder), or I might have given the cow another shot with my second gun before she turned to run. Although evidently severely wounded, she still managed to get over the ground at a great rate, and entered the bush at least 100 yards in advance of myself and the Bushman, who were following at our best pace, the Kafirs carrying my guns being a considerable distance behind. Just within the edge of the jungle was one very thick patch, unlike the greater part, covered with foliage, and behind this the wounded buffalo turned and stood at bay waiting for her pursuers. Not thinking of this stratagem (a very common one with both buffaloes and elephants), and imagining her to be a considerable distance ahead, I ran into her very horns before I saw her, and she at the same time seeing me at once charged, with eyes on fire, and her nose stretched straight out, grunting furiously. Luckily she was not standing head on, but broadside to me, and so could not come straight at me, but had first to turn round the bush. This gave me time to spring through the bushes to one side, as she rushed past, when she immediately made at the Bushman, who, springing into a small sapling, just swung his body up out of reach as she passed beneath. So close was she, that, as the calabash full of water, which he had been carrying slung on an assegai, fell to the ground behind him, she smashed it to atoms, either with her feet or horns, just as, if not before, it touched the ground. After this she turned and stood under the very slender tree on which the Bushman hung, looking up at him, and grunting furiously, but not attempting to butt the tree down, which I think she could have accomplished had she but tried. At this instant the Kafir who carried my ten-bore rifle, reaching the scene of action unperceived by the buffalo, fired at and missed her, on which she again retreated behind the bush from whence she had first charged. By this time, however, I had my second elephant-gun in my hands, and creeping up gave her another bullet on the point of the shoulder, just as she caught sight of me and was again turning to charge. On receiving this second ball, she fell to the ground, and snatching up an assegai, and followed by several of the Kafirs, we ran in and despatched her before she could rise. She proved to be a dry cow in splendid condition."

He killed several good bull elephants in the Chobe bush and had some narrow escapes, once nearly losing his life owing to the caps missing fire. What delighted him most was the abundance of other game he saw. He believed the sable antelopes here carried finer horns than in any part of South Africa, south of the Zambesi, and often wished afterwards he had shot one or two, but when he encountered them he was always after elephants, so he did not fire. The best specimen of this grand animal he killed in Northern Mashunaland three years later, and its horns measured 44½ ins. in length, but he always thought that somewhere in Africa there were greater sable antelopes than this, and one day, in later years, he found in the museum at Florence a wonderful single horn of 60 inches. For years he tried to find out where it came from without success. Now we know it must have been sent from Angola, Portuguese West Africa, for on the Quanza river some remarkable specimens have been obtained, reaching up to 63 inches, but it is feared that they are few in number there, and nearly extinct.

Near the Chobe on some marshy flats he found the lechwe antelope for the first time and killed some good examples, and he accurately described[1] the curious movements of these antelopes.

" When first they make up their minds to run, these lechwe buck stretch out their noses, laying their horns flat along their backs, and trot like an eland, but on being pressed break into a springing gallop, now and then bounding high into the air like impalas. Even when in water up to their necks they do not swim, but get along by a succession of bounds with great rapidity, making a tremendous splashing and general commotion. Of course when the water becomes too deep for them to bottom they are forced to swim, which they do well and strongly, though not as fast as the natives can paddle, and in the rainy season, when the country is flooded, great numbers are driven into deep water and speared before they can again reach the shallows where they can touch ground. It is owing to their being thus driven about and harried by the natives in canoes, I suspect, that they are so wild, as I don't think they can often have heard the sound of a gun before."

In September he was very lucky with the elephants, killing five each day on September 4th and September 8th. Altogether he shot twenty-four in 1874.

" During the intensely hot weather in September and October, just before the rains fall, elephants soon become fatigued if driven about and exposed to the fierce sun. When they get hot and tired they insert their trunks into their mouths and draw out water from their stomachs, which they dash over their breasts and shoulders to cool themselves ; and when the supply of water is exhausted they will sometimes throw sand over their bodies, which one would suppose would only make them hotter than they were before. Though, as I have said, elephants get knocked up comparatively soon when hunted during the hot weather, yet, as may be imagined, it is killing work following them

---

[1] " A Hunter's Wanderings," pp. 137–138.

on foot at that season, in deep sandy ground and under a
tropical sun, and with nothing to drink but a very limited
allowance of water carried in a gourd, which soon gets
lukewarm from the intensity of the heat."[1]

On September 11th he made a start for home, reaching
Daka on September 26th, after an absence of three months.
He then went east to trade at Wankie, where he got 300 lbs.
of good ivory. In December he trekked south to the Tati,
where he shot his first lion. Thus it was three years before
Selous actually shot a lion in Africa—a fact that may seem
somewhat strange, but not so much when we consider the
nocturnal habits of these animals. I knew a man in East
Africa who lived in a district where lions are far more
abundant than they were in South Africa, who, though
constantly shooting and travelling in lion haunts, had never
once seen one of these beasts in the course of several years.

Selous' first lions were evidently of the fighting order, as
they always are, when pressed by a mounted man.[2]

" On this occasion, as Dorehill and myself were riding
through a patch of bush, our ears were suddenly saluted
with a muffled growling that we did not immediately
interpret. The next instant, however, Hartebeest rushed
forward, pointing with his assegai, and shouting, ' Isilouan !
isilouan ! ' (lions ! lions !). I saw nothing, but galloped
through the bush in the direction he pointed, Dorehill
heading a little to the right. A few moments later, coming
to a more open part, I saw two large lionesses trotting along in
front of me. Upon hearing me behind them, they both
stopped, and standing broadside to me, turned their heads
and looked towards me. Pulling in my horse, I jumped to
the ground, upon which they started off again at a gallop.
I fired at the hindermost one as she ran, and evidently
struck her, for she threw up her tail and gave a loud growl.
They now went into a patch of short mopani bush, beyond
which the country was open forest, with no underwood.
At first they trotted out into this open forest, but the
wounded one not seeming to like it, turned, and squatting

---

[1] " A Hunter's Wanderings," p. 181.
[2] *Ibid.*, pp. 187–189.

on the ground, crept back like a cat, with her shoulders above her back, and her eyes all the time fixed upon me, until she reached a little thorn-bush, under which she stretched herself at full length, and lay watching me with her head couched on her outstretched paws. All this time the other lioness was standing in the open, and I was just going to dismount and fire at her, when, turning towards me, she trotted a few steps forwards, and then, throwing her tail two or three times straight into the air, came galloping forwards, growling savagely. Turning my horse's head I pressed him to his utmost speed, closely pursued by the lioness. I do not know how near she got, but her loud purring growls sounded unpleasantly close. As soon as the growling stopped, I knew she had given up the chase, and so rode round in a half-circle to get a view of her. She then trotted to a large mopani tree, in the shade of which she stood. When I rode to another tree about sixty yards off, she lowered her head and stood looking at me, snarling savagely, with her tail held straight in the air. I think that she had done her best to catch me, as her flanks were heaving like those of a tired dog, with the exertion of her run. Feeling sure that she would charge again as soon as she recovered her breath, I steadied myself and fired from the saddle, but missed her. She never took the slightest notice of the shot, but continued snarling and growling. Resting the butt of my rifle (a single ten-bore muzzle-loader) on my foot, I now reloaded with all expedition, and fired again, the lioness all this time having preserved the same position, standing exactly facing me. This time I struck her right in the mouth, knocking out one of the lower canine teeth, breaking the lower jaw-bone, and injuring her neck. She fell to the shot instantly, and lay quite still. I thought she was dead, but took the precaution to reload before riding up to her. On my dismounting and walking towards her, she raised herself on her fore-quarters, when I gave her a ball in the shoulder which effectually settled her. Dorehill now came up with the Kafirs. He had seen the other lions, a male and two females, for there were five altogether, but they had given him the slip in a

H

patch of thick bush. We now went to look for the one I had first wounded, but though there was a little blood under the bush where she had been lying, we could discover no further trace of her, and the ground being very hard no sign of her spoor was visible, even to the keen eyes of the Bushmen. So, after skinning the one I had killed, which was in beautiful condition, we returned to the waggons."

At Tati Selous received his first letters from home since he left the Diamond Fields three years previously, and after reading their contents he decided to go home, and so turned his face southward on February 1st, 1875.

CHAPTER IV

1876–1878

THE years 1872–1874 were undoubtedly the most
strenuous of Selous' life, for after his return to
South Africa in 1876 he used the horse in the
greater part of his journeys in the interior, except on such
trips as he made into the " fly," when he seldom met with
elephants. He landed again at Algoa Bay on March 15th
1876, and at once organized another trip into the interior,
taking four months before he reached the Matabele country
by bullock waggon. Here he met his old friend Dorehill,
Lieutenant Grandy, R.N., and a Mr. Horner, and as it was
too late to make an extensive trip after elephants the party
spent the remainder of the year in short hunting trips down
the Tati, Shashi, and Ramokwebani rivers. Much of this
time was spent in hunting giraffes, and he gives many lively
accounts of this exhilarating sport, also of hunting buffaloes
and the larger antelopes. One day on the Ramokwebani
Selous and his friends had a thrilling hunt after an old male
lion which gave much trouble. Selous broke the animal's
shoulder with the first shot and then followed into thick
bush in which the lion kept retreating. For that evening
he was lost as night came on, but next day Selous tried his
dogs, which seemed disinclined to face the quarry. The
lion, however, was soon found, as a wet night had made
" spooring " easy, and he kept up a continuous roaring,
which is unusual. Grandy and Horner had shots, after
which the lion continued his retreat from one thicket to
another, but roaring at intervals.[1]

" As it was, however, I was peering about into the bush
to try and catch sight of him, holding my rifle advanced in

[1] " A Hunter's Wanderings," pp. 244–245.

front of me, and on full cock, when I became aware that he was coming at me through the bush. The next instant out he burst. I was so close that I had not even time to take a sight, but, stepping a pace backwards, got the rifle to my shoulder, and, when his head was close upon the muzzle, pulled the trigger and jumped to one side. The lion fell almost at my very feet, certainly not six feet from the muzzle of the rifle. Grandy and Horner, who had a good view of the charge, say that he just dropped in his tracks when I fired, which I could not see for the smoke. One thing, however, I had time to notice, and that was that he did not come at me in bounds, but with a rush along the ground. Perhaps it was his broken shoulder that hindered him from springing, but for all that he came at a very great rate, and with his mouth open. Seeing him on the ground, I thought that I must have shattered his skull and killed him, when, as we were advancing towards him, he stood up again. Dorehill at once fired with a Martini-Henry rifle, and shot him through the thigh. On this he fell down again, and, rolling over on to his side, lay gasping. We now went up to him, but, as he still continued to open his mouth, Horner gave him a shot in the head. I now examined my prize with great satisfaction. He was an average-sized lion, his pegged-out skin measuring 10 ft. 3 in. from nose to tip of tail, sleek, and in fine condition, and his teeth long and perfect. Grandy and Horner must both have missed him when they first fired, as we could find no mark of their bullets on the skin ; so that when he charged the only wound he had was the one I had given him on the previous evening. This bullet had merely smashed his shoulder-blade and lodged under the skin just behind it. The bullet with which I so luckily stopped him when charging had struck him fair on the head, about half an inch above the right eye ; here it had cracked the skull, but, without penetrating, had glanced along the bone and come out behind the right ear. I believe that this shot must have given him concussion of the brain and caused his death, and that when he stood up after it was merely a spasmodic action, for the shot that Dorehill gave him was only a flesh wound through the thighs, and the last shot that Horner gave him in the head as he lay on the ground had passed beneath the brain-pan."

At the Ramokwebani Selous met for the first time George Westbeech, the well-known trader, who had for years traded in the far interior as a pioneer. He principally worked the ivory business on the Zambesi and all its confluents north and south. In 1871 he opened up a lucrative business with Sepopo, king of the Barotsi, and between that year and 1876, when Sepopo was assassinated, he brought out no less than 30,000 lbs. of ivory. He also traded much with the Portuguese on the Zambesi, and his operations extended as far north as the Mashukulumbwe country. Selous, as well as all travellers in the interior at this period, had a great respect for Westbeech, and bears testimony to his high character and integrity in dealings with the natives. He regarded him as a fine type of the best class of English pioneer, and is scathing in his denunciation of "stay-at-home aborigines' protectionists, who, comfortably seated in the depths of their armchairs before a blazing fire, are continually thundering forth denunciations against the rapacious British colonist, and the 'low, immoral trader,' who exerts such a baneful influence upon the chaste and guileless savages of the interior. I speak feelingly, as I am proud to rank myself as one of that little body of English and Scotch men who, as traders and elephant-hunters in Central South Africa, have certainly, whatever may be their failings in other respects, kept up the name of Englishmen amongst the natives for all that is upright and honest. In the words of Buckle, we are neither monks nor saints, but only men."

Late in 1876 Selous went down to the Diamond Fields to fetch some property, and trekked south via Bamangwato. This occupied five months before he returned to Matabeleland. On December 6th he had an adventure with lions at Pelatse. He was awakened at 2.30 by his boy, January, who told him there was something on his horse. It was, however, too dark to see to shoot, but he crept near and saw two lions leave the dead horse. He then crawled close to the carcase and another lion rose and sprang away. Just as daylight came in, however, he saw a lion lying " between me and the horse, its tawny body pressed flat upon the yellow sand and its great head couched upon its outstretched paws." He fired at it at a distance of twelve paces and the lion rolled over, recovered, and, made off. When day broke he followed the wounded lion for several miles, but never found it again. A few days later some Bushmen found the lion dead and took the skin, but Selous never recovered it, as he had by this time gone south.

In " A Hunter's Wanderings," " The Lion in South Africa " (Badminton Library), and " The Gun at Home and Abroad," Selous gives the most complete account of the lion and its habits and mode of hunting that has been written by any hunter of wide experience.

It is somewhat curious to notice that three first-class authorities, namely Selous, Finaughty, and Neumann, who all had a wide experience with lions, buffaloes, and elephants, all differ entirely as to the respective danger in dealing with these formidable animals. Selous considered that the lion was much the worst when cornered, Finaughty is emphatic that the buffalo is by far the most dangerous opponent, whilst Neumann gives the elephant first place. Each hunter had ample opportunities for gauging the fighting qualities of these animals, and all agree that they are very dangerous, and give numerous examples from their own experience, so that we are still left in doubt as to the real issue. The experience of men who have only seen and shot a few lions, buffaloes, and elephants is not of much value, because these beasts are judged according to their behaviour in special cases, but Selous shot many of all kinds when rifles were clumsy and inefficient, and even when armed with the most accurate and powerful weapons, and yet adheres to his point, that the lion never refuses battle when once he is stopped, whilst buffaloes and elephants almost invariably try to get away unless severely wounded. It is possible, however, that in past times lions in South Africa were more savage than they are to-day in East Africa and Somaliland, just as probably they were more prone to attack without provocation in the days when Jules Gerard hunted lions in French Algeria. At any rate this is the opinion of Sir Frederick Jackson, an experienced hunter in East Africa, who, although admitting he had not had a wide experience with lions, seems to think they always try to sneak off whenever they can—even when wounded. William Judd, perhaps the most experienced hunter of all game in East Africa, and a man who has also killed many lions in South Africa, places the buffalo first as the most dangerous animal, and his opinion is worthy of the highest consideration.

Selous bases his argument on the following :—

" That more accidents have happened in encounters with buffaloes than with lions is not that the former is a more dangerous animal than the latter, but because, for every lion that has been killed in the interior, at least fifty buffaloes have been brought to bay."

All of which is perfectly true.

Whilst on the subject of the comparative danger of various wild beasts it may be interesting briefly to summarize the views of other experienced hunters. Cuninghame and Tarlton place the elephant and the lion equal first, with the buffalo third. Sir Frederick Jackson and William Judd say the buffalo is easily first as a dangerous foe ; whilst Captain Stigand assigns the danger in the following order, viz. : lion, elephant, rhinoceros, leopard, buffalo. Sir Samuel Baker makes a more curious order—elephant, rhinoceros, buffalo, and lion the last. Oddly enough, only one hunter, namely Drummond, places the rhinoceros as the worst, but it must be remembered that when he hunted in South Africa heavy rifles were scarce and somewhat inadequate.

Nevertheless, despite all these very divided opinions, it is generally agreed amongst all professional hunters, both Boers and British, with whom I have discussed the question, both in East and South Africa, that the buffalo is perhaps the most dangerous animal, because he is so hard to stop and offers generally so sudden, so determined, and so unfavourable a target when actually charging.

When actually wounded and charging there is little doubt that the buffalo is the toughest of all, because he bursts out suddenly from a concealed spot and presents no vulnerable target, and I know from actual experience how helpless a man feels when one of these brutes comes grunting fiercely at his heels. Of course no man of sense does go poking about in dense bush after a wounded buffalo, but then all hunters are foolhardy sometimes and trouble ensues. We hate to leave a wounded animal, especially if it carries a good head. Thus have nearly all the numerous fatal accidents happened. A charging elephant is nearly always turned by a frontal shot, whereas a buffalo is never stopped unless it is mortally hit, but the chief danger in elephant-hunting seems to be (so Neumann thought) from outside sources—that is from vicious cows in the same herd which may be encountered suddenly. Neumann was an exceedingly brave man, and in his first trips was only armed with an ordinary ·256 Mannlicher throwing a solid bullet. His method was to creep right in amongst a herd and shoot the best bull through the heart. This often did not kill it at once, and rendered him liable to be charged suddenly by other members of the herd. Wherefore he rightly estimates that his own form of hunting was the most dangerous of all African hunting. When he got a double ·450 high-velocity Rigby he killed elephants much more easily and did not have nearly so many narrow escapes. It therefore seems to be the case that, armed with modern weapons, the hunter of elephants runs no especial risk if he does not try in the first instance to get too close to his quarry and gives it a side shot in the right place, whilst in the case of a charging animal the lion is the easiest to stop and the elephant the easiest to turn and the buffalo the hardest to kill. Yet if a quiet shot can be got at a buffalo bull before he has seen the hunter there seems to be little if any danger to the hunter.

Men who have encountered thousands of buffalo have told us that they have never seen an unwounded buffalo charge and that this only occurs when the hunter suddenly meets one face to face in the bush. But even this is not quite correct.

Speaking of buffaloes and their aggressiveness, Selous says : " Although many accidents happen in the pursuit of these animals, yet, in my opinion, the danger incurred in hunting them is marvellously exaggerated. Having shot nearly two hundred buffaloes to my own rifle, and followed very many of them when wounded into very thick bush, I think I have had sufficient experience to express an opinion on the subject." He suggests that, in the majority of cases when disasters occurred from a sudden attack, apparently without provocation, the buffalo which charged had probably been wounded by another hunter, and cites many instances to confirm this. Moreover, it may be added that buffaloes in old age often become deaf and lie in the bush until suddenly encountered by a man. Then a charge generally ensues because the meeting was unexpected.

Although Selous held that lions are the most dangerous of all opponents, by his own accounts his escapes from infuriated buffaloes were quite as numerous as those from the great cats.

Whilst hunting on the Chobe in 1877 he knocked down a young bull from a herd which gave him a very bad five minutes. As he was standing close to the bull, which he saw was only stunned, it suddenly rose to its feet and seemingly took no notice of a bullet fired point-blank into its chest. Selous ran past the bull, which catching sight of some of the Kafirs at once charged them, grunting furiously.[1]

" I was now by my tree, watching events and putting another cartridge into my rifle. The buffalo having missed my boys, who had all climbed into or were standing behind trees, soon slowed down to a trot, but was evidently still eager for revenge, as he came round in a half-circle with nose upraised and horns laid back. I was just going to fire at him, when he must have got my wind, for he suddenly swung round and, seeing me, came on at a gallop as hard as he could. He was about one hundred yards off when he started, and when he was some sixty yards from me I fired

---

[1] " A Hunter's Wanderings," pp. 433–434.

for his throat ; but he neither stopped nor swerved nor showed in any way that he was hit, but came straight on. I had plenty of time, and could have swarmed up the branchless stem of the sapling by which I was standing, and got out of his reach with the greatest ease ; but, as my legs were bare, I knew that such a course meant the loss of a lot of skin, so I determined to dodge him. I was young and active in those days, and full of confidence in my nerve, so, holding the stem of the tree in my left hand, I leant out as far as possible and awaited the onset. When he was very near me—so close, indeed, as to preclude the possibility of his being able to swerve and pass on the other side of the tree—I pulled my body with a sudden jerk up to and beyond the stem, and, shooting past the buffalo's hind-quarters, ran as hard as ever I could to another tree standing in the direction from which he had come. I knew that by this manœuvre I should gain a good deal of ground, as, even if my adversary had followed me, the pace at which he was going was such that he would not have been able to turn till he had got some way past the tree where I had given him the slip. Had he come round after me I should now have climbed for it ; but, as I expected, when I dodged from under his very nose and shot past behind him he lost me entirely and ran straight on. He did not, however, go far, but stopped and lay down, and I killed him with another bullet."

Again on the Chobe in 1879 he wounded an old bull, which he followed through open bush. The buffalo was, however, concealed as usual, and charged suddenly at ten yards' distance.

" I had no time to raise the rifle to my shoulder," he says, " but swinging it round to my hips, just pulled the trigger, and at the same time sprang to one side. At the same moment I was covered with a shower of sand, and some part of the buffalo, nose or horn or shoulder, touched my thigh with sufficient force to overthrow me, but without hurting me in the least. I was on my feet again in a moment, ready to run for it, but saw that my adversary was on the ground bellowing, with a hind-leg, evidently broken, dragging out behind him. Before he recovered himself I despatched him with a bullet through the lungs."

In April, 1877, Selous again reached Tati and, after a visit to Lobengula, at once trekked north to the Zambesi in the hope of securing elephants. This time he was accompanied by Mr. Kingsley, an Englishman, and Mr. Miller, a young colonist who was a first-rate shot. He had also several native hunters in his service. However, the whole trip resulted, as far as elephants were concerned, in a complete failure, only Miller killing two male animals. At Gerva he met his old friends Dorehill and Horner, who had both been seriously ill with fever, while his good friend Lieutenant Grandy had died from the same cause.

When Selous reached the Chobe he found that the elephants had all disappeared, but does not state the cause, which I have since ascertained was probably due to the great drives organized by Sepopo, Chief of the Barotsi, in the triangle of the Chobe-Zambesi delta. Apropos of this, my friend McLeod of McLeod gave me the following account. In 1875 he, with Dorehill and W. Fairlie, trekked up from the south and left their waggons at Pandamatenka on the Zambesi. Here they crossed the river and went in on foot, intending to hunt in the Barotsi country. After good sport with game, Sepopo received the party kindly and invited them to a great elephant drive which annually took place in September in the junction formed by the meeting of the Chobe and Zambesi rivers. Many thousands of natives took part in this great hunt. A line of fire enclosed the base of the triangle, into which several hundred elephants had been driven, whilst some thousands of natives in canoes lay in the rivers on each flank to cut off elephants and shoot and spear them in the water as they broke out. When all was in readiness the lines from the base fires advanced and the elephants began to break back and the shooting began. " Such a fusillade," remarked McLeod, " more resembled a battle than a hunt ; the firing was of the wildest description, and so inaccurate that we were in constant danger of losing our lives. At the end of the day only nine elephants were killed by our party and the natives

round us, whilst the majority broke through our cordon
and that of the fire behind and escaped. A considerable
number, however, were speared and shot on the rivers on
each flank. Several men were killed and wounded in the
attack."

The following year (1876) another great hunt of similar
character took place, and late in the season Sepopo was
assassinated and the whole country thrown into a state of
anarchy.

These great hunts, scaring the elephants out of the whole
district, would account for Selous' bad luck in 1877, but he
seemed to have enjoyed himself hunting buffalo, of which
he killed no fewer than forty-five in four months on the
Chobe. He states that he experienced a few dangers and
one rather narrow escape.

Selous, although he did not consider the buffalo so
dangerous an antagonist as the lion, had his full share of
adventures with them. His escape from an old bull which
killed his horse under him, on the Nata river in May, 1874,
was almost miraculous, for a buffalo seldom leaves his
victim once he has got him down.

He found two old buffalo bulls and galloped within three
yards of them, and the rifle missed fire. After another chase
one of the bulls, getting annoyed, stood and offered a good
shot, and the cap again played the hunter false.[1]

" Putting on a third cap, I now kept it down with my
thumb, and was soon once more close behind him, and had
galloped for perhaps a couple of minutes more, when,
entering a patch of short thick mopani bush, he stopped
suddenly, wheeled round, and came on at once, as soon as
he caught sight of the horse, with his nose stretched straight
out and horns laid back, uttering the short grunts with
which these animals invariably accompany a charge.

" There was no time to be lost, as I was not more than
forty yards from him ; so, reining in with a jerk and turning
the horse at the same instant broadside on, I raised my gun,
intending to put a ball, if possible, just between his neck
and shoulder, which, could I have done so, would either

---

[1] " A Hunter's Wanderings," pp. 279–281.

have knocked him down, or at any rate made him swerve, but my horse, instead of standing steady as he had always done before, now commenced walking forward, though he did not appear to take any notice of the buffalo. There was no time to put my hand down and give another wrench on the bridle (which I had let fall on the horse's neck), and for the life of me I could not get a sight with the horse in motion. A charging buffalo does not take many seconds to cover forty yards, and in another instant his outstretched nose was within six feet of me, so, lowering the gun from my shoulder, I pulled it off right in his face, at the same time digging the spurs deep into my horse's sides. But it was too late, for even as he sprang forward the old bull caught him full in the flank, pitching him, with me on his back, into the air like a dog. The recoil of the heavily-charged elephant-gun with which I was unluckily shooting, twisted it clean out of my hands, so that we all, horse, gun, and man, fell in different directions. My horse regained its feet and galloped away immediately, but even with a momentary glance I saw that the poor brute's entrails were protruding in a dreadful manner. The buffalo, on tossing the horse, had stopped dead, and now stood with his head lowered within a few feet of me. I had fallen in a sitting position, and facing my unpleasant-looking adversary. I could see no wound on him, so must have missed, though I can scarcely understand how, as he was so very close when I fired.

" However, I had not much time for speculation, for the old brute, after glaring at me a few seconds with his sinister-looking bloodshot eyes, finally made up his mind and, with a grunt, rushed at me. I threw my body out flat along the ground to one side, and just avoided the upward thrust of his horn, receiving, however, a severe blow on the left shoulder with the round part of it, nearly dislocating my right arm with the force with which my elbow was driven against the ground, and receiving also a kick on the instep from one of his feet. Luckily for me, he did not turn again, as he most certainly would have done had he been wounded, but galloped clean away.

" The first thing to be done was to look after my horse, and at about 150 yards from where he had been tossed I found him. The buffalo had struck him full in the left thigh ; it was an awful wound, and, as the poor beast was evidently in the last extremity, I hastily loaded my gun and put him out of his misery. My Kafirs coming up just then, I started with them, eager for vengeance, in pursuit of the buffalo, but was compelled finally to abandon the chase, leaving my poor horse unavenged."

Curiously enough, McLeod met with an almost identical accident on the Nata in 1875. The buffalo struck the horse behind in his charge, and horse, rifle, and rider were all thrown to the ground. Although McLeod was lying helpless, the buffalo confined its fury to the horse and struck it with his horns till life was extinct. Then, without looking at McLeod, who had been thrown into a thorn-bush, it galloped away.

Selous gives several instances of the tenacity of life and viciousness retained to the last moment of the buffalo.[1]

" Once, in 1874, when hunting with George Wood near the Chobe, we came upon an old buffalo bull lying down in some long grass. My friend gave him a bullet as he lay, upon which he jumped up and stood behind some mopani trees, only exposing his head and hind-quarters on either side their stems. After eyeing us for a few seconds he turned and went off at a gallop, but before he had gone many yards, Wood fired at him with his second gun and knocked him over ; he was on his legs again in a moment, and, wheeling round, came straight towards me at a heavy gallop, his nose stretched straight out and grunting furiously. When he was about twenty yards from me I fired with my large four-bore elephant-gun and struck him fair in the chest. This staggered but did not stop him, for, swerving slightly, he made straight for the Kafir carrying my second gun ; this the man at once threw down and commenced climbing a tree. The buffalo just brought his right horn past the tree, and scraping it up the trunk so as to send all the loose pieces of bark flying, caught the Kafir a severe

---

[1] " A Hunter's Wanderings," pp. 282–283.

blow on the inside of the knee, nearly knocking him out of the tree. The sturdy beast then ran about twenty yards farther, knelt gently down and, stretching forth its nose, commenced to bellow, as these animals almost always do when dying ; in a few minutes it was lying dead."

Buffaloes wounded by man or lions are always dangerous.

" One cold winter morning in 1873, I left my camp before sunrise, and had not walked a quarter of a mile skirting round the base of a low hill, when, close to the same path I was following, and not twenty yards off, I saw an old buffalo bull lying under a bush. He was lying head on towards us, but did not appear to notice us. My gun-carriers were behind, having lingered, Kafir-like, over the camp-fire, but had they been nearer me I should not have fired for fear of disturbing elephants, of which animals I was in search.

" As I stood looking at the buffalo, Minyama, one of my Kafirs, threw an assegai at it from behind me, which, grazing its side, just stuck in the skin on the inside of its thigh. Without more ado, the ugly-looking old beast jumped up and came trotting out, with head up and nose extended, evidently looking for the disturbers of its peace, and as Minyama was hiding behind the trunk of a large tree, and the rest of the Kafirs had made themselves scarce, it at once came straight at me, grunting furiously. I was standing close to a very small tree, not more than six inches in diameter, but as I was unarmed, and to run would have been useless, I swarmed up it with marvellous celerity. The buffalo just came up and looked at me, holding his nose close to my feet, and grunting all the time. He then turned and went off at a lumbering canter, and I then, for the first time, saw that he had been terribly torn and scratched on the hind-quarters and shoulders by lions. Had he tried to knock my little sapling down, he might, I think, easily have accomplished it ; as it was, my legs being bare, and the bark of the tree very rough, I had rubbed a lot of skin off the insides of my knees and the calves of my legs."[1]

Buffaloes, if the ground is hard, can go at a great pace and can outrun a horse for some distance. It once took

---

[1] " A Hunter's Wanderings," p. 283.

me a chase of five miles before I got up with a big bull on whose head I had set my desires. " In 1873," writes Selous, " a buffalo cow, although severely wounded, ran down in the open a horse Lobengula had lent me, and on which my Hottentot driver was mounted ; she struck the horse as it was going at full speed between the thighs with her nose, and, luckily striking short, knocked it over on one side and sent its rider flying, but before she could do further damage a bullet through her shoulders from George Wood incapacitated her for further mischief."

He seems to have been much depressed at this time as to his prospects of making a living—at any rate as an elephant-hunter and trader. " Nothing[1] has gone right with me since I left England, nor do I think it ever will again. I was born under an unlucky star, for even if I do not suffer from personal and particular bad fortune, I seem just to hit off the particular year and the particular part of the country for my speculation when and where everything has gone to rack and ruin. Had I left England in October, 1875, instead of February, 1876, I should in all human probability have done fairly well, and been able to return to England at the beginning of the next year (1878), for last year 40,000 lbs. of ivory were traded at the Zambesi alone, and every hunter did well. This year, owing principally to Sepopo's assassination, only 2500 lbs. have been traded, and not a hunter has earned his salt. But, mind you, I do not yet despair ; I am still well to the good, and, if I can only get to a country which is not worked out, I will soon get a few pounds together." Later the same year he writes to his father (October 17th, 1877) : " On this side of the river elephant-hunting is at an end, all the elephants being either killed or driven away. I am now going to try and go down the Zambesi to Tete—a Portuguese settlement, and from there to the new missionary settlement at Lake Nyassa."

After returning to Pandamatenka in 1877, Selous went down the Zambesi with a Mr. Owen and with donkeys, bent on trading and hunting in the " fly " north of the river.

[1] Letter to his mother.

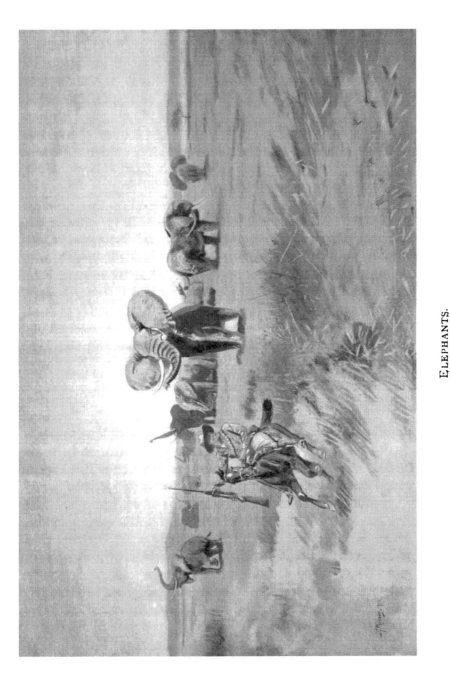

ELEPHANTS.

Eight days later he crossed at Wankie's Town and reached Mwemba's kraal—that chief being an important local chief of the Batongas. Mwemba was much pleased to see the travellers, as he stated they were the first white men he had ever met. The donkeys, too, were new beasts to him.

We need scarcely follow Selous' wanderings in the pestilential climate of the Zambesi valley during the next few months. He was completely disappointed in finding elephants, and both he and his companion suffered severely from fever in the deadly climate. All down the river he had daily evidence of the evil doings of the Portuguese, who employed the Shakundas to capture and enslave Batongan girls for their use and subsequent trade in human flesh. The price paid for a girl was usually an old musket or about twenty rupees. Near the mouth of the Kafukwe the travellers met Canyemba and Mendonca, head chiefs of the Shakundas, who appeared to be a proper pair of scoundrels, but small-pox was raging here, so Selous and Owen did not stay for long, but went north into the Manica country on December 13th. Hence they got up to the high country and shot a little game, including some konze (Liechtenstein's hartebeest), the first Selous had seen.

On January 6th they reached the kraal of Sitanda, head chief of the Manica country. " We found the old fellow a slight-built old Kafir, with an astute thin-featured face, sitting outside his hut with about a dozen cronies. When his people first come up to him to report any news, they roll on their backs in the dust before him, and subsequently, when talking to him, lie down on their sides and rub one shoulder in the dust at the conclusion of every sentence."

The Kafukwe country looking unpromising for elephants, Selous then resolved to go north to the Mashukulumbwe country, but this was prevented by the breakdown of Owen, who became seriously ill with fever. A few days later, after hunting lechwes in a swamp, Selous himself became ill, and for a fortnight both the travellers experienced all the trials of malarial fever. Sitanda was of course delighted, and hoped they would soon die and he could annex all their trade goods. He, in fact, refused them all help in the way

I

of food and porters in the manner usual to a savage who thinks he has white men in his power. The chief had given orders to all his people not to help the unfortunate invalids, no matter what payment was offered. Finally, poor Selous was reduced to " buying," for 320 loaded cartridges, one Kafir boy from a Portuguese. " The Portuguese told me I must watch him well in the daytime, and tie him up at night ; however, I explained to him, through one of my boys, that, although I had bought him, I did not want to keep him for a slave, and that if he would carry for me as far as the Zambesi, he might go where he liked afterwards, or continue working with me for wages."

On January 24th Selous and Owen left this " accursed spot where we had spent eighteen miserable days." Ill and weak they staggered south, and five days later " the slave " ran away with a valuable breech-loading elephant-gun. This, however, was recovered, but not the whole stock of Martini-Henry cartridges and corn which was essential to existence.

Thoroughly worn out, they reached the Zambesi at last on February 18th. No game had fallen to their rifles, as both were too ill to hunt.

After getting more provisions and carriers from Mendonca the party struck south, but after April 1st Owen was so weak that he had to be carried. Selous, however, improved a little when he reached the healthier country, but was still weak and unsuccessful in what little hunting he did. More-over, the Banyais carrying Owen struck work, so Selous decided to leave him in charge of his faithful Basuto servant Franz and himself to push on to the waggons at Inyati and to send back help to his friend. On April 17th, he bade good-bye to Owen, and reached Inyati on May 4th, sending seven men to the Gweo, where Owen rested, and they eventually brought him out safely to the Matabele country.

After this unfortunate trip Selous was much depressed in mind, feeling that the whole country south of the Zambesi was played out for the trader and the hunter. Writing to his mother from Tati (May 28th, 1878), he expresses all his gloomy anticipations—doubtless the after effects of fever from which he had not yet recovered. " I am afraid that if I ever get home again you will find me much changed for the worse in temper and disposition. Continual never-ending misfortune in small matters and the failure of every speculation has changed me from a tolerably light-hearted fellow into a morose sad-tempered man. It is all very well to say that one can but do his best and that sort of thing, but in this world a man's merit and worth are measured solely according to his success and by no other standard. During the last year almost everybody has been ruined, and all the smaller traders sold up. Next year I am going to try a new country to the north of Ovampoland in South-Western Africa. Things cannot be worse there than they are here, and from all I can learn probably much better. If there is nothing to be done there, I am sure I don't know what I shall do, but think of trying the Western States of North America. To try farming in this country with the luck against one would never do, for there is not one but twenty diseases to which all sorts of live stock are subject ; all of them unknown in America and Australia."

Selous was far from well after this trying trip, and it took him two months to recover from its effects, so it was not till August that he set off again, after getting permission from Lobengula, to hunt in the Mashuna country, where he hoped to join his friends Clarkson, Cross, and Wood, who had gone north in the previous June.

On August 20th he left Inyati, in company with Mr. Goulden (Clarkson's partner), and trekked north. On the 30th he reached the Gwenia, where he found the old Boer hunter Jan Viljoen and his family. Here he had some sport with sable antelopes, and moved on the next day and reached the Umniati on September 6th, and on September 8th the Gwazan, where he shot a bull sable. After crossing the Sweswe, where he found the Neros, well-known Griqua elephant-hunters, he heard that his friends were on the Umfule river, two days north. Here he learnt that Clarkson and Wood had killed eight bull elephants in one day, September 8th ; so was anxious to join them as soon as possible after this exciting piece of news.

On reaching the encampment of his friends he heard they were away on the Hanyane river, so he at once decided to follow them. Next day Selous killed a sable bull and met his friends close to the scene of the elephant slaughter of the previous Sunday. Clarkson and Wood had already killed forty elephants, and had to record the death of Quabeet, Wood's head Kafir, by a tuskless bull elephant. Selous gives some particulars of this unhappy event in a letter to his mother (December 25th, 1878) : " Mr. Clarkson came across a troop of elephants and commenced shooting at them. Whilst killing one he heard another screaming terrifically, and galloped in that direction but saw nothing. In the evening Quabeet was missing, but no one thought anything could have happened to him except that he had lost himself. On the second day, however, as he did not turn up, Clarkson bethought him of the continuous scream-ing he had heard, and remembered to have seen a gigantic tuskless bull turn out by himself, whose spoor he resolved to follow the next morning. This he did, and soon found the place where the elephant had chased a man ; there he found Quabeet's gun, and near it the odds and ends of skin he had worn round his waist and finally what remained of Quabeet. The poor fellow had been torn into three pieces. The elephant must have held him down with his foot and then torn him asunder with his trunk."

On September 14th the party found a herd of cow ele-phants and shot six, and on September 17th they all went north-east to the mahobo-hobo forests which lie between the Umsengasi and Hanyane rivers to look for elephants. The same evening they found two old bulls near the Umbila river. Selous quickly killed three bulls and a cow. " The fourth I tackled," he says, " cost me six bullets and gave me a smart chase, for my horse was now dead beat. I only got away at all by the skin of my teeth as, although the infuriated animal whilst charging trumpeted all the time like a railway engine, I could not get my tired horse out of a canter until he was close upon me, and I firmly believe that had he not been so badly wounded he would have caught me. I know the shrill screaming sounded unpleasantly near."

Immediately after this episode the herd of elephants showed signs of exhaustion. " The poor animals were now completely knocked up, throwing water (taken from their stomachs) over their heated bodies as they walked slowly along." But the hunters stuck to them until their cartridges were exhausted ; all, that is to say, except Selous, who had still thirteen left.

Selous then selected a big cow for his next victim, and experienced one of the narrowest escapes of his whole adventurous life.[1]

" Having picked out a good cow for my fifth victim, I gave her a shot behind the shoulder, on which she turned from the herd and walked slowly away by herself. As I cantered up behind her, she wheeled round and stood facing me, with her ears spread and her head raised. My horse was now so tired that he stood well, so, reining in, I gave her a shot from his back between the neck and the shoulder, which I believe just stopped her from charging. On receiving this wound she backed a few paces, gave her ears a flap against her sides, and then stood facing me again. I had just taken out the empty cartridge and was about to put a fresh one in, when, seeing that she looked very vicious, and as I was not thirty yards from her, I caught the bridle and turned the horse's head away, so as to be ready for a fair start in case of a charge. I was still holding my rifle with the breech open when I saw that she was coming. Digging the spurs into my horse's ribs, I did my best to get him away, but he was so thoroughly done that, instead of springing forwards, which was what the emergency required, he only started at a walk and was just breaking into a canter when the elephant was upon us. I heard two short sharp screams above my head, and had just time to think it was all over with me, when, horse and all, I was dashed to the ground. For a few seconds I was half-stunned by the violence of the shock, and the first thing I became aware of was a very strong smell of elephant. At the same instant I felt that I was still unhurt and that, although in an unpleasant predicament, I had still a chance for life.

[1] " A Hunter's Wanderings," pp. 339-340.

I was, however, pressed down on the ground in such a way that I could not extricate my head. At last with a violent effort I wrenched myself loose, and threw my body over sideways, so that I rested on my hands. As I did so I saw the hind legs of the elephant standing like two pillars before me, and at once grasped the situation. She was on her knees, with her head and tusks in the ground, and I had been pressed down under her chest, but luckily behind her forelegs. Dragging myself from under her, I regained my feet and made a hasty retreat, having had rather more than enough of elephants for the time being. I retained, however, sufficient presence of mind to run slowly, watching her movements over my shoulder and directing mine accordingly. Almost immediately I had made my escape she got up and stood looking for me, with her ears up and head raised, turning first to one side and then to the other, but never quite wheeling round. As she made these turns, I ran obliquely to the right or left, as the case might be, always endeavouring to keep her stern towards me. At length I gained the shelter of a small bush and breathed freely once more."

After a time he recovered his rifle and again attacked a cow which he thought was his late assailant, and killed her with two more shots, but she proved to be a different beast.

Selous did not escape quite scatheless from this encounter, for his eye was badly bruised and the skin all rubbed off the right breast. His horse, too, was badly injured, though he recovered after two months. Altogether, on this great and exciting day, no fewer than twenty-two elephants, realizing 700 lbs. of ivory, were killed by Selous, Clarkson, and Wood.

On September 24th the hunters killed five old bull elephants near the Hanyane, and shortly afterwards, elephants becoming shy, the party broke up, Cross, Goulden, and Wood going to the Umfule, and Clarkson and Selous remaining near the Hanyane. Both parties were, however, quite unsuccessful in hunting bull elephants, either in the neighbourhood of these rivers or in short trips they made into the " fly " region along the Umniati, Sebakwe, and Se-quoi-quoi rivers.

After enjoying some sport with the various large antelopes and witnessing an exciting chase and attack made by
a single hunting-dog on a sable antelope, the party turned
northwards and reached Gwenia, where the Viljoens were
camped, on December 11th, just as the heavy rains set in.

Here Selous had a piece of good luck. A lioness attacked
the Viljoens' cattle at ten o'clock one morning and went off
with a calf. The dogs, however, were at once loosed, and
soon brought the marauder to bay. Jantje, a Hottentot,
and one of the Viljoens' Kafirs ran at once to the scene of
tumult, when both of them fired and missed, but Selous
got an easy chance at forty yards, and killed her with a
bullet through the shoulders. On December 25th he wrote
to his mother telling her that his plans for the following
year were uncertain. He hoped to go " to the country
north of Lake Ngami, but may spend the winter with the
Volunteers against the Zulus if the war comes on."

CHAPTER V

1879–1880

LIKE all big game hunters Selous always dreamed of a land teeming with game where other hunters had not been and scared the game away. He saw by this time that the old hunting-grounds, at least as far as elephants were concerned, were finished, and that he must find for himself a new field to exploit if such a place existed. The difficulties, however, even to such a man as himself, were immense, because the "fly" debarred him to the east and north, whilst to the west was nothing but a waterless desert where no elephants could live. If therefore he was to find the virgin country it must be far to the north where he could not take his waggons. The country on which he had set his heart was the Mashukulumbwe, and though no hunters had been there, he heard from natives that it was full of elephants. In 1877 he had tried to reach it, but owing to the hostility of the Portuguese and local chiefs beyond the Zambesi, and the subsequent illness of himself and his friend, he had been obliged to abandon the venture. Now, however, in 1879, he conceived a plan to cross the desert to Bamangwato, when he hoped to kill gemsbuck, which had so far eluded him, and to hunt on the Chobe, which always held a peculiar attraction for him, then to leave his waggons and visit the unknown portions of the Barotsi country and strike east to the Mashukulumbwe. He expected that this journey would extend over two or three years, so in January he trekked south to Klerksdorp in the Transvaal, where he laid in stores and ammunition for the long trip.

On April 14th he reached Bamangwato and obtained permission from Khama to travel through the Kalahari to the Mababe river. This time young Miller again accompanied him as well as another young colonist of German extraction named Sell. Khama sent with Selous a grumpy disagreeable old Kafir named Ai-eetsee-upee (the man who knows nothing) to look after the waggons. Five other coloured men completed the party.

On May 4th they reached the Botletlie river. " This," says Selous, " is one of the most abominable spots I have yet visited : one small mud hole from which a little filthy water was all we could get for ourselves or the oxen, yet on the map this river looks like a young Mississippi."

On May 8th to the west of the Botletlie, Selous reached an encampment of bushmen, who told him there were giraffes in the bush close at hand. An old bull was soon found. " I gave the giraffe four shots," says Selous, " and then, seeing that he was done for, galloped round him, upon which he stood reeling under a tree, and I was just pulling my horse in, when a lion, a lioness, and two half-grown cubs jumped out of the bushes just in front of me and trotted slowly away. Just at this moment, too, I saw four stately giraffe cows walk out of the bush in single file about 500 yards ahead. The lion, after trotting a few paces, turned round and stood, broadside on, looking at me, offering a splendid shot. I was on the ground in a moment and gave him a bullet just behind the shoulder. With a growl he galloped away for about 100 yards, and then rolled over on his side, stone dead. I just rode up to assure myself of the fact, and then galloped on after the giraffe cows." Two of these he also killed.

On May 10th he saw the first gemsbuck, " the antelope of all others of which I longed to shoot a fine specimen," but after wounding one he lost it. Next day, however, he killed a young cow.

On May 28th they reached the so-called " fountain " of Sode-Garra, where the bushmen told him that the country to the north was impassable owing to no rain falling the previous summer. Never having known the untutored savage to tell the truth Selous imagined that the bushmen were lying, and so decided to risk it and trek on. The poor oxen then had a terrible time ; they got no water for two days and nights except a little moisture at one spot. On the fourth day they reached the sand-belts and pans just south of the Mababe flats, and still there was not a drop of water. It was here two years previously the famous Boer elephant-hunter Martinus Swartz and ten members of his family died of fever, only six individuals surviving out of a party of seventeen.

At these dried-up pans, however, Selous found some comparatively fresh spoor of buffalo and that meant there must be water at no very great distance. Accordingly, he abandoned the waggons and accompanied by bullocks, horses, dogs and Kafirs went north to the great plain known as the Mababe flat. Here they saw grass fires at a distance of about twelve miles, but the presence of numerous zebras indicated that there was water still nearer. Old Jacob, one of his Kafirs, now said there was a small vley close at hand. " We went to look," writes Selous, " and five minutes later found a long shallow vley full of water. I could have hugged the dirty old man with delight. What a sight it was to see the poor thirsty oxen come trotting down to the pan, as soon as they smelt the longed-for water, and rush knee-deep into it ! What a sudden relief the sight of that pool of muddy water was, too, and what a weight of fear and anxiety it lifted from our hearts ! Only an hour before it had seemed that I was doomed to lose all my live stock— nearly everything I possessed in the world—from thirst ; and now the danger was past, and not a single ox had given in." Next day the oxen were sent back and brought the waggons to the vley.

On June 4th he encountered three lionesses, at one of which he had a running shot which knocked her over. Soon a second lioness stood and turned to bay, and Selous killed her dead with a shot in the head just as she was on the point of charging. He then returned to the first wounded animal and gave her a shot through the lungs. Two days later whilst stalking giraffes he met two full-grown lions lying under a bush.[1]

" I now turned my attention to the second lion. As,

[1] " A Hunter's Wanderings," pp. 382–383.

owing to the grass, I could not see him clearly, I mounted my horse and gave him a shot from the saddle, as he lay half-facing me, gazing towards me with anything but a pleasant expression of countenance. Whether he realized the misfortune which had befallen his comrade or not I cannot say, but he certainly had an angry, put-out sort of look. As I fired, a loud roar announced that the bullet had struck him, and I could see that he was hard hit. He now sat on his haunches like a dog, holding his head low, and growling savagely. In this position he exposed his chest, so hastily pushing in another cartridge, I jumped to the ground before he could make up his mind what to do, and firing quickly, struck him in the centre of the breast, just under the chin. This rolled him over, and riding up, I saw that he was in his last agonies, so left him, and took a look at the first I had shot, a magnificent old lion with a fine black mane, and a skin in beautiful condition, and of a very dark colour all over. All this, which has taken so long to relate, must have occupied less than a minute of time, and the lions being both dead, I again turned my attention to the giraffes."

Two of these, a bull and a cow, he chased and killed.

A few days later Selous' friend, H. C. Collison, arrived in his camp. Collison, with French, had also trekked north across the thirst-land, and lost several of their oxen on the way. Moreover, to add to these disasters, Clarkson, an intimate friend of all three, had been struck by lightning and killed near Klerksdorp shortly after their departure for the interior. Speaking of Clarkson, to whom he was much attached, Selous says : " A better fellow never stepped. Short of stature, but very strong and active, he was, like most colonists, a capital shot and first-rate rough-rider, qualities that could hardly fail to make him a successful hunter. Morally speaking, too, he was upright and honourable in his dealings with his fellow-men, cool in danger, and as plucky as a bull-dog. May his spirit find a good hunting-country in the next world ! "

A few days later Collison, French and Selous established a permanent hunting-camp on the Mababe river and went

north on foot into the " fly." Owing to the size of the party
they soon separated, French and Miller going to the Sunta
river, whilst Collison, Sell and Selous went on up the
Machabe, but afterwards they met on the Chobe. Miller
and Selous then passed on to Linyanti, where they killed
four elephants, many buffaloes, and several of the small
spotted and striped bushbucks peculiar to the Chobe. Here
Selous tried unsuccessfully to kill a specimen of the sitatunga
antelope by hunting in a canoe at dawn amongst the reed
beds, but only saw one female, although he found lying dead
a fine male killed by a rival.

On August 23rd Selous obtained permission to hunt
elephants in the angle of the Chobe and the Zambesi from
the Barotsi chief Mamele. After a visit to the waggons to
get stores and ammunition he returned to the Chobe angle
with French and Miller. Close to Mamele's town the party
met four lionesses, one of which Selous shot. Buffaloes at
this time were in immense herds feeding out in the open all
day, even amongst the native cattle, and Selous shot several
to provide meat for the Kafirs.

It was not until September 24th that the party found any
elephants, and then Selous and Miller killed a young bull,
four large cows and a heifer. Poor French on this day
wounded and lost a cow, and contrary to advice, followed
it into the bush. He was never seen again, and died of
thirst in the bush. For days Miller and Selous tried to find
his tracks, but without avail. The loss of his good friend
made a deep impression on Selous, and for years afterwards
he never spoke of French, to whom he was greatly attached,
without showing signs of emotion. To have lost two of his
best friends in one year depressed him greatly, and to this
were added constant attacks of malarial fever which made
him very weak.

However, at the time he always hoped that French might
have reached some place of safety on the river and be alive.
So Selous continued to hunt for elephants until one day
" Boy," French's gun-bearer, crawled into camp and gave
an account of his master's death. It appeared that after
hunting for days in the bush in the wrong direction poor

French collapsed, and as he was dying wrote on his rifle the words " I cannot go any further ; when I die, peace with all." French's two boys, " Boy " and " Nangora," then walked all night and struck the river at Linyanti. " For several nights," says Selous, " I never slept, as the vision of my lost friend wandering about and dying by inches continually haunted me."

Seriously ill as he was, Selous then went to Linyanti, hoping to recover the body of his friend and give it decent burial, and Mamele promised to send all his people out to look for it when the rains came, but it was never found. Selous himself was so depressed in mind and worn with fever that he did not care to hunt any longer on the Chobe, so made for his waggons, which he reached on October 11th, where he found Sell dangerously ill. Miller, too, was attacked with malaria but soon recovered.

It was now necessary to wait for the rains, but as they did not come Selous, tired of shooting wildebeest and zebra on the Mababe flats, once more returned to the Chobe to look for elephants. He went as far as Maimi's town, and as the rain was now threatening he retraced his steps. By the middle of November he again reached the waggons, and the much desired rains at last fell. The party got to the Botletlie with ease, but between that river and Bamangwato the oxen again suffered terribly and were nearly lost owing to thirst. Later, in December, Selous reached the Diamond Fields, and was there attacked by a low fever which nearly cost him his life ; in fact, nothing but the unremitting attention and care of his friends, Mrs. Frederick Barber and her daughter, Mrs. Alexander Baillie, rescued him from death.

Meanwhile, owing to political blunders, South Africa and all its white and black races were in a ferment, and the Zulu War in full progress. The usual cause of England's wars with savages was acts of rapine or insolence on the part of natives living in wild country where the black or red man predominated in numbers and a small white population was threatened with danger. No such reason, however, was the cause of the Zulu war in 1879. Since 1861 the Natal colonists had lived alongside the Zulus in perfect amity, and the colonists " felt no real alarm concerning the Zulus until the idea was suggested to them by those in authority over them." [1]

The real cause, apart from the fact that the Natal farmers were annoyed that at their side dwelt a great black population they could neither tax nor force to work for them, was the aggression of the Transvaal Boers in a small portion of territory owned by Cetawayo, the Zulu king, and lying on the Transvaal border. There were two disputed boundary lines. The one between Zululand and the Transvaal to the south of the Pongolo river, and the other between the Zulus and the Swazis, to the north of and parallel with the Pongolo river.

The Swazis had always been hereditary enemies of the Zulus, and there was bitter feeling between the two races. Nevertheless the real cause of both disputes was the acquisitiveness of the Boers. In the case of the territory on the second boundary line they professed to have obtained by cession from the Swazi king in 1855 a strip of land to the north-east of the Pongolo river, so as to form a barrier between the Swazis and the Zulus ; but the Swazis denied having ever made such a cession. It is doubtful, however, whether the Swazis had any power to have made such a contract, even if it had been made, because the territory in question was occupied until 1846 by two Zulu chiefs, Puttini and Langalibalele. These chiefs, however, had been driven out of Zululand by Umpande (Panda), then king of the Zulus.

As time went on efforts were made to induce Cetawayo to allow the boundary territory to be occupied by the Boers, but the king sagely replied that as we had suggested that this territory belonged to Zululand, and he wished it for his own people, he did not see how it could belong to two parties. A boundary commission was, however, eventually formed, and asserted that neither party had a claim to the whole, whilst distinctly stating that no cession of land had been made by the Zulu king past or present.

[1] " History of the Zulu War," by Miss Colenso and Col. Durnford.

Other minor causes of the Zulu war were the raids of Umbilini, a Swazi chieftain living under Cetawayo's protection, and the forcible capture in Natal of Zulu brides and girls who had run away to escape disagreeable marriages.

On December 11th, 1878, the Zulus were presented with an ultimatum, of which the demand for the disbandment of the Zulu army was the principal clause. Cetawayo agreed to some of the demands but asked for time to consult his Indunas as regards demobilization. This was, however, refused. It would appear that even Cetawayo was anxious to avoid war if possible, for at his side stood John Dunn, who well knew the power of England. Lord Chelmsford had, however, completed his preparations for war, and on January 12th crossed the border into Zululand. Then followed the disaster of Isandlwana, the splendid defence of Rorke's Drift, the battle of Ngingindhlovu, in which the Zulus lost heavily, and in July the great battle of Ulundi, which finally broke the Zulu forces.

Selous always enjoyed meeting people who had taken part in events in the recent history of South Africa, and one day he met at my house General Sir Edward Hutton, who told us the following story of the capture of Cetawayo.

" After the defeat of the Zulus at Ulundi," remarked Sir Edward, " they scattered in all directions and we sent out small patrols throughout the country to search for the king. On this occasion the Zulus behaved in the most magnanimous manner. Although they could with ease have annihilated the majority of these patrols, not one was attacked, for they felt that the supreme test had been passed and their army utterly defeated. I believe that one day after the battle of Ulundi it would have been safe for an English lady to have walked across Zululand unmolested, so noble was the behaviour of the natives. I was attached to a patrol under Major Marter, K.D.G., and we came up with the king at Nisaka's kraal in the Ngome Forest.

" Cetawayo was seated in a hut attended by two of his chief wives. Marter entered the hut with myself and explained to the king that his presence was required by Sir Garnet Wolseley, and that he must come at once.

Cetawayo promptly refused. Marter took out his watch and stated that he would give him five minutes to decide. The black monarch still refused to move. ' I will now give you five minutes more,' said Marter, ' and then if you are still obstinate I shall set fire to the hut.'

" The King remained obdurate. Then Marter drew from his pocket a box of matches, and I still seem to see clearly the expression on Cetawayo's face as he listened to the scraping of the match on the box. Cetawayo, who was an immense man, and at the moment perfectly naked, then rose with great dignity and stalked out of the hut. Here he threw a large kaross over his shoulder and stood there looking every inch a king.

" ' Where are you taking me ? ' he observed.

" ' That I cannot tell you,' replied Marter.

" ' Well, I refuse to go,' came the answer.

" The King was then seized by soldiers and put upon a litter and thus carried with his wives to a waggon which was awaiting."

Selous was much interested in this story, and then told us the following interesting tale which I never heard him repeat before or later. It has always been a puzzle to me how he knew Cetawayo, for after many enquiries amongst his family and friends I have been unable to learn when he visited Zululand, for otherwise he could not have known the Zulu king. Yet the fact remains that he distinctly said on this occasion that he had met the black monarch in some of his past wanderings.

" I had known Cetawayo formerly, and when he was confined in Robben Island shortly after the conclusion of the war, I thought I would go down one day when I was in Cape Town and have a chat with him. I found him much as I had known him, but more corpulent and somewhat depressed. After some general conversation I said :

" ' Well, Cetawayo, what do you think of John Dunn now ? '

" This I knew was a sore point with the king, for he had treated John Dunn like a brother and given him wives, slaves and lands as one of his own head indunas. Dunn had afterwards deserted him and given all his help and information to Sir Garnet Wolseley.

"Cetawayo thought deeply for a few moments, and then said, ' One very cold and stormy night in winter I was seated before a large fire in my hut when there was a noise without as if someone was arriving. I asked the cause from my attendants, and they told me a white man in a miserable state of destitution had just arrived and claimed my hospitality. I ordered the slaves to bring him in, and a tall splendidly made man appeared. He was dressed in rags, for his clothes had been torn to pieces in fighting through the bush, and he was shivering from fever and ague. I drew my cloak aside and asked him to sit by the fire, and told the servants to bring food and clothing. I loved this white man as a brother and made him one of my head indunas, giving him lands and wives, the daughters of my chiefs. *Now Shaunele (the sun has gone down), and John Dunn is sitting by the fire but he does not draw his cloak aside.'* "

Such is the black man's reasoning, and can we controvert it with uplifted heads?

After the Zulu war McLeod asked some of the chiefs why they went to war with us. They replied, " The Right of the Strong. Now you have proved you are the strongest we will look up to you and follow you." Except for one trifling insurrection under Denizulu, which was quickly nipped in the bud, the Zulus have since accepted our suzerainty.

The following example of the intellect and common-sense of the South African native is given to me by McLeod of McLeod, who was in charge of the Swazis both in the Zulu war and the subsequent attack on Sekukuni, the paramount chief of Basutoland.

McLeod called upon Ubandini, the Swazi king, to raise some 8000 levies. This army was then about to set out for Basutoland, there to join our forces under Sir Garnet Wolseley. The following conversation took place :—

McL. " It is agreed that your people may have all the cattle they can capture, but the English Government

K

insists that on no account are your men to injure the Basuto women and children."

Ubandini thought deeply for a moment, and then re-marked, " Mafu (the McLeod's native name), do you like rats ? "

McL. " No."

U. " In fact you kill them whenever you can."

McL. " Yes."

U. " But surely you spare the females and little rats ? "
No answer.

The black man will do much from fear or for utilitarian motives, but to him as a rule charity simply does not exist. One day in 1874 an old man came to Sepopo, the paramount chief of the Barotsi, and claimed his help. Sepopo, who was drinking beer with a white trader, turned to some of his men and said : " He's a very old man ; can he do any work ? " Being answered in the negative he ordered his servants to take the old man down to the river and hold his head under water. On being informed that the un-fortunate victim was dead he coolly said : " Then give him to the crocodiles," and then went on chatting quietly and drinking beer with his white friend. The whole affair was a matter of no importance.

Of the intentions and views of the Zulus and the Boers at this time Selous writes to his mother, January 25th, 1880, and it is interesting to notice that at this time his attitude towards the Boers was not so sympathetic as it eventually became on more intimate knowledge.

" Last year when I went in hunting I thought to have done well, as I obtained leave to hunt in a country where a few years ago elephants were very plentiful. But, alas, during the last two years Moremi's hunters from Lake Ngami have overrun the whole district and effectively driven away the elephants, so that I have again made an unsuccessful hunt. I shall now give up hunting elephants, as it is impossible to make it pay. However, I must make one more journey into the interior, which I intend to be my last. If I keep my health it will be a long one, for I intend to cross the Zambesi again and endeavour to penetrate through the Mashukulumbwe country to Lake Bangwolo, for which purpose I have bought twelve donkeys that will carry my traps and make me independent to a great extent of native carriers.

" During the last four years, though I have led a life of great hardship and privation, yet I have lost much money and almost ruined a good constitution ; to throw away a little more money and health after what has already gone, will not much matter, and the former I may not lose at all, for I may shoot elephants, indeed, most likely I shall. I intend publishing a book, and think that a journey into a country where no one has ever been before would greatly enhance its value. My plans are liable to modification owing to fever, tsetse flies, and various minor circumstances.

" The Zulu war is over. You think it was unjustifiable, but it was not so, for so long as the military power of the Zulus remained unbroken there could be no peace in South Africa and the white inhabitants of Natal and the Transvaal would have had an assegai constantly dangling over their heads. Sir Bartle Frere knew this, and no doubt manœuvred so as to bring on a war, a war which he knew to be inevitable sooner or later. Of course but little glory has been gained, and one cannot but admire and pity the Zulus, who made a brave but unavailing resistance to our men armed with far superior weapons. I think they are far better off than before, and are not burdened with the cruel despotism of Cetawayo. It seems that after all there will be a disturbance with the Transvaal Boers. I hope not, but of course, if they force it upon themselves, their blood will be upon their own heads. I do not admire them ; mentally they are, I should think, the most ignorant and stupid of all white races, and they certainly have not one tenth part of the courage of the Zulus. Physically they are immensely big as a rule and capital shots, but there can only be one end for them to an open rupture with the British authorities, death and confiscation of property which will leave another legacy of hatred between Dutch and English inhabitants of this country for many years to come."

Early in 1880 Selous, having completely recovered from his attack of fever and settled up French's affairs, turned his attention to the preparations for his big expedition across the Zambesi. Difficulties, however, arose which foiled all his plans. In the first place the Matabele were supposed (officially) to be in a disturbed state, so it was necessary for Selous to go to Pretoria to obtain from Sir Owen Lanyon, the administrator of the Transvaal, permission to carry a good supply of ammunition. This, however, Sir Owen blankly refused. The secretary to the administrator was Mr. Godfrey Lagden (afterwards Sir Godfrey Lagden, Governor of Basutoland for many years, and a close friend of Selous). Sir Godfrey thus writes to me :—

" Selous approached me to get the Governor's permit to proceed with firearms through a forbidden or restricted route to Matabeleland, then closed owing to political reasons. This route was dangerous to travel in consequence of the threatening attitude of Lobengula. I was able to help in a measure—who could refuse to help so bold and charming a personality ?—but not to the full measure he wanted. He went away saying : ' I want you some day to come and trek with me, and enjoy as you do the beautiful big game as well as the small without killing it. Meanwhile I must away, and as a permit cannot take me over the Crocodile river, I must swim it in spite of crocodiles and Matabele.' "

The refusal of a permit to carry sufficient ammunition undoubtedly caused him to abandon the long journey— that is to say, for the time being—and in his letters home at this period he is once again depressed at the financial outlook and the difficulty of making a living. " I hope to be in England," he says (March, 1880), " by the end of the year. I shall then go in for writing a book, for which I may get a little money. I know that people have got good sums for writing bad books on Africa, full of lies, though I do not know if a true book will sell well. My book at any rate will command a large sale out here, as I am so well known, and have a reputation for speaking nothing but the truth."

Before going home he decided to go to Matabeleland and

join his friends Collison, J. S. Jameson, and Dr. Crook in a hunting trip to the Mashuna country.

Here it is necessary to say a few words concerning Selous' friend, J. S. Jameson, for in later days he took a prominent part in the page of African history.

James Sligo Jameson was born at Alloa, N.B., on 17th of August, 1856. His father, Andrew Jameson, was the son of John Jameson, who founded the business in Dublin. From his early youth he evinced a great taste for sport and natural history, with a desire to travel and doing something big. After schooldays at Dreghorn and the International College, Isleworth, he began to read for the army, but soon abandoned his intention, and his father being a rich man he went on his travels in 1877 to Ceylon, Calcutta, Singapore, and Borneo, where he made a good collection of birds and insects. In 1878 he went to South Africa and hunted on the borders of the Kalahari in Montsioa's veldt until 1879, when he returned to Potchefstroom and outfitted for an extensive trip to Matabeleland and the Zambesi in 1880. Whilst at Potchefstroom he carried despatches to Sir Garnet Wolseley at Pretoria and then returned, completed his preparations, and trekked north across the Limpopo to Matabeleland, where later on he met Selous.

In the spring of 1881 Jameson returned to England with a fine collection of heads, birds and insects, and the following year, in company with his brother, J. A. Jameson, he went to the upper waters of the Mussel Shell river in Montana and hunted successfully bear, sheep, wapiti, mule deer and antelope. In 1883 he again hunted in the Rockies with his brother on the North Foot of Stinking Water, then a great game country, and killed thirty-six mountain sheep, buffalo, bears and wapiti.

In 1884 he travelled in Spain and Algeria, and in 1885 married Ethel, daughter of Major-General Sir Henry Durand.

It was in January, 1887, that the English public were interested in the proposed expedition for the relief of Emin Pasha—Gordon's friend—under the command of H. M. Stanley. The whole idea was one that appealed to Jameson's chivalrous nature, and as it seemed to offer good opportunities for collecting specimens of big game, birds and insects in a part of Africa that was practically unknown, he offered a thousand pounds to be allowed to accompany the expedition as an officer acting under Stanley's orders. This offer was at once accepted.

" Why all the ambitions of my lifetime should have been concentrated at this time, with a seemingly prosperous issue, I know not ; but I assure you that I did not accept the position without weighing well all there was for and against it. Ever since childhood I have dreamt of doing some good in this world, and making a name which was more than an idle one. My life has been a more or less selfish one, and now springs up this opportunity of wiping off a little of the long score standing against me. Do not blame me too much."[1]

After a wearisome journey up the Congo, Stanley decided to make a base camp at Yambuya on the Aruwimi, and to leave there all the sick and useless Soudanese and Zanzibari soldiers and porters, extra stores, etc., and to push on himself to the Ituri forest and Lake Albert with the main expedition. Two officers had to be left in charge at Yambuya, and to his great disgust Jameson found that he was one of those selected for this uncongenial task. Almost from the first the whole outfit suffered from semi-starvation. The site of the camp was badly chosen, the natives were more or less hostile, and Jameson and his gallant friend, Major Barttelot, were often at their wits' ends to feed their men and keep down the continuous death-rate.

Stanley, it seems, had promised to return in November, and that if he did not return he had arranged with Tippu-Tib, the Arab chieftain, ivory and slave-trader, and actual master of the Upper Congo, to permit a thousand porters to bring on the rearguard and join him at Lake Albert.

At last things became so desperate that Jameson himself went up the Congo, a twenty-four days' journey, to see Tippu-Tib to try and induce him to supply the men with

[1] Letter to Lady Durand, Jan. 22nd, 1887, from " Story of the Rear Column," p. 31.

which to cross Africa—even offering a bond for five thousand pounds on his and Major Barttelot's private account if Stanley's word was not considered sufficient. Tippu-Tib seems to have behaved well, and accompanied Jameson back to Stanley Falls, from which he and Barttelot presently started with some four hundred unruly Manyema savages.

We need not follow poor Jameson's troubles in the ensuing months of June to August, 1888, when, the move failing, owing to ceaseless thefts, desertions and small-pox, Jameson at last reached Unaria and Barttelot returned to Stanley Falls. Barttelot was then murdered, and Jameson returned to Stanley Falls, where he found it impossible to re-organize the expedition without monetary help, which at the time he could not obtain. There being no prospect of doing anything in the way of crossing Africa, and no word or orders having been received from Stanley, Jameson then went down the river to Bangala in order to obtain some reply from the Emin Relief Committee. Tippu-Tib indeed offered himself to go with Jameson, but demanded £20,000 —a sum which at the time it was not possible for Jameson to guarantee. On this journey Jameson got wet and caught a chill which soon developed into acute fever. He was a dying man when his good friend Herbert Ward lifted him from the canoe at Bangala, and he only lived for a few days.

Jameson was to all who knew him well of a generous and gentle nature, full of thought for others and a man of high courage.

At the end of May, 1880, Selous reached Bulawayo and met his friends, and left a few days later for the hunting veldt, where they had fine sport with all sorts of game except elephants. On July 24th Jameson and Selous left their waggons on the Umfule river and went in on foot with thirteen natives into the " fly " country to the north. This was a rough, hilly country where rhinoceros were numerous in the hills and hippopotami in the river. The country was quite unknown, but the object of the hunters was to strike east to the Hanyane and follow it down to the Portuguese town of Zumbo on the Zambesi. At Lo

Magondi's kraal they decided to abandon the Hanyane route and to follow the Umfule to its junction with the Umniati.

On July 31st they reached a pool and killed several hippopotami, and the hunters and natives were soon revelling in meat and fat. The next day Selous killed a very fine buffalo bull. In a few days they reached the Umniati and entered the first Banyai village. The party got game almost every day, and on August 10th Selous killed another fine buffalo bull. On the Umniati the natives engaged in the practice of enclosing a space of the river over 200 yards broad and 400 yards in length to confine a herd of hippopotami so as to starve them to death. In one of these the travellers saw ten unfortunate animals which had been enclosed for about three weeks. Occasionally one was speared by the natives when it became exhausted.

On August 17th Jameson and Selous turned homewards towards their waggons, and whilst travelling through the bush suddenly came upon two fine bull elephants. Jameson was in great excitement, as they were the first he had ever seen. The elephants passed broadside and both hunters fired, but the beasts made off. After several more shots—Jameson having got hold of his big rifle—both hunters killed their quarry, then following the course of the Umzweswe for some distance, where Jameson got his first lion, and by striking east to the Umfule river, they got back to their waggons on August 30th.

In a letter to his mother (November 2nd, 1880) Selous says : " I will send you an account of a lion that came to our camp whilst we were away and did a bit of mischief, causing the death amongst other things of Mr. Jameson's servant, a white man named Ruthven." No details of this unfortunate incident are, however, available.

Jameson and Selous continued hunting until November, and then trekked out to Bulawayo. In December Selous bade farewell to Lobengula and reached Bamangwato at the end of the month. Early in 1881 war broke out in the Transvaal, so Jameson and Selous travelled along the borders of the Kalahari desert to Griqualand and reached the Diamond Fields. Here Selous disposed of his waggon, oxen and horses, travelled to Port Elizabeth, and took ship for England. As soon as he landed he heard that " the wretched war with the Transvaal—a war that will leave a legacy of hatred for generations to come to be equally divided between the Dutch and English colonists in South Africa—had been concluded by a most humiliating peace, and a more disgraceful page added to the history of England than any that have yet been written in its annals."

On April 17th, 1877, Sir T. Shepstone, on behalf of H.M. Government, annexed the Transvaal. It is true that for a long time the management of the affairs of the Boer Republic had been going from bad to worse. Its government had no longer powers to enforce laws or to collect taxes. Nevertheless, many thought our action was unjust as long as their affairs did not affect us. On one point, however, we had a right, for the conduct of the Boers to the native tribes had been abominable. One of the causes alleged for our interference was the desultory war carried on with great brutality by the Boers against Sekukuni, chief of the Bapedi. This war was brought on by the encroachment of the Boers on the Bapedi, just as the Zulu war was brought on by similar causes. The object of the Boers in their attacks on native races was firstly the acquisition of territory, and secondly the capture of children to be brought up as slaves.

When the annexation was announced, the Zulus rejoiced greatly, but their joy was soon dashed when they found that, far from removing the bitter trouble of the boundary question, the English had turned against them in this matter. They were sore at our having espoused the cause of their enemies, the Boers, whom they had refrained from attacking for many years, when they could have done so with impunity, without coming into collision with the English. Even at this time they still believed in us ; but considered that Sir T. Shepstone in undertaking the government of the Boers, had become a Boer himself.

At first the Boers took the annexation quietly, and sent two commissions to London, in 1877 and 1878, with a memorial signed by thousands of Boers stating their rights in the matter, in order to avoid war, but obtained no satisfaction from the Secretary of State for the Colonies. A considerable feeling of unrest therefore remained after their return, and the Boers went into laager near Pretoria, where Sir Bartle Frere met them on September 10th, 1879. The Boers then complained bitterly of the annexation and of the manner in which it had been carried out. The answer given on the 29th of September by Sir Garnet Wolseley was that we intended to keep the Transvaal.

On the 12th of December there was a meeting of over six thousand Boers at Wonderfontein, and many resolutions were passed which in the main proclaimed their continued independence. At the end of 1879, however, the Home Government established a sort of Executive Council for the Transvaal which consisted of both Boers and Englishmen. In March, 1880, the first legislative assembly under Her Majesty's rule was opened at Pretoria by Colonel Owen Lanyon, and for a short time after this the Home Government was assured that the agitation amongst the Boers was dying out, whereas in reality it was only the calm before the storm.

On November 11th some disaffected Boers forcibly stopped an execution sale for non-payment of taxes. Soon after this the Boers gathered and refused to pay taxes. This led to collisions, and Sir Owen Lanyon ordered up troops to Potchefstroom. On December 13th, 1880, the first shot was fired and England began to reap the fruit of her disastrous policy. The result of the war of 1881 and the subsequent peace made by Gladstone immediately after the disaster of Majuba are too well known to need recapitulation.

As soon as Selous arrived in England he began preparing for the Press an account of his travels which was published by Richard Bentley & Son in the same year under the title of " A Hunter's Wanderings in Africa."[1]   As was expected

---

[1] Mrs. Jones (Miss A. S. Selous), who did the illustrations for his first book, writes to me: " I fear I must own to these illustrations, but at least they were a proof of what my brother was to me—my hero always— I never could have gone through such an ordeal otherwise, for I knew nothing about animals. Still I do not regret them, although the sight of them on the screen was always acutely painful to me ! You were his greatest friend, so you will understand."

by his friends, but not himself, it achieved an immediate success and stamped the author at once not only as a great hunter, naturalist and explorer, but as one who could narrate his experiences in an entertaining fashion. Since Baldwin's " African Hunting and Adventure," published in 1863, there had been no first-class book on South African sport, so Selous' book was welcomed by all men who love the rifle and the wilderness. If he made a mistake it was in publishing the lists of game shot by himself between January, 1877, and December, 1880. They amount to such a formidable total that, both at the time and subsequently reviewers attacked him for what they call " this wholesale senseless slaughter." Selous was wont to reply to this charge by saying that the greater part of the meat killed was consumed by his own followers and hungry natives who would do nothing for him unless he killed some animal for food.[1] This is very true, but it must be admitted there was enormous waste on some days when four or five giraffes or elephants were killed. Selous, however, was no different from other hunters of all time, and thought that in the case of very abundant species they would last for ever, or in the case of others—such as the great game—if he did not shoot them somebody else would. Nevertheless, he was far more considerate than the majority of the early hunters, and never shot an animal except for a definite purpose. Between the years 1860–1870 the destruction of game in South Africa was very great, but the real disappearance of the large fauna probably dated from the introduction of the modern breech-loading rifle, roughly about 1875, and the commencement of the sale of hides for commercial purposes. It will give the reader a better idea of what this wholesale destruction meant when I state that one dealer in Kroonstad (Orange River Colony) told me by reference to his books that between the years 1878–1880 he exported nearly two

---

[1] Writing in 1892 Selous says : " As I have lately been accused of slaughtering game for sport, I will take this opportunity of saying that during this journey (Autumn, 1892), though I walked for days amongst innumerable herds of wild animals, I only fired away twelve cartridges from the day I left Salisbury until the date of my return there, and that, as is my usual practice, I never fired a shot except for the purpose of supplying myself and my party with meat."

million skins of springbuck, blesbok and black wildebeest. He, it is true, was the principal dealer in hides for that part of the Vaal river district, but there were many others who also exported very large numbers. It has been abundantly proved that game of all kinds must disappear at the advent of railways and modern weapons. In a new country every man carries a rifle and uses it, whilst history teaches us that nothing has ever been done to save the game until it is on the verge of extinction. East Africa, alone of all countries, made adequate Game Laws in time, but how long the game will last there, near railways, is a doubtful point, for the settlers have now taken matters into their own hands and are destroying the game wholesale on the pretext of wanting the grass for the cattle. This is done indiscriminately by all settlers whether they have cattle or not. Considering that Big Game shooting parties furnish a good part of the revenue (over £10,000 annually in shooting licences) of British East Africa, and that the country, except for coffee, black wattle and hemp, all of which grow where there is little or no big game, is mostly unsuitable for ranching, the state of things is deplorable.

There are many who sneer at Big Game shooting, and are opposed to the slaughter of animals, but if we look upon this sport in a wider sense, in its magnificent opportunities for training the body and developing the best qualities in men of the right stamp, and in the matter of shooting, endurance and the organization of material, we will find that the balance is on the right side. There is, in fact, no outdoor exercise to compare with it, whilst the man who delights in slaughtering large numbers of animals purely for the lust of taking life is extremely rare.

CHAPTER VI

1881-1885

WHEN Selous returned to South Africa in November, 1881, it was with the fixed intention of abandoning his wandering life. The chase of the elephant which, above all wild animals, furnished some pecuniary return, had now become so precarious, owing to the scarcity of the animals, that even men like Selous could not make a living at it, so when his friend Mandy, who was doing well in Cape Colony as an ostrich-farmer, suggested to him that he should enter the same profession, he decided that the advice was good. Accordingly when he returned to the Cape he at once visited Mandy, whom he found far from flourishing. His employer had died and ostrich-business was at a low ebb commercially, so Selous, who had several orders for specimens of the larger game from dealers and museums, once more turned his thoughts towards the north, and was soon again on his way to the happy hunting grounds. At Kimberley he bought a fine grey horse named " Diamond " (which, after proving his excellence, fell a victim to the usual horse-sickness), and then proceeded to Klerksdorp in the Transvaal, where he hoped to take over his friend Collison's Matabele boys. These he found ready to go with him, as well as Morris, the waggon-driver, and an excellent Griqua lad named Laer, who was later of much assistance in skinning and preparing specimens. From an old Matabele pioneer named Leask he bought a waggon and a good span of oxen, and also laid in a good stock of provisions. Just as he was starting, a missionary named Arnot begged for a passage to Bamangwato, which was at once granted. Passing through the Manica district of the Transvaal, Selous met one of the old

Boer Voortrekhers, by name Friedrich de Lange, who showed him a curious " snake-stone " which was supposed to have the power to cure snake-bite. De Lange valued this stone highly, and stated that its efficacy was invariable, and that it had already cured several people and horses that had been bitten by snakes. Selous himself was able to confirm de Lange's belief in the talisman, for he had met the daughter of one Antony Forman, who as a child had been severely bitten by a cobra, and whose life was saved by applying the stone, which was applied twice before it drew out the poison. Selous met the girl—then sixteen years of age—in 1877 and she showed him the old scar. Apparently the rough side of the stone adhered to the wound until a certain amount of poison had been absorbed and then it fell off. Several applications were necessary. It is probable that this remarkable stone had been brought from India.

Passing along the Crocodile river, where a drought set in and drove the game to the neighbourhood of the river, Selous managed to kill a few good specimens of hartebeest and wildebeest which he preserved. Diamond proved a splendid shooting horse, but another mount, Nelson, which was at first intractable, eventually became a valuable animal, as he successfully survived the prevalent sickness. This horse, though somewhat slow, did Selous yeoman service for several years, and he eventually sold it to Lewanika, chief of the Barotsi, in 1888.

At this time Selous hunted industriously to make a good collection of butterflies, and after many years he did make a very complete collection, which he presented to the Cape Town Museum. The curator of this museum was the late Mr. Trimen—a man for whom Selous had a great respect—who was ever delighted to receive any novelties, and many were the new species discovered by these two active entomologists. Selous, in fact, had all his life collected butterflies, and did so almost to the day of his death in German East Africa, for it was nothing to him to chase agile insects in the heat of the day, when other men only thought of rest and refreshment. The capture of some new species was to him always a great event, and though others, less interested than himself, wondered at his taking so much trouble about a wretched butterfly, he had all the absorbing pleasure of finding some new thing, the ambition of all true naturalists.

One day, whilst butterfly hunting, he found an ox bogged in the mud of the river. The poor beast had been badly bitten by crocodiles, which are perhaps more numerous in the Limpopo than in any river in South Africa, except perhaps the Botletlie. Numerous goats and calves belonging to natives were annually destroyed there, whilst in 1876 a Boer hunter named Berns Niemand met his death from these reptiles whilst crossing the river.

At the Notwani river, on March 5th, Selous decided to visit Khama and ask his permission to travel along the Limpopo and up the Mahalapsi river to Matabeleland. He rode by night, and " off-saddled " to give his horse a rest and feed for half an hour.

" I had been lying thus upon the ground for perhaps a couple of minutes, listening to the slight noise made by my horse as he cropped the short dry herbage. Suddenly the sound ceased. For a few seconds I lay dreamily wondering why it did not recommence ; but as there was still silence, I rolled quickly over on my stomach, and, looking under the bush to ascertain why my horse had stopped feeding, I saw that he was standing in an attitude of fixed attention, with ears pricked forward, intently gazing towards the road. I instantly turned and looked in the same direction, and as instantly saw on what the horse's eyes were fixed. There, not thirty yards away, and right in the open, a lioness, looking large and white in the brilliant moonlight· was coming up at a quick and stealthy pace, and in a half-crouching attitude. In an instant I was on my feet, and the lioness, probably observing me for the first time, at once stopped and crouched perfectly flat on the ground. The saddle and rifle lay out in the moonlight right between me and the lioness, though nearer to me than to her. It was not a time to hesitate. I knew she must be pretty keen set, or she would have retreated upon seeing me ; and I felt that if I remained where I was, she would resume her journey towards my horse, which might end in my having to carry the saddle back to the Notwani. Obviously the only thing to be done was to get hold of my rifle ; so I walked quickly forward into the moonlight towards where it lay against the saddle. I must confess that I did not like advancing towards the lioness, for I knew very well of what hungry lions are capable ; and there is nothing like experience to damp the foolhardy courage of ignorance. However, whilst I took those dozen steps she never stirred ; but just as I stooped to grasp my rifle she sprang up with a low purring growl, and made off towards some thorn-bushes to her right. I fired at her as she ran, and, though I certainly ought to have hit her, I must have missed, as she neither growled nor changed her pace. But I was fairly well pleased to have driven her off, and lost no time in loosening my horse's hobbles and saddling him again."

After this adventure and visiting Khama, who as usual acceded to his request, he passed on north to Matabeleland, and in June formed a hunting camp on the tributary of the river Bili in the well-watered valleys and verdant forests of Northern Mashunaland.

On June 20th he set a gin for hyenas which had been troublesome. Soon after midnight his dogs began barking and retreated into camp, which they would not have done before a hyena. Then some heavy animals came galloping past and Blucher, a favourite dog, was missed. Since the animal had uttered no sound Selous concluded he had been seized by the head and carried off by a lion. For a time all was quiet, and then the boys began shouting and said that a lion had come through the thorn-fence and taken the skin of a sable antelope that had been drying on a frame. This proved to be the case, and this very bold lion or others then returned a second time and carried off another wet skin.

Yet a third time the lion entered the camp and attacked the skins, one of which he commenced drawing within thirty yards of the camp. All this time Selous had never been able to get a clear shot, but as soon as dawn came he

BUFFALOES ALARMED

saddled his horse and soon saw a lion and lioness lying on an open bank close to the stream, but they moved off in the uncertain light. For that day the lions won.

That night an enclosure was built, baited, and a gin placed at each entrance, but later only a hyena met its death. At sundown poor Blucher, terribly mangled, crawled into camp, but though every attention was given him, he died some weeks later. The next day, however, better luck prevailed. Some Kafirs found a lion, and Selous getting a close shot from the back of his horse killed it with a bullet in the head. On the way back to camp another lion was put up and bolted through the forest.

This lion he wounded badly and lost for a time, but on further search it was found and charged the hunter savagely. The lion then stopped.

" The position was now this : the lion was standing with open mouth, from which blood was flowing, growling savagely, and looking like nothing but a wounded and furious lion, whilst right in front of him, and within thirty yards, stood Laer's refractory pony, backing towards the lion, and pulling with him Laer, who, of course, was looking full into his open jaws, which he did not seem to admire. I think I shall never forget the momentary glimpse I had of his face. He was at that time only a lad of about fifteen or sixteen years of age, and there is no wonder that he was frightened—but frightened he most certainly was : his hat had fallen off, his mouth was wide open, and his eyes staring, and he was pulling desperately against the horse, which was steadily dragging him nearer to the lion. I was a little to the right of Laer and a little further from the lion, but not much, and he looked alternately at the two of us. I am sure it was simply want of strength that prevented him from coming on and mauling either Laer or the pony, for before I could raise my rifle he sank down on the ground, but still kept his head up, and, with his mouth wide open, never ceased growling or roaring (I do not know which is the better word). Of course I fired as quickly as I could, the circumstances not admitting of any delay. I aimed right for his open mouth, and at the shot his head fell so

L

suddenly, and in such a way, that I knew the bullet had reached his brain." [1]

During the next six weeks Selous shot and preserved many fine specimens of the larger African antelopes for the British Museum, Cape Museum, and London dealers. At this time he met his old friend Dorehill, who was also on a shooting trip. He had with him his young wife, who was probably the first English lady to travel in the interior of Mashunaland. On the way to visit him at his camp Selous killed a leopard which was feeding at mid-day on the carcase of a black rhinoceros killed by Dorehill—a very unusual circumstance.

At this time Selous determined to visit Tete on the Zambesi, going there via the Hanyane river, and to cross the intervening country which was then quite unknown. After leaving his waggons on August 6th, he crossed the Manyami, accompanied by Laer, some natives, and one pack donkey, and passed numerous Mashuna villages on the hills, and so across to Umkwasi to the remarkable hills of Chikasi, where rocks several hundred feet high rise from the level plains. The country here was beautiful and the climate that of an English June, though colder at night. Here Selous lost his only donkey, killed by a hyena.

After crossing the Mutiki and the Dandi rivers, where no game was seen, and reaching Garanga, where guides were obtained, all the party now descended to the Zambesi valley. At the Kadzi river there was a considerable amount of game and swarms of tsetse flies, and so, following the course of the Umsengaisi, Selous reached the Zambesi at Chabonag on August 17th.

Here he decided to make for Zumbo.

After reaching Zumbo, formerly a centre of trade in gold dust and now a trade base for ivory, which mostly came from the Loangwa valley to the north, Selous, after mapping various new features in this region, struck south again. He had difficulty with his guides and, as always happens in the intense heat of the Zambesi valley, was again struck down with fever. He struggled on, however, on foot until Sep-

---

[1] " Travel and Adventure in S.E. Africa," pp. 37–40.

tember 10th, when Laer turned up with one of his horses, and on September 14th reached his camp, where in the fine air he soon mastered the fever. Early in October he reached the Matabele country and travelled to Klerksdorp, where he despatched his collections to Cape Town and England.

After laying in a fresh stock of provisions and trading goods he again set out for the interior, and in May, 1883, made his permanent camp on the banks of the Manyami river in Mashunaland. After unsuccessfully searching for elephants to the north and west, he crossed the Manyami to the Mazoe river, and from thence proceeded to the eastern bank of the Sabi river, close to the Portuguese frontier, where he hoped to obtain specimens of the now rare white rhinoceros and Liechtenstein's hartebeest. So far the last named was only known from specimens taken at and north of the Zambesi river, so that it was possible that the Sabi hartebeest might be slightly different.[1]

On the 11th of July Selous made a start for the south-east, and on the way knocked down a good specimen of the striped eland which, however, he was destined to lose, as he had lost his knife and had not another cartridge to kill it with. The next day he shot a splendid wart-hog, which cut his dog Punch rather badly, and which for many years was the best specimen in his museum. Next day he emerged on to the high open grassy downs between the Manyami and the Mazoe rivers. The climate of this delightful region, which has an elevation from 4500 to 6000 feet, is the best in Mashunaland and has an equable temperature throughout the year except in the months of June and July, which are rather cold. Running streams intersect the plateau in all directions and small patches of forest afford wood and shelter to passing travellers. Fifty years before this beautiful country was heavily populated by peaceful Mashunas, but about 1840 the bloodthirsty Matabele overran the district and slaughtered everyone except a few which were kept for slaves.

In 1883 it was a great country for eland, roan antelope,

---

[1] Selous, however, did not kill any on this trip. I shot one near the Sabi in 1893 which proved to be identical with the northern race.

and ostriches, several fine specimens of which fell to Selous' rifle. One of these, a female roan with horns 2 ft. 7 in. over the curve, still remains the record for females of this species. Near the river Chingi-Ka he killed a fine bull eland, which he left with some Mashunas who, however, skinned and cut it up during the night. This threw Selous into a rage, and he seized their bows and arrows and assegais and threw them on the fire, and then to their astonishment and annoyance made a bonfire of the rest of the carcase.

On July 30th he reached the river Impali, a tributary of the Sabi. Here was a Mashuna town where all the men carried bows and arrows and the women were tattooed on the forehead, cheeks, breasts and stomach. The next day Selous found tracks of the antelope he had come to hunt, but on this and following days he had no luck in finding them, though some days afterwards he killed a bull rhinoceros. He then returned to his camp on the Manyami, and continued to hunt there till November, and then started south-west on his return home. The day after leaving the Manyami, whilst crossing a tributary of the River Sarua, the wheel of one of his waggons collapsed, and knowing that a Boer and an Englishman were close at hand, Selous determined to go to their camp, borrow a wheel and bring his waggon on, and make the new wheel in a place where he would have the pleasure of talking to some white men. That day Selous rode across country to the camp of Grant and Karl Weyand, and when Laer turned up they received the news that the waggon driver had met five lions on the road. Selous then felt sorry he had not gone by this route, for Laer described the big lion of the party as the most magnificent he had ever seen. Next day Selous rode back to his camp, and on the way he had an exciting adventure with a leopard which he wounded as it ran into the bush. The now angry beast hid in the cover but disclosed its whereabouts when the hunter came close. " However, I had seen whereabouts he was lying, and so determined to fire a shot or two to make him show himself ; but before I could do so he again raised his head with another snarl, and immediately after came straight out at me, and at such a pace that before I could turn my horse and get him started the leopard was right under his tail. He chased me for some sixty or seventy yards before he stopped, coming right into the open and keeping close up the whole time. I pulled in as quickly as I could, and before the plucky little beast regained the bush gave him a second shot which quickly proved fatal. When charging and chasing me this leopard growled and grunted or roared exactly like a lion under similar circumstances, and made just as much noise."

The next day Laer turned up with the wheel, across which lay the fresh skin of a lion he had killed. It appeared that the previous evening when the waggon-driver and a native boy named April were sitting by the fire a lion rushed into the camp and attacked one of the oxen. April fired at it and missed, but Laer, though only a boy, put in another cartridge and took a shot which was fatal.

The following day some men whom Selous had sent into the " fly " to look for elephants returned and reported " a big lion close by." Immediately Selous was out and after him with his dogs, which were led. He had not, however, gone far when he saw the lion lying flat on the ground at right angles to where he was riding. As his horse would not stand, he dismounted.

" All this time the lion had never moved, nor did he now, but lay watching me intently with his yellow eyes. Nothing stirred but his tail, the end of which he twitched slowly, so that the black bunch of hair at its extremity appeared first on one side of him, then on the other. As I raised my rifle to my shoulder I found that the fallen tree-trunk interfered considerably with the fine view I had had of him from my horse's back, as it hid almost all his nose below the eyes. In the position in which he was now holding his head I ought to have hit him about half-way between the nostrils and the eyes. which was impossible ; anywhere above the eyes would have been too high, as the bullet would have glanced from his skull, so that it required a very exact shot to kill him on the spot. However, there was no time to wait, and, trying to aim so that the bullet should just clear the fallen log and catch him between the eyes, I fired. With a loud roar he answered the shot, and I instantly became aware that he was coming straight at me with open mouth and flaming eyes, growling savagely. I knew it was hopeless to try to get another cartridge into my single-barrelled rifle, and utterly useless to try to mount, more especially as my horse, startled by the loud hoarse grunts and sudden and disagreeable appearance of the charging lion, backed so vigorously that the bridle (to a running ring on which a strong thong was attached, the other end being fastened to my belt) came over his head. I had a strong feeling that I was about to have an opportunity of testing the accuracy of Dr. Livingstone's incredible statement that, for certain reasons (explained by the Doctor), a lion's bite gives no pain ; but there was no time to think of anything in particular. The whole adventure was the affair of a moment. I just brought my rifle round in front of me, holding the small of the stock in my right hand and the barrel in my left, with a vague idea of getting it into the lion's mouth, and at the same time yelled as loud as I could, ' Los de honden, los de honden,' which being translated means, ' Let loose the dogs.' In an instant, as I say, the lion was close up to me. I had never moved my feet since firing, and whether it was my standing still facing him that made him alter his mind, or whether he heard the noise made by my people, who, hearing my shot, immediately followed by the loud growling of the lion, were all shouting and making a noise to frighten the lion from coming their way, I cannot take upon myself to say ; but he came straight on to within about six yards of me, looking, I must say, most unpleasant, and then suddenly swerved off, and passing me, galloped away."[1]

The dogs then ran him to bay alongside a big anthill.

" As soon as he saw me he paid no further heed to his canine foes, but stood, with his eyes fixed on the most dangerous of his assailants, growling hoarsely, and with his head held low between his shoulders—just ready to charge, in fact. I knew my horse would not stand steady, so jumped off, and taking a quick aim fired instantly, as it does not do to wait when a lion is looking at you like this,

[1] " Travel and Adventure in S.E. Africa," pp. 130–133.

and when he may make up his mind to come at any moment. Usually they jerk their tails up over their backs, holding them perfectly stiff and rigid, two or three times before charging. They sometimes charge without doing this, but they never do it without charging. My bullet inflicted a mortal wound, entering between the animal's neck and shoulder and travelling the whole length of his body. He sat down like a dog on his haunches immediately after, and was evidently done for, as he lolled his tongue out of his mouth and growled feebly when the dogs bit him in the hind-quarters."[1]

The pegged-out skin of his lion measured ten feet eleven inches, and it proved to be the third largest Selous ever killed.

In mid-December Selous went out to Bulawayo and there found himself involved in a row with Lobengula, who unjustly accused him of killing hippopotami. The Matabele apparently had some superstition regarding these animals and believed that a drought would follow the killing of a number of these animals unless the bones were returned to the river. Doubtless some slaughter had taken place owing to the activities of a certain trader who made a business in sjamboks.

When Selous met Lobengula he was at first quite friendly, and when the hunter told him he had not killed a single hippopotamus that year the king said there was no case against him. A few days later, however, he was summoned to the king's presence and Selous heard there was likely to be trouble. The case lasted three days, during which time the white men accused had to sit outside the kraal in the pouring rain.

Concluding his attack on Selous, Ma-kwaykwi, one of the head indunas, said :

" ' It is you, Selous, who have finished the king's game.' He went on : ' But you are a witch, you must bring them all to life again. I want to see them—all, all. Let them all walk in at the kraal gate, the elephants, and the buffaloes, and the elands.'

[1] " Travel and Adventure in S.E. Africa," pp. 133–134.

" I stood up and called out :   ' All right ; but when the lions come in, will you, Ma-kwaykwi, remain where you are to count them ? '

" This caused a general laugh at Ma-kwaykwi's expense, and quite stopped his flow of eloquence."

Finally Selous had to pay sixty pounds.   This fine he always considered to be a robbery.

As soon as the case finished Selous went to Klerksdorp and sent his collections to England.   He was sore at his treatment by Lobengula, and so determined to avoid Matabeleland and to hunt in the northern parts of Khama's territory this year.   One day at Klerksdorp he met Walter Montague Kerr bent on a long expedition through Matabeleland and Mashunaland to the Zambesi, and the two hunters travelled together as far as Bulawayo.   Here they separated, Kerr going north and eventually crossing the Zambesi, where the illness, privation, and hardship he underwent so undermined his health that his early death resulted.   He published an interesting book on his travels[1] which is, however, now little known.

At this time Selous was much depressed owing to the low state of his finances, for although he had been able to support himself entirely by trading and his rifle since 1871, he had made nothing and his whole assets were represented by horses, oxen, waggons and general outfit.   His mother, too, frequently urged him to give up South Africa, and either come home or try another country, but to this he turned a deaf ear and only expressed his wish to worry on till better times came.   Writing to her on April 6th, 1884, from Bamangwato, he says :—

" This country is now in a terrible state financially, bankrupt from Cape Town to the Zambesi.   Nothing that is not exportable has any real value, for nothing can be turned into money.   Thanks to my specimens I have during the last two years, in spite of more than reasonable losses, even for Africa, done very well, but all that I have made is represented by waggons, salted horses, cattle, rifles, etc., for all of which I have paid large prices, but which, if I

[1] " The Far Interior."

wished to realize and leave the country, would bring me in
scarcely enough to pay my passage to England. It is all
very well to tell a man to leave such a country and try
another. It would be the wisest thing to do, no doubt, but
it is a thing that few men are capable of doing. What you
say of Edward Colchester (friend of his youth) returning to
Australia and beginning life again at thirty-nine is not at
all to the point. He would simply be returning again to his
old life, for which he has never ceased to pine ever since he
came home and settled down in England. I was very interested in what you told me about Spiritualism, but are you
sure that William Colchester really saw his child (recently
deceased) and touched and spoke to him? In Sergeant
Cox's accounts of Materializations the figure seen is that of
the medium, and I have never yet seen an authentic account
of any other Materialization. At present I believe nothing
(about Spiritualism), but am *inclined* towards Materialism,
but at the same time time I do not believe everything, and
am in a state of doubt. If I felt sure—quite sure—that I
was merely material, I think I should before long take a
good dose of laudanum and stop the working of my inward
mechanism, for life, on the whole, is a failure—to me, at
any rate—who, I think, am naturally of rather a sad turn
of mind, though I can quite understand it being very
different to sanguine hopeful people. However, as I feel
doubtful upon the subject, I certainly shall not have recourse
to violent measures but shall protect my vital spark as
long as I can. I think I told you about Jameson being
struck down by a sort of paralytic stroke and not being
able to come out this year to hunt.

"I am very sorry indeed, for being with Jameson, who is,
of course, a rich man, I should have been free from the
constant anxiety which now overhangs me like a black
cloud as to whether I shall be able to pay my debts. It is
so very easy to lose a hundred pounds in live stock, from
sickness, drought, hunger, etc., and so hard, so very hard,
to make it. Last year I paid Mr. Leask nearly £1600. This
year I only owe a few hundreds and am at present well to
the good, as I have nearly £2000 worth of property."

Selous left Bamangwato in April, 1884, and trekked across the desert north-west to the Mababe veldt. He was fortunate enough to find for once plenty of water, owing to thunderstorms, and he did not experience any great hardships as he did in 1873 and 1879. In June he established his main hunting camp near the north end of the Mababe flats. The bushmen here told him of the activities of a man-eating lion who had recently killed several men. Selous at once set out to look for him, and soon found one of the unfortunate victims, torn to pieces and partially eaten. But the lion seems to have left this district, and the hunter was unable to find him, since he did not commit further depredations.

Selous did not remain long on the Mababe. In August he retreated to Sode Gara and Horn's Vley, where he killed some good specimens of giraffe, hartebeest, gemsbuck, and ostrich. Then he moved eastward for a while, and afterwards went south to Tati, which he reached in late November, and so on to Bulawayo, where he remained for the winter, sending his specimens out on a trader's waggon.

After visiting Lobengula, who demanded a salted horse valued at sixty pounds for the right to hunt in Mashunaland, Selous set off again to the north-east. He took with him four horses and thus quaintly describes a new cure for a hopeless " bucker."

" I almost cured him," he says, " of bucking by riding him with an adze handle, and stunning him by a heavy blow administered between the ears as soon as he commenced, which he invariably did as soon as one touched the saddle ; but I never could make a shooting horse of him, and finally gave him to Lobengula, in the hope that he would present him to Ma-kwaykwi or some other of his indunas against whom I had a personal grudge."

Selous now went to the Se-whoi-whoi river, where two years previously he killed the last two white rhinoceroses he was destined to see. These great creatures had now become exceedingly scarce in Africa south of the Zambesi, and are now quite extinct in all South Africa except in the neighbourhood of the Black Umvolosi in Zululand, where, according to latest reports (1917), there are twelve which are fortunately strictly preserved. In 1886 two Boers in Northern Mashunaland killed ten, and five were killed in Matabeleland in the same year. After this date they seemed to be extremely rare. I saw the tracks of one near the Sabi in 1893, and the same year Mr. Coryndon killed one in Northern Mashunaland.

When he reached the high plateau of Mashunaland and got to the Umfule and Umniati rivers Selous found game plentiful, and was soon busy collecting specimens. After a visit to the Zweswi he passed on to the Lundaza, a tributary of the Umfule. Here he found a large herd of elephants. He was, however, badly mounted on a sulky horse, as his favourite Nelson had been injured, and this greatly handicapped him, as well as causing him twice to have some hairbreadth escapes.

On the great day on which he killed six elephants he had numerous adventures. First he shot at and wounded a large bull which he could not follow, as an old cow charged him viciously and gradually overhauled his sulky horse ; but on entering thick bush he avoided her and soon got to work on two fresh bulls which he killed. He then dashed after the broken herd and soon came face to face with an old cow, who chased him so hard that he had to leap off his horse to avoid her. Curiously enough, the elephant did not molest his horse, but getting the wind of the hunter, charged him and was eventually killed. Selous then followed the retreating herd, and only at first succeeded in wounding two large cows, one of which charged him, when he had again to abandon his horse, but after some trouble he killed them both.

Later, on the Manyami, he found another small herd and killed a big bull and a cow. The bull charged him fiercely but swung off on receiving a frontal shot, and was then killed with a heart shot. Later in the year he went south to the Sabi and was lucky enough to kill five Liechtenstein's hartebeest, which he had failed to get on his previous hunt for them.

In December he returned to Bulawayo. On the way, whilst travelling with Collison, James Dawson, and

Cornelis van Rooyen, a noted Boer hunter, an incident occurred which showed the power of a sable antelope in defending itself from dogs. Van Rooyen fired at a bull, and all the dogs rushed from the waggon to bring the wounded animal to bay. When the hunter got up and killed the sable it was found that the gallant antelope in defending itself with its scimitar-like horns had killed outright four valuable dogs and badly wounded four more. The strength and rapidity with which a sable bull uses its horns is a wonderful thing to see. When cornered either by a lion or dogs the sable lies down and induces the enemy to attack its flanks. Then like a flash the horns are swept sideways and the attacker pierced. I lost my best dog by a wounded bull in 1893. He was killed in an instant, both horns going right through the whole body, between heart and lungs. In the same year I found in a dying condition a splendid bull sable, badly mauled by a lion, and incapable of rising, but the lion himself, an old male, was found dead about a hundred yards away by some Shangan natives. I saw the claws and teeth of this lion, but the skin was not preserved as the lion had been dead some days when it was found. There is little doubt that both the sable and the roan antelopes are dangerous when cornered. A Matabele warrior was killed by a wounded cow sable in 1892, and Sergeant Chawner of the Mashunaland police was in 1890 charged by a slightly wounded bull roan which missed the rider but struck his horse through the neck and so injured it that it had to be shot. A similar incident also happened to Mr. George Banks in 1893.

CHAPTER VII

1886–1889

D URING the year 1886 Selous did but little hunting and shooting, though he twice made short visits to Matabeleland both before and after a journey home to England, where he remained for several months. In the following year he was employed to act as guide and hunter to Messrs. J. A. Jameson,[1] A. C. Fountaine,[2] and F. Cooper,[3] on a long trip to Mashunaland, in which all concerned had wonderful sport. The party killed twelve lions, and discovered the remarkable limestone caves of Sinoia and the subterranean lake whose waters are cobalt blue.[4]

A main camp was established on the Upper Manyami, and from there hunts were organized in all directions. The travels of the four Englishmen occupied the greater part of the year.

It was during this expedition that one day whilst chasing four koodoo bulls Selous charged straight into one of the pitfalls made by the natives for trapping game. The impact was so great that the horse broke his back and Selous himself so injured the tendons of one of his legs that he was unable to walk for three weeks afterwards. In such a life as he had, much of which was spent in rough country, racing game at full speed on horseback, it was unavoidable that the hunter should meet with numerous falls. He was, however, so tough and clever that in most

---

[1] J. A. Jameson, a brother of J. S. Jameson.

[2] A. C. Fountaine, of Narford Hall, Norfolk.

[3] Frank Cooper, of Bulwell Hall, Notts, another well-known big game hunter of his period who had had in previous years excellent sport with wapiti in Colorado, where he and his brother secured some remarkable heads.

[4] For Selous' own account of these caves and their discovery see " Proc. Geographical Soc.," May, 1888.

cases he escaped unhurt, but once, when chasing a black rhinoceros on the Manyami river in 1883, he had a bad fall and smashed his collar-bone, and on another occasion, in October, 1880, whilst chasing a bull eland, he dashed at full speed into a dead tree branch. Even after this he killed his game, but on reaching camp became half-unconscious with concussion of the brain. There was a deep wound on the side of his eye which destroyed the tear-duct, leaving a cavity which eventually healed up, but a year after, one day in London, he coughed up a piece of wood that must have been driven right through the tear-duct till it reached the passage at the back of the nose. The scar on his face seen in all later photographs of Selous was caused by the recoil of his first elephant-gun, which his native servant had inadvertently loaded twice.

Of the expedition of 1887, when Selous hunted with J. A. Jameson, A. C. Fountaine, and Frank Cooper, no complete record seems to have been kept, but Selous narrates a few of their adventures in his articles in the Geographical Society's Journal[1] (1888), and in " Travel and Adventure in South-East Africa," pp. 445–7, he gives some details of their wanderings.

It was not the habit of Selous to give up any scheme, however difficult, once he had set his heart upon it. We have seen how often his plans for reaching the " Promised Land " beyond the Zambesi had been foiled, but he never abandoned the idea and resolved to put it into execution whenever the opportunity should occur. At last, in 1888, he found himself free to make another attempt. He was in good health and possessed an ample supply of money to purchase material, which in the case of the long journey involved was a necessity.

He left Bamangwato on April 9th, 1888, with two waggons, five salted horses, and sixteen donkeys. His intention was to go first to Lialui and take up his residence with Lewanika for at least a year. Panda-ma-tenka was reached on the

---

[1] Selous was a regular contributor to the Geographical Society's Journal. In course of time the Society honoured his discoveries by giving him the Cuthbert Peek grant, the Back Premium and the Founder's Gold Medal.

16th of May, and there Selous learned that the country to
the north was in a very unsettled condition owing to rival
claims to the chieftainship of Barotsiland, and that it might
be months before he got across the Zambesi. Soon after,
he met his old friend George Westbeech, who strongly
advised him not to enter Barotsiland, but to take advantage
of an invitation from Mr. Arnot, who was established in the
Garanganzi country, which was said to be full of elephants.

Accordingly Selous left his waggons and set off down the
Zambesi, intending to cross the river at Wankie's Town and
strike north along his old route of eleven years before. In
the light of his subsequent adventures amongst the Mashukulumbwe it is here necessary to say something of his
coloured companions on this eventful trip. There was
Daniel, a Hottentot waggon-driver ; Paul, a Natal Zulu ;
Charley, an interpreter who had been trained amongst
Westbeech's elephant-hunters ; and two of Khama's men.
All these were well armed with modern breechloading rifles.
Besides these men he had four Mashunas who had served
him on former expeditions, and whom he could trust in an
emergency. Other boys were hired at Panda-ma-tenka,
and with these and the donkeys carrying the outfit Selous
set forth for Wankie's Town with complete confidence.

Having arrived at Wankie's Town in eight days, the
donkeys having been safely towed across the river, troubles
now began. Daniel, the Hottentot, developed fever and
died in four days, and then the boys whom he had hired at
Panda-ma-tenka deserted. Selous, however, managed to
get on with his own small lot, and even hired a few Batongas.
But soon old Shampondo, the Batonga chief of the district,
came and demanded further presents, bringing at the same
time a small Batonga army to enforce his views. For a
moment there was nearly trouble, as Selous' " boys "
loaded their rifles at the threatening aspect of the natives,
but their master, with his usual tact in dealing with savages,
saved the situation, though he was not allowed to proceed
without further extortion. Selous knew that later he would
have to pass through the territory of Mwemba, " the biggest
scoundrel " amongst the Batongas, so he importuned

Shamedza to give him porters and to help as far as the Zongwi river, and this the chief did.

The reason of these extortions was that the Batonga chiefs were afraid of the white men because of their own evil deeds. Although they had seen no Europeans since Dr. Livingstone, his brother, and Kirk, several Jesuit fathers had been as far as the Zambesi and had died or been maltreated. David Thomas had also been murdered by the Batongas, as well as a Portuguese trader. Selous knew that if he followed the Zambesi as far as the Kafukwe he was certain to be attacked and probably murdered. Accordingly he decided to strike due north to the Mashukulumbwe in spite of their evil reputation.

Next day he reached the Muga and the following crossed the Kachomba river, and on the third day came to the Mwedzia, where he was able to hire a few useful men. During the following day he marched over what he describes as the " roughest country to walk over in the whole world," stony and barren conical hills devoid of game or water. On the third day he emerged into better country covered with forest and good grass, and here at a village he picked up a guide to take him to Monzi, a Batonga chief, who lived on a high plateau which was said to abound in game.

The following day he reached the plateau and saw abundance of zebra, Liechtenstein's hartebeest, blue wildebeest, roan antelope, and eland. Later he interviewed old Monzi, who told him he had seen no white man since the visit of Dr. Livingstone thirty-five years before. The natives were very friendly, as Selous gave them an eland and a zebra he had shot, and all seemed to go well. At Monzi's the traveller got two guides to take him to the Kafukwe, and at the second village he struck he found himself for the first time amongst the naked Mashukulumbwe. Here a lot of Sika-benga's men (Barotsi) arrived with a crowd of armed Mashukulumbwe, and said they had come to buy ammunition. The attitude of the natives was suspicious, and when Selous refused either to sell them powder or to go with them, they said : " You will live two days more, but on the third day your head will lie in a different place from your body."

Selous, however, paid no heed to their threats, and that day proceeded on his journey, telling his guides to proceed east to the Mashukulumbwe villages and intending to camp in the open veldt. Paul and Charley, who both had experience with natives north of the Zambesi, agreed that this was the best policy, but "we unfortunately allowed ourselves to be dissuaded and led into the jaws of death by our ignorant guides." These men said the party would find no water on the plateau but only in the villages, so there they went.

At the second village the natives were frightened, and, avoiding this place, they pressed on over a veldt teeming with game to the Ungwesi river. Here Selous camped at a village where, after preliminary shyness, the natives seemed fairly friendly and showed the hunter where to camp and get wood and water. At the Magoi-ee Selous found himself in a highly populated district and camped at a village where lived Minenga, the chief of the district. That worthy insisted on Selous camping alongside the village and would take no refusal. Accordingly Selous found himself in the lions' den, as it were, and felt he must brave it out now if anything went wrong, so he set to work to make a "scherm" of cornstalks and plant-poles to secure the donkeys.

After a while things did not look so bad, as the natives abandoned their spears and came and joined in a dance with the Batonga boys. Then, too, the women and girls came down and ate with Selous' men—usually a sure sign of peace. By nightfall Selous viewed the whole scene and felt he had no cause for alarm, and felt he had quite gained the goodwill of these savages. At nine o'clock, when Selous was already in bed, Minenga sent him a message to come to drink, but, as he was tired, he did not go. In the light of subsequent events, Selous was glad he had not accepted the invitation, for he would certainly have been murdered. The dance and noisy musical instruments were intended to drown any noise that might have occurred.

Next day Selous hunted, and later, when in camp, was surrounded by great crowds of natives which, however, left at sundown.

M

" I could not sleep, however, and was lying under my blanket, thinking of many things, and revolving various plans in my head, when about nine o'clock I observed a man come cautiously round the end of our scherm and pass quickly down the line of smouldering fires. As he stopped beside the fire, near the foot of Paul and Charley's blankets, I saw that he was one of the two men who had accompanied us as guides from Monzi's. I saw him kneel down and shake Paul by the leg, and then heard him whispering to him hurriedly and excitedly. Then I heard Paul say to Charley, ' Tell our master the news ; wake him up.' I at once said, ' What is it, Charley ? I am awake.' ' The man says, sir, that all the women have left the village, and he thinks that something is wrong,' he answered. I thought so too, and hastily pulled on my shoes, and then put on my coat and cartridge-belt, in which, however, there were only four cartridges. As I did so, I gave orders to my boys to extinguish all the fires, which they instantly did by throwing sand on the embers, so that an intense darkness at once hid everything within our scherm.

" Paul and Charley were now sitting on their blankets with their rifles in their hands, and I went and held a whispered conversation with them, proposing to Paul that he and I should creep round the village and reconnoitre, and listen if possible to what the inhabitants were talking about. ' Wait a second,' I said, ' whilst I get out a few more cartridges,' and I was just leaning across my blankets to get at the bag containing them when three guns went off almost in my face, and several more at different points round the scherm. The muzzles of all these guns were within our scherm when they were discharged, so that our assailants must have crawled right up to the back of our camp and fired through the interstices between the corn-stalks. The three shots that were let off just in front of me were doubtless intended for Paul, Charley, and myself, but by great good luck none of us was hit. As I stooped to pick up my rifle, which was lying on the blankets beside me, Paul and Charley jumped up and sprang past me. ' Into the grass ! ' I called to them in Dutch, and prepared to follow. The discharge of the guns was immediately followed by a perfect shower of barbed javelins, which I could hear pattering on the large leathern bags in which most of our goods were packed, and then a number of Mashukulumbwe rushed in amongst us.

" I can fairly say that I retained my presence of mind perfectly at this juncture. My rifle, when I picked it up, was unloaded ; for, in case of accident, I never kept it loaded in camp, and I therefore had first to push in a cartridge. As I have said before, between our camp and the long grass lay a short space of cleared ground, dug into irregular ridges and furrows. Across this I retreated backwards, amidst a mixed crowd of my own boys and Mashukulumbwe.

" I did my best to get a shot into one of our treacherous assailants, but in the darkness it was impossible to distinguish friend from foe. Three times I had my rifle to my shoulder to fire at a Mashukulumbwe, and as often someone who I thought was one of my own boys came between. I was within ten yards of the long grass, but with my back to it, when, with a yell, another detachment of Mashukulumbwe rushed out of it to cut off our retreat. At this juncture I fell backwards over one of the ridges, and two men, rushing out of the grass, fell right over me, one of them kicking me in the ribs and falling over my body, whilst another fell over my legs. I was on my feet again in an instant, and then made a rush for the long grass, which I reached without mishap, and in which I felt comparatively safe. I presently crept forwards for about twenty yards and then sat still listening. Standing up again, I saw that the Mashukulumbwe were moving about in our camp. It was, however, impossible to see anyone with sufficient distinctness to get a shot, for whenever one of the partially-extinguished fires commenced to burn up again it was at once put out by having more sand thrown over it.

" But I now thought no more of firing at them. I had had time to realise the full horror of my position. A solitary Englishman, alone in Central Africa, in the middle of a hostile country, without blankets or anything else but what he stood in and a rifle with four cartridges. I doubt whether Mark Tapley himself would have seen anything cheerful in the situation. Could I only have found Paul or Charley or even one of my own Kafirs, I thought my chance of getting back to Panda-ma-tenka would be much increased, for I should then have an interpreter, I myself knowing but little of the languages spoken north of the Zambesi. I now began to quarter the grass cautiously backwards and forwards, whistling softly, in hopes that some of my own boys might be lying in hiding near me ; but I could find no one, and at length came to the conclusion that all those of my people who had escaped death would make the most of the darkness and get as far as possible from Minenga's before day-dawn, and I decided that I had better do the same."[1]

He therefore decided to strike for Monzi's, the first village where he dared to show himself. First he made his way down to the ford on the Magoi-ee, but luckily observed a party of men watching there. Selous then retreated some 300 yards down stream and swam the river, which he well knew was swarming with crocodiles.

" The Mashukulumbwe I saw had now made up the fires, upon which they were throwing bundles of grass, by the light of which I presume they were dividing my property. I turned my back upon this most melancholy spectacle and, taking the Southern Cross for my guide, which was now almost down, commenced my lonely journey."

Selous' own account of his wanderings in his retreat from the Mashukulumbwe to the Zambesi makes some of the most interesting reading to be found in any book devoted to true adventure. Here he was, alone in Africa, only furnished with his rifle and four cartridges, a knife, and a few matches, and he had to overcome at least three hundred miles or more before he dared approach a village. It was a position that might have depressed any man except a genuine veldtsman, for that danger from all natives was to be feared was a certainty, since they would not hesitate to attack a single man whose life was wanted, just as one dog

[1] " Travel and Adventure in S.E. Africa," pp. 221–224.

always chases another running behind a cart. All night long he walked, keeping a watchful eye for lions, and at the hill Karundu-ga-gongoma next day he searched for spoor to see if any of his boys had come that way, but there was no fresh sign, so he lay all day under a tree watching the ford of the river. Here he heard voices, and thinking they might be his own men he concealed himself and listened. Presently two heads appeared above the grass and he recognized two Mashukulumbwe by their cone-shaped head-dresses. They were evidently discussing the imprint of the hunter's shoes left on the sand. Selous was ready to shoot both if they saw him, but it was some relief when they turned and went back the way they had come. Hunger now began to assert itself, and the wanderer determined to shoot anything he could find, but, as his stock of cartridges was so small, he had to make a certainty of each shot. Luckily at this moment a single wildebeest came by within thirty yards and furnished an abundant supply of meat.

After a good dinner and the sun had set, Selous, shouldering his rifle and a supply of meat, again struck south. At dawn, perished with cold, he reached the last Mashuku-lumbwe village, and, being near Monzi's, he determined to risk trouble, and entered the village. Here he found an unarmed boy, who furnished him with water, but even as he drank it he heard whispering in a hut close by and saw a man come out stealthily and vanish in the darkness. Presently this man returned with a gun in his hand, and later Selous heard him testing a bullet with the ramrod. All was quiet for a time, however, and Selous sat dozing over the fire. Then he awoke with a start, to find that two unarmed men had arrived and sat by the fire close to him. They questioned him and he endeavoured to answer them.

" In endeavouring to do so to the best of my ability, I kept gradually turning more towards them, till presently my rifle lay almost behind me. It was whilst I was in this position that I heard someone behind me. I turned quickly round to clutch my rifle, but was too late, for the man whom I had heard just stooped and seized it before my own hand touched it, and, never pausing, rushed off with it and disappeared in the darkness. I sprang up, and at the same moment one of the two men who had engaged me in conversation did so too, and, in the act of rising, dropped some dry grass which he had hitherto concealed beneath his large ox-hide rug on to the fire. There was at once a blaze of light which lit up the whole of the open space around the fire. My eyes instinctively looked towards the hut which I had seen the man with the gun enter, and there, sure enough, he sat in the doorway taking aim at me not ten yards from where I sat. There was no time to remonstrate. I sprang out into the darkness, seizing one of the pieces of wildebeest meat as I did so ; and, as the village was surrounded with long grass, pursuit would have been hopeless, and was not attempted. My would-be assassin never got off his shot."[1]

Bad as his position had been, it was now far worse with the loss of his rifle. His only hope was that Monzi might prove friendly, so, after travelling all night, he reached Monzi's village. When that old chief heard his story he said, "You must leave my village immediately. They will follow you up and kill you. Be off! Be off instantly." Monzi was not so bad as the rest, he filled Selous' pockets with ground-nuts, and sent three men to take him a short distance, and these men strongly advised him not to trust the Batongas, in whose country he now found himself. After a meal it occurred to him that it would be a good plan to make south-east to Marancinyan, the powerful Barotsi chief, and throw himself on his protection. This chief was a friend of George Westbeech, the Zambesi trader, but the difficulty was to find his village. Somewhat unwisely, as it turned out, Selous visited some Batonga huts and asked a man the footpath to Sikabenga's (Marancinyan) kraal. This man at once roused the village, and a dozen armed men pursued and came up to Selous, who faced them, but these men proved not unfriendly, and even showed him the right track to follow.

At last he reached Marancinyan's kraal and found the

[1] " Travel and Adventure in S.E. Africa," p. 232.

chief to be a tall, well-built young fellow, and, as he spoke Sintabili fairly well, conversation was easy. He did not treat the wanderer well, "yet had it not been for him I should in all probability have been murdered by the orders of his uncle. This, however, I only learnt some time afterwards, and though for three days I must have lived constantly in the very shadow of death, I had no idea at the time that my life was in danger."

In three days Marancinyan told Selous that his life was in danger and that the Mashukulumbwe had followed, demanding his death, and that he must leave at once and go to a small Batonga village close by and wait there till sundown, when he would bring guides.

Disturbed and suspicious at this news, Selous knew the Mashukulumbwe would never dare to threaten the well-armed Barotsi. However, he saw he must comply and trust to the Barotsi chief's promise. Accordingly he went off, but as Marancinyan did not appear Selous returned to his kraal and thus boldly addressed him : " What do you mean, Marancinyan, who say that you are George Westbeech's friend and the friend of all white men, by sending me to sleep among your dogs ? Have you given orders to murder me in the night ? If you want to kill me, you can do so here in your own town." This seemed to have upset the chief, who again repeated that Selous' life was in danger and that if he would go and sleep at the Batonga village he would for certain bring guides to lead him to Panda-ma-tenka.

On the following morning the chief fulfilled his promise, and next day Selous reached a Batonga village under one Shoma. Here he found a friend who gave him fresh guides, and also heard the welcome news that ten of his boys had slept in a village close by and were making for the village of Shankopi far to the south. Here, five days later, Selous met with the remnant of his party, who had for long given him up for lost. They were very glad to greet their master, and " patted me on the breast and kissed my hands." In the night attack it appears that twelve men were killed and six more wounded out of the whole twenty-five. Everyone had had narrow escapes.

" Paul, the Zulu, got through the first rush of our assailants unhurt, but was nearly drowned in crossing the river, where he lost my single 10-bore rifle. Charley also got out of the scherm unwounded, and, making his way to the river, there fell in with two of our boys, and with their assistance crossed safely with rifle, cartridge-belt, and clothes. I found that we had all done the same thing, namely, held to the south through the night, across country. Charley said he was close to me when I shot the wildebeest ; he heard the shot, and ran with the two boys in the direction, but never saw me. I fancy he must have passed me whilst I was cooking the meat, as I was then in a deep hollow. He too had been seen and pursued in the daytime near the village where my rifle was captured, but again escaped in the long grass. This had also happened to the survivor of the two Mangwato men, who, being likewise alone and unarmed, had incautiously approached a village. He said that one man got close up to him and threw three assegais at him, one of which cut his right hand. At last, however, he outran him and escaped. Neither Paul, Charley, nor the rest had gone near Monzi's, or any other village, being afraid of the inhabitants, but had kept through the veldt, and only cut into our trail beyond the hill U-Kesa-Kesa. Here Charley shot a zebra, and was shortly afterwards joined by Paul, who had then been three days without food. Farther on Charley shot another zebra, and here he and Paul remained for three days more, hoping that I would turn up, and collecting all the other survivors of our party."[1]

After this all danger and most of the hardship were past. They got provisions, and in a few days crossed the Zambesi, and three days later reached the waggons at Panda-ma-tenka. Thus it took the party about three weeks to cross three hundred miles of country since the night of the attack by the Mashukulumbwe.

In time Selous was able to piece together the reasons why he was attacked by the Mashukulumbwe. The actual cause of the trouble was due to Sikabenga's uncle, who sent a party of men north after Selous to get powder from him

[1] " Travel and Adventure in S.E. Africa," p. 241.

at all costs, even if they had to kill him. These were the men Selous met the day he left Monzi's. Then the hunter refusing them powder, they followed him up and induced the Mashukulumbwe to attack him. One of the Barotsi warriors was left in a village beyond Monzi's, having fallen sick, and this was the man who tried to shoot Selous and failed.

Sikabenga, who had acted on his uncle's instructions, but was really anxious to save the white man's life, was therefore in a quandary when Selous appeared and threw himself on his protection, and especially so when he expected the loot from Selous' camp to arrive at any moment. That was why he was so anxious to get him out of the village, for if Selous had observed Sikabenga's complicity in the attack that chief would have been obliged to order his murder. But Sikabenga himself did not long survive in this land of battle, murder, and sudden death, for a Matabele impi crossed the Zambesi in August, 1889, and killed him and most of his people.

Most men, having gone through such exciting experiences, would have been content to have given African savages a wide berth for a long period afterwards, but not so Selous, whose reckless disposition he himself describes as " nearly equal to that of the Wandering Jew." But a few days elapsed and he was again planning a journey across the Zambesi to visit Lewanika, the head chief of the Barotsi, with the purpose of selling to him some of his salted horses and getting permission to hunt elephants in the unknown country north of the Kabompo river in the following year.

After shooting five elands to furnish meat at his main camp during his absence, Selous crossed the Zambesi, towing his horses behind a canoe. From here he moved westwards to the Ungwesi river. After crossing the Kasaia the horses ran away, but were recovered after they had passed through some belts of " fly " country, but as the day was cloudy and a high wind blowing no serious results were to be feared. When the horses turned up, the party moved on to Sesheki, where Selous met two missionaries, branch workers belonging to Mr. Coillard's mission, long established in Barotsiland.

After leaving Sesheki's the road led through "fly" country, which was traversed by night, and, crossing the Loanja, a dull, comparatively gameless country was traversed, until the party reached Sefula and Lialui in the main Barotsi valley. Here Selous met Mr. and Mrs. Coillard, who did so much for this country and who survived the pestilential climate for many years.

Selous was well received by Lewanika, who was perhaps the most enlightened black chief in all South Africa with perhaps the exception of Khama. With him he did some good trading. It was interesting to observe the attitude of the natives to their chief when an audience was granted.

" When strangers came in, they saluted the chief most ceremoniously. First they would kneel down in a row, and after clapping their hands, bend their heads forward until their foreheads touched the ground, when the head was moved slowly from side to side ; then, raising their heads again, they would look towards the chief, and throwing their arms quickly and wildly into the air would shout twice in unison, and in slow measured tones, the words ' So-yo, so-yo.' This ceremony would be twice repeated, when, after clapping their hands again, they would get up and retire."

Selous found the Barotsi valley enervating and far from interesting, although birds were numerous in the swamplands. Cranes, storks, avocets, spoonbills, herons, bitterns, egrets, wattled and spur-winged plovers, stilts, dotterel, and curlew were abundant and afforded him some amusement in watching their habits, but the large game, except lechwe, were rare. Beyond Sinanga to the west the scenery became more beautiful, and here the hunter found tracks of elephants and large herds of buffalo. He also visited the Falls of the Gonyi, which few travellers had ever seen. At the mouth of the River Nangombi his boatmen killed a huge reed-rat, like an immense guinea-pig, which Selous believed was an animal new to science. Next day a disaster befell one of the canoes, which was sunk in twelve feet of water by a hippopotamus, and the traveller was only able to recover a small portion of its valuable cargo. Soon after this he turned back and reached his waggons on the 12th of October, going south in December, and reaching Bamangwato early in January, 1889.

CHAPTER VIII

1889-1892

EARLY in 1889 Selous met Frank Johnson at Bamangwato and was asked by him to act as guide for a gold prospecting expedition to the upper regions of the Mazoe River. As it was then impossible to conduct such an expedition through Matabeleland, Lobengula having closed all the roads, Selous, accompanied by Mr. Burnett and Mr. Thomas, an experienced miner, travelled by sea to Quilimani, in Portuguese territory, and then to Lokoloko on the Quaqua by boat, and thence overland to Mazaro on the Zambesi. From here the party travelled up-stream to Tete, where the Governor, Senhor Alfredo Alpuina, neither helped nor hindered them to any extent. Selous had orders to mark out gold-bearing areas in Portuguese territory, but from the first had difficulty with his porters (Shakundas), who were fearful of meeting the natives of Motoko, with whom the Portuguese had been at war.

On August 18th the travellers left Tete, and went first towards Zumbo and then south to the Kangadzi and Kansawa rivers, where they met a troop of lions, one of which, a lioness, Burnett killed. On September 1st twenty-nine out of forty-two carriers bolted, and their loss was more or less made good by men from surrounding villages. At the kraal of a chief, Maziwa, they were subjected to the usual extortion, which excited the remaining Shakunda carriers to practise a little blackmail. Things got so bad that Selous decided to destroy a good part of his trade goods and to push on in spite of Maziwa's threats. A short retreat was, however, necessary, and the remaining Shakunda carriers, except one who remained faithful, were dismissed. From Rusambo a fresh start was made. Near the head of the Umkaradsi

Valley Selous found a fine unnamed mountain, which he called Mount Darwin, after the illustrious naturalist, and then pushed on to Mapondera's kraal, which was in the centre of a gold-bearing district. Mapondera, chief of the Makori-kori, was a powerful chief, and from him Selous obtained a mineral concession, and got him to sign a paper to the effect that he considered himself in no way under Portuguese rule. This was important, for at this time the Portuguese, although holding none of the country, considered that they owned Mashunaland.

Having concluded his business, Selous decided to try and fix the actual source of the Mazoe, which was then unknown. Accordingly, he and Burnett started off on their wanderings, leaving Thomas, who was ill with fever, at Mapondera's kraal.

We need not follow the travels of Selous and his companions in their subsequent journeys, for Selous' own survey of this country and his remarks on Mount Hampden and its neighbourhood, are published in the Journals of the Royal Geographical Society Suffice it to say, that on October 10th Selous and Burnett returned to Rusambo, after having carefully surveyed the adjoining country. The party then struck down the Ruenya river, where they killed some hippopotami, and reached Tete again on October 23rd. Here Selous had a stormy interview with the Governor, who accused him of being an agent of the British Government, and demanded the document made between himself and Mapondera. This, however, Selous declined to agree to, but eventually gave him a copy. After this the party had no further trouble, and reached Cape Town early in December.

At this time (1890) all circumstances seemed to point to the fact that unless the British Government took possession of Mashunaland the Portuguese intended to do so. In 1888 Lord Salisbury had proclaimed it to be within the sphere of British influence, and said that he would not recognize the claims of Portugal unless that country could show occupation. It was therefore, in Selous' opinion at any rate, clear that the Portuguese expeditions of 1889 made against local chiefs in the North-East, were undertaken to prove conquest and ownership, for at this time no Englishman was domiciled nearer Mashunaland than Matabeleland.

In view therefore of coming trouble Selous, who was then aware of Rhodes' schemes, wrote this letter to the " Selous Syndicate," setting forth the extreme importance of establishing occupation at once by British pioneers, or the valuable country of Mashunaland would be lost to us. On reaching Cape Town he at once proceeded to Kimberley, and was delighted to find that Mr. Rhodes fully concurred with his views, and was determined that the country should be occupied in the cause of the British South African Company during the coming year (1890). Selous then laid before him his idea of cutting a road passing from the south-east of Matabeleland due north to the Portuguese frontier. This scheme Rhodes did not at first approve of,[1] but he afterwards accepted it in its entirety.

" It is due to Mr. Cecil Rhodes alone," writes Selous, " I cannot too often repeat, that to-day our country's flag flies over Mashunaland. He alone of all Englishmen possessed at the same time the prescience and breadth of mind to appreciate the ultimate value of the country, combined with the strong will which, in spite of all obstacles, impelled the means and the power successfully to carry out the scheme of its immediate occupation. What the acquisition of this vast country means is as yet scarcely apparent to the great majority of Englishmen, perhaps to none who are not acquainted with the history of South Africa during the present century, or who have not watched the giant strides which have taken place in its development during the last twenty years. But, in the not distant future, when quick and easy communications into Mashunaland have been established, and the many difficulties which now hamper the development of this the youngest of British colonies have been overcome, then I think Englishmen will be able

[1] Rhodes' original plan was to attack Lobengula with a small force. This, Selous pointed out to him, would be certain to lead to disaster since Rhodes' infcrmation as to the strength of the Matabele was obviously incorrect. It is therefore clear that Selous in over-persuading him to abandon this method rendered him and the nation a considerable service.

to appreciate what they owe to Mr. Rhodes for inaugurating a new departure in South African history, and securing for his countrymen the first ' show in ' in a country which must ultimately become a very valuable possession."

By the end of 1889 Rhodes drew up his plan of occupation, which was approved by Sir Henry Loch, High Commissioner for South Africa, and other authorities. The guidance of the expedition was left entirely in the hands of Selous. The route of the road to be cut was from the Macloutsie river, over the high plateaux of Fort Charter and Salisbury, and north to Manica.

In January, 1890, Selous wrote his letter to the " Times," which gave a very complete survey of the Portuguese and British claims, as well as a general description of the country it was proposed to occupy.

In February and March he made a flying visit to Bulawayo, where he saw Lobengula, who gave him a message for Cecil Rhodes. Writing from Palapswi, on March 26th, he says : " I got back the day before yesterday from Matabeleland and leave to-morrow for Kimberley. I am the bearer of a message from Lobengula to Mr. Cecil Rhodes. He promises to come to an understanding with Mr. Rhodes as to the opening up of Mashunaland if Rhodes will go up to Bulawayo and arrange with him personally. I am going to try and persuade Mr. Rhodes to accompany me back to Bulawayo immediately. I hope he will be able to go, and trust some satisfactory arrangement may be come to. Still, I distrust Lobengula and his people. Things are in such a condition just now regarding Matabeleland and Mashunaland that it is quite impossible to tell what may happen. Everything may be settled peaceably (or forcibly) this year. Or again, the High Commissioner may forbid any expedition to be made this year against the wish of Lobengula. The question is a very strange one. The Charter was granted to the South African Company on the strength of their having obtained a concession from Lobengula for the mineral rights in Matabele- and Mashunaland. These rights were really bought, and a lot of money was paid to Lobengula directly, and to his people indirectly, by the agents of the Company.

Now it seems as if Lobengula was inclined to disallow Europeans to work for gold, either in Matabele- or Mashunaland. In order to avoid trouble, the Company now wish to waive their rights in Matabeleland proper, where they would necessarily come in contact with the Matabele people, and to exploit and develop Mashunaland, a country to which the Matabele have no just title. In order to do this without coming into contact with Lobengula and his people, the Company now wish to make a road to Mashunaland that shall not touch Matabeleland at all, but pass to the south of that country, and it is quite possible that Lobengula and his people, fearing to let whites get beyond him and establish themselves in Mashunaland, will try and prevent this road being made. At present the political situation in England is a most ridiculous one as regards Mashunaland. Lord Salisbury has warned the Portuguese out of it, saying that it is to him the sphere of British influence, and now Lobengula will not allow British subjects or any white men to enter his country as long as he can keep them out. I abhor the Matabele, yet I would not have them interfered with or their country invaded without a *casus belli* ; but that they should keep Europeans out of Mashunaland is preposterous."

In March, 1890, Selous was sent up to Palapswi with instructions to get men from Khama to cut a waggon-road to the eastern border of his country. He was, moreover, to be assisted by some Matabele in this critical work, and so visited Lobengula at Bulawayo to explain the objects in view. Lobengula, however, denied having ever given Dr. Jameson any promise about assisting in the making of the road, and firmly asserted that he would not allow it to be made. He said that he would not discuss matters with any of Rhodes' emissaries, and that if there was to be any talk the " Big White Chief " himself must come to visit him. Wherefore Selous returned to Kimberley and saw Mr. Rhodes, who sent Dr. Jameson, and with him Selous then returned to Tati.

Meanwhile a considerable force, about four hundred white men, had been gathered at the Macloutsie with the intention of occupying Mashunaland, whether the Matabele liked it or

ON THE MASHUNA PLATEAU.

not. Selous himself was sent eastward to pick out a good line for a waggon-road as far as the Shashi and Tuli rivers—which survey he concluded by May. It was during one of these journeys he was lucky enough to find and kill the best koodoo bull he ever saw, a magnificent specimen, 60 inches long on the curve and 45⅜ straight. By the 10th of June the waggon-track to Tuli was open.

The pioneer expedition now moved, with the scouts in front ; the Matabele threatened to attack, but did not do so, and Selous, with his scouting parties in advance and covered by Khama's mounted men, commenced cutting the long road from the Macloutsie to Mount Hampden, a distance of four hundred and sixty miles. As each section of the road was cut the main expeditionary force followed after. About the worst section was between the Umzing-wane and the Umshabetse rivers, a desolate thirst-land ; but this was passed in three days. This territory, which I visited in 1893, was claimed by the Matabele, and includes the King's private hunting-ground, and the pioneers expected every moment to be attacked ; so every precaution was taken, the mounted men keeping a sharp watch and the axe-men doing the cutting.

From the Umshabetse river Selous wrote to his mother (July 13th, 1890) : " I am here with an advanced party of the pioneer force—forty men—all mounted. We have already cut nearly 120 miles of road from the B.S.A. Company's camp on the Macloutsie river, and are now on the borders of the Banyai country. We are already far to the east of all the inhabited part of Matabeleland and are now going north-east, always keeping more than 150 miles as the crow flies from Bulawayo. So far we have seen nothing of the Matabele. We are, however, taking every precaution against surprise, and always have scouts out in front and several miles behind us on the road who do not come in till after dark. We keep watch all night, too, with relays of guards. Should a large impi come down to attack us, we shall simply abandon our waggon and retire on the main body, which is now coming on, on the road we have made. Our main body is composed of four hundred good men,

N

besides fifty native mounted scouts supplied by Khama. If we can get two hours' notice of the approach of the Matabele, just sufficient time to have all the waggons put into ' laager ' on the old Boer plan, Lobengula's men can do nothing to us.   If they attack us in ' laager ' they must suffer fearful loss.   The young men want to fight, but Lobengula and the older men want peace.   However, do not be downhearted, dearest mother.   Personally, I hope there will be no fighting."

On July 18th the main column caught up the roadmakers at the Umshabetse river, and on August 1st the Lunti river was reached.   Selous now scouted ahead and found an easy road to the plateau ahead, and by " Providential Pass " the expedition eventually emerged from the forest into the open country.

Whilst they were cutting the road from the Lunti to Fort Victoria an ultimatum was received from Lobengula by Colonel Pennefather that he must turn back at once, unless he "thought he was strong enough to go on," and warning him to expect trouble if he did so.

By this time, however, Lobengula had lost his best chance of attacking the expeditionary force, for they had now emerged on the open downs ; yet it is a wonder he managed to keep his young men in check.   Had he attacked in the bush country it is doubtful if our forces, even if they had not met with a reverse, would have been able to proceed.   At any rate intense excitement prevailed in Matabeleland, and many new impis of warriors were formed ready to take action.

On September 1st the expedition reached the source of the Umgezi, where Fort Charter was established ; so that by September 30th the Company had a continuous chain of forts and posts over eight hundred miles from Tuli to Fort Salisbury.   Here Selous left the expedition, as he was the only man who knew the surrounding country, and it was essential for him to go with Mr. A. R. Colquhoun to confer with Umtasa, the chief of Manica.   On September 14th a treaty was agreed to by which the British South Africa Company acquired and took possession of a large area of auriferous country—much to the annoyance of the Portuguese, who claimed it. Treaties were concluded with all the other chiefs except Motoko, whom Selous visited early in November. The Portuguese, however, did not give up their claims without some show of force, for when Major Forbes went down to take over parts of Manica he had trouble with the Portuguese, and had to arrest Colonel d'Andrada and others, to avoid bloodshed ; and for safety sent his prisoners to Fort Salisbury.

Before reaching Salisbury at the end of November, Selous spent three months altogether in travelling through the northern and eastern districts of Mashunaland and concluding treaties of amity with all the native chiefs. This, besides mapping and literary work—describing the country —occupied his time till the middle of December, when he again visited Motoko, chief of the Mabudja, to obtain a treaty of friendship, as well as a mineral concession, in which he was quite successful. In October he wrote home from Mangwendi's kraal praising the climate of Eastern Mashunaland, and evidently in high spirits at the great success of the pioneer expedition. " The opening up of Mashunaland seems like a dream, and I have played a not unimportant part in it all, I am proud to say. The road to Mashunaland is now being called the ' Selous Road,' and I hope the name will endure, though I don't suppose it will. At any rate, the making of the road was entrusted *entirely* to me and I did my work to everyone's satisfaction. An old Boer officer said to me, just before the expedition started, ' I think that the expedition without Mr. Selous would be like a swarm of bees that has lost its Queen and does not know where to go to.' Yet it is too bad of me to sing my own praises, but I do feel most proud at the share I had in putting it through, *the whole idea, too, of making the road at all and thus circumventing the Matabele and gaining possession of Mashunaland was my own.* I proposed it to Rhodes in Kimberley on my return from the Zambesi last December. At first he did not like the idea ; but after thinking it over, resolved to try and carry it out, with the result that Mashunaland is now practically a British province.

" Before the rainy season is over, the Company will probably have come to some definite understanding with Lobengula, who, by the by, recognized my importance in the expedition by sending down a message to Sir Henry Loch, the High Commissioner, that ' Selous had turned his oxen and his horses into his (Lobengula's) cornfields.' "

Writing from Motoko's kraal on November 16th, he says : " Before coming here, I have had no difficulty with any of the other chiefs, but here I have had a lot of worry and trouble. My great difficulty is that the whole country is really ruled, not by the chief (Motoko) but by one whom they call the ' Lion-God.' This appears to be a hereditary office, and the holder of it lives away by himself in the mountains, and is looked upon with superstitious dread and reverence by the Chief and his people. However, I have now got things on a friendly footing, but I shall have to go back to Fort Salisbury, in order to get certain articles to appease the ' Lion-God,' and then return here before I shall finally be able to conclude the treaty with Motoko. I am under engagement to the Company till the end of next August, and do not think I shall take a fresh engagement, as I am anxious to get home. Having passed the best part of my life in the wilderness and amongst savages, I should now like to see something of civilized countries, with perhaps an occasional short trip into an out-of-the-way place. If I live to be an old man, I should like to re-visit this country, thirty or forty years hence, by railroad."

In January, 1891, he returned to Umtali, where he received orders to cut a road from that place to Lower Revui, and afterwards to lay a new road from the Odzi river to Salisbury. February was the wet season, so it was with some difficulty that he set about his task on the Odzi in company with Mr. W. L. Armstrong. On May 3rd, however, he had made one hundred and fifty miles of road to Salisbury, riding three strong horses to a standstill in his numerous peregrinations. Then news reached him of further trouble with the Portuguese, and he was asked by Mr. Colquhoun to take two waggon-loads of stores and ammunition to the small British garrison isolated at Manica, where there was an imminent prospect of fighting. Whereat he expresses his views clearly as to his own inclinations as regards soldiering. "Now I am not a fighting man, and neither look forward with enthusiasm to the prospect of being shot, nor feel any strong desire to shoot anyone else."

However, he regarded the matter, as he always did when called upon, as a duty, and left at once for Manica with Lieutenant Campbell and twenty ex-pioneers. On May 13th the party reached Umtali, where they heard that the Portuguese had made a sortie from Massi-Kessi, and had attacked Captain Heyman's camp near Chua. The Portuguese troops, numbering one hundred whites and blacks from Angola, however, had shot so badly that no one was hit and soon lost heart and bolted back to Massi-Kessi, which was soon after occupied by our forces. To his mother he wrote from Umtali, May 20th, 1891 :—

"I got down here on the 13th by the new road I have made for the Company, with about twenty men and two waggon-loads of provisions, and we were astonished to hear that a fight had already taken place near Massi-Kessi on the afternoon of the 11th, and I will now tell you what has actually taken place. It appears that on the 5th of this month the Portuguese reoccupied Massi-Kessi, with a force consisting of about one hundred white soldiers and three or four hundred black troops. Thereupon Captain Heyman went over from here (Umtali Camp) to near Massi-Kessi with fifty men and a seven-pounder cannon, and a lot of Umtasa's men, to protest against the invasion of Umtasa's country. Two days later, Captain Heyman and Lieutenant Morier (a son of Sir Robert Morier, British Ambassador at St. Petersburg) went down to Massi-Kessi with a flag of truce, to interview Ferreira, the Commander of the Portuguese forces, and the Governor of Manica. Ferreira told him that he was at Massi-Kessi, in accordance with the terms of the *modus vivendi* which the Company's forces were breaking, by being at Umtali, and said that he would drive the Company's men out of the country. Captain Heyman then said that he had better not do anything before the expiration of the *modus vivendi*, to which he replied that he would attack him whenever he thought fit to do so. Captain Heyman's position was on a hill about five miles from Massi-Kessi. On the 10th, I think, one of the Portuguese officers came up with a flag of truce, evidently to see what number of men Captain Heyman had with him. He only saw about fifteen, as all the rest were lying down in the long grass, and it must have been from his report that an attack was resolved upon. Captain Heyman told me that he was immensely surprised to see the Portuguese troops swarming out of Massi-Kessi at about 2 p.m. on the 11th. They advanced in two bodies, led by the Portuguese officers. Captain Heyman first fired a blank charge with the cannon to which they paid no attention, and then seeing that they meant business the firing commenced in earnest. The firing lasted two hours. The Portuguese officers did all they could to get their men on, and behaved very well indeed ; but their men evidently did not relish the business, and after making two attempts to reach a hill which would have commanded Captain Heyman's position, broke and fled back to Massi-Kessi. Not a single man of the Company's force was hit, but the Portuguese lost an officer (Captain Bettencourt), and it is believed about twenty men. Early next morning Captain Heyman sent a man down to Massi-Kessi with a flag of truce, offering the services of the doctor, and when he got there he found the place deserted. For some unaccountable reason the Portuguese had deserted the place, leaving nine machine-guns, ammunition, and stores and provisions of all kinds behind them. It is thought that a panic set in amongst the black troops, and the white Portuguese were afraid to remain behind without them. The whole affair is very inglorious to the Portuguese arms, and will have a great effect on their prestige with the natives. Of course Massi-Kessi was seized and looted by the northern barbarians, and has now been blown up and destroyed. Everybody is longing for another Portuguese expedition to come up, as then there will be a chance of more loot. What will happen now it is impossible to say, but I think that the British Government must step in, and either order the Company to leave Manica, or else support it against the Portuguese, in which case they will be unable to do anything of importance. They will now, I think, have great difficulty in getting up here, as the natives are all hostile to them and all their carriers will have to be brought from other parts. The country, too, is a very difficult one to travel through. I shall be very glad when things are settled, as Mashunaland will be kept back until they are. I have been down with Colonel Pennefather, as I told you, on a reconnaissance about thirty miles beyond Massi-Kessi, on the track of the Portuguese, and they have evidently beaten a hasty retreat."

Immediately after this fiasco Selous went down to Umliwan's kraal, situated between the Pungwi and the Busi rivers, to fetch away the abandoned waggons. One night, whilst on the return journey, the camp was attacked by five lions and an ox killed. Next morning Selous, of course, went after them, but failed to get a shot. The following night he made a small hut close to the carcase of the ox, and into this Selous and Armstrong crept at sunset, and the night's adventure as described by Selous[1] is one of the best stories he ever wrote. The lions kept continually returning to the carcase. Several shots were fired and two lionesses and a hyena killed, but one wounded lion succeeded in escaping.

Although he says little of it at the time, Selous did an immense amount of tramping to and fro, all footwork because of the " fly," in the unhealthy country, both contiguous to and in the Portuguese territory about the Pungwi and Busi rivers in 1891 and 1892, in the hope of finding a road to the East Coast that would be free from the tsetse fly and where waggons could pass. In this he was unsuccessful, and he was reluctantly forced to admit that a railway would be the only method of transport to the coast, and that until this was made no progress was possible. However, his journeys carried him for the first time into the last great haunt of game south of the Zambesi, for at this time the whole of the territory in the neighbourhood of these rivers was one huge game reserve which, owing to its unhealthiness, was seldom visited by sportsmen or even meat-hunters. And so it continued till 1896, when the rinderpest swept off

[1] " Travel and Adventure in S.E. Africa," pp. 417-425.

nine-tenths of the koodoos, elands and buffalo. Since that day the game recovered in a measure, and even to-day there is more game there than anywhere south of the Zambesi, but it contains a shadow of its former abundance at the time when Selous first visited it. Practically Selous was the first white man to see this great assembly of game and to hunt them, for the Portuguese were not hunters and never left the footpaths. He found vast herds of buffaloes in the reed-beds, bushbucks as tame as in the Garden of Eden stood gazing at a few yards and did not fly at the approach of man, whilst out on the plains there was a constant procession of Liechtenstein's hartebeest, blue wildebeests, tsessebes, water-bucks, zebras, and here and there were always scattered parties of reedbucks, oribis, and the smaller antelopes. Wart-hogs and bush-pigs were equally tame and confiding, and hippopotami disported in the rivers and lagoons in broad daylight, and there was not a night that several troops of lions were not heard roaring. Yet curiously enough, in spite of the abundance of the last-named, Selous only saw three individuals, one of which he killed after it had charged twice. This, he says, was the last of "thirty-one lions I have shot."[1] This number does not tally with the statement, "I have only shot twenty-five lions when entirely by myself,"[2] but the discrepancy is accounted for by the fact that he killed six lions between 1893 and 1896.

The opening up of the new country proceeded rapidly till June, 1892, when Selous wrote to his mother from Salisbury :—

" The telegraph wire is now at Fort Charter, and before the end of next month the office will be opened here in Salisbury, and Mashunaland will be in telegraph communication with the whole of the civilized world. This, if you come to think of it, is really a magnificent piece of enterprise. We are having the most lovely weather up here, although it is the middle of summer and the rainy season ; nice cool cloudy days, with showers of rain occasionally, but nothing worth speaking of. The Government buildings

---

[1] "African Native Notes and Reminiscences," p. 311, 1908.
[2] Badminton Library. "The Lion in S. Africa," p. 316, 1894.

are progressing rapidly. We now have an abundance of vegetables here. Everything thrives marvellously, potatoes, cabbage, onions, shalots, radishes, lettuces, etc. etc. Wheat sowed in August last by the head of the Africander Bond deputation, ripened and was cut in four months and a few days from the date of sowing, and has been sent down to Cape Town. Major Johnson's agricultural expert pronounced it to be as fine a sample of wheat as he had ever seen, and says he will be able to raise two crops a year. In fact, the country is now proved to be an exceptionally fine one for both agriculture and stock-farming, in spite of Mr. Labouchere and Lord Randolph Churchill. The gold prospects are also improving, and many of Mr. Perkins' prognostications have already been falsified. I think there is no doubt that this country will have a grand future, but the development will be very slow for some time yet ; in fact, until a railway has been made from the East coast, at least as far as Manica. Once this railway has been built, however, the country must be developed very quickly, I think. All impartial persons agree that the climate on this plateau is cooler and altogether more enjoyable than that of Kimberley and many other parts of civilized South Africa ; but, of course, directly one leaves the plateau and gets into the low bush-country towards the Zambesi, the East coast, or the Transvaal, fever is rife during the rainy season. Unfortunately, most of the gold-belts are in this unhealthy zone, and until the bush is cut down, the land cultivated, and good houses are built round the mines, miners will suffer from fever in the bad season ; but this is the same in all new countries. I am now going down to make a road from Manica to the other side of Massi-Kessi, so as to be ready from our side to meet the tramway or railway which the Mozambique Company have undertaken to make from the Pungwi river. My intention is to leave the Company's service in June next, and in August I shall go down to the East coast, and hope to be in Johannesburg in October, and in England before the end of the year. I do not intend to revisit Mashunaland for several years, but I shall have considerable interests there, which will increase in value as the country develops. I intend to visit America, to see the World's Fair, in 1893, and should like to visit Japan at the same time. I consider myself independent, as I can live on the £330 a year which my de Beers shares produce, and I have a good many more properties which may turn out valuable."

Selous continued making roads until May, 1892, when there being no further work for him to do, he terminated his engagement with the British South Africa Company, and went down to Beira, and so to Cape Town and England, which he reached on December 17th, 1892. Before leaving, however, he did a little hunting, and killed his last lion on October 3rd, and his last elephant, a splendid old bull, with tusks weighing 108 lbs. the pair, on October 7th.

It was in December, 1891, that Selous killed his finest lion, a splendid animal with a good mane, and one whose pegged-out skin measured over eleven feet. This lion had done much damage at Hartley Hills, breaking into stables and kraals, and destroyed many horses and goats. This was an unusually daring beast, and efforts to destroy him had been of no avail. Whilst dining with Dr. Edgelow one night, Selous heard his driver, John, fire from his camp close by, and called out to ask the cause. The driver replied that a lion had just killed one of the loose oxen. Nothing could be done that night, but at dawn Selous took the spoor in the wet ground, but lost it on the dry veldt. Next evening he made a shelter against a tree.

" As the shooting-hole between the overhanging branches of the tree behind which I sat only allowed me to get a view directly over the carcase of the ox, I arranged another opening to the right, which gave me a good view up the waggon-road along which I thought the lion would most likely come, and I placed the muzzle of my rifle in this opening when I entered my shelter. As the night was so light, I thought it very likely that my vigil might be a long one ; for even if he did not wait until the moon had set, I never imagined that the lion would put in an appearance until after midnight, when the camp would be quite quiet. Under this impression, I had just finished the arrangement of my blankets, placing some behind me and the rest beneath me, so as to make myself as comfortable as possible in so confined a space, and was just leaning back, and dreamily wondering whether I could keep awake all night, when, still as in a dream, I saw the form of a magnificent lion pass rapidly and noiselessly as a phantom of the night across the moonlight disc of the shooting-hole I had made to the right of the tree-stem. In another instant he had passed and was hidden by the tree, but a moment later his shaggy head again appeared before the opening formed by the diverging stems. Momentary as had been the glimpse I had of him as he passed the right-hand opening, I had marked him as a magnificent black-maned lion with neck and shoulders well covered with long shaggy hair. He now stood with his forelegs right against the breast of the dead ox, and, with his head held high, gazed fixedly towards my waggon and oxen, every one of which he could, of course, see very distinctly, as well as my boy John and the Kafirs beside him. I heard my horse snort, and knew he had seen the lion, but the oxen, although they must have seen him too, showed no sign of fear. The Kafirs were still laughing and talking noisily not fifty yards away, and, bold as he was, the lion must have felt a little anxious as he stood silently gazing in the direction from which he thought danger might be apprehended.

" All this time, but without ever taking my eyes off the lion, I was noiselessly moving the muzzle of my little rifle from the right-hand-side opening to the space that commanded a view of his head. This I was obliged to do very cautiously, for fear of touching a branch behind me and making a noise. I could see the black crest of mane between his ears move lightly in the wind, for he was so near that had I held my rifle by the small of the stock I could have touched him with the muzzle by holding it at arm's length. Once only he turned his head and looked round right into my eyes, but, of course, without seeing me, as I was in the dark, and, apparently, without taking the slightest alarm, as he again turned his head and stood looking at the waggon as before. I could only see his head, his shoulder being hidden by the right-hand stem of the tree, and I had made up my mind to try and blow his brains out, thinking I was so near that I could not fail to do so, even without being able to see the sight of my rifle. I had just got the muzzle of my rifle into the fork of the tree, and was about to raise it quite leisurely, the lion having hitherto showed no signs of uneasiness. I was working as cautiously as possible, when without the slightest warning he suddenly gave a low grating growl, and turned round, his head disappearing instantly from view. With a jerk I pulled the muzzle of my rifle from the one opening and pushed it through the other just as the lion walked rapidly past in the direction from which he had come. He was not more than four or five yards from me, and I should certainly have given him a mortal wound had not my rifle missed fire at this most critical juncture, the hammer giving a loud click in the stillness of the night. At the sound the lion broke into a gallop, and was almost instantly out of sight."

This was a terrible misfortune, but next morning Selous tracked the lion up a watercourse and soon found him.

" John was looking about near the edge of this shallow water, and I had turned my horse's head to look along the bank higher up, when the unmistakable growl of a lion issued from the bushes beyond the rivulet, and at the same time John said, ' Daar hij ' (there he is). I was off my horse in an instant to be ready for a shot, when he turned round and trotted away, and John ran to try and catch him. I thought the luck was all against me, as I expected the lion would make off and get clean away ; but I ran forward, trying to get a sight of him when he suddenly made his appearance in the bush about fifty yards away, and catching sight of me, came straight towards me at a rapid pace, holding his head low and growling savagely. I suppose he wanted to frighten me, but he could not have done a kinder thing. He came right on to the further bank of the little stream just where it formed a pool of water, and stood there amongst some rocks growling and whisking his tail about, and always keeping his eyes fixed upon me. Of course, he gave me a splendid shot, and in another instant I hit him, between the neck and the shoulder, in the side of his chest, with a 360-grain expanding bullet. As I pulled the trigger I felt pretty sure he was mine. With a loud roar he reared right up, and turning over sideways fell off the rock on which he had been standing into the pool of water below him. The water was over three feet deep, and for an instant he disappeared entirely from view, but the next instant regaining his feet stood on the bottom with his head and shoulders above the surface. I now came towards him, when again seeing me, he came plunging through the water towards me, growling angrily. But his strength was fast failing him, and I saw it was all he could do to reach the bank, so I did not fire, as I was anxious not to make holes in his skin. He just managed to get up the bank, when I finished him with a shot through the lungs, to which he instantly succumbed."[1]

Selous has always been regarded by the British public as the first lion-hunter of all time. They would like to have seen him travelling round with a large circus and a band giving demonstrations of shooting lions from horseback à la Buffalo Bill, but nothing was further from his own ideas than such a showman's display. Being as truthful as he was modest, he always entirely disclaimed any great prowess as a lion-hunter and said what was true—that many men had killed a far greater number of lions than himself. It was only on particular occasions like the last adventure described that he went out of his way to shoot lions that had become troublesome and dangerous, but at all times he never declined a fight when he was lucky enough to meet lions, whether he was himself afoot or accompanied by dogs. If he had wished to make a great bag of lions, doubtless he could have done so ; but he never wished to pose as a lion-hunter like Jules Gerard and others, and so his total bag was modest. Actually, he himself shot thirty-one lions and assisted in the destruction of eleven others. Even his good friend, H. A. Bryden, usually so accurate in his statements, says : " He was easily the greatest lion-hunter of his time," and the general public, taking the cue from many writers, say a thing is so-and-so and the statement becomes standard-

---

[1] Badminton Library. " The Lion in S. Africa," p. 343.

ized. But, after all, it is only a very few men who know the real facts of any case, and they often have a habit of holding their tongues. Doubtless, if Selous had enjoyed the opportunities of the Brothers Hill, he would have been just as active and successful in destroying lions as they—if he had not been killed in the process. Selous, as a matter of fact, had no more genius for hunting than that enjoyed by many others. He was an admirable hunter, but just as unable to spoor a lion on dry veldt as other white men—that gift alone belonging to certain black races. The title, therefore, of being "the greatest lion-hunter"—even if we admit the desirability of using superlatives—seems to belong to the man or men who by perfectly fair means and taking risks—the same as Selous himself did—have shot the greatest number of lions. Wherefore, I give a few particulars.

As Selous himself has said, probably the greatest lion-hunter within his experience of South Africa was Petrus Jacobs, who killed in his life—chiefly with the assistance of dogs—well over one hundred lions, and was himself badly mauled when he was over seventy-three years of age.

Probably the greatest all-round hunter of African game now living is William Judd, now a professional hunter in British East Africa. In South and East Africa he has killed forty-eight lions and been in at the death of forty-three others. In giving me these particulars, he says: " I have never had any really narrow squeaks from lions with the exception of the time I was out with Selous on the Gwasin Guishu plateau " (see " Field," May 28th, 1910). It may be remarked that this immunity is due to the fact that he is a magnificent shot. He considers the Buffalo a far more dangerous opponent. A. B. Percival, Game Warden, is said to have shot fifty lions during his residence in British East Africa.

In Somaliland, hunting almost exclusively for lions, Colonel Curtis in one season killed twenty-seven, and in the same time Colonel Paget and Lord Wolverton nearly as many. Captain Mellis also in one season accounted for twenty-one lions, and several other British sportsmen have killed twenty in one trip in that part of Africa.

What a man does and what he could actually do in the way of lion-killing is perhaps beside the question. A great lion-hunter like Sir Alfred Pease, both an admirable shot and a superb horseman, has only killed fourteen lions and joined in eleven " partnerships," but this in no way represents the number of lions he *could* have killed had he wished to do so. Being of an unselfish disposition it was ever his pleasure, since he had killed all the specimens he wanted, to give his friends who were anxious to shoot lions every opportunity of doing so. In fact, on many occasions, at his farm on the Kapiti Plains, he himself " rounded up " the lions for other men to kill, and simply looked on—standing ready in case of trouble. " Lions were so plentiful at my place on the Athi," he writes, "that one party killed in one day (1911–12) fourteen lions. I have often spared a fine lion to give a guest a chance, and have never seen him again. The finest lion I ever saw was an enormous black-maned fellow. I prevented my son-in-law from firing at him, as I wished President Roosevelt to get him during his stay with me. Subsequently, I think a German got his skin; but in reality, I believe H. D. Hill killed him after a German party and the Brothers Hill had fought a great battle with him near Lukania."

Sir Alfred then goes on to give particulars of the astounding performances of the Brothers Harold D. Hill and Clifford Hill, who if they wished it—which they probably do not—are justly entitled to the right of being called the first of modern lion-hunters. " Harold Hill managed my farm in British East Africa for several years. He told me a year ago that he had, since he had been there, 1906–15, on my farms of Theki and Katanga, and on his own and his brother's farms—Katelembo and Wami—killed himself one hundred and thirty-six lions. I think this figure will include a very great number of what I should call ' partnerships,' for his brother Clifford must have killed as many or more than Harold, for he has done more actual hunting.[1] Clifford Hill

[1] In a letter to me from East Africa, March 12th, 1918, Harold Hill states that he has been in at the death of 135 lions and that his brother Clifford has seen 160 lions shot. In most cases, he admits, he and his brother generally allowed some friend to have his first shot.

acted as professional hunter to many 'safaris,' but you could absolutely rely on any statement he made, although it is not likely that he believed, himself, in counting heads of game killed. I should not be surprised if these two brothers have not been in at the death of over three hundred lions during their residence in East Africa."

"Some years ago Lord Delamere had, I think, killed between fifty and sixty lions. Many of these (over twenty) were killed in Somaliland. Some of these were 'ridden,' and others may have been killed at night, but Delamere was, nevertheless, a keen and fearless hunter."

Commenting on the different methods of hunting lions in Somaliland and British East Africa, Sir Alfred says :—

"The Somaliland method of hunting (i.e. following a fresh spoor on hard ground till the lion was viewed) was, in my opinion, the best test of skill and sporting qualities, since you tracked and did the whole thing on your own initiative. Personally, I enjoyed most the B.E.A. work. You saw much more of the beasts, and I loved galloping and rounding them up for others to kill as much as I enjoyed anything in my whole life."

Paul Rainey's methods of hunting lions with a large pack of hounds can hardly come into the true category of lion-hunting where risks are taken. The dogs, it is true, were often killed or wounded ; but as a friend who had taken part in these hunts remarked, " It was just like rat-hunting, and about as dangerous." It is true that one man, George Swartz (formerly a German waiter at the Norfolk Hotel, Nairobi), was killed in one of these hunts, but the accident was singular. Swartz was a very bold fellow and moved close in in thick bush when the dogs had a lion at bay one day in the Kedong in 1912. The lion " broke bay," and either intentionally charged Swartz or ran over to him by chance as he worked the cinema-camera. The beast gave the man one bite in the stomach and then left him, but the unfortunate fellow died shortly afterwards of his wounds. Paul Rainey claims to have killed over two hundred lions with his dogs.

It has always been the custom amongst hunters that he

THE BATTLE OF THE STRONG.

who draws first blood from any animal—even if it is only a scratch—is entitled to the beast when subsequently killed. It is a good law on the whole, but there are many instances where it is scarcely justified—that is to say, when the first shooter has done little beyond slightly injuring the animal, if a dangerous one, and the second hunter has stood "all the racket," and killed the beast at the risk of his life. Here is such an example given to me by Sir Alfred Pease :—

"I lent my rifle (a ·256 Mannlicher) to a friend, also my horse to gallop and 'round up' a lion, whilst I kept watch on a bush where another had hidden, not being able—owing to dongas—to get round him. My friend soon jumped off and fired two or three shots at the first lion, which worked round and came and lay down under a thin thorn-bush less than a hundred yards from my position. I then went towards the bush and the lion charged me. I fired twice with a 10-bore gun at about sixty and fifteen yards, and the beast— a very fine black-maned lion—fell dead to my second barrel.

"My friend now came up, and to my disgust said excitedly, 'My lion!' I said, 'Mine, I think?' He said, 'No; I had first blood!' I had no idea the lion had been hit, but when we examined him there was a ·256 hole in his back ribs. I was rather sore, as I had stood the racket; but *it was the rule*. I killed the second lion in a quarter of an hour. We did not quarrel, however, and he gave my daughter the skin of the first lion, which was nice of him."

However, if he did kill a considerable but not a remarkable number of lions, Selous will always remain the greatest authority on the subject, for in his numerous writings he has given us accounts of sport and natural history in connection with this animal that are quite unequalled by any other writer. In all the descriptions and the accounts of its habits he accumulated a vast mass of material, mostly new and original—which is without a blemish, without a single incorrect statement. These writings by Selous, especially his admirable notes in "African Nature Notes and Reminiscences," and the small monograph on "The Lion," by Sir Alfred Pease, constitute a complete record of the natural history and sport connected with this interesting animal.

o

To clever and broad-minded people in other lands it may be a wonder that so excellent a field naturalist as Selous was not granted a State allowance, to pursue his work as a pioneer and naturalist, so as to relieve him of the constant strain on his slender resources. We know that in France, Germany, Austria, Italy, America and Japan such a thing would have been done long ago ; but foreigners have no knowledge of our various Governments' neglect of science, or of the miserable pittances they allowed to the various scientific bodies for such a purpose in this country. Heaven alone knows what inventions, amounting in value to vast sums, have been literally driven out of England by this abominable stinginess, and sold to other countries, which in time became our deadliest enemies in trade and war. And so in turn our scientific societies, each and all of which considered their own branch the most important, have pursued a policy of neglect and jealousy towards all young workers in whatever branch they showed exceptional originality.

The officials of the British Museum are poorly paid, and they and the Zoological Society, having little or no money to expend on researches of importance in foreign lands, have to go and beg from the general public whenever any expedition is being sent abroad.

In America, where matters are worked on broad-minded principles, field zoology is now recognized as being as important as purely scientific zoology, and ample funds are given to all genuine collectors outside the body corporate, and the advancement of general knowledge is all that is desired. The result is that more excellent work in this branch of science is being done to-day in New York and Washington than in all other countries. It is true they have ample funds for such purposes and these are generously distributed ; but there are no jealous cliques there, and the spirit in which the work is done is wholly admirable.

Perhaps the only scientific society that has received great monetary help is the Royal Geographical Society, and when Arctic or Antarctic expeditions are launched the public has always responded magnificently. I have often wondered why, for beyond the individual effort of bravery on the part of the gallant members of these expeditions, the scientific and material results of these expeditions are very small compared with those of one well-conducted expedition to Central Asia or Africa, which in time has often given considerable scientific results, as well as knowledge of new countries that have become the homes of white men. From the time of Denham and Clapperton to Selous what has ever been done for our African explorers ? Absolutely nothing. These grand men have taken quite as great risks as Arctic or Antarctic travellers, have explored thousands of square miles of new country and done it all out of their own pockets, often ruining themselves in purse and health. An Antarctic expedition costs the British nation anything from £30,000 to £50,000, and its leaders receive knighthoods, and other official distinctions, but we never heard Livingstone called anything but a wandering missionary, or Selous aught but a big game hunter ; nor has any Government taken the smallest notice of them. Yet these two men, by their courage, tact in dealing with natives, personal influence, skill in mapping and eventual advice to those in authority, did more, both for Science and the Empire, than all the expeditions to the wildernesses of perpetual snow and ice.

It must not be supposed that Selous, had he wished, could not have obtained some of these material rewards which are valued by most men. He was not without influential friends, both at home and in Africa, but his natural modesty forbade him to make use of them. One man above all others should have made it his duty to have helped him, but let us see how he acted.

Cecil Rhodes was a big man—big in almost every way except in the matter of gratitude—and when he found that Selous was—to use an Americanism—such an " easy mark," he exploited him to the limit of his capacity. Rhodes knew that without Selous' immense local knowledge and tact with the native Mashuna chiefs his best-laid schemes might go astray, so he played on his patriotism, and promised him many things, not one of which he ever performed.

Selous was, in fact, the whole Intelligence Department, and when he cut the road north with such rapidity it really gave Lobengula no time to act until it was too late. So that the first expedition, which might easily have been a failure, turned out an unqualified success.

" Let me introduce you to Mr. Selous," said Rhodes to a member of the Government at a big luncheon party in 1896, " the man above all others to whom we owe Rhodesia to the British Crown." These were fine words, and a fine acknowledgment of Selous' services. But what happened afterwards, and were Rhodes' promises to him kept ? When the Empire builder found his tool was of no further use, he absolutely ignored him, and could never find time even to see him. To his cynical mind gratitude simply did not exist. Selous was just one of the pawns in the game, and he could now go to the devil for all he cared.

If others gained gold and titles out of the efforts of Selous and the Chartered Company, these mushroom successes strut their uneasy hour and are soon forgotten ; but Selous left behind him an imperishable name for all that was best in the new lands, which is well voiced in the words of Mr. A. R. Morkel, in a letter to the Selous Memorial Committee (1917) :—

" The natives around my farm all remember him, though it is well over twenty-five years since he was last here ; and it is a pretty good testimony to his character, that wherever he travelled amongst natives, many of whom I have talked to about him, he was greatly respected and esteemed as a just man. We, settlers of Rhodesia, will always have this legacy from him, that he instilled into these natives a very good idea of British justice and fairness."

We need express no surprise that the man who did the most hard work was left unrewarded, for such is life. It is on a par with the experience of a gallant officer in a Highland regiment who, after nearly three years of intense warfare in the front line (1914–17), and still without a decoration of any kind, although twice wounded, came to Boulogne, where he met an old brother officer, who had been there in charge of stores for one and a half years, wearing the D.S.O. and M.C. ribbons. " I am not a cynical man," he remarked to me, " but I must say that for once in my life I felt so."

CHAPTER IX

1893-1896

SELOUS had been hunting something all his life, yet he never seems to have lost sight of the possibility that a little fellow with a bow and arrow might one day take a shot at him. Perhaps in earlier days he feared him a little, but when, one January day in 1893, he went to Barrymore House, his mother's home at Wargrave, the small archer was there waiting in ambush and found a very willing victim. The immediate cause of the attack was the fact that Miss Gladys Maddy, a daughter of the Rev. Canon Maddy, was staying with Selous' mother. This was one of Selous' lucky days, for in a short time, since the attraction seems to have been mutual, he decided to try and win the lady as his wife. In this he was quite successful, and by the spring they were engaged. Meanwhile the hunter, being now well known to the public, had arranged to make a lecturing tour in the United States, under the auspices of Major Pond, and had hoped that this would be finished by late September, when he would be able to do a hunt in the Rockies afterwards. All arrangements had been completed and he had already taken his passage to America when the news of the Matabele rising arrived in England. He at once cancelled all his engagements and took the first steamer to South Africa.

After the Pioneer expedition to Mashunaland in 1890 had proved a success the country seemed in so quiet a state that the police force there was in 1891 disbanded. This was doubtless a great mistake. The Matabele were not the kind of people to take the position of a conquered race with equanimity. Their whole history showed them to be a virile fighting people who up till now had conquered all native races in their vicinity, and believed themselves to be superior to the white, with whom they had not as yet been fairly tested in battle. This primal fact, and the gross mismanagement on the part of the Chartered Company (which Selous himself admits) of the cattle question, produced a feeling of bitterness on the part of the Matabele, who, being above all things cattle-owners, and not slaves who had been conquered, resented the regulation exacting paid labour from every able-bodied man. The confiscation, too, of their cattle and the manner in which the confiscation was carried out added fuel to the fire. These circumstances, combined with the fact that the Matabele nation had not been beaten in war, were the causes for the outbreak in 1893. The Matabele, in fact, were still too raw to appreciate the advantages (sic) of civilization. They did without them. The assegai and the raid were to them still the heart of life. From the time of Umsilikatzie till now their forays amongst their more or less defenceless neighbours had, comparatively speaking, been one continuous success, even the fairly powerful Bechuanas under Khama were in a constant state of dread. Within a few years they ravaged all the country up to the Zambesi, and even sent two expeditions right across the waterless Kalahari to attack the Batauwani of Lake Ngami. These were indeed bold enterprises, as the marauders had to traverse nearly four hundred miles of desert almost devoid of game and only inhabited by a few bushmen. This first expedition, in 1883, was only partially successful, whilst the second one met with complete disaster. The Batauwani got wind of the impending attack and sent their women and children and cattle beyond the Botletlie river. They then ambushed the Matabele and killed many of them, whilst large numbers were drowned in trying to cross the river. Not a single head of cattle was captured, and hundreds of Lobengula's best warriors died from starvation, thirst, and exhaustion on the return journey, whilst only a remnant of the army got back to Bulawayo. One smaller party of Matabele went north by the Mababe river and eventually got back to Matabeleland by the northern route.

It was between 1883 and 1890 that the Matabele were most active in attacking their weaker neighbours. Sometimes with diabolic cunning they "nursed" the various Mashuna chiefs until the latter became rich in cattle and ivory and were ripe for slaughter. This they did to Chameluga, a powerful sorcerer, whom Lobengula professed to esteem and even to fear, but this favouritism was, after all, only an assumed pose, for in 1883 an army was sent to destroy the Situngweesa, of whom Chameluga was chief. The chief was summoned to Bulawayo, but was met at the Tchangani river, and all his party slaughtered with the exception of a young wife named Bavea, who was taken prisoner, but afterwards escaped to the north. Before his death, however, Chameluga had just time to send a young son to warn his people, and they took flight into the hilly country between the Mazoe and Inyagui rivers, and only a few were destroyed by the raiding Matabele who had followed their spoor. In 1888 an impi raided the Barotsi and killed the chief Sikabenga and most of his tribe.

In 1890 the Matabele also attacked and almost completely destroyed the large Mashuna tribe whose ladies were so wonderfully tattooed, and which Selous described as seeing east of the Sabi on his visit there in 1885. Selous does not mention this in his book, although he must later have been well aware of the fact.

In 1893 I found that all the plain and forest country here was swept clear of natives, but to the east of the Sabi there were villages of Gungunhlama's Shangans living on the tops of the kopjes, their little grass huts hanging to the sides of the cliffs like bunches of martins' nests. They told me that in 1890 a big impi of Matabele had annihilated the Mashunas that formerly lived there, and they themselves, even in their aerial fastnesses, lived in constant dread of attack.

Although the Matabele had not moved during the advent of the Pioneer Expedition to Mashunaland in 1890, Lobengula and his chiefs had been in a state of smouldering unrest since that time, and the best authorities considered that they intended to attack Bulawayo, Salisbury, and Victoria,

where many of the settlers and some troops had taken
refuge and gone into " laager " in the early part of 1893.
All signs pointed to a conflict, and when I reached the
Middle Drift of the Limpopo in May of that year, I was
strongly advised by the police officer in charge, Sergeant
Chauner (afterwards killed), to return to the Transvaal. As
he had no orders to stop me, and as I found my Boer friend,
Roelef van Staden, ready to go on, I went north across the
Umsingwani and shot some koodoos in Lobengula's pet
preserve. This led to trouble, as we were captured by
twelve Matabele warriors, who came to our camp and
insisted on our accompanying them to the king's kraal. Of
course we knew what this meant in wartime. Perhaps we
should be killed, and at the least it would involve a loss of
my whole outfit. So we sent most of the Boers and all the
women and children back to the Drift and vanished east-
wards in the night with our horses and a light waggon. In
the morning some Matabele came after us and shouted that
they intended to kill us and all the English that year, but
a few shots fired over their heads dispersed them. Baulked
of their prey the brutes then returned and assassinated a
dozen poor Makalaka Kafirs with whom we had encamped.

After our departure to the hunting-ground to the east,
only one Boer family, the Bezedenhuits, Mr. George Banks,
Captain Donovan, and a Mr. Mitchell,[1] of the 15th Hussars,
got into Mashunaland from the Transvaal, as the Matabele
soon made their unsuccessful attack on Victoria and communications with the north were stopped. We had various
adventures, but passed safely through the Matabele without
being detected on our return. Mr. George Banks went West
and Captain Donovan struck North and joined the British
forces, whilst Bezedenhuit went out through the Lower
Drift after a small fight with the Matabele.

In 1893 Selous returned to South Africa, went up country
by the Bamangwato route, and joined the Chartered Company forces there in September. From Fort Tuli he wrote
on September 30th :—

---

[1] This unfortunate gentleman went to hunt hippopotami at the mouth
of the Limpopo. Neither he nor any members of his outfit were ever
heard of again and they may have been wiped out by the Matabele.

" I reached here last Sunday and met Dr. Jameson.
News has just come in that the Matabele have attacked a
patrol near Fort Victoria, and in a fortnight's time the
Company's forces will be in a position to retaliate. At Dr.
Jameson's request I have remained with the force here,
which in case of necessity will co-operate with the Mashunaland column and attack the Matabele simultaneously from
the West, when they advance from the East. In the meantime I am going on a small scouting expedition with two
companions to examine the country along the western
borders of Matabeleland."

On this scouting trip he met with no adventures and he
returned to Tuli on October 11th. On October 19th he
started northward with Colonel Goold Adams' column. On
November 2nd his column met with its first opposition near
Impandini's kraal, when the Matabele made an attack on
some waggons coming into camp. " There was a bit of a
fight," Selous wrote to his mother, " and the Matabele were
driven off with considerable loss. I was unfortunate enough
to get wounded. As I am in very good health, this wound
is not at all dangerous, though, of course, it makes me
very stiff and sore all down the right side, but I shall soon
be all right again." Of the details of this day he wrote a
more complete account to his future wife.

" Owing to the miserable state of the oxen, a portion of
the waggons did not get up to us on November 1st, but were
left behind at a distance of about three miles from our main
column and the oxen sent on to the water. After drinking
they were sent back at once, and early on the morning of
November 2nd the waggons came on. Soon afterwards we
heard heavy firing and knew that the convoy was attacked.
As there were but few men with the convoy, assistance was
urgently needed, we knew, and the alarm was at once
sounded and the horses called in. I got hold of my horse
long before the troop horses came in, and, saddling him up,
galloped back alone to help the fellows with the waggons.
They were not far off, and were being attacked on all sides
by the Matabele, who were keeping up a hot fire and closing
in on both flanks and from the rear. Our fellows were

sticking to it well, though in small numbers. My appearance, I think, checked the Matabele a little, as, seeing one horseman gallop up, they naturally thought more were at hand. However, as I was very near them, and firing away at them, they fired a lot of shots at me. The whistling of the bullets made my horse very restive, and presently one of them hit me. The wound, however, is not dangerous. The bullet struck me about three inches below the right breast, but luckily ran round my ribs and came out behind, about eight inches from where it entered. The Matabele came right up to our camp, some being shot within three hundred yards of the laager with the Maxim. They were then beaten off and a good many of them killed, and had it not been that they got into a lot of thickly wooded hills close behind our camp their loss would have been much heavier. Our loss was two white men killed, and three wounded, including myself, and of our native allies two killed and several wounded. Before I came up the Matabele had captured a waggon, which they burnt, and killed Corporal Mundy, who was in charge of it. Sergeant Adahm was killed and two other men wounded after the Matabele had been driven off from the camp and whilst they were fighting them in a hill.

" Yesterday we pushed on and took up a splendid position here, where if we are attacked we shall be able to give a good account of ourselves."

The campaign of 1893 against the Matabele was short and a complete success. A compact force, part of which had gone up through the Transvaal, and part from the north, and consisting of 670 white men, of whom 400 were mounted, moved up under the command of Dr. Jameson. It was under the guidance of Nyemyezi, a Matabele chief who was bitterly opposed to Lobengula, and the force travelled unmolested until they reached the Tchangani river, where they were attacked by some 5000 Matabele of the Imbezu and Ingubu regiments, who were heavily defeated. On hearing this news Lobengula fled from Bulawayo and recalled his son-in-law, Gambo, from the Mangwe Pass, which gave opportunity to the southern column, under

Colonel Goold Adams, to whom Selous was attached as Chief of the Scouts, to move up and join Dr. Jameson's column. When this southern force of Matabele heard of the disaster on the Tchangani to their picked regiments they retired to the Matoppo hills and surrendered without fighting.

Meanwhile Lobengula continued to retreat north of the Tchangani, closely pursued by Major Wilson and his column, which, getting too far from his support, was surrounded and annihilated with his small force at the Tchangani river. Soon after this the powerful Matabele, forced into the trackless bush in the rainy season, and seeing their women and children dying of starvation and fever, surrendered in detail and accepted the liberal terms offered them. The whole campaign was settled by two battles, in which they attacked the white men in laager and suffered many reverses. The fighting spirit of the natives, however, was only scotched but not killed, as subsequent events showed.

On November 11th Selous gives some interesting details of the general progress of the campaign after the Matabele had attacked them and been driven north. " The Matabele generalship has been abominably bad. They never did what they ought to have done, and we took advantage of their opportunities. The strong British column from the East, advancing through open country, with a large force of mounted men and a large number of machine guns, simply carried everything before it, and on the two occasions when they attacked the ' laager ' the machine guns simply mowed them down. No one, knowing their abominable history, can pity them or lament their downfall. They have been paid back in their own coin.

" Our column advancing from the West had very great difficulties to contend with, as the whole country on that side is covered with thick bush and broken hills. Had the Matabele here made a determined opposition we could never have got through, and should probably have met with a disaster. But the large army opposed to us retired without fighting as soon as they heard that the King's forces had made an unsuccessful attack on the laager near

Bulawayo, and so we came in here (Bulawayo) without further trouble.

" So the campaign is virtually over, and the fair-haired descendants of the northern pirates are in possession of the Great King's kraal, and the ' Calf of the Black Cow '[1] has fled into the wilderness."

Writing from Bulawayo, where he went into hospital, November 27th, 1893, he says :—

" I am still here, but hope to get away now in a few days. My wound is getting on famously, and will be soon quite healed up. If I had not been in such good health it might have given a lot of trouble and taken a long time. These people (the Matabele) are thoroughly cowed and demoralized, and must be having a very bad time of it, as they are now living in the bush and must have very little to eat, and heavy rain is falling every day and night, which will not add to their comfort. The King has fled to the north, but his people seem to be dropping away from him, and I don't think he knows exactly what to do. Yesterday messengers came in here from him saying he was willing to submit, as he did not know what else to do and could go no further. If he surrenders he will, of course, be well treated, but removed from Matabeleland. His people evidently now wish to surrender and live under the government of white men, but there are such a lot of them that they will take up the whole country, and it would, I think, be much better if the King would go right away across the Zambesi and form a new kingdom for himself, just as his father fled from the Boers of the Transvaal and established himself in this country. If he would do that a large number of his people would go with him and the warlike element in this country would be removed, whereas, if they once come back, although they will be very humble at first, they may give trouble again later on."

A very true prophecy.

In December, 1893, Selous left Bulawayo, as he thought, for ever, having no intention to return to South Africa.

[1] Lobengula's native name.

He arrived home in England in February, 1894, and was married to Miss Marie Catherine Gladys Maddy, in her father's parish church at Down Hatherly, near Gloucester, on April 4th. Many old friends assembled at the Charing Cross Hotel to honour his marriage, and in a speech he said that his career as a Rugby boy had helped not only to support the fatigues which he had had to contend with, but to despise the strong boy who bullied the weak one and to admire the strong who guarded the weak. He thought that if any of those present should ever go to Matabeleland he would not hear anything that he had done but would become an Englishman as well as a Rugby boy. His Rugby friends subscribed together and gave him a handsome memento in the shape of a silver salver and ewer, and he was very proud of this gift.

Selous and his wife then went abroad for the honeymoon, passing through Switzerland and Italy. After a very pleasant visit to Venice they journeyed to Budapest, and on to their friends the Danfords, at Hatzeg in Transylvania, where Selous did a little egg-collecting. After some time spent in the mountains they went on down the Danube to Odessa, and so to Constantinople, where they made the acquaintance of Sir William Whittall, with whom Selous made plans to hunt in Asia Minor in the autumn of 1894. Selous and his wife then returned to England in July, and after his autumn trip to Smyrna, which is detailed later, he returned to Surrey and bought the land and arranged plans for renovating the house at Worplesdon which was afterwards his home. The original house was not large, but possessed a good area of land, flanked by a pretty and clear stream, and this plot was eventually made into a charming garden which Mrs. Selous has devoted care and energy to render beautiful and homelike. In later years a good orchard was added. The house was greatly added to and improved in 1899. At the same time as the house was being built a museum was erected close by, and in this all Selous' treasures, brought from his mother's house at Wargrave, were stored. As time went on it was found to be too small for his rapidly increasing collection, so in later years another wing was added, which made the whole building perhaps the largest private museum of its kind in Great Britain.

It was in August, 1894, that Selous went north for his first experiences of Highland sport. His destination was the Island of Mull, where for a fortnight he enjoyed the chase of the seal, the otter, and the wild goat, on the estate of Loch Buie, at the invitation of the Maclaine of Lochbuie. He thus describes his first search for seals and otters :—

" On August 16th, 1894, accompanied by the keepers MacColl and Nottman, I visited Loch Spelve in search of seals and otters. Skirting the shores of the loch in a small boat, we soon espied two seals lying out on a rock. They, however, winded us and slipped into the water, when we were still a long way off. We then went ashore and put the three terriers into a cairn which the keepers knew otters to be partial to, and from the behaviour of the dogs we soon became aware that one of the animals was somewhere about. Knowing that if the dogs succeeded in drawing the otter from the rocks it would make for the sea, I took up my position amongst the slippery seaweed covered with stones near the water and waited full of expectation. However, the otter resisted all the overtures of the terriers and would not bolt. Then MacColl, the wily, produced some evil-smelling fuse and, setting light to it, pushed it into a hole amongst the stones. The effect was magical, for the otter bolted at once almost between MacColl's legs. Instead, however, of coming towards the sea, it made back through the wood and took refuge in another cairn. From the second place of refuge another piece of fuse soon dislodged it, and this time making for the sea, it came past me in the open, travelling over the seaweed-covered rocks at no great pace. My first barrel knocked it over, but it quickly recovered itself, only to be again knocked down by my second left-hand barrel. This time it lay dead, and proved to be a fine bitch otter in excellent coat, weighing 14½ lbs. and measuring 3 ft. 6 ins. in length."

In January, 1895, he again went to Loch Buie and shot his first woodcock and other Highland game, and in January, 1897, he got his first pair of ptarmigan. It was in Ben Alder

Forest that he killed his first Highland stags, but the chase of red deer as conducted in Scotland did not, as we should expect, greatly appeal to him.

In September, 1894, Selous and his wife reached Bournabat near Smyrna, where he remained a short time as the guest of H. O. Whittall. From here, accompanied by his wife and the Whittalls, Selous made a short trip into the interior, with the intention of finding haunts of the wild goat (*Capra aegagrus*). After an interesting journey amongst the Turks and Yuruks he returned to the sea-coast, where in the Musa Dagh he did some hunting, but was unsuccessful in finding the old billies, only killing one male with small horns. On October 3rd he returned to Smyrna, and then went straight into the Ak Dagh to look for the long-faced red deer. These animals are now scarce and difficult to hunt in the dense forests, and he only succeeded in coming up to one good fourteen-pointer, which he killed with a long shot on October 19th.

He was, however, somewhat fascinated with this hunting in Asia Minor, for though the game was comparatively scarce and hunting difficult, owing to the rough nature of the ground and abundance of local hunters, yet it satisfied his idea of what is called " high-class sport." Selous never liked to admit failure with any animal, so at the end of January, 1895, he again made a trip to Asia Minor in the hope of getting good specimens of the wild goat and, if possible, the black mouflon (*Ovis gmelini*). This time he decided to hunt the Maimun Dagh, a great mass of mountains situated close to the Smyrna railway. For a fortnight he toiled up and down its steep and parched cliffs, and then at last he saw and got a shot at one of the patriarchs with long horns. This goat he wounded very badly and lost, but some days later a Turk saw a large goat fall from a cliff and remain suspended by its horns in a tree, where he despatched it. This was without doubt the fine male which Selous had lost, and he was lucky enough to obtain the head. A few days later he found another grand billy, alas with only one horn. This he also killed and lost, but found it the next day. Two other fair specimens made up his bag, so on the whole the expedition was quite successful. Then he returned to England in February.

Although so recently married, Selous found that living in England was too expensive, and this, combined with the " call of the wild," which never left him, evolved a new spirit of restlessness and desire once more to live in the open veldt and to see the game. To this was added the request of an old friend, Mr. Maurice Heany, who asked him to go into Matabeleland and assist him in the management of a land and gold-mining company. After consulting his wife, who was willing to share the troubles and difficulties of the new country, Selous accepted the post, which was to occupy him for two years.

Accordingly Selous and his wife left England in March, 1895, and after spending two months in Cape Colony and the Free State, where he shot some springbuck, blesbuck, and black wildebeest for his collection, he took ship to Beira and then went by rail to Chimoio, where he met his waggon and oxen, and passed on via Salisbury, the Hanyane river, to Bulawayo. At the Sebakwe river he fired at what he thought was a jackal, but on arriving near the animal, which he expected to find dead, as he had heard the bullet strike, he was suddenly charged by a leopard. The angry beast passed right under his stirrup-iron, and after going thirty yards stopped and sat on its haunches. Another shot at once killed it.

The Selous now left for Essexvale, the farm of his company, and took up their quarters in a rough wood and mud two-roomed house which was to be their home until the wire-wove bungalow, which had been sent out from England in sections, should arrive and be erected. It was whilst travelling to Essexvale that Selous met his old friend, Mr. Helm, the missionary, who by his long residence amongst the Matabele was thoroughly conversant with native views. Mr. Helm said that on the whole the natives had accepted the new regime, but that they were highly incensed at the confiscation of their cattle by the Chartered Company. The natives at first were told that after all the cattle had been branded with the Company's mark and handed back to the natives, only the king's cattle would be confiscated. " This promise," says Selous, " was made under the belief that nearly all the cattle in Matabeleland had belonged to the king and that the private owners had been but few in number." This was a great mistake, for nearly every chief induna and men of any position had possessed large herds of their own.

At Bulawayo Selous found a ruined kraal, since it had been burnt and deserted by the Matabele after their defeat in 1893. The site of the new town had been marked out by the settlers, who had camped close by, and a general air of hope and prosperity hung over the scene of the new British town that was shortly to arise from the ashes of the past. No difficulties with the natives were apprehended, and farms and town-sites were at a high value. No one, in fact, dreamed that in a few months the whole country would be overwhelmed in the calamity of the rinderpest—a cattle disease that swept from Abyssinia to the Cape and killed in its course nearly the whole stock of cattle, as well as many fine species of game, such as buffalo, eland, koodoo, etc. Added to this the Matabele again rose, burnt the farms, and in many cases murdered all the new settlers and carried destruction throughout the whole country north of the Limpopo. To add to these horrors a bad drought and an unusual plague of locusts rendered farming and transport practically impossible.

There were some 70,000 cattle at this time in the hands of the natives, and a final settlement was made by which the Chartered Company retained two-fifths, giving the remaining three-fifths to the natives, a settlement by which for the time being the natives appeared satisfied.

All through the autumn and winter of 1895 life passed quietly at Essexvale. The new house arrived, and was erected just before the rains set in on a high position eighty feet above the Ingnaima river. The Company bought 1200 head of cattle which were distributed amongst the natives. Five thousand gum-trees were raised from seed and planted on some forty acres of ploughed land, the other products including maize and fruit trees of various kinds.

P

All this time the natives appeared to be happy and contented, whilst Umlugula, a relation of Lobengula, and a great chief under his rule, now living some eighteen miles away, constantly visited Selous and seemed as quiet as the rest, although he was actively plotting the rebellion which was shortly to break out. Selous afterwards thought that the cause of the insurrection was the withdrawal of the Matabeleland Police Force and their munitions of war, and its subsequent capture by the Boers in the ill-starred " Jameson Raid."

The first cloud of trouble appeared in February, 1896, when news was spread that the " Umlimo," or god of the Makalakas, who lived in a cave in the Matoppo hills, had said that the white man's blood was about to be spilt. It was also rumoured that Lobengula was not dead, as previously reported, but was coming with a large army from the north-east and west. Umlimo also claimed to have sent the rinderpest which at this date had already reached Northern Matabeleland.

So far, however, there were merely rumours, and old residents in the country, with the single exception of Mr. Usher, believed that nothing was to be feared. Mr. Jackson, a native commissioner, thought that if the natives rose a certain danger was to be expected from the Matabele Police, who had been armed with Winchesters and were kept for the purposes of law and order, and in this he was right, for half of this body revolted and attacked their former employers.

The " Umlimo " was a kind of native hereditary priest whose family are supposed to inherit supernatural powers. His family are known as the children of the god and all are supposed to commune with the unseen deity. He lived in the Matoppo Hills, where the people visited their " god " and consulted him. He was supposed to speak all languages, and could moreover roar like a lion, bark like a dog, and do other wonderful things. There seemed to have been other Umlimos in other tribes, and it is somewhat strange that this " deity " of the despised Makalakas should have been possessed of such influence over the powerful Matabele.

Lobengula at any rate constantly visited and even feared this man, and there is no doubt that Lobengula and his chiefs made full use of him in the present instance to excite the natives.

In the middle of March Selous was appointed to inspect the Umsingwani and Insiza district and try and stop the spread of the rinderpest to the south, and in this he was powerless, as trek-oxen further carried the infection. At Dawson's store on March 22nd he heard that a native policeman had been killed and that the murderers with their women and children had fled to the Matoppo hills. This was the first overt act of the rebellion.

Immediately after this two attacks were made on the native police, and Selous found when he arrived home that some Matabele had borrowed axes from Mrs. Selous, and had left with them ostensibly to repair their cattle-kraals, but in reality to attack the settlers. The following night three miners, Messrs. Foster, Eagleson and Anderson, carrying on work at Essexvale, were attacked and murdered as well as several other Europeans in the neighbourhood. Next day most of the Essexvale cattle were driven off by the natives, so that there was now no doubt that a rising was imminent. Selous therefore took his wife into Bulawayo for safety, and returned at once with an armed force of thirty-eight men, intending if possible to recover his cattle ; but by this time the flame of rebellion had spread to the whole of the north, and numerous white men, women and children had been brutally murdered.

At least nine-tenths of the Matabele natives were now in arms against the whites, who were very badly equipped and in sore straits for arms, ammunition, cattle and horses. Their position was somewhat desperate, but, as ever before and since, the settlers nobly responded to the call to arms, although there was really no organized force worth speaking of. However, about five hundred good men and true assembled at Bulawayo, from which it was almost impossible to move owing to the absence of horses. This force only had some 580 rifles, but a good supply of ammunition—1,500,000 rounds. There was also a ·303 Maxim and an old gun or two. This is all they had with which to resist some 10,000 Matabele, of which at least one-fifth had breechloading rifles and plenty of ammunition. The tactics of the Matabele, however, were indifferent, and it is somewhat incomprehensible that they never blocked the main road to the south or attacked waggons or coaches moving along it.

Of the 1000 white men in Bulawayo only about 300 were available for active operations, as 400 had always to be kept for the defence of the women and children in the town : but in addition to this force a regiment of native boys, mostly Zulus, was organized by Colonel Johan Colenbrander,[1] and did excellent scouting work. This little force of white and black eventually drove the Matabele from the neighbourhood of Bulawayo and rescued many small isolated detachments, whilst keeping the enemy at bay until the arrival of Sir Frederick Carrington, who eventually completed their rout.

But to return to the movements of Selous after he revisited his farm. He was not long in finding part of his stolen cattle and burning the kraal where they were found. Then he searched for the rebels and found them in the act

---

[1] Col. Johan Colenbrander, as his name implies, was of Dutch origin. He was born at Pinetown, Natal, in 1859. At the age of twenty he was a skilled shot and hunter, and kept a general store in Swaziland close to the King's kraal. His first wife Maria was then the only white woman in Swaziland. She was a beautiful woman, one of the daughters of Mr. John Mullins, of Natal, and was an expert rider and rifle-shot. Colenbrander was a born hunter and fighter and took part in all the recent wars in South Africa. He was also an excellent linguist, speaking fluently several native dialects. He served with distinction in the Zulu War, and in 1889 and again in 1890 accompanied the Matabele envoys to England as guide and interpreter. From 1895 he held several positions under the Chartered Company. In 1893 he remained with Lobengula as peace envoy when the Pioneers entered Mashunaland. In 1896 he organized and officered " Colenbrander's Boys," and in the second Boer War in 1901 he took command of Kitchener's Fighting Scouts and rendered good service, being mentioned in despatches and receiving the C.B. His second wife was Yvonne, daughter of Captain Loftus Nunn, and she died after two years of marriage, whilst his third wife Kathleen, daughter of Mr. James Gloster, survives him. Colenbrander all his life liked to go where sport, life, war and adventure called, and was ever a loyal friend to Britain. As a hunter Selous reckoned him as one of the most experienced in South Africa. He was unfortunately drowned in Feb., 1918, whilst taking part in a cinema performance representing the Zulu War. As he was crossing the Klip river his horse became restive, and he threw himself off and tried to swim to the bank ; when on the point of being rescued he threw up his arms and sank.

of driving off more cattle. These he attacked and recovered some 150 cattle belonging to Colenbrander. Selous then returned to Essexvale on March 26th, and left the herd of cattle there in charge of loyal natives because he feared they would be attacked by rinderpest if he drove them into Bulawayo. This, however, may have been a mistake, since Inxnozan, a native Matabele warrior, and some three hundred of his men came in a few days and burnt the farm and carried off all the cattle.

Selous then took his men to Spiro's Store in the Matoppo hills in the hope of finding or rendering assistance to Mr. Jackson, the native commissioner, who was reported to have been murdered with the whole force of native police. He was now entering the Matabele stronghold, where large forces of the enemy were likely to be encountered. He put his best men out to scout ahead. In a gorge in the hills the enemy were found in some force, and Selous' men drove them off after some sharp fighting. Selous himself was fired at at a distance of fifteen yards, but fortunately the shot missed. Cattle to the number of one hundred were found, and Selous endeavoured to drive them, but the enemy again attacked, when four horses were killed and two men wounded. After this small fight he returned to Bulawayo, where he was delighted to find his friend Mr. Jackson, who had been given up for dead. Soon afterwards Selous went on patrol and visited the Mangwe laager, and on the way saw much of the ravages of the rinderpest. At one spot at a farm near Bulawayo "acres of carcasses were lying festering in the sun."

Various patrols, under Colonel the Hon. Maurice Gifford, Captain Brand, Captain Van Niekerk, Captain Grey and others all had sharp fighting with the Matabele, and relieved many isolated bodies of white men.

In April Selous was appointed Captain of the " H " troop of the Bulawayo Field Force, and went out to clear the road and establish forts at Fig Tree and Mangwe. First he erected a very strong little fort called Fort Molyneux. Further on, at Fort Halstead, he made another, and at the Matoli river a third. All this he did with the Matabele army

lying on the Khami river, about twelve miles west of Bulawayo, whilst another large army was in the Elibaini hills
close by. Yet they did not attack Selous' patrols or fort
builders, and did not approach Bulawayo until the middle
of April, when a small fight occurred between the scouts
under Grey and Van Niekerk and a large body of the enemy.
The scouts then returned. Shortly after this Selous joined
in patrols with Captain Macfarlane and Captain Bisset in
trying to dislodge the enemy from positions close to the
town, and in the last-named attack on the Umguza the
Matabele lost heavily. During this fight, and whilst firing
hard, Selous' pony ran away and he was soon surrounded by
large numbers of Matabele.

The incident is best related in his own words :—[1]

" A few bullets were again beginning to ping past us, so
I did not want to lose any time, but before I could take my
pony by the bridle he suddenly threw up his head and
spinning round trotted off, luckily in the direction from
which we had come. Being so very steady a pony, I imagine
that a bullet must have grazed him and startled him into
playing me this sorry trick at such a very inconvenient
moment. ' Come on as hard as you can, and I'll catch your
horse and bring him back to you,' said Windley, and started
off after the faithless steed. But the steed would not allow
himself to be caught, and when his pursuer approached him
broke from a trot into a gallop, and finally showed a clean
pair of heels.

" When my pony went off with Windley after him,
leaving me, comparatively speaking, *planté là*, the Kafirs
thought they had got me, and commenced to shout out
encouragingly to one another and also to make a kind of
hissing noise, like the word " jee " long drawn out. All this
time I was running as hard as I could after Windley and my
runaway horse. As I ran, carrying my rifle at the trail, I
felt in my bandolier with my left hand to see how many
cartridges were still at my disposal, and found that I had
fired away all but two of the thirty I had come out with, one
being left in the belt and the other in my rifle. Glancing

[1] " Sunshine and Storm in Rhodesia," pp. 161–163, published by
Rowland Ward and Co.

round, I saw that the foremost Kafirs were gaining on me fast, though had this incident occurred in 1876 instead of 1896, with the start I had got I would have run away from any of them.

" Windley, after galloping some distance, realized that it was useless wasting any more time trying to catch my horse, and like a good fellow came back to help me ; and had he not done so, let me here say that the present history would never have been written, for nothing could possibly have saved me from being overtaken, surrounded, and killed. When Windley came up to me he said, ' Get up behind me ; there's no time to lose,' and pulled his foot out of the left stirrup for me to mount. Without any unnecessary loss of time, I caught hold of the pommel of the saddle, and got my foot into the iron, but it seemed to me that my weight might pull Windley and the saddle right round ; as a glance over my shoulder showed me that the foremost Kafirs were now within a hundred yards of us, I hastily pulled my foot out of the stirrup again, and shifting my rifle to the left hand caught hold of the thong round the horse's neck with my right, and told Windley to let him go. He was a big, strong animal, and as, by keeping my arm well bent, I held my body close to him, he got me along at a good pace, and we began to gain on the Kafirs. They now commenced to shoot, but being more or less blown by hard running, they shot very badly, though they put the bullets all about us. Two struck just by my foot, and one knocked the heel of Windley's boot off. If they could have only hit the horse, they would have got both of us.

" After having gained a little on our pursuers, Windley, thinking I must have been getting done up, asked me to try again to mount behind him ; no very easy matter when you have a big horse to get on to, and are holding a rifle in your right hand. However, with a desperate effort I got up behind him ; but the horse, being unaccustomed to such a proceeding, immediately commenced to buck, and in spite of spurring would not go forwards, and the Kafirs, seeing our predicament, raised a yell and came on again with renewed ardour.

" Seeing that if I stuck on the horse behind Windley we should both of us very soon lose our lives, I flung myself off in the middle of a buck, and landed right on the back of my neck and shoulders. Luckily I was not stunned or in any way hurt, and was on my legs and ready to run again, with my hand on the thong round the horse's neck in a very creditably short space of time. My hat had fallen off, but I never let go of my rifle, and as I didn't think it quite the best time to be looking for a hat, I left it, all adorned with the colours of my troop as it was, to be picked up by the enemy, by whom it has no doubt been preserved as a souvenir of my presence among them.

" And now another spurt brought us almost up to John Grootboom and the five or six colonial boys who were with him, and I called to John to halt the men and check the Matabele who were pursuing us, by firing a volley past us at them. This they did, and it at once had the desired effect, the Kafirs who were nearest to us hanging back and waiting for those behind to join them. In the meantime Windley and I joined John Grootboom's party, and old John at once gave me his horse, which, as I was very much exhausted and out of breath, I was very glad to get. Indeed, I was so tired by the hardest run I had ever had since my old elephant-hunting days, that it was quite an effort to mount. I was now safe, except that a few bullets were buzzing about, for soon after getting up to John Grootboom we joined the main body of the colonial boys, and then, keeping the Matabele at bay, retired slowly towards the position defended by the Maxim. Our enemies, who had been so narrowly baulked of their expected prey, followed us to the top of a rise, well within range of the guns, but disappeared immediately a few sighting shots were fired at them.

" Thus ended a very disagreeable little experience, which but for the cool courage of Captain Windley would have undoubtedly ended fatally to myself. Like many brave men, Captain Windley is so modest that I should probably offend him were I to say very much about him ; but at any rate I shall never forget the service he did me at the risk of his own life that day on the Umguza, whilst the personal gallantry he has always shown throughout the present campaign as a leader of our native allies has earned for him such respect and admiration that they have nicknamed him ' Inkunzi ' (the bull), the symbol of strength and courage."

After this exciting incident, Selous, having lost his horse, managed to get another, and assisted Captain Mainwaring in repairing the telegraph wires to Fig Tree Fort, which had been cut. He then rejoined his troop, which arrived from Matoli. On the way they found the bodies of two transport riders killed by followers of Babian and Umsheti.[1]

Selous then built Fort Marquand on the top of a kopje, which commanded the road and a splendid view of the surrounding country. After a brief visit to Bulawayo he again went north to build a fort at the Khami river, and afterwards visited Marzwe's kraal, which had been attacked by an impi.

On his return to Bulawayo he found the large column commanded by Col. Napier despatched to the Tchangani river to meet the column coming from Salisbury under Colonel Beal, with which was Cecil Rhodes. This column, the largest sent out from Bulawayo, inflicted severe punishment on the Matabele. On May 20th the Salisbury column was met, and after considerable fighting the whole force returned to Bulawayo, having suffered but small loss. On the way a number of the mutilated corpses of white men and women were found and buried. The history of these murders Selous relates in his book on the campaign.[2]

Shortly before the arrival of the Field Force and Salisbury Column, Colonel (now Sir Herbert) Plumer had arrived with a strong body of troops from the south, and the back of the rebellion was broken, for this gallant officer attacked the enemy and drove them from the neighbourhood of Bulawayo, whilst in June General Sir Frederick Carrington, who had now taken over the supreme command, cleared the districts surrounding the Matoppo hills, and then to the north and east, the rebels retreating as the patrols advanced.

[1] Lobengula's Prime Minister, whom I met in 1893 and whose portrait I executed for the " Daily Graphic " in that year.

[2] " Sunshine and Storm in Rhodesia."

On June 7th Selous proceeded with Colonel Spreckley's patrol to Shiloh, where but little resistance was encountered, and on the 4th of July the campaign may be considered at an end, when the Bulawayo Field Force was disbanded. Thus ended one of the many little native wars in which British colonists, nobly assisted by Boer contingents, overcame under great difficulties a strong and well-armed nation of savages, who, if they had been properly organized, might easily have overwhelmed our small forces. The Matabele, the last strong savage power in South Africa, were beaten by good " morale " and tenacity on the part of the whites, who were incensed at the brutal savagery displayed by their enemies, for if they had not fought for their lives not only they but all their wives and children would have been murdered. Mr. Labouchere's choice phrase, " that the natives are being shot down like game at a battue, with apparently *as little danger* to the shooters as to those killing hares and rabbits," was as great a travesty of the case as it was mendacious.

Selous, at any rate in 1896, was a firm believer in the future of what is now called Southern Rhodesia, and at that date wrote : " It is known throughout South Africa that Matabeleland and Mashunaland are white men's countries, where Europeans can live and thrive and rear strong healthy children ; that they are magnificent countries for stock-breeding, and that many portions of them will prove suitable for Merino sheep and Angora goats ; whilst agriculture and fruit-growing can be carried on successfully almost everywhere in a small way, and in certain districts, especially in Mashunaland and Manica, where there is a greater abundance of water on a fairly extensive scale.

" As for the gold, there is every reason to believe that out of the enormous number of reefs which are considered by their owners to be payable properties, some small proportion at least will turn up trumps, and, should this proportion only amount to two per cent, that will be quite sufficient to ensure a big output of gold in the near future, which will in its turn ensure the prosperity of the whole country."

He moreover predicted that when the railway reached

Bulawayo success would be assured, but that this success would be destroyed if the British South Africa Company's Charter was revoked and the affairs of the colony administered by Imperial rule. Whether these hopeful views, honest as they are, have been fulfilled, still remains to be seen.

Shortly after the British occupation of Mashunaland the Chartered Company made an immense effort to " boom " the country and induce settlers and investors to become interested in it. The papers were filled with accounts of the " New Eldorado," whose gold mines were to rival the Rand, and whose lands were to teem with flocks and herds of sheep and cattle on a scale that would make Canada and other parts of South Africa look quite small. The effect was to drive up the Chartered £1 Shares to over £7, and to create some apprehension in the minds of the few old South Africans who really knew the assets of what is, as a matter of fact, a country of only average possibilities. Its successful gold mines have, after years of test, proved only of moderate wealth, and these are only few in number, whilst the farming industry that was to have supplied the wants of all the local population as well as great quantities of cattle for export, has not yet proved a great success. In fact, after twenty years, the gallant Rhodesian farmers are still living on hope. There are too many adverse features against the man who farms stock in Rhodesia, even if he possesses capital, whilst the settler without money has no earthly chance to make good. Through all these years every effort has been made by the Chartered Company to induce the right kind of settler to go there, but on the whole their efforts have not met with any great success, or, after all this time, we should not read the usual note of hope in the " Times " report of the " Mashunaland Agency," November 17th, 1917 :—

" Test shipments of frozen meat have already been made from Rhodesia to England, and the results were favourably reported on by experts. It would seem, in short, that South Africa and Rhodesia may well become successful competitors in the meat supplies of the world, and this Company has already secured an early start in this development of an important industry.   We have recently added sheep-breeding to our ranching operations, although at present on a small scale only."

The high rate of freight and expense of transport from an isolated region like Rhodesia will be the great difficulty in the future, even if they can raise the stock, and the country will have to compete with Canada, New Zealand, and South America, all countries which have now good, cheap, well-organized methods of transport and shipment.   It must not be supposed that Rhodesia has suffered altogether from a lack of the right kind of settlers.   On the contrary, the most cheerful, industrious type of gentleman-farmer has tried to " make good " there and when backed by capital has just managed, after years of toil, to make both ends meet.   If the reader wishes to know the absolute truth about conditions of life there let him ask some of the old settlers who are independent in opinion and have no land to sell, and let him read the novels of Gertrude Page and Cynthia Stockley, and he will glean a far more accurate picture of life in Southern Rhodesia than from any company reports or blue books.   Romance is often truth, whilst complete distortion may lie in official dreams.

The British South African Company is ever active in trying to get the right kind of settlers in Southern Rhodesia and we have no fault to find with them for that if they were to put them in healthy, fertile areas, but what are the actual prospects of success there compared with other British colonies.   They too have a post-war land-scheme of offering ex-soldiers a free land-grant of 500,000 acres.   It sounds generous, but if it is to grant free blocks of land (in Scotland) of the class offered to ex-soldiers without capital by the Duke of Sutherland, I feel very sorry for the poor soldiers. All the land of any value in South Rhodesia is already taken up by settlers, whilst a great part of the country is totally unfit for " white man " colonization.

The following is written by a lady now resident as a farmer's wife in South Rhodesia, and gives accurately the various pros and cons and the prospect of success to-day in that colony.

" Do not resign your position as any kind of brass hat to come out here, if making money is your aim and object. Even our wealthiest farmers are not on the way to being plutocrats. After all, we are 6000 miles from our best market. But should fate or fortune land you here, you who love the sky and the open road, and the starry solitudes of an African night, the clear-cut outline of granite hills against a sapphire sky and the fragrance of a flower-jewelled veld, the whirr of startled birds and the crash of game as it bounds through the bush, I think you would find it difficult to return to the troglodyte life of London.—ETHEL COLQUHOUN JOLLIE." (" The Field," April 6th, 1918.)

When the boom in " Things Rhodesian " was at its height, some truth of the real state of affairs seemed to have reached British investors. Henry Labouchere doubtless got hold of a good deal of perfectly correct information and much that was decidedly otherwise. With his characteristic audacity in exposing all shams he, in a series of articles in " Truth," ruthlessly attacked the Chartered Company and all exploiters and " boomers " of the new territory. Much of what he wrote was the truth, but with it all, most of his criticisms were too scathing and hopelessly inaccurate. Amongst those classed as rascals who came under the lash of his pen was Fred Selous, a man who knew no more about business than a child, and who was not associated in the smallest degree with any financier, and who had never written one word about the country he was not prepared to substantiate. To those who knew Selous and his perfect immunity from all stock-dealing transactions the whole thing was simply ridiculous, but the Great Public, after all, is too often prone to believe any libel if it is constantly repeated. In consequence Selous was much depressed by these attacks and resented them bitterly, for he knew he was wholly innocent, yet being advised that he would not advance his position by replying in the newspapers he resolved to bide his time and reply to them *in toto* in a work he had under preparation (" Sunshine and Storm in Rhodesia ").

Mr. Burlace (of Rowland Ward, Ltd., who had bought the

rights of his new book) met Selous at Plymouth on his arrival in 1896, and fortunately persuaded him not to mention controversial matters to the numerous pressmen who were there and wished to hear what he had to say concerning Mr. Labouchere's articles. Selous was, however, still anxious to thresh out the whole matter in his book, but Mr. Burlace, who has very considerable business knowledge and a firm conviction that the public do not care two straws about controversial matters after the subject is, so to speak, "dead," gave him good advice to avoid the discussion as far as possible and to let the public learn by a man's own character, past and future, who speaks the truth. That was sound logic, and Selous profited thereby, although he did answer many of Labouchere's gross libels on the Bulawayo Field Force.

In many ways Rowland Ward and the members of his staff were good friends to Selous for a considerable part of his life. They bought his specimens at a good price, looked after his affairs at home before he married, and helped him in a hundred ways. Rowland Ward purchased the rights of Selous' new book, "Travel and Adventure in South-East Africa," and gave the author a good sum of money for his work. If "A Hunter's Wanderings" made Selous known to the public, "Travel and Adventures in South-East Africa" assured his reputation, made money for him when he badly wanted it, and fixed a definite value to his future books and the numerous contributions he made to scientific and sporting literature. "Sunshine and Storm in Rhodesia," published by Rowland Ward and Co., was also a success and gave the public a clear and truthful account of the second Matabele war and did much to enhance the author's reputation. This book he dedicated to his wife "who, during the last few months, has at once been my greatest anxiety and my greatest comfort."

It had long been one of Selous' ambitions to add to his collection the heads of that rare and beautiful antelope, the Nyala, or Angas's bushbuck, *Tragelaphus angasi*, whose habitat was the dense bush stretching along the coast from St. Lucia Bay, Zululand, to the Sabi river in Portuguese territory, east of Mashunaland. It has also more recently been found in Nyassaland. Wherefore, as soon as he left Matabeleland and reached Kimberley, he left his wife and went to Delagoa Bay, intending to hunt this animal for a short time in the dense thickets which border the Pongolo and Usutu rivers in Amatongaland. Only three Englishmen previously had had personal acquaintance with this somewhat rare antelope, namely, Angas who discovered it, Baldwin in 1854, and Drummond, 1867–1872, all of whom wrote of its great beauty, cunning nature, and the pestilential climate in which it lived.

In Delagoa Bay Selous was fortunate enough to meet a certain colonist named Wissels, who owned a small trading station near the junction of the Pongolo and Usutu rivers, right in the heart of the habitat of the Nyala. Wissels was returning home next day in his sea-going boat and Selous made some swift preparations and accompanied him. In two days he reached the Maputa and proceeded overland, with three women carriers, to Wissels' station, where he found numerous freshly captured skins and horns of the animal he had come to hunt. For the next few days, in pouring rain, he crept through the bush with native hunters, and was fortunate enough to bag three fine male and two female Nyala, a pair of which are now in the Natural History Museum in London ; the heads of the two other males are in the collection at Worplesdon. He was somewhat disappointed not to shoot the rare little Livingstone's Suni, one of which he saw, as it was one of the few rare antelopes he did not possess. After a long tramp of eighty miles through deep sand he reached Delagoa Bay on October 7th, and then returned to Kimberley, and so to England, not, however, completely escaping the inevitable attacks of fever which are the lot of all who hunt the Nyala in the feverish swamps and thickets of the East Coast.

CHAPTER X

1896–1907

AS soon as Selous and his wife returned home at the end of 1896 he finished off the notes he had made concerning the second Matabele War, and delivered them to Rowland Ward & Co., who published his book, " Sunshine and Storm in Rhodesia," shortly afterwards. From this time forward he did a considerable amount of literary work, which, being in demand, gave him sufficient money to satisfy many of his more pressing wants at home, as well as supplying funds for the numerous short trips he now made every year. Owing in a large measure to the kindly help and advice given to him by a South African friend, his finances were now put on a sound basis, and he was able to look forward to being able to live at home in comfort without being denied those short periods of wandering which to him were part of his existence. Of course there were always ups and downs due to market fluctuations, and when things went wrong for a while he would have fits of depression that he would be unable to hunt any more ; but these always passed away sooner or later when the clouds lifted and some new piece of work commanded a good price. There is little doubt that a man enjoys best that for which he has worked. All Selous' later hunts were the outcome of his industry with the pen, and in some measure from lectures, so he experienced some joy in the working, for it meant to him the camp fire and the open road.

In reading of his almost continuous wanderings after this date it must not be supposed that he was not happy in his home life. As a matter of fact no man considered himself more blessed by fortune in the possession of wife and children, and every fresh expedition, when he felt impelled

LIONS CHASING A KOODOO BULL.

as it were to go to the wilds, was fraught with misgivings and anxieties for his loved ones at home. It was always a wrench when the time came. He wrote once to Roosevelt on this point, and received the following sympathetic answer :—

". . . After all, there is nothing that in any way comes up to home and wife and children, in spite of the penalty one has to pay for having given hostages to fortune. I know just exactly how you feel about the 'two hearts.' Having a wife and six children, of whom I am very fond, I have found it more and more difficult to get away ; for the last eight years, indeed, my hunting trips have merely been short outings. I am of course very much interested in my work here ; but I cannot say how I long at times for the great rolling prairies of sun-dried yellow grass, where the antelopes stand at gaze, or wheel and circle ; for the splintered cottonwoods on the bank of some shrunken river, with the wagon drawn up under them, and the ponies feeding round about ; for the great pine forests, where the bull elk challenge, and the pack-train threads its way through the fallen timber. I long also for the other wilderness which I have never seen, and never shall see, excepting through your books, and the books of two or three men like you who are now dead. It may be that some time I can break away from this sedentary life for a hunt somewhere ; and of all things possible to me, I should like to take this hunt among the big bears of Alaska, and try to work out their specific relationship. But I don't know whether I shall ever get the chance ; and of course this sedentary life gradually does away with one's powers ; though I can walk and shoot a little yet. Politics is a rather engrossing pursuit, and, un-fortunately, with us it is acute in the Fall, at the very time of the best hunting ; and as my children grow older I am more and more concerned with giving them a proper training for their life-work, whatever it may be. I don't yet accept the fact that I shall never get the chance to take some big hunt again, and perhaps it may come so I shall be able to ; and meanwhile I do revel in all the books about big game, and when I can get out to my ranch even for ten days, I

Q

enjoy it to the last point, taking an old cow-pony and shambling off across the grassy flats for a few days' camping, and the chance of an occasional prong-buck.

" I am glad you like to chat with me even by letter. Ever since reading your first book I have always wanted to meet you. I hope I may have better luck next year than I had this. You will of course let me know if you think I can be of any help to you in your Canadian trip.

" The Colonel X. whom I wrote to you about is, I am quite sure, what we should term a fake, although I also have no doubt that he has actually done a good deal of big game hunting ; but I am certain that, together with his real experiences, he puts in some that are all nonsense. Did you ever read the writings of a man named Leveson, who called himself ' the Old Shikari ' ? He was undoubtedly a great hunter ; yet when he wrote about American big game, I know that he stretched the long bow, and I am very sure he did the same about African big game. He everywhere encountered precisely those adventures which boys' books teach us to expect. Thus as soon as he got to Africa, he witnessed a vicious encounter between black rhinoceroses and elephants, which would have done credit to Mayne Reid ; exactly as Colonel X. relates the story of a fearful prize-fight, in which a captive English Major slays a gorilla, against which he is pitted by a cannibal king—dates, names and places being left vacant.

" What do you know of that South African hunter and writer named Drummond ? He wrote very interestingly, and gave most vivid descriptions of hunting-camps, of the African scenery, and of adventures with lions and buffaloes ; but his remarks about rhinoceroses made me think he was not always an exact observer, especially after I had read what you said.

" By the way, did I ever mention to you that Willie Chanler's party was continually charged by black rhinoceroses, and his companion, an Austrian named Von Höhnel, who stayed with me once, was badly mauled by one."

Like most schoolboys with a taste for natural history and

an adventurous disposition Selous had, as we have seen, been an industrious bird-nester. In his youth he had commenced to make a collection of European birds' eggs, and this taste, usually abandoned by most boys in after-life, was in him only dormant. When he set out to do anything he generally carried it through to the end ; and so when opportunity came again, as it did after his wanderings in South Africa were finished, he seized it with avidity. He was much too good a naturalist to collect eggs wholesale, as some collectors unfortunately do, but contented himself with one or two clutches taken by himself. His contention was, I think, a correct one, that if only one clutch of eggs of a bird is taken, the same bird either sits again and lays a fresh set of eggs or makes a new nest. So little or no harm is done.

Being a member of the British Ornithologists' Union he knew all the regular egg-collectors, and soon obtained the best information where various species were to be found. Each year as April came round he packed his bag and, occasionally accompanied by some local enthusiast, he went to all the best resorts of rare birds in England, Scotland, the Orkneys, Asia Minor, Spain, Hungary, Holland, and Iceland.

Thus in 1897 he commenced the egg-hunting season by going to Smyrna in February with the intention of taking the nests of the large raptorial birds which there breed very early in the year. The point he made for was the Murad Dagh, a range of mountains in the interior of Asia Minor, where he knew the short-toed, golden and imperial eagles, and the black and griffon vultures nested. He also had some hopes that he might secure one of the big stags before they dropped their horns. On his journey he suffered much from the cold in the mountains, and was also at first unsuccessful in finding any of the big stags, who seemed to have been hunted out of the range. He saw three fine stags but did not succeed in finding one of those which he had wounded. He then returned to Smyrna and went into the Maimun Dagh again. Here he took the eggs of black vulture, griffon vulture, short-toed eagle and lämmergeier. Getting tired of

this range he went on to the Ak Dagh, where he took one
golden eagle's nest, three griffon vultures' eggs, and two of
black vultures. He also shot a young red deer, with which
was a fine old stag that had just dropped its horns. He
returned to England in March.

In England he commenced his nesting operations in April
by hunting Thatcham Marsh (near Reading) for water-rails'
nests, and took two. Then he went on to the Scilly Isles for
sea-birds.

He says, in a letter to me : " I am going to Brabant if I
can obtain a permit from the Dutch Government to collect
a few eggs, and after that to Scotland, where I shall remain
until it is time to leave for America." In Scilly, he says :
" I got eggs of the Greater and Lesser Black-backed Gulls,
Herring Gull, Manx Shearwater, Oyster-catcher, and Ringed
Plover, but found no Terns breeding." On June 8th he
decided to put off his trip to Holland, as it was too late. I
then gave him particulars where he could get Arctic, Lesser
and Sandwich terns in Scotland, and also obtained permission for him to take two Capercaillie nests. All of these
he obtained.

In any collection of hunting trophies, the gems of all
collections (with perhaps the exception of the red deer of
Europe and the great sheep and goats of Central Asia) are
the great deer of North America, and Selous had for long
envied the possessors of such fine specimens of moose,
wapiti and caribou as had been obtained in the seventies
and eighties of the last century. It is true that as good
moose and caribou can be killed to-day as ever ; but the
great wapiti, owing to their curtailed range, are gone for
ever, so a hunter to-day must be content with inferior
specimens. In 1897 three or four specimens of wapiti were
allowed to be killed in the restricted area south of the
Yellowstone Park, and it was with the intention of killing
these as well as other North American game that Selous
turned to the West in August, 1897.

In his youth Selous, like other boys of similar tastes, had
devoured the works of Ballantyne, Mayne Reid, Catlin, and
Kingston, relating to fact and fiction, and had always

desired to visit America as one of his lands of dreams. But it was not civilized America that appealed to him. Cities are the same all the world over. It was the land of vast plains and tractless forests swarming with game that appealed to him ; and if he could not, alas, now find such a hunter's paradise, he could at least see something of the little that was truly wild which was left and perhaps obtain a few fair specimens for his collection. Once, it is true, he had actually taken his passage to America. That happened in 1893, but the outbreak of the Matabele war in that year had caused him to alter his plans and he went back to South Africa instead.

Selous had a good friend, W. Moncrieff, who owned a small cattle ranch in the heart of the Big Horn Mountains in Wyoming. Here in the adjoining forests and mountains still lived a remnant of the bears, wapiti, mule-deer and sheep that had formerly been so abundant, and the local knowledge enjoyed by Moncrieff enabled him to furnish Selous with the best information. Accordingly he left England accompanied by his wife, and, passing through Canada, reached the ranch on the last day of August. Next day the party on horses, accompanied by a waggon with one Bob Graham as a guide, struck into the mountains and, after passing over the main range of the Big Horns, descended into the Big Horn basin. This is covered with sage brush, and is still the home of a few prong-horned antelopes, two of which, one a good male, Selous succeeded in shooting.

The hunters then proceeded up the south fork of Stinking Water, and established a main camp in the forests, where a few very shy wapiti males were still to be found. For twenty days Selous toiled in a mass of dense and fallen timber before he carried his first wapiti head back to camp. Wapiti are in fact now both shy and scarce, and a man must persevere and work continuously, at least early in the season, before even one fair specimen can be found, but Selous greatly enjoyed the grandeur and wildness of the scenery, and being still in the prime of life the exertion of daily toil did not in any way affect his energy. On September 29th he shot his first mule-deer buck. A little snow came and helped to make tracking easier. Then Selous had some luck, and he killed four wapiti, two in one day, and a fifth near Davies' ranch on October 28th. Near the same place too he killed one of the few remaining white-tailed deer-bucks in Wyoming, but its head was rather a poor one, that of an old male " going-back." Selous wrote an account of this trip to Roosevelt, then Assistant Secretary to the American Navy, and received (November 30th, 1897) the following reply :—

" Your letter made me quite melancholy—first, to think I wasn't to see you after all ; and next, to realize so vividly how almost the last real hunting-grounds in America have gone. Thirteen years ago I had splendid sport on the Big Horn Mountains which you crossed. Six years ago I saw elk in bands of one and two hundred on Buffalo Fork ; and met but one hunting expedition while I was out. A very few more years will do away with all the really wild hunting, at least so far as bear and elk are concerned, in the Rocky Mountains and the West generally ; one of the last places will be the Olympic Peninsula of Oregon, where there is a very peculiar elk, a different species, quite as big in body but with smaller horns, which are more like those of the European red deer, and with a black head. Goat, sheep, and bear will for a long time abound in British Columbia and Alaska.

" Well, I am glad you enjoyed yourself, anyhow, and that you did get a sufficient number of fair heads—wapiti, prong-buck, black-tail, and white-tail. Of course I am very sorry that you did not get a good sheep and a bear or two. In the north-eastern part of the Park there is some wintering ground for the elk ; and I doubt if they will ever be entirely killed out in the Park ; but in a very short while shooting in the West, where it exists, will simply be the kind that can now be obtained in Maine and New York ; that is, the game will be scarce, and the game-laws fairly observed in consequence of the existence of a class of professional guides ; and a hunter who gets one good head for a trip will feel he has done pretty well. You were in luck to get so fine a prong-buck head.

" Do tell Mrs. Selous how sorry I am to miss her, as well

as you. I feel rather melancholy to think that my own four small boys will practically see no hunting on this side at all, and indeed no hunting anywhere unless they have the adventurous temper that will make them start out into wild regions to find their fortunes. I was just in time to see the last of the real wilderness life and real wilderness hunting. How I wish I could have been with you this year ! But, as I wrote you before, during the last three seasons I have been able to get out West but once, and then only for a fortnight on my ranch, where I shot a few antelope for meat.

" You ought to have Hough's ' Story of the Cowboy ' and Van Dyke's ' Still Hunter.' Also I think you might possibly enjoy small portions of the three volumes of the Boone and Crockett Club's publications. They could be obtained from the ' Forest and Stream ' people at 346 Broadway, New York, by writing. Have you ever seen Washington Irving's ' Trip on the Prairie,' and Lewis and Clarke's Expedition ? And there are two very good volumes, about fifty years old, now out of print, by a lieutenant in the British Army named Ruxton, the titles of which for the moment I can't think of ; but I will look them up and send them to you. He describes the game less than the trappers and hunters of the period ; men who must have been somewhat like your elephant-hunters. When I was first on the plains there were a few of them left ; and the best hunting-trip I ever made was in the company of one of them, though he was not a particularly pleasant old fellow to work with.

" Now, to answer your question about ranching ; and of course you are at liberty to quote me.

" I know a good deal of ranching in western North Dakota, eastern Montana and north-eastern Wyoming. My ranch is in the Bad Lands of the Little Missouri, a good cattle-country, with shelter, traversed by a river, into which run here and there perennial streams. It is a dry country, but not in any sense a desert. Year in and year out we found that it took about twenty-five acres to support a steer or cow. When less than that was allowed the ranch became overstocked, and loss was certain to follow. Of course where hay is put up, and cultivation with irrigation attempted, the amount of land can be reduced ; but any country in that part of the West which could support a steer or cow on five acres would be country which it would pay to attempt to cultivate, and it would, therefore, cease to be merely pastoral country.

" Is this about what you wish ? I have made but a short trip to Texas. There are parts of it near the coast which are well-watered, and support a large number of cattle. Elsewhere I do not believe that it supports more cattle to the square mile than the north-western country, and where there are more they get terribly thinned out by occasional droughts. In Hough's book you will see some description of this very ranching in Texas and elsewhere. I really grudge the fact that you and Mrs. Selous got away from this side without my even getting a glimpse of you."

As he had only shot two wapiti with fair heads and one mule-deer with average horns, Selous decided to have a second hunt in the Rockies, with the object of obtaining better specimens. In November, as a rule, there is heavy snow in the mountains, and this has the effect of driving the game down out of the heavy timber into more open ground where " heads " can more easily be seen and judged. Accordingly in October, 1898, Selous went to Red Lodge in Montana and there met the hunter Graham. This time he went up the north fork of Stinking Water to the forest and about twelve miles east of the Yellowstone Park. Mild weather, however, throughout November was all against seeing any quantity of game, so Selous was again somewhat disappointed with the results of this hunt.

After this trip, in 1898, he wrote to me :—

" Come here yourself as soon as you can. *Vous serez toujours le bienvenu.* A damned newspaper reporter (an American, who came here whilst I was in London, and would not go away until he had seen me) said I have got some good wapiti heads, but I only got one *fair* one. I got four wapiti bulls altogether, but two had very small heads— not worth taking. I got four mule-deer stags, one with a very nice head and a second not at all bad. I also shot another lynx ; but I had very unfortunate weather, hardly any snow, and when I left the Mountains the wapiti were still up in their early autumn range."

Selous was rather disappointed in not obtaining better wapiti heads, and wrote in his book ("Travels East and West") that bigger heads of deer could now be killed in Hungary than in the Rockies. Commenting on this, Roosevelt, in a letter to him at a later date, says :—

"By the way, I was in the winter range of the deer (Colorado), and I have never seen them so numerous. They were all black-tail (mule-deer). Every day I saw scores, and some days hundreds. There were also elk (wapiti). I did not shoot either deer or elk, of course ; but I saw elk-antlers shot last fall, ranging from 52 to 56 inches in length. I think you were a few years ahead of time (although only a few years) when you stated that already bigger antlers could be secured in Hungary than in the Rockies."

In this doubtless Roosevelt was correct ; but Selous had hunted in a district where all good heads had been picked off, and the range and feed of wapiti had been so curtailed that even at this date and now it is practically impossible to obtain a good specimen.

In April, 1899, he went with his wife to Wiesbaden, returning in June. In October he paid a short visit to his friend, Mr. Danford, in Transylvania, where he killed some good specimens of chamois—one, a female, having horns 11 inches long. In November he came home again, and having some thought of hunting elk in Norway in the following year, wrote to me in November, 1899 : "I want to hear all about your hunt in Norway, so come over here at once. I am very glad to hear you were so successful with the elk and bear, and should much like to have a try next year, if I could stand the work, which I have always heard is very hard." This hunt, however, failed to materialize.

One of Selous' beliefs was that it was impossible for men to hold wide sympathies and to lead others towards the light unless they had been through the grinding-mill of experience in other lands. His broad-minded outlook made him a cosmopolitan in one sense of the word, for he found good and something ever to learn from the men of all nations ; yet withal at heart he was intensely English of the English, and believed in our destiny, as a nation, as a guiding light to universal understanding. His view was that no man had any right to express an opinion on another nation unless that man had lived amongst the people he criticized *and could speak their language.* Such a theory would no doubt be unpopular, but it is right. In international differences all kinds of people express their views in contemporary literature just because they happen to have the ear of the public ; but how many of these really know anything about the people they criticize. A popular cry is raised, and the mob follow like a flock of sheep. An instance of this was the complete misunderstanding of the causes of the Boer War and Boer nation. There were not half a dozen men in England or Africa to tell the public at home the true state of things, and when they did express their views they were quickly drowned in a flood of lies and misrepresentations by interested politicians and gold-magnates who held the press. Men like Selous and Sir William Butler, because they told the absolute truth, were dubbed " Pro-Boers," when in reality they were the best examples of " Pro-English " Englishmen. They simply could not be silent amongst the welter of falsehoods, and only tried to stem the flowing tide of mendacity. Their strongly expressed view that the war would *not* be a walk-over for us, and that we were fighting a gallant foe who deemed themselves right in defending their country, which had been most distinctly given back to them by inviolable treaties (made by the Gladstone Government), was correct, and that they would fight desperately and to a large extent successfully was abundantly proved by subsequent events. If Selous made a mistake it was in allowing certain letters to the " Times " and " Morning Post " to appear *after the war had commenced.* I have reason, however, to believe that these letters were written and sent in prior to the commencement of hostilities, and that they were " held over " to a time when their appearance was, to say the least of it, unfortunate.

In justice to Selous, however, it must be said that after this he kept silent, nor did he ever utter a word publicly in the matter. He felt that we were now hopelessly involved, and that anything he could say would be of little use. Though he felt sad and disappointed over the whole matter, he was far too much a patriot to do other than wish success to our arms, though he ever hoped that some amicable settlement would evolve out of the whole disastrous affair. Afterwards too he often expressed his appreciation of the noble way in which the subsequent British Government treated the Boers, both at the conclusion of peace and the liberal manner in which we sought to bury the hatchet—a manner which unfortunately has not always met with success amongst the older Boer irreconcilables. Men like Botha and Smuts have proved that our later policy has been broad-minded and humane, and that in time we shall amalgamate in one South African Dominion a nation absolutely loyal to the British Crown ; but it will be a long time before the malcontents have lost all their bitterness and a new generation understands what is meant by a Greater South Africa.

His true feelings as regards the war are thus stated in a letter to me, November 5th, 1899 :—

" This war is a most deplorable business ; but of course, as you say, we *must* bring it to a successful conclusion now at whatever cost ; but think what South Africa will be like when it is over. However, it is useless talking about it. My letters to the ' Times ' have raised a great deal of ill-feeling against me in this country."

And again, writing January 1st, 1900, he says :—

" I am very depressed about this war. It is a bad business, and justice is not on our side. There was a lot of dirty work done by the capitalists to bring it about, and no good can come of it for this country. I have seen several letters written by Jan Hofmeyr during the last few months, beginning before the war. They are very interesting, and I hope will be published some day. They seem to explode the idea of the leaders of the Cape Africanders having been in a conspiracy of any kind with the Pretoria lot."

From 1872 onwards Selous had known and studied the Boers intimately. He had lived and hunted with them from the Orange Free State to Matabeleland, and had found them a simple race of hunter-farmers, intensely patriotic and hopelessly conservative. He knew that "they are neither angels nor devils, but just men like ourselves," and that the views of the British, German and Jew storekeepers and traders of the Transvaal and Orange Free State were hopelessly wrong, because they did not know the real back-veldt Boers of the country, who made up the majority of the Nation. He himself had never received anything but kindness and straight dealing from them, and was therefore able to appreciate their indignation and outbursts of fury when a second annexation was contemplated by our Government. He replies to the charge that life for Englishmen was impossible in the Transvaal after the retrocession to the Boers of that country in 1881 : " Mr. Rider Haggard has told us that he found it impossible to go on living in the Transvaal amid the daily insults of victorious Boers, and he also tells us that Boers look upon Englishmen with contempt, and consider them to be morally and physically cowards. I travelled slowly through the Transvaal by bullock-waggon shortly after the retrocession of the country in 1881, and visited all the farmhouses on my route. I met with no insults nor the least incivility anywhere, nor ever heard any boasting about Boer successes over our troops, though at that time I understood the ' Taal ' well. In common with all who really know the Boers, who have lived amongst them, and not taken their character at second-hand, I have always been struck by their moderation in speaking of their victories over our soldiers. As for the Boers having a contempt for Englishmen as individuals, that is nonsense. They hate the British Government, and knowing their history, I for one think they have ample reason for doing so. But the individual Englishman that they know, they take at his real value. There are of course, unfortunately, certain Englishmen in Johannesburg, or people who are now put down as Englishmen, who could not but appear as contemptible to a Boer as they would do to most people in this country. But, on the other hand, I could name many Englishmen and Scotchmen, men who have been honest and upright and fearless in all their dealings with their neighbours, who have been held in immense respect by all the Boers of their acquaintance. These men, however, lived amongst the Boers, spoke their language, and took a sympathetic interest in their lives ; whilst one of the troubles of the present situation in the Transvaal is that the Uitlander population of Johannesburg is, in its sympathies, its mode of life, and all its hopes and aspirations, as wide as the poles asunder from the pastoral Boers, with whom it never mixes, and whom it therefore does not understand." (Letter to the " Times," October 24th, 1899.)

This was also exactly my own experience as recently as 1893, when I lived entirely and trekked with Boers for a year. Never was I ever treated except with the greatest kindness both by my own intimate friends or casual acquaintances, once I had learnt to speak the " Taal," nor did I ever hear them " crow " over their victories of 1881. There was, however, always the latent fear that the British Government would again play them false, and they would be once more forced to fight us ; but with individual Englishmen they liked and trusted there was no sign of animosity.[1]

In June, 1900, Selous was asked to sign a protest, issued by the " South Africa Conciliation Committee," inaugurated by W. L. Courtney (editor of the " Fortnightly Review "). In the following letter, however, written to the Secretary, he manifests his sound common-sense in separating the " causes of the war " from what could be done at the moment when our forces were actually fighting and likely to prove victorious. His grievance was with the authorities

[1] As an instance of this I may mention that the greater number of the " hunting " Boers I lived with and knew well were captured in the Middelburg district in 1900 by a party of Steinacker's horse, who surprised the commando at dawn. All were captured except Commandant Roelef Van Staden, my former hunter, one of the finest men it has ever been my good fortune to meet in any land. He fought his way out singlehanded and escaped. When brought into camp these Boers were well treated by Colonel Greenhill-Gardyne (Gordon Highlanders), who asked them if they knew me, to which they replied that I was the only Englishman they had ever known and that they would consider it a favour if he would kindly send a message of friendship to me, detailing their capture and certain misfortunes that had befallen some of their families in the war. They were also particularly anxious that I should know that Van Staden had escaped. This letter I treasure, for it shows that the Boers have no personal animosity to those who have once been their friends.

who brought about the war and the methods which had been employed to make it, and not with the conduct thereof or its natural effects. Wherefore he refused to sign the protest, and gave his reasons as follows :—

" August 3rd, 1900.

" I have left your circular so long unanswered because I have been thinking over it very deeply, and because, although I realize most fully the force of all the arguments that can be used against the annexation of the Boer Republics, I still think that those who sign the protest ought to be able to propose some scheme of settlement which holds out a better prospect of future peace. I personally can think of no such scheme. Had honourable terms been offered to the Boers, and the independence of their countries been assured to them with certain necessary limitations, immediately after the occupation of Pretoria, there might have been great hope for the future peace of the country, but all that has occurred, not only in the Transvaal and Orange State, but also in the Cape Colony, must have caused such a feeling of exasperation amongst the Dutch Africanders against the British Government, that I cannot but feel that the granting of a limited independence to the Boer Republics would not now produce rest or peace. Things have gone too far for that now, and it seems to me that Great Britain will only be able to hold South Africa in the immediate future by force. I am of course convinced of the truth of all you say in the protest, that the annexation of the Boer Republics is ' contrary to the public declarations of Her Majesty's Ministers, alien to all the best traditions of a freedom-loving country, burdensome to the resources of the nation, and wholly distasteful to the majority of our fellow-subjects in South Africa,' but that does not blind me to the fact that the race hatred that has been engendered by this war is so deep and so terrible that the granting of independence to the Boer Republics would be more immediately disastrous to British supremacy in South Africa than unjust annexation accompanied by the garrisoning of the country with large numbers of troops.

Annexation or no annexation, I firmly believe that sooner or later the people who actually live in South Africa—as distinguished from those whose only interest in the country is the exploitation of its mineral wealth—will govern the country, and, if they wish it, have their own flag, and throw off all allegiance to Great Britain. I would gladly sign any protest against the policy which brought about the war, one of the results of which is this ill-omened annexation of independent states, but I am beginning to think, with John Morley, that annexation was an almost necessary result of a war pushed to the bitter end. I am very sorry to have troubled you with so long a letter, but I wish you to understand that, although my views as to the iniquity of the policy which brought about the war will always remain the same, and although I think the annexation of the two Boer Republics a piece of injustice and a national disgrace, and would most willingly have signed a protest against it three months ago, I now feel the exasperation caused by the war is so great that the independence of the Boer Republics might very possibly be used against British supremacy in South Africa. It is a very distressing outlook, and I can see no light in the future ; but still I do not feel justified in signing the present protest. I beg to thank you for the last two leaflets you sent me, Nos. 53 and 54. The publication of Colonel Stonham's evidence, as to the humanity of the Boers, ought to have a very good effect if it could be made widely known."

After this the war drew on slowly to its eventual finish in 1901, Selous' only public contribution being a letter to the " Speaker," which was used by the South African Conciliation Committee in its efforts to influence the Government, and part of this letter, which deals with the effects of the war on the Boer population and the future, is worth quoting :—

" Should it, however, be determined to erase the Boer Republics from the map of Africa and to carry on the war to the point of practically exterminating the able-bodied male population of these two sparsely-peopled States, let it not be thought that the surviving women will bring up

their children to become loyal British subjects. Let Englishmen remember that the men who prophesied that within a
short time after the war was over the Boers would become
reconciled to the British, whom they would then have learnt
to respect, are the same people who also told us that the war
would be a very short and simple campaign, as the Boers
were a degenerate, cowardly race, who could no longer shoot
at all well, and who would be sure to disperse to their
homes after the first battle, if only a hundred of them were
killed. These were the sort of predictions which were very
commonly heard in this country a few months before the
war commenced, and they were the utterances of men
wholly ignorant of the Boer character.

"As showing that there are people whose opinions are
entitled to respect who think differently, I will now quote
from memory a passage in a letter lately written by a
well-known and well-educated Dutch Africander to a friend
in this country : ' Those people who expect that the Boers
will soon forgive and forget this war, and settle down quietly
under the British flag, are most terribly mistaken. I think
I know my own countrymen, and I believe that if, after this
war is over, the independence of the Republics is destroyed,
the historic episode of Hamilcar making Hannibal swear
eternal enmity to Rome will be re-enacted in many a farm-
house throughout the Transvaal and Orange Free State.
The Boer women will teach their children to hate the very
name of England, and bid them look forward to the day
when their country will be freed from British domination.'
These words, even if the idea they express is somewhat exaggerated, are worthy of attention when it is remembered
how rapidly the Boers increase in numbers and fighting
strength." (" The Speaker," 1900.)

After this he only expressed his views to a few personal
friends, such as President Roosevelt, who was in close
sympathy with his hopes that peace on a fair basis might
soon be restored. In reply to one of his letters, Roosevelt,
writing March, 1901, says :—

" It makes me melancholy to see the Boer War hanging
on. Your limit of eighteen months (the time Selous stated

THE WANDERING MINSTREL.

it would last) is rapidly approaching. Of course there can be only one ending; but it is a dreadful thing to have the ending come only by the exhaustion of the country and of the fighting men. How I wish you could be made administrator of all South Africa. Somehow I feel that you could do what no other man could do, and really bring about peace. I begin to be afraid you have been right about this war. I hope we shall see things go right hereafter."

It is interesting too to study both Roosevelt's and the American attitude towards our policy in the Boer War. In reply to Selous' explanation of the whole matter the American statesman thus writes (March 19th, 1900) :—

" I appreciate very deeply the trouble you have taken in writing to me ; although in a way your letter has made me feel very melancholy. My idea of the questions at issue has been mainly derived from the ' Spectator,' a paper that I take and always like, and which impresses me as being honestly desirous of getting at the true facts in any given case. I paid especial heed to what it said because of its entire disapproval of Cecil Rhodes and the capitalist gang. Moreover, a friend of mine, Ferdinand Becker, who was in the Transvaal and who saw very clearly the rights and wrongs of each side, and for whose judgment I have great respect, insists that as things actually were the war was inevitable, *that there had to be a fight, and that one or the other race had to be supreme in South Africa.* By the way, much of the pro-Boer feeling here is really anti-English, and as I have a very warm remembrance of England's attitude to us two years ago, I have of course no sympathy with such manifestations. So I thought after Montague White's visit to me that I should like to hear the other side from someone whom I could thoroughly trust, and I appealed to you. It is largely an academic curiosity on my part, so to speak, for the answer of the English Premier to the communication of transmissal sent by President McKinley with the letters from the Presidents of the two Republics shows that any mediation would be promptly rejected. I do not suppose that the end can be very far distant now, unless there is a formidable uprising in the Cape Colony, for it would look as

R

if there had never been fifty thousand Boers under arms, and Roberts has four times that number of troops in South Africa. Evidently the Boers are most gallant fighters, and quite as efficient as they are gallant.

" I had been inclined to look at the war as analogous to the struggles which put the Americans in possession of Texas, New Mexico, and California. I suppose the technical rights are about the same in one case as in the other ; but, of course, there is an enormous difference in the quality of the invading people ; for the Boers have shown that they have no kinship with the Mexicans. In Texas the Americans first went in to settle and become citizens, making an Outlander population. This Outlander population then rose, and was helped by raids from the United States, which in point of morality did not differ in the least from the Jameson raid—although there was at back of them no capitalist intrigue, but simply a love of adventure and a feeling of arrogant and domineering race-superiority. The Americans at last succeeded in wresting Texas from the Mexicans and making it an independent Republic. This Republic tried to conquer New Mexico but failed. Then we annexed it, made its quarrels our own, and did conquer both New Mexico and California. In the case of Texas there was the dark blot of slavery which rested on the victors ; for they turned Texas from a free province into a slave republic. Nevertheless, it was of course ultimately to the great advantage of civilization that the Anglo-American should supplant the Indo-Spaniard. It has been ultimately to the advantage of the Indo-Spaniard himself, or at any rate to the advantage of the best men in his ranks. In my regiment, which was raised in the South-West, I had forty or fifty men of part Indian blood and perhaps half as many of part Spanish blood, and among my captains was one of the former and one of the latter—both being as good Americans in every sense of the word as were to be found in our ranks.

" If the two races, Dutch and English, are not riven asunder by too intense antagonism, surely they ought to amalgamate in South Africa as they have done here in

North America, where I and all my fellows of Dutch blood are now mixed with and are indistinguishable from our fellow Americans, not only of English, but of German, Scandinavian, and other ancestry.

" The doubtful, and to my mind the most melancholy, element in the problem is what you bring out about the Englishman no longer colonizing in the way that the Boer does. This is a feature due, I suppose, to the enormous development of urban life and the radical revolution in the social and industrial conditions of the English-speaking peoples during the past century. In our Pacific States, and even more in Australia, we see the same tendency to the foundation of enormous cities instead of the settlement of the country districts by pioneer farmers. Luckily, America north of the Rio Grande and Australia definitely belong to our peoples already, and there is enough of the pastoral and farming element among us to colonize the already thinly-settled waste places which now belong to our people. But the old movement which filled the Mississippi valley at the beginning of this century with masterful dogged frontier-farmers, each skilled in the use of the rifle and axe, each almost independent of outside assistance, and each with a swarm of tow-headed children, has nearly come to an end. When Kentucky, at the close of the eighteenth century, was as populous as Oregon 100 years later, Kentucky did not have one-tenth of the urban population that Oregon had when she reached the same stage. Now, urban people are too civilized, have too many wants and too much social ambition, to take up their abode permanently in the wilderness and marry the kind of women who alone could be contented, or indeed could live in the wilderness. On the great plains of the West, when I was in the cattle business, I saw many young Easterners and young Englishmen of good families who came out there ; but not one in twenty, whether from the Atlantic States or from England, married and grew up as a permanent settler in the country ; and the twentieth was usually a *déclassé*. The other nineteen were always working to make money and then go home, or somewhere else, and they did not have their womankind with them. The 'younger son' of whom Kipling sings is a picturesque man always, and can do very useful work as a hunter and explorer, or even a miner, but he is not a settler, and does not leave any permanent mark upon any true frontier-community with which I am acquainted. After the frontier has been pushed back, when the ranchman and the cowboy and the frontier-ganger, who are fitted for the actual conditions, have come in, then the 'younger son' and the struggling gentleman-adventurer may make their appearance in the towns. Of course, there are exceptions to all of this, but as a rule what I have pointed out is true. I have seen scores—perhaps hundreds—of men from Oxford and Cambridge, Harvard and Yale, who went into cattle-growing on the Great Plains, but they did just as I did; that is, worked with greater or less success at the business, gained an immense amount of good from it personally, especially in the way of strength and gratifying a taste for healthy adventure, learned much of human nature from associating with the men round about, and then went back to their own homes in England or New York or Boston, largely because, when it came to marrying and bringing up children, they could not well face the conditions ; and so the real population of the future in the valleys of the upper Missouri, the Platte, and the Rio Grande, will be composed of the sons of their companions, who were themselves descendants of small farmers in Texas, Missouri, and Illinois, or of working-men from Scandinavia and Germany.

" Pardon this long letter, which has wandered aside from the thesis with which it started. I hope that the language of the more highly civilized people will, in spite of the evil influences of to-day, gradually oust the ' Taal,' or whatever you call Boer Dutch in South Africa, and that when the conquest of the two Republics is succeeded by the full liberty which I understand the Cape Dutch enjoy, there will come a union in blood as well as in that between the two peoples who are so fundamentally alike.

" I am looking forward to the receipt of the three books you have been so very kind as to send me. I do know a certain amount about the Boers from the time of their great trek onward, for it has always seemed to me to be one of the most fascinating bits of modern history."

In the spring of 1900 Selous went on a bird-nesting trip to the forest and marshes of the Danube in Hungary, and was successful in getting the eggs of many new species for his collection. When he arrived home in June he found his finances in low water, owing to enlarging his house, and so feared he would be unable to make an extensive autumn hunt, but later on things improved, and he was able to go West after all.

In September, 1900, he went to Canada to hunt moose, and arrived at Mattawa, Ontario, on September 24th. On this trip he was fortunate in securing the services of George Crawford, a half-breed Indian, who was probably the best moose-caller and hunter in that province. In spite of the number of American hunters who at this time made the districts of Kippewa and Tamiskaming their favourite hunting-grounds, Crawford always knew where to go to secure moose, and it was not long before Selous reached a hunting-ground, about three days north of Mattawa, on Lake Bois Franc, where he killed two fine bulls. After this short trip he went to Snake Lake to try and secure a good white-tailed deer stag, but was not very successful, as he only secured a four-year-old buck with moderate horns. On October 26th he landed in Newfoundland and, being supplied with bad information, went by railway from Port-aux-Basque to Howley, a station on the main line, where the annual slaughter of caribou took place late in the season.

It was not long before Selous found that the so-called " sport " of shooting caribou on migration as they crossed the line in their southern migration was not sport at all, and that frequently, owing to the number of bullets flying in all directions fired by enthusiastic meat-hunters, the shooting was likely to result in human as well as cervine casualties. Moreover, hardly any good stags come south with the mass of does and immatures, so, taking his guide Stroud and an old man named Robert Saunders he left the place in disgust and went south to the Terra Nova river, intending to strike into the heart of the country and, if possible, catch up the main body of the migrating deer before they cast their horns and reached their winter-quarters near the south coast. But he was too late, and after an onerous tramp, during which he penetrated beyond the limits reached by other white men, he was forced to return owing to lack of food, but not before his sharp eyes had seen numerous trees stripped by "summering" stags in the neighbourhood of St. John's Lake. These signs convinced him that the local movements of the deer were unknown even to the hunters in Newfoundland, and that the big stags would probably be found in autumn in the heart of the island, and not on migration in the north. In this he was quite correct. He did not, however, go home without a specimen, for he killed one nice stag on his journey inland.

Accordingly he made plans to hunt in the neighbourhood of St. John's Lake in the following autumn of 1901, and procuring two canoes from Peterborough in Ontario, and enlisting the services of Saunders and his cousin John Wells, he ascended the rocky Terra Nova river in September. To the reader it may seem easy to go seventy miles in a canoe upstream, but the fact that previous hunters had not been there proves that there were difficulties. No Newfoundland boats in fact would withstand the rocky benches of this swift-flowing river, so progress can only be made for the most part by wading and dragging the canoes, whilst the hunter has to force his way through dense forest, so thick at times that an axe has to be used for progress to be made before reaching the higher plateaux, where lakes and streams are easily passed. Once on Lake St. John, all was easy, and Selous found game abundant and a small migration of big stags already in progress.[1]

Moreover, Selous was lucky enough to have struck a good year for "heads." In less than eight days he shot his five stags, two of which carried remarkably fine heads—one, in fact, a forty-pointer, which he killed by a long shot close to his camp, being one of the finest specimens ever killed in the island by any sportsman. Selous often spoke after-

---

[1] This is very unusual, for in four seasons' hunting there, I never found the deer move at so early a date as September 15th.

wards of this trip as being one of the pleasantest he ever had in his life.

He writes, October 6th, 1901 :—

" I am back from Newfoundland. I had a short but very successful little trip into quite new country, thanks to my canoes, and shot the five stags my licence entitled me to kill very quickly. I have got one really remarkable head, a second, very handsome, with beautiful double brow-antlers, and very fine tops ; and a third, a pretty regular head of medium size—the other two not much to boast about. But my two good heads are really fine, and when you see them you will never rest till you go to my new ground and get more like them. I can give you all particulars when we meet, and have arranged that my guide—hardly the right word, as we got into country where he had never been in his life and where he says no one has ever yet hunted, except a few Micmac Indians who were out after caribou, but trapping beavers along the rivers—shall keep himself unengaged for you up to June next."

In December we had some good days together in Shropshire, at Sir Beville Stanier's, shooting partridges, and at Swythamley with the Brocklehursts killing driven grouse in a blizzard. Selous, though then over fifty, was much fitter and more active than many a man of twenty-five, and the way he walked and talked was a joy to behold. After dinner he would begin telling stories, and at 1.30 was still hard at it when most of us were dying to go to bed. Nothing could curb his enthusiasm once a congenial topic was started, and his avidity was such both for acquiring and dispensing knowledge that time itself seemed all too short.

Early in January, 1902, he went to Smyrna for the purpose of egg-collecting, with the added expectation of getting a shot at a stag or wild goat, and on March 5th writes :—

" I got back from Asia Minor last week, with a good series of eggs of the White-tailed Eagle and one Lämmergeier's egg. I found two Lämmergeiers' nests, both with young birds, but I got an addled egg which I was able to blow. I had no shooting, though I made an attempt to get a shot at a stag, but there was so much snow in the mountains that the Turks would not take pack-ponies in for fear of getting snowed up."

On August 11th we were all at Swythamley again enjoying the hospitality of Sir Philip Brocklehurst and having some very excellent shooting. One day we shot the park and killed 1170 rabbits, and a notice of this event given in the "Field," as 585½ brace of grouse, a good bag, indeed, for Staffordshire, was a statement so far from the truth that we easily traced it to the old squire's love of nonsense.

Having some time at his disposal in September, Selous resolved to take a short run out to Sardinia for the purpose of adding specimens of the Mouflon to his collection. Most of the English hunters who have killed this very sporting little sheep have pursued it in March, at which time of year the Mouflon are mostly hidden in the tall " Maquia " scrub (*Erica arborea*), where they are difficult both to find and to stalk. Someone, however, had given Selous the hint that if he went to Sardinia in late September he would see the sheep on the open hills, when they would probably afford much better sport. This was quite true, but unfortunately for the hunter the autumn of 1902 was one of the wettest on record, and Selous, after the first few days of good weather, when he killed three fair rams, lived for a fortnight in pouring rain and discomfort in a leaky tent, and had eventually to give up the chase in disgust. He came back, however, with a high admiration for the intellectual abilities of the little Mouflon, and resolved at some future date once again to visit the "elevated farmyard,"[1] as someone has termed these mountains of "the Isle of Unrest."

On November 17th he left on his first trip to British East Africa, taking the German boat at Marseilles to Mombasa. As this trip was somewhat experimental he made no large plans and merely wished to get a few specimens of the common species of mammals found there. This he hoped to do by making short trips in the neighbourhood of the line. At

---

[1] On the hills of Genna Gentu, the principal home of the Mouflon in Sardinia, the native shepherds allow their cattle and herds of sheep and goats to graze amongst the wild sheep and this constant disturbance keeps all creatures constantly on the move.

this time, even so near civilization, British East Africa was truly a big game paradise.

Writing to Abel Chapman concerning this, Selous says :—

" My trip to East Africa last year (1902–1903) cost me just £300, but I think I did it cheaper than most people. I got fairly good heads of Coke's, Neumann's, and Jackson's Hartebeests, Topis, Impala, Bushbucks, Oribis, Steinbucks, and Cavendish's Dik-diks. I did not get a Jackson's Wildebeest as, although there were thousands all along the line when I went up country, when I came back to try to get one, they had migrated south. I saw lots of Common and Defassa Waterbucks, but no good heads, so never shot one. Also hundreds of Elands. I did not actually see a Rhino., but often got quite fresh spoor ; but I did not want to shoot one of these animals as I have good specimens from South Africa."

He reached home in March, 1903, and the spring of this year was, as usual, spent in egg-collecting. He writes, June 30th :—

" I have just finished my egg-collecting season. I got a Dotterel's nest on the top of Ben Wyvis, also a couple of Ptarmigans' nests, which are difficult to find. I got too several nests of Grasshopper Warbler, Wood Wren, and Pied Flycatcher in Northumberland, but I had a very good local man to help me."

The year 1904 was a very busy one for Selous, and the following letter to me gives some idea of his energy in hunting for the eggs of birds of which he has not yet taken specimens.

" During the last few days I have been marking Kingfishers' nests on the Thames and Water Rails' nests in Thatcham Marsh, for Major Stirling (of Fairburn), who has been very kind to me in Scotland and helped me to get all sorts of good eggs. I have got him two Kingfishers' nests marked that I am sure have eggs in them, and also two Water Rails' nests. One of these had six eggs in it yesterday. We go to Wargrave for the Kingfishers to-morrow, and to Thatcham for the Water Rails on Thursday. On Friday I am off to North Wales, where I hope to get a

Chough's nest. During the first half of May I shall be here, and will come over to see you during that time. On May 15th I start for Ross-shire, to get Crossbills, and then on to Orkney to get eggs of Hen Harrier, Short-eared Owl, Twite, etc. On May 26th I must be at Ravenglass, in Cumberland, to get a couple of clutches of Sandwich Terns' eggs (by permission), and the next day on the Tyne for Pied Flycatchers, Grasshopper Warblers, etc. Then back to Orkney early in June for Merlins, Black Guillemot, Eider Duck, etc. Then I think I shall try for a Scoter's nest near Melvick, in Sutherlandshire, and I wind up the season with a trip to St. Kilda with Musters to get eggs of Fork-tailed Petrel and Fulmar. Are there any old orchards about you ? If so, we might look them over for a Hawfinch's nest about May 10th. I am not going to lend any of my heads to the Crystal Palace people. They wrote to me about it, but I have declined to send them any heads."[1]

Later in the year he wrote one of his characteristic letters, speaking of his successes in egg-hunting and expressing his sorrow at the death of our mutual friend, Sir Philip Brocklehurst :—

" I am now home again from my egg-collecting trip to the north. I have had a fairly successful season. I got two Choughs' nests in North Wales in April, and several Water Rails' near here in a nice little swamp I know of. In Orkney I got Hen Harrier, Short-eared Owl, Merlin, Eider Duck, Dunlin, Golden Plover, Rock Pipit, and Twite. I have also taken this year in Northumberland and Cumberland nests of Wood Wren, Grasshopper Warbler, Pied Flycatcher, Great Spotted Woodpecker, Sandwich Tern, and Shell Duck. Now I want a nest of Lesser Spotted Woodpeckers. There are a few about here, but I cannot find out where they nest. I am going to the Crystal Palace to-morrow, and shall see your Caribou heads there I hope. Now I want you to help me. I am President of our village cricket-club, and have got together a team to play them on July 9th (Saturday). I am experiencing great difficulty in getting an eleven to-

---

[1] Later he was persuaded to lend his heads for the exhibition, but few visitors saw the collection.

gether. Will you help me and play for me on that day ?
If so, please come here in time for lunch. We do not play
till 2.30 p.m. Now can you come ? Do, if you can, and
bring another man with you. Please let me know about
this as soon as possible, as I must now begin to hustle to get
my team together. Isn't it sad to think that poor old Sir
Philip Brocklehurst has gone ? If we ever go to Swythamley
again, things can never be as they were in the old Squire's
time. I feel his loss very much. If you are at home now I
should like to come over and see you and have our usual
' crack,' my dear Johnny."

Just before leaving for Canada on July 14th he writes :—

" What with people coming to see us here, garden-parties,
cricket, political meetings, etc., there seems to be no time
for anything. I hope you will have a good time Whale-
hunting in August in the Shetland Isles. Write us a good
account of it and make some good pictures."

Leaving England on July 14th, 1904, Selous reached
Dawson City, on the Yukon, on August 8th. He went via
Vancouver, and much enjoyed the pleasant voyage up the
North Pacific coast, which abounds in islands and forests,
and in scenic effect is much superior to Norway, which it
resembles. Here he joined a party of sportsmen who
had chartered a flat-bottomed steamer to take them up the
north fork of the MacMillan river, a branch of the Yukon.
There was, however, a delay of ten days, and as Selous could
not endure inactivity he spent the time, with the help of a
half-breed Indian and a pack-horse, in the Ogilvy Mountains,
where he found and killed a male caribou of the variety
which I have recently described under the name of *Tarandus
rangifer ogilvyensis*, one of the many sub-specific races of
reindeer of the North American Continent as yet somewhat
imperfectly known. Selous then returned to Dawson, and
the hunting party being assembled on the little steamer, a
start up-stream was made on August 21st. After proceeding
some distance up the Yukon, the Pelly, and then the Mac-
Millan for five days through shallow and tortuous channels,
the steamer could go no further. At Slate Creek two
Americans, Professor Osgood the Zoologist, and Carl Rungius

the artist of mammals, left to establish a hunting-camp there, whilst Selous and his friend, Mr. Charles Sheldon, a well-known hunter and field naturalist, passed up the north fork of the MacMillan, the rest of the party going up the south fork. Selous soon killed a moose cow for meat, and in a few days Sheldon, reconnoitring up in the mountains, found a good camping-place on the edge of timber-line, so Selous and his friend then left the canoes and carried their heavy packs up the mountain. Whilst doing so Louis Cardinal, the half-breed hunter, spied a bull moose lying in the scrub, and Selous soon worked down to it and killed it at short range. Sheldon's chief object of pursuit was the wild sheep of these ranges, *Ovis fannini*, whilst Selous' was to obtain good moose and caribou, and, if possible, grizzly bears and sheep.

In the first two days Selous killed a fine caribou bull of the sub-specific race *Tarandus rangifer osborni*, a fine form of reindeer that exists from the Itcha Mountains in British Columbia to the east of the Kenai Peninsula. This variety, which is only found west of the Rocky Mountains, intergrades to the south with *Tarandus rangifer montanus* of southern British Columbia, and to the north-west with *Tarandus rangifer stonei* of the Kenai peninsula. It is by far the finest of the American caribou, with the exception of the nearly extinct race, a branch of *Tarandus rangifer labradorensis*, which belongs to the north-east corner of Labrador, and carries fine massive horns from 50 to 61 inches long, but not furnished as a rule with many points.[1] Selous was much cheered in getting so easily two fine specimens of this great deer at once. One night in the middle of September a fine display of the Aurora Borealis with its magnificent tongues of flame was observed, and Selous rightly says, " I count these splendours of the Arctic sky as amongst the most marvellous of all the wonders of the world," an opinion all who have seen them will endorse.

In the next few days Selous killed another bull moose, but not a large one, carrying a head with a span of 50 inches,

---

[1] I was so fortunate as to kill one of these caribou in the Tanzilla Mountains on the borders of Alaska, with fifty-three points, in 1908, but this was quite an exceptional head of an unusual type.

and then an old bull with horns evidently going back. At last dawned a day of great good fortune, for the hunter met and killed a great bull whose horns have seldom been equalled by any taken out of the Yukon Territory. The horns, measuring 67 inches across, a width not often surpassed even in the Kenai peninsula, were very massive, and carried 41 points ; the skull and horns weighed over 75 lbs. " Altogether," he says, " it seemed to me I had at last obtained a trophy worth a king's ransom," for to a hunter such as he no bag of gold or diamonds would have seemed more precious.

Meanwhile his friend, Charles Sheldon, had not been so fortunate as he usually was in finding the big sheep rams, and had only shot a few immatures and females and young for the extensive collection he afterwards formed for American museums, and, as the season was now late and the prospect of the " freeze up " imminent, the two hunters abandoned their hunting-camp and started down-stream on the return home. After some disappointments, one in which Sheldon lost a fine bull moose owing to a missfire, Selous and his companion reached Plateau Mountain, where Osgood and Rungius, who had enjoyed some good sport with moose and caribou, were again met. The whole party then went down-stream, and had some difficulty in getting through the ice which was now forming, but reached Selkirk safely on October 7th. On the whole this had been a very successful trip for Selous, but he was a little disappointed in not getting sheep, grizzly, and black bears.

His own account of the whole trip is as follows :—

" My dear Johnny,—Just a line to tell you that I got home again from the Yukon country yesterday (November 7th). I shall have a lot to tell you about it when we meet. The original trip that I was invited to join fell through, as neither the governor of the Yukon Territory was able to go nor my friend Tyrrel who invited me to join the party. There was a lot of delay, and eventually three Canadians, three Americans, and myself hired a small flat-bottomed steamer to take us up the Pelly and MacMillan rivers. This took much longer than was expected, and it was not till

August 30th that we got to the furthest point to which the steamer could take us. Then we all split up, and an American (Charles Sheldon, an awfully good fellow, whom I hope I shall be able to bring over to see you one of these days) and myself (we had chummed up on the steamer) tackled the north fork of the MacMillan river. We had each a twenty-foot canoe and one man. My man was a French half-breed, and Sheldon's a white man, both first-rate fellows. We had a very ' tough ' time getting the canoes up the river, as the stream was fearfully strong and the water very cold. We were in the water most of every day for six days, often up to our waists, hauling the canoes up with ropes. Then we reached the foot of a big range of mountains. The day we left the steamer bad weather set in and we had 18 days of filthy weather, sleet and snow, and the whole country covered with snow. On September the 6th or 7th we packed up into the mountains, carrying everything on our backs to close up to timber-line (about 5000 feet in this northern country, the point where we left the timber being about 2500 feet above sea-level). No Indians to pack, no guides, no nothing, and damned little game either, though we were in an absolutely new country, where there are no Indians at all, and only four trappers in the whole district, and these men never go up into the high mountains. There were any quantity of beavers up the north fork of the Mac-Millan. The trappers have not yet touched them and they are wonderfully tame. We could find no sheep rams in the mountains, only small flocks of ewes and kids. Moose after September 18th were fairly numerous, but by no means plentiful. I only saw three caribou, one a very good bull, whose head will, I think, interest you. I believe it is the kind that Merriam calls Osborn's caribou, a very large heavy animal, with horns rather of the Barren Ground type, but finely palmated at the top. I shot four bull moose and spared two more. One of my moose has a right royal head, and pays me well for all my trouble. The spread across the palms, with no straggly points, is 67 inches, and it has 41 points (23+18). My second best head measures 58½ inches across the palms, with 22 points(11+11). I boxed my heads in Vancouver, and hope to get them some time next month, and you must come and see them as soon as they are set up."

In the autumn of 1905 he went on his third trip to Newfoundland, in order to see something more of the interior of the island and to shoot a few caribou. The country he now selected was that in the neighbourhood of King George IV Lake, a district that had only previously been visited by two white men, Cormack, its discoverer, in 1822, and Howley in 1875. This is not a difficult country to reach, as canoes can be taken the whole way, and there are no bad " runs " or long portages. The autumn of 1905 was, however, perhaps the wettest on record, and it poured with rain every day, whilst, as to the caribou stags, they carried the poorest horns in any season, owing to the severity of the previous winter. In this trip, in which he was accompanied by two excellent Newfoundlanders, Joseph Geange and Samuel Smart, Selous saw large numbers of caribou, but did not obtain a single good head, and though he enjoyed the journey, the trophies killed were somewhat disappointing, and especially so as he had broken into quite new country.[1]

Selous' own account, in a letter to me, November 22nd, is as follows :—

" By the time you get this letter I shall be at home again, or at any rate in London. I have to commence my lecturing on December 4th, but if I can get a spare day before then I will come over and see you. My experience in Newfoundland was much the same as yours. I saw a lot of caribou, but no very large heads. I had, too, terribly bad weather, almost continuous rain and sleet storms on the high ground near George IV Lake. By-the-bye, Mr. Howley tells me that to the best of his belief I am the third white man who has visited that lake. The first was Cormack, who named it a long time ago, and the second Mr. Howley, who was there in 1875. The caribou in the country between King George's Lake and the head of the Victoria river live there. I saw

---

[1] This year I was hunting in the Gander forests about 75 miles southeast of King George IV Lake and saw an immense number of caribou stags, but only one with a first-class head, a 35-pointer, which I was fortunate enough to kill. Later in the season I saw most of the heads killed in the island and there was not a good one amongst them.

non-travelling deer there, all the herds were stationary, feeding or lying down in one spot all day long. Lots of trees too along the river, where the stags had cleaned their horns. Packing in from Lloyd's river to the north-west, I struck some splendid caribou-ground. Here the deer were all on migration southwards. As a matter of fact, I did very little systematic hunting, but a lot of tramping, always carrying a 40 lb. pack myself. I have got one very pretty head of 36 points, very regular and symmetrical, but not large. In a storm of driving sleet it looked magnificent on the living stag. I have another head I like, and some others of lesser merit, one of them for the Natural History Museum. I have preserved a complete animal for them."

OSBORN'S CARIBOU.

CHAPTER XI

1906–1907

IN April, 1906, Selous went all the way to Bosnia just to take the nest and eggs of the Nutcracker, and those who are not naturalists can scarcely understand such excessive enthusiasm. This little piece of wandering, however, seemed only an incentive to further restlessness, which he himself admits, and he was off again on July 12th to Western America for another hunt in the forests, this time on the South Fork of the MacMillan river. On August 5th he started from Whitehorse on the Yukon on his long canoe - journey down the river, for he wished to save the expense of taking the steamer to the mouth of the Pelly. He was accompanied by Charles Coghlan, who had been with him the previous year, and Roderick Thomas, a hard-bitten old traveller of the North-West. Selous found no difficulty in shooting the rapids on the Yukon, and had a pleasant trip in fine weather to Fort Selkirk, where he entered the Pelly on August 9th. Here he was lucky enough to kill a cow moose, and thus had an abundance of meat to take him on the long up-stream journey to the MacMillan mountains, which could only be effected by poling and towing. On August 18th he killed a lynx. At last, on August 28th, he reached a point on the South Fork of the MacMillan, where it became necessary to leave the canoe and pack provisions and outfit up to timber-line. Here almost immediately he killed a cow caribou for meat, and a comfortable camp was soon made. During the following days Selous hunted far and wide, and found that Osborn's caribou was as plentiful in these ranges as his friends in the previous year had found them. He killed six splendid bulls, one of which is now to be seen, mounted whole, in the Natural History Museum, and in a short time got all the specimens he wanted. One day he saw a large black animal, which he took to be a bear, coming towards him, and eventually killed it at a distance of 400 yards. It proved to be a black variety of the wolf—a somewhat rare animal to kill with the rifle, and curiously enough he killed another a few days later.

Before leaving the mountains he shot a good bull moose and missed another, whilst going down-stream, at 30 yards. A second shot, however, killed the animal, and gave the hunter another fine specimen with horns 63 inches across. Selous reached Selkirk on September 20th, and so had no difficulty in getting out before the ice formed.

As soon as he got home he wrote to me telling of the results of his trip, and I give it as showing the sympathetic nature of his disposition for the sorrows of others :—

" The first part of your letter awoke afresh all my sympathy for you and poor Mrs. Millais in your sorrow for the loss of your dearly beloved child. I suppose you can never hope to forget what you once possessed and can never have again, nor would you wish to do so ; but time is merciful, and whilst never forgetting the sweetness of disposition of your dear child, the sorrow for her loss will gradually hurt you less and less. At least I trust it will be so. I am so glad to hear that you have got such a splendid lot of caribou heads this year. You well deserve them, for you have taken a lot of trouble to get them. You must now have quite a unique collection of Newfoundland caribou heads. I got one good moose this year $63\frac{1}{2}$ inches spread (measured by Mr. Burlace the other day) and another pretty head of 52 inches spread. Besides these two I only saw one other bull moose—a fair-sized head. I saw a good many caribou, but no large heads. Every big bull I saw seemed to have a well-grown head. On August 29th I saw a single old bull and shot him. The next day I saw another bull with ten cows and shot him. These heads were both in velvet, but fully grown out and the velvet just ready to peel off. On September 1st I saw another single bull and shot him ; and on the following day got another close to camp. Both these bulls had their horns quite clean of velvet, not a shred left on any part. I then went away to another range of mountains to look for sheep and moose, returning again to the caribou-ground about the middle of September. On my first day I came across four splendid old bulls all together. They all had big heads, and I got close to them and could have shot them all, but I let two of them go after killing the other two, which seemed to me to have the finest horns. Whilst I was skinning the animals I had shot (with my half-breed Indian) three more big bulls *and a hornless cow* came and lay down on a knoll about 400 yards away. One of these seemed to have very large horns ; but I thought that six was enough, so I let them alone. I think three or four of the heads I have got are pretty good, but much better no doubt could be got if one waited till they got into large herds after the rutting season. Burlace makes my longest head 57¼ inches, another is 55 inches, and two others just over 51 and 50. Two of them have an inside spread of 48 inches. One head is of quite a different type to the other five. It is only about 40 inches long and very like a Newfoundland head with beautiful tops. Besides the caribou and moose I only got two wolves—very fine ones, and one of them black. I saw no bears at all, and only female sheep. I am going away on Saturday, December 1st, lecturing (with a two days' interlude at Beville Stanier's), and shall not be home again from Scotland till December 15th. On December 17th I go away again till the 20th ; but after that I shall be at home for a long time. Let me know when you get your heads home, and I will then come over to look at them, and you must come and see my Yukon heads as soon as I get them from Ward's."

In May, 1907, he went to Asia Minor to take the eggs of sea and raptorial birds, living on or near the Mediterranean coasts.

In June he wrote : " I was very pleased to see the letter you wrote to the ' Field ' about poor Arthur Neumann. I had thought of writing something myself, but did not know

him as well as you did.   I shall never cease to regret his loss.
I look upon him as the last of the real genuine hunters of
African big game."

Arthur Neumann, the celebrated elephant - hunter, was
born at Hockliffe Rectory, in Bedfordshire, in 1850.   In
1868 he went to Natal and later to Swaziland, and acted as
interpreter during the Zulu war in 1879.   From 1885–1887
he hunted much in South Africa, and after a time went to
East Africa, where he helped to survey the line from the
coast to Lake Victoria Nyanza.   After another visit to
South Africa he made his first journey after elephants to
the East of Mount Kenia and killed large numbers of bull
elephants.

In 1896 he was badly injured by a cow elephant, and
returned to Mombasa in October, 1896.   In 1899 he took
part in the second Boer war, and in 1902 returned to East
Africa and had another successful hunt, getting some
immense tusks.

In 1903–1904, hunting in Turkana, Turkwel and the
Lorian swamp, he killed many elephants, and made his last
expedition in 1905–1906, when his ivory realized £4500 on
sale in London.   He was a pioneer like Selous, and wherever
he went made a favourable impression on the native—
helping greatly to advance our hold on British East Africa.
He died suddenly in 1907.

In August, 1907, Selous went on a little hunt after
reindeer in Norway, as the guest of his old friend, Captain
P. B. Vanderbyl, a hunter who has had perhaps as great a
general experience of big game hunting as any man living.
In this trip Selous shot five good stags in seven days'
hunting, but was not so fortunate as to get a first-class
specimen, although some of his heads were good.   Of this
trip Captain Vanderbyl kindly sends me the following note :

" Although friends of many years' standing, Selous and I
only did one shooting-trip together, and that was after
Reindeer in Norway.   We sailed from Hull to Stavanger in
August, 1907, and marched in with pack-ponies a few miles
from the head of the Stavanger Fjord to Lyseheien, where
a small shooting-box had been recently erected.

" Owing to a five years' close season which had just terminated we found the reindeer fairly numerous, and not too difficult to approach, but as they always feed up-wind, and cover a lot of ground, we had some days to walk long distances before spying any.

" We arrived at Lyseheien a few days before the opening of the season, and spent the time walking after ryper, of which we used to get 12 or 15 brace a day, and although Selous was never a good shot with the gun, he showed the same keenness after the birds as he did for any form of sport. He had to leave Norway a few days before I did, in order to see his boys before they returned to school.

" We were quite successful on this trip, and secured thirteen stags between us, with some good heads among them. When not hunting, we beguiled the time with some French novels Selous produced, and I never knew of his liking for this kind of literature before.

" We both enjoyed the trip thoroughly, and were surprised to find so wild and unfrequented a hunting ground within about three days journey of London."

During this season I was camped on the highest part of the range, some thirty miles to the north. A heavy snowstorm, lasting for six days, occurred on September 1st, and drove all the deer south-west to Lyseheien, which accounted in some measure for the excellent sport enjoyed by my friends.

Reindeer are at all times subject to these sudden local migrations, and the very uncertainty of the sport makes it somewhat fascinating and difficult. In Norway it is now difficult to secure a good reindeer head for this reason, and the fact that indiscriminate poaching, even on what is called strictly preserved ground, prevails.

During the winter of 1907 and early in the following year Selous devoted himself to finishing his book " African Nature Notes and Reminiscences " (published by Macmillan & Co. in 1908), a work which he wrote principally at the instigation of his friend, Theodore Roosevelt. In this he devotes the first two chapters to his views on protective coloration and the influence of environment on living organisms. For lucidity and accuracy of treatment he never wrote anything better or more clearly discounted the views of theoretical naturalists. It is a model of conclusive argument backed by sound data. Commenting on his remarks ex-President Roosevelt thus gives his opinions on the subject (November 1st, 1912) :—

" It is a misfortune that in England and America the naturalists should at the moment have gotten into an absolutely fossilized condition of mind about such things as protective coloration. Both the English and the American scientific periodicals are under the control of men like Professor Poulton and others who treat certain zoological dogmas from a purely fetichistic standpoint, exactly as if they were mediæval theologians. This is especially true of their attitude toward the doctrine of natural selection, and incidentally toward protective coloration. There is much in natural selection ; there is much in protective coloration. But neither can be used to one-twentieth the extent that the neo-Darwinians, such as Mr. Wallace and the rest, have used them ; indeed these neo-Darwinians have actually confused the doctrine of natural selection with the doctrine of evolution itself.

" Heller is coming home soon. He has just written me from Berlin, where he saw our friend Matzchie who, you doubtless remember, has split up the African buffalo into some twenty different species, based on different curves of the horns. Matzchie told Heller that he had read my statement that of the four bulls I shot feeding together near the Nairobi Falls, the horns, according to Matzchie's theory, showed that there were at least two and perhaps three different species (among these four bulls from the same herd). Well, Matzchie absolutely announces that doubtless there *were* two species among them, because the locality is on the border-line between two distinct types of buffalo, that of Kenia and that of the Athi ! I think this is one of the most delightful examples of the mania for species-splitting that I have ever seen. On the same basis Matzchie might just as well divide the African buffalo into a hundred species as into twenty ; and as for the elephant he could make a new species for every hundred square miles.

"Apparently your 'African Nature Notes' was 'hoodooed' by my introduction and the dedication to me ; but I cannot help hoping that you will now publish a book giving your experiences in East Africa and up the White Nile. Without the handicap of my introduction, I think it would do well ! Seriously, the trouble with your ' African Nature Notes ' is that it is too good. The ideal hunting-book ought not to be a simple record of slaughter ; it ought to be good from the literary standpoint and good from the standpoint of the outdoor naturalist as well as from the standpoint of the big game hunter. Stigand's books fulfil both the latter requirements, but he has not your power to write well and interestingly, and he has a rather morbid modesty or self-consciousness which makes him unable to tell simply and as a matter of course the really absorbingly interesting personal adventures with which he has met. Unfortunately, however, the average closet naturalist usually wants to read an utterly dry little book by some closet writer, and does not feel as if a book by a non-professional was worth reading—for instance, I was interested in London to find two or three of my scientific friends, who knew nothing whatever about protective coloration in the field, inclined to take a rather sniffy view of your absolutely sound and, in the real sense, absolutely scientific, statement of the case. On the other hand, the average man who reads hunting-books is too apt to care for nothing at all but the actual account of the hunting or of the travelling, because he himself knows no more about the game than the old Dutch and South African hunters whom you described used to know about the different ' species ' of lion and black rhinoceros. Nevertheless I am sure that your ' African Nature Notes ' will last permanently as one of the best books that any big game hunter and out-of-doors naturalist has ever written. Charles Sheldon was saying exactly this to me the other day. By the way, I hope he will soon write something about his experiences in Alaska. They are well worth writing about. I am much irritated because Shiras, some of whose pictures I once sent you, will not make any use of his extraordinary mass of notes and photographs of

American wild game and the rarer creatures of the American forests and mountains.

" I am sending you herewith a rather long pamphlet I have published on the subject of protective coloration. Thayer answered the appendix to my ' African Game Trails,' in a popular Science Monthly article, re-stating and amplifying his absurdities. Men like Professor Poulton treat him with great seriousness, and indeed Professor Poulton is himself an extremist on this subject. I thought it would be worth while going into the subject more at length, and accordingly did so in the bulletin of the American Museum of Natural History, and I send you a copy. I shall also send one to Stigand. Do write me about your experiences."

Roosevelt was in a measure responsible for this excellent book, and it was due to his encouragement that Selous undertook its publication. He sent it in parts to his friend, who thus summarizes the author's literary style :—

" I have been delighted with all the pieces you sent me, and have read and re-read them all. Do go on with your lion article. I earnestly wish you would now write a book describing a natural history of big game. You are the only man alive, so far as I know, who could do it. Take S.'s book, for instance, which you sent me. It is an excellent book in its way, but really it is only a kind of guide-book. The sole contribution to natural history which it contains is that about the wolves and the big sheep. But you have the most extraordinary power of seeing things with minute accuracy of detail, and then the equally necessary power to describe vividly and accurately what you have seen. I read S.'s book, and I have not the slightest idea how the sheep or the ibex or the deer look ; but after reading your articles I can see the lions, not snarling but growling, with their lips covering their teeth, looking from side to side as one of them seeks to find what had hurt it, or throwing up its tail stiff in the air as it comes galloping forward in the charge. I can see the actual struggle as the lion kills a big ox or cow buffalo. I can see the buffalo bulls trotting forward, stupid and fierce-looking, but not dangerous unless molested, while they gaze from under their brow-armour of horn at the first white man they have ever seen. I can see wild hounds, with their ears pricked forward, leaping up above the grass to see what had shot at the buffalo they were chasing.

" I was immensely interested in your description of these same wild hounds. And what a lesson you incidentally give as to the wisdom of refraining from dogmatizing about things that observers see differently. That experience of yours about running into the pack of wild hounds, which, nevertheless, as you point out, often run down antelopes that no horse can run down, is most extraordinary. I am equally struck by what you say as to the men who have run down cheetahs on horseback. Judging from what Sir Samuel Baker saw for instance, cheetahs must be able to go at least two feet to a horse's one for half a mile or so. I wonder if it is not possible that the men who succeeded in running them down were able to get a clear chase of two or three miles so as to wind them. If different observers had recorded the two sets of facts you give as to the speed of the wild hounds under different conditions, a great many people would have jumped to the conclusion that one of the two observers, whose stories seemed mutually contradictory, must have been telling what was not so.

" Let me thank you again for the real pleasure you have given me by sending me these articles. Now do go on and write that book. Buxton and I and a great many other men can write ordinary books of trips in which we kill a few sheep or goat or bear or elk or deer ; but nobody can write the natural history of big game as you can."

Selous' intimacy with the President was of that charming character which unfortunately we now only associate with early Victorian days. They wrote real letters to one another of that heart-to-heart nature which only two men absorbed in similar tastes, and actuated by a similar intellectual outlook, can send as tributes of mind to mind. Such letters are ever a joy to the recipient ; but once Selous seems to have over-expressed his concern, when the President was attacked and wounded by a would-be assassin. The answer is both characteristic and amusing.

" My dear Selous, I could not help being a little amused by your statement that my ' magnificent behaviour, splendid pluck and great constitutional strength have made a great impression.' Come, come, old elephant-hunter and lion-hunter ! Down at the bottom of your heart you must have a better perspective of my behaviour after being shot. Modern civilisation, indeed, I suppose all civilization is rather soft ; and I suppose the average political orator, or indeed the average sedentary broker or banker or business-man or professional man, especially if elderly, is much overcome by being shot or meeting with some other similar accident, and feels very sorry for himself and thinks he has met with an unparalleled misfortune ; but the average soldier or sailor in a campaign or battle, even the average miner or deep-sea fisherman or fireman or policeman, and of course the average hunter of dangerous game, would treat both my accident and my behaviour after the accident as entirely matter of course. It was nothing like as nerve-shattering as your experience with the elephant that nearly got you, or as your experience with more than one lion and more than one buffalo. The injury itself was not as serious as your injury the time that old four-bore gun was loaded twice over by mistake ; and as other injuries you received in the hunting-field."

CHAPTER XII

1908–1913

ON March 20th, 1908, President Roosevelt wrote to Selous and announced his intention of taking a long holiday in Africa as soon as his Presidency of the United States came to an end, and asked Selous to help him. So from this date until the following March, Selous busied himself in making all the preparations and arrangements of a trip the success of which was of the greatest possible delight to Roosevelt and his son Kermit, and advantage to the American museums of Natural History, which benefited by the gift of a magnificent series of the East African and Nile Fauna.[1] Selous threw himself into the task with characteristic energy, with the result that the President had the very best advice and help. Roosevelt was at first adverse to taking a white man as caravan-manager, but Selous overruled this and proved the wisdom of employing such men as Cuninghame and Judd (for a short period), who are by far the most experienced hunters in East Africa, for Roosevelt and his son had then nothing to do but hunt and enjoy themselves, whilst all the burden of camp-arrangements was taken off their shoulders. Writing on November 9th, 1908, Roosevelt expresses his gratitude, and in his letter gives some insight into his policy of the " employment of the fit."

" Perhaps you remember the walk we took down Rock Creek, climbing along the sides of the Creek. On Saturday

---

[1] The collection of Birds and Mammals made by the Roosevelt expedition is now for the most part in the American Museum of Natural History at New York and at Washington. It is probably the best collection ever made by one expedition in Africa, and the book which the President wrote —" African Game Trails "—will always remain one of the best works of reference on the subject.

I took fifty officers of the general staff and War College on that same walk, because I thought the older ones might need a little waking up. I was rather pleased to find that they all went pretty well, even when we waded the Creek where it was up to our armpits, and climbed the cliffs. My dear Selous, it does not seem to me that I would have taken this trip (to Africa) without your advice and aid, and I can never begin to thank you for all you have done."

President Roosevelt was also delighted with the prospect that he would have Selous' company in his forthcoming voyage to Africa. Writing December 28th, 1908, he says :—

"Three cheers ! I am simply overjoyed that you are going out. It is just the last touch to make everything perfect. But you must leave me one lion somewhere ! I do not care whether it has a black mane or yellow mane, or male or female, so long as it is a lion ; and I do not really expect to get one anyhow.[1] I count upon seeing you on April 5th at Naples. It makes all the difference in the world to me that you are going, and I simply must get to Mac-Millan's during part of the time that you are there.

"I have written Sir Alfred Pease that I shall leave Mombasa just as soon as I can after reaching there ; go straight to Nairobi, stay there as short a time as possible, and then go direct to his ranch. I particularly wish to avoid going on any hunting - trip immediately around Nairobi or in the neighbourhood of the railroad, for that would be to invite reporters and photographers to accompany me, and in short, it would mean just what I am most anxious to avoid.

" Do let me repeat how delighted I am that you are to be with me on the steamer, and I do hope we will now and then meet during the time you are in British East Africa. I should esteem it an honour and a favour if you would accompany me for any part of my trip that you are able, as my guest."

No doubt to regular African hunters it is far better and

----

[1] President Roosevelt realised his hopes. In two days, between Sir Alfred Pease's farm and the railway (Kapiti Plains), he and his son Kermit killed seven lions. They also killed several others in the Sotik.

more enjoyable that they should pursue their wanderings unaccompanied by a white guide, but to any man, however experienced in other lands, success in Africa in a "first trip" certainly depends much on the local knowledge of the white hunter who accompanies the expedition, if expense is no object. A man may know all about hunting elsewhere, yet would make the most egregious mistakes in Africa, and perhaps never see the animals he most wishes to possess if he went only accompanied by a black shikari, so Selous made a point of insisting that Roosevelt should have the best local guidance at his command. Thus he writes to Sir Alfred Pease, who was then resident in East Africa :—

"*September 26th*, 1908.

"MY DEAR SIR ALFRED,

"Since I received your letter I have heard again from President Roosevelt. He tells me that he has heard from Mr. Buxton,[1] and that Mr. Buxton thinks that he ought not to engage a white man to manage his caravan. He quotes me the following passage from Mr. Buxton's letter: 'If you wish to taste the sweets of the wilderness, leave the Cook tourist element behind, and trust to the native, who will serve a good master faithfully, and whom you can change if not up to your standard.' The President then goes on to say that he is puzzled ; but that his own judgment now '*leans very strongly*' towards engaging a white man, and as I know that several men who have recently travelled in East Africa have also strongly advised him to do so, I feel sure that he will decide to engage Judd or a man named Cuninghame, who has also been strongly recommended to him. I must confess that I fail to follow Mr. Buxton's argument. The objection to being a Cook's tourist is, I always thought, because one does not like to be one of a crowd with many of whom you may be entirely out of sympathy, and how on earth the fact that he had a white man to look after all the details of his caravan, instead

---

[1] Mr. Edward North Buxton also did much to help the President in his forthcoming trip.

of a native headman, would give his trip the flavour of a Cook's tour, or prevent him in any way from tasting the sweets of the wilderness, I entirely fail to understand. Rather, I think, it would enhance the sweetness and enjoyment of his trip by relieving him of all the troublesome worries connected with the management of a large caravan. First of all, I believe that both Judd and Cuninghame would have a wider knowledge of the whole of East Africa than any native headman. The President would say, ' Now I want to go to the Gwas N'yiro river, where Neumann used to hunt, or to the country to the north of Mount Elgon, or to the country where Patterson saw all those rhinoceroses, giraffes and other game last year.' His manager would then work out the amount of provisions it would be necessary to take for such a trip, the number of porters necessary, engage those porters, and in fact make all the necessary arrangements to carry out the President's wishes. He would then arrange the loads, attend to the feeding of the porters, the pitching of camp every evening, and give out stores to the cook, and generally take all the petty details of the management of a caravan off the President's hands. As regards hunting, the manager of the caravan would never go out with the President unless he asked him to do so. He, the President, would go out hunting with his Somali shikari, a staunch Masai or other native to carry his second rifle, and natives to carry the meat and trophies of any animal shot. Of course, if when going after lions, elephants or buffaloes, he would like to have his white manager with him, all well and good, and it would be an advantage if such a man was an experienced hunter and a steady, staunch fellow who could be depended on in an emergency. Now, as I have said before, I feel sure that the President will finally decide to engage either Judd or Cuninghame, and the question is which is the better of those two men. I know neither of them—for although I seem to have met Cuninghame years ago, I do not remember him. I never heard of Judd until Bulpett spoke to me about him, nor of Cuninghame, until the President wrote and told me that Captain and Mrs. Saunderson had strongly advised him to engage him. He was also advised to engage Cuninghame by an American who was lately in East Africa, and now I have just got a letter from Cuninghame himself, a copy of which I enclose you to read. Please return it to me as I have sent the original to the President and asked him to get Mr. Akeley's opinion. As soon as I received this letter from Cuninghame, I went to London and saw Mr. Claude Tritton. He (Mr. Tritton) told me he knew both Judd and Cuninghame well, and thought them both thoroughly competent men. What do you think about it ? Do you know Cuninghame, or can you find out anything as to the relative value of these two men—Judd and Cuninghame ? MacMillan evidently knows both of them, and he is coming home in a month or six weeks' time. I have written all this to the President, and asked him to wait until we find out more about the two men ; but suggesting that should he finally decide to engage either Judd or Cuninghame, leaving it to us to decide which was the better man, we should wait to hear MacMillan's opinion, but then write and engage one or the other, and ask him to pick out himself the best Somali shikaris, gun-carriers and special native headmen, whom he could have ready by a given date (this is your suggestion, and I think an excellent one, as probably both Judd and Cuninghame know some good and reliable men and have had them with them on hunting-trips). In the meantime I told the President that I would answer Cuninghame's letter, in a strictly non-committal way, but telling him that I would write again in a couple of months' time, and that he *might* be wanted to manage the President's early trips. Let me know what you think of all this. I am now convinced that the President will take either Judd or Cuninghame with him. My arguments may have had some weight with him, for I am strongly in favour of his doing so, but other people have also given him the same advice. On the other hand, he has heard Mr. Buxton's arguments on the other side, and he may decide to be guided by them. But Mr. Buxton's views are, I think, not generally held by men who have travelled extensively in Africa, and I think the President will finally decide to engage either Judd or

Cuninghame, and if so we must try and ensure his getting the best man. I trust that the weather is now somewhat better in Scotland, and that you have had some good sport.

" Believe me,
" Yours very truly,
" F. C. SELOUS.

" P.S.—As Cuninghame is now starting on a trip which will last three or four months, he will be back at Nairobi early next month, and if engaged by the President, would then have plenty of time to look out for Somalis, and other picked natives, before the President's arrival in Africa."

Selous himself went on the hunt in East Africa with his friend, W. N. MacMillan, who was resident in East Africa. He left England on April 1st, 1909. Just before starting, he gives his ideas on the prospects of hunting in the rainy season.

" MY DEAR JOHNNY,
" Just a line to bid you good-bye before I start for East Africa. I would have written to you long ago, but I have been continually looking forward to coming over to see you before I left England ; but the bad weather has always prevented me from doing so. I am going out to East Africa at the very worst time of year, as heavy rains have still to come in May and June. The consequence will be that when I get there the whole country will be smothered in long grass, just as it was when I was in East Africa last, game will be very scattered, and there will be a very small chance of getting a lion. I would never have entertained the idea of going at this season but for the fact that I am going out as the guest of Mr. MacMillan (who has a large ranch near Nairobi), and my expenses will be very small. It just came to this, that I had to go now—as President Roosevelt wanted me to meet him at Naples and travel with him to Nairobi—or not at all ; but I don't look forward to much success, and the risk of getting fever is always very much greater when hunting in the rainy season, than in dry weather. Very heavy rains have been falling this season all

MT. KENIA FROM THE SOUTH.

over North and South Rhodesia, and in British Central Africa, as well as in East Africa. Every trip I have made during the last few years has been marred by rain. My last trip to East Africa was very much spoilt by rain and long grass, then the trip to Sardinia, as well as the last ones to Yukon and Newfoundland, were much spoilt by rain. I hope that you have now quite recovered from the effects of the pleurisy you caught last year in British Columbia. Are you going anywhere this year I wonder ? ''

Selous' first trip with MacMillan was successful in his getting several new species for his collection, but what he most wanted was a good black-maned lion. He was, however, unsuccessful in this. Mr. Williams, a member of his party, found three lions one day and killed two of them somewhat easily. The third charged and seized the unfortunate hunter by the leg, severely biting him. His life, however, was saved by the bravery of his Swahili gun-bearer, who gave the lion a fatal shot as it stood over his master. Mr. Williams was carried to hospital in Nairobi, where he lay between life and death for some time, and then completely recovered.

At the beginning of September, 1910, the Second International Congress of Field Sports was held at Vienna in connection with the Exhibition. The First Congress met at Paris in 1907, when the British delegate was Lord Montagu of Beaulieu, while, at Vienna, Selous was appointed by Sir Edward Grey, then Secretary of State for Foreign Affairs, as the official delegate from this country. The Congress was divided into three separate sections, dealing respectively with the Economic Importance, the Science and Practice, and the Legislation of Field Sports. The meetings of these three sections were held simultaneously, and the British delegate confined his attention to Section III (Legislation). In this section he was instrumental, with the cordial support of his French colleague, Comte Justinien Clary, President of the St. Hubert Club of France, in securing the passing of an important resolution in favour of the International Protection of Migrating Birds (especially the quail and woodcock).

T

At the Exhibition Great Britain was represented by a very fair collection of Big Game heads. Selous sending his best Koodoo, Wart Hog, White Rhinoceros, and Alaskan Moose, all exceptional specimens.

Selous was delighted with all he saw of the Great Hunting Exhibition, by far the finest of its kind ever offered to the public. I had hoped to meet him there, as I was going to hunt in Galicia, but found he had left for home. After describing the exhibition he wrote to me :—

" Warburton Pike wishes me to tell you that he will show you round the Exhibition. The Hungarian, Austrian and old German stags' heads are simply wonderful, but there are so many that it is bewildering. Weidmann's Heil."

Warburton Pike, here mentioned, was a splendid specimen of an Englishman, who was to British Columbia and Arctic Canada what Selous himself was to Africa. In his person existed a type of pioneer as modest as courageous. His travels and privations in the Arctic barren grounds made him known to most people in Canada, whilst his unselfish devotion and unfailing kindness to his fellow colonists endeared him to thousands of " voyageurs " who battled with the forces of Nature in the far North-West. He had a little mine amongst the Jack pines above Dease Lake where he lived, in the four working months, chiefly on tea, game and " flapjacks." Here he wrested from a refractory soil about as much gold as would have satisfied a Chinaman. Nevertheless, he toiled on year after year, because he had faith and the grit that bites deep even when common sense says, " Is it good enough ? '

Every spring saw " Pikey " full of hope, dragging his canoe with two Indians up the rain-drenched valley of the Stikine for 200 miles, and then on with pack-horses to his mine, another 100 miles, and every fall he raced downward to the sea, disappointed, but undefeated. When people met him in Vancouver, they would say, " How goes it, Pikey ? " Then his kind face would light up. " Splendid," he would reply, though he had hardly enough money to buy bread and butter.

Yet no one ever appealed to Warburton Pike in vain, for

on the rare occasions when he had a little money he invariably gave it away to his less fortunate friends. Every wastrel and miner on the Pacific slope knew " Pikey " and asked his advice and help, which was ever forthcoming, and in the eyes of the colonists he was the man who embodied the type of all that was best.

From Vancouver to the Yukon and from St. Michaels to the Mackenzie, the name of Warburton Pike was one to conjure with, and though comparatively unknown in England, his noble spirit will never be forgotten in the homes of all those who knew and loved him. Like all good men, he came to England in 1914, to play his part in the Great War, and I think it broke his heart when he found no one would employ him. He suffered a nervous breakdown, and in a fit of depression he took his own life in the summer of 1916. He published a few books, among which the best-known is " Through the Sub-Arctic Forest."

Selous had long cherished a desire to add to his great collection of African trophies a specimen of the Giant Eland of the Lower Sudan. An expedition for this purpose, however, without outside aid would have been to him too expensive a trip, so he made certain arrangements with Lord Rothschild and the British Museum which helped to alleviate the financial strain. After this had been successfully effected, he left on January 19th, 1911. Thus he writes of his plans on the eve of departure :—

" MY DEAR JOHNNY,

" Just a line in frightful haste to thank you for your kind letter and all your good wishes. If I am successful in finding the Elands, I fear I shall not be able to get a head for my own collection, as if I get permission to shoot more than those I want for the N.H. Museum, I must get a specimen for Rothschild, who will give me £70 for it, and I don't think they will let me get one for Rothschild and another for myself in addition to those I want for the Museum. I have, however, first to find the Elands and then shoot and preserve them, and to do the latter all by myself, with only raw savages to help me will be a hard job in the climate of the

Lado, where I am going to look for my game. I shall probably be more sure of finding the Elands to the south of Wau, in the Bahr-el-Ghazal Province, but the journey there would be much more expensive, and my means are very limited. I hope to get a free passage from Khartoum to Lado in the Government steamer I have been very much interested in Buxton's new Koodoo-like antelope, but what nonsense it is to call it a ' Mountain Inyala.' It does not resemble an Inyala in any way. It is of course quite a distinct species. I don't know if I shall be able to get anything for myself at all this trip. The white-eared Kob and Mrs. Gray's Kob are only found near Lake No, near the junction of the Bahr-el-Ghazal with the Nile, but going by steamer to and back from Lado, the steamer does not stop there, only steams through their district, and there is only one steamer a month. I shall look forward very much to seeing your new book on American big game on my return from the Sudan. With your own illustrations it cannot fail to be a very attractive and interesting work. The climate of the Lado they tell me is bad, unhealthy, intensely hot and enervating, but I hope I keep pretty well, and come back all right."

When he reached Cairo, he had an interview with Sir F. Wingate, to whom he had letters of introduction from Sir E. Grey. He then went on to Khartoum, where he met Mr. Butler, who was then in charge of big game matters connected with the Lower Sudan. Mr. Butler advised him to go to Mongalla, as the best and most accessible place at which to find the Giant Eland, since Wau had been much hunted, but Selous thought that the Tembera country would be the best, because few travellers had ever been there, and it could only be reached by a toilsome journey from the river with pack-donkeys. Accordingly he took the steamer going south. At Rejaf the vessel stopped to take in wood, and there met another steamer whose occupants informed him of the death of poor Phil Oberlander, who had just been killed by a buffalo near the village of Sheikh Lowala. It appears that this unfortunate fellow, who had just killed a fine Giant Eland at Mongalla, and was on his way home up the river, had stopped at a village near

Mongalla for a day or two, to try to get a buffalo, of which there were some herds in the neighbourhood. He had landed and very soon found a good herd. His shots wounded a big bull, which left the herd and retreated into the thick bush. Oberlander at once followed, but unfortunately forgot to reload his heavy rifle. The usual thing happened, and the wounded bull charged suddenly from one flank, and instead of reports two clicks ensued. The bull rushed at Oberlander, knocked him to the ground and literally beat his body to a pulp. Later in the day the bull was found lying dead. Its head was recovered by Mr. Butler, who sent it to the Vienna Museum, for which Oberlander had collected industriously for several years.

I first met Oberlander on the steamer going to Alaska, in September, 1908. He then called himself Count Oberlander, a title which I believe he had no claim to. He was a strange creature, full of assurance, and with a very complete contempt for British and American game-laws, and apparently oblivious of the fact that without their institution he would not have been able to obtain the specimens he so earnestly desired to capture. His one idea seemed to be to get specimens anyhow, and that a letter from the authorities of the Vienna Museum and an unlimited expenditure of cash would overcome all difficulties. In this he was partly right and partly wrong, for when he shot numerous female sheep and kids in the mountains of Cassiar he reckoned without the long arm of the law and the vigilance of the hawk-eyed Bryan Williams, our game warden in Vancouver, who promptly had him arrested and heavily fined.

As an example of his impudence he told us the following story, which I afterwards found was true in all details. One day in August, 1908, he went to the National Park at Yellowstone, and coolly informed two of the game wardens that he had come there to shoot a buffalo. At first the latter regarded the matter as a joke, but, finding he was in earnest, they told him that if he did not clear out they would confiscate his guns and arrest him. Unabashed, Oberlander said :

" Well, you need not get huffy. I will give you £250 for that old bull," pointing to an old patriarch within a wooden enclosure. The shaft, however, went home, for the game wardens at once reported the matter to their chief.

Now, £250 was a very nice sum, and it was quite within the realms of possibility that the old bull would die a natural death within the next year or two and that the dead carcase might be worth perhaps £50. Facts, therefore, were facts, which seemed to appeal to the business instincts of the park authorities, so next day Oberlander was informed that he might shoot the buffalo as soon as his cheque was forthcoming. Oberlander at once handed over the money and killed the bull, shooting him through the bars of the cage, and he showed us an excellent photograph of this doughty deed with no little satisfaction.

Oberlander afterwards hunted in Cassiar, Mexico, East Africa, and the Arctic regions, before going on the expedition up the Nile that was to prove fatal to him. In him the Vienna Museum lost a good friend, but he could scarcely be considered a good type of sportsman.

We need not follow Selous' wanderings in the parched uninteresting forest country about Tembera, where for nine weeks, in company with a native chief named Yei, he hunted the small herd of Giant Elands somewhat unsuccessfully. At last he killed a good female, but had no luck in securing a big male. On March 7th he went north to Rumbek, and on March 28th he and Captain Tweedie went north to a small river and shot nine Kobs. On April 4th he again left Rumbek and returned south for another hunt for the Elands, which was again unsuccessful. On April 29th he arrived at the Nile and turned homewards.[1]

" I cannot pretend," writes Selous, " I enjoyed my excursion in the Bahr-el-Ghazal Province. In the first place, I was unsuccessful in the main object of my journey. Then the deadly monotony of the landscape, the extraordinary scarcity of game, and the excessive heat of the climate, all combined to make my trip very wearisome and uninterest-

---

[1] Selous gave a full account of his trip in articles in the " Field," July–September, 1911.

ing." He came away, however, with a very deep admiration for the gallant band of young Britons who were doing the work of the Empire in the wilds of Africa.

At the end of this trying hunt he was far from well, and was unable to ride, so he had to tramp the whole way to the Nile on foot. Arrived at Rumbek the medical officer there discovered the cause of his ill-health, so, as soon as he arrived in England he saw Mr. Freyer, who recommended an operation. "I got over the operation," he writes to Abel Chapman, " wonderfully well, and simply healed up like a dog. In fact, I was the record case for healing up in ten years amongst Freyer's patients." I went to see him in a nursing home in London, and heard all about his Lado trip, which was rather a sore subject with him, but, with his usual determination, he was only full of ideas to go back again and make a success the next time. In August we both went again to Swythamley, as the guests of young Sir Philip Brocklehurst, and had a very pleasant time amongst the grouse on the Derbyshire hills. Afterwards Selous stayed for a time in the Isle of Wight, with his wife and boys, and later in the autumn he travelled to Turin Exhibition of hunting and shooting, as one of the British jurors.

Later in 1911 Selous again left for British East Africa, to go on another hunt to the Gwas N'yiro river, with his friend MacMillan. Before leaving he wrote to President Roosevelt, intimating that he feared he was now too old for the hard work entailed by African hunting, which called forth the following comfortable advice (Sept. 11th, 1911).

" MacMillan lunches here Thursday. I am very glad you are going out with him to Africa. He is a trump ! I am rather amused at your saying that you will not take any risks with lion now, and that you do not think your eyes are very good. I would not trust you !—seriously. I always wished to speak to you about the time that you followed the lioness which crouched in a bush, and then so nearly got Judd, who was riding after you. I think you were taking more of a chance on that occasion than you ought to have taken. It is not as if you had never killed a lion, and were willing to take any chance to get your first specimen. That I could quite understand. But you have killed a great many, and you ought not to do as poor George Grey did last year, and get caught through acting with needless recklessness.[1] I know you will not pay any heed to this advice, and, doubtless, you regard me as over-cautious with wild beasts, but, my dear fellow, at your age and with your past, and with your chance of doing good work in the present and future, I honestly do not think you ought to take these risks unless there is some point in doing so.

" You say you are too old for such a trip as that with MacMillan. Nonsense ! It is precisely the kind of trip which you ought to take. Why, I, who am far less hardy and fit, would like nothing better than to be along with you and MacMillan on that trip. But you ought not to take such a trip as that you took on the Bahr-el-Ghazal. It would have meant nothing to you thirty years ago ; it would mean nothing to Kermit now ; but you are nearly sixty years old, and though I suppose there is no other man of sixty who is physically as fit as you, still it is idle to suppose that you can now do what you did when you were in the twenties. Of course I never was physically fit in the sense that you were, but still I was a man of fair hardihood, and able to hold my own reasonably well in my younger days ; but when I went to Africa I realized perfectly well, although I was only fifty, that I was no longer fit to do the things I had done, and I deliberately set myself to the work of supplying the place of the prowess I had lost by making use of all that the years had brought in the way of gain to offset it. That is, I exercised what I think I can truthfully say was much intelligence and foresight in planning the trip. I made it for a great scientific National museum (which was itself backed by private capital), and made it at the time when the fact that I had been President gave me such prestige that the things were done for me which ought to have been done, but were not done, for you last

---

[1] George Grey, brother of Lord Grey of Falloden, an excellent hunter and charming personality. He was killed by a lion on Sir Alfred Pease's estate in 1910.

spring. Then I took along Kermit, who, in the case of the bongo and koodoo and Northern Sable, was able to supply the qualities that I once had had and now lacked. In consequence, while everything was done to make my trip successful and comparatively easy, I am yet entitled to claim the modest credit that is implied in saying that I took advantage of the opportunities thus generously given me, and that I planned the trip carefully, and used the resources that my past had given me, in the way of notoriety or reputation, to add somewhat to my sum of achievement. On your trip you also had genuine bad luck, and the trip was not long enough, and the opportunities were not sufficiently numerous, to allow the good and bad luck to even up, as they will on such a long trip as mine. For instance, it was simply luck in my case that got me some of my game ; but then it was simply luck, also, that I did not get some other things ; and so it about evened up.

" My own physical limitations at the moment come chiefly from a perfectly commonplace but exasperating ailment—rheumatism. It not only cripples me a good deal, so that I am unable to climb on or off a horse with any speed, but it also prevents my keeping in condition. I cannot take any long walks, and therefore cannot keep in shape ; but I am sufficiently fortunate to have a great many interests, and I am afraid, sufficiently lazy also thoroughly to enjoy being at home ; and I shall be entirely happy if I never leave Sagamore again for any length of time. I have work which is congenial and honourable, although not of any special importance, and if I can keep it for the next seven or eight years, my youngest son will have graduated from college, so that all the children will be swimming for themselves, and then I am content not to try to earn any more money.

" Fond though I am of hunting and of the wilderness and of natural history, it has not been to me quite the passion that it has been to you, and though I would give a great deal to repeat in some way or some fashion, say in Central Asia or in Farther India, or in another part of Africa, the trip I made last year, I know perfectly well that I cannot do it ; and I do not particularly care for smaller trips. If it were not for our infernal newspaper-men, I should go off for a week or two this fall bear-hunting in the Louisiana cane-brakes ; but I know I should be pestered out of my life by the newspaper-men, who would really destroy all my pleasure in what I was doing. I have found that I have to get really far off in the wilderness in order to get rid of them, even now, when I am no longer a person of public prominence. I never cared for the fishing-rod or the shot-gun, and I cannot afford to keep hunters. But you, my dear fellow, are still hardy, and you can still do much. I have never understood why your ' African Nature Notes ' did not have a greater financial success. It is a book which will last permanently, and will, I am sure, have an ever-increasing meed of appreciation. I reread it all last winter, and Sheldon, as I think I told you, mentioned to me the other day that he regarded it as the best book of the kind that had ever been written.

" Kermit is, at the moment, in New Brunswick getting moose, caribou, and beaver for the National Museum. I think I told you that he got four sheep, three of them for the Museum, on his recent trip into the Mexican desert. He made it just as you have made so many of your trips, that is, he got two Mexicans and two small pack-mules, and travelled without a tent, and with one spare pair of shoes and one spare pair of socks as his sole luggage. Once they nearly got into an ugly scrape through failure to find a water-hole, for it is a dangerous country. Kermit found that he could outlast in walking and in enduring thirst, not only the Mexicans but the American prospectors whom he once or twice met."

The reference in his letter to the lioness " which crouched in a bush, and then so nearly got Judd," refers to an incident that happened in the Gwas N'yiro bush in Selous' former hunt with MacMillan (1909), and this little adventure was related to me by William Judd himself. It appears that Selous and Judd were out together one day and disturbed two lionesses, which disappeared in thick forest. Selous at once galloped after them and outdistanced Judd, who

came somewhat slowly cantering behind, as he did not wish
to interfere with Selous. All at once, from the side of the
path, Judd saw a great yellow body come high in the air
from the side of the game-trail. He had no time even to
raise his rifle from the position across the saddle-pommel,
but just cocked it up across and pulled the trigger. One of
the lionesses, for such it was, had apparently crouched and
allowed Selous to pass, and had then hurled herself upon
the second hunter. By a fine piece of judgment, or a happy
fluke, Judd's bullet went through the lioness's eye and
landed her dead at his feet. His horse swerved. He fell
off, and found himself standing beside the dead body of his
adversary. Selous then returned, and was astonished to find
Judd standing over the dead animal in the path he had so
lately passed. I saw the skin of this lioness in Judd's house,
near Nairobi, in 1913, and noticed the little bullet hole over
the eye. If the missile had gone an inch higher it is doubtful
if the hunter would have escaped with his life, or at any rate
without a severe mauling.

After the trip with MacMillan, 1911–1912, Selous writes
(June 23rd, 1913) :—

" My dear Johnny,—I wonder where you are and what you
are doing. Some one told me the other day that you were
going to Africa on a shooting-trip this year. I had quite an
interesting time with MacMillan, and got a few nice things
to add to my collection. I got three nice Lesser Koodoos
on the lower Gwas N'yiro river as well as Gerenuks, good
Beisa, and Impala—though nothing exceptional—very
good specimens of the small races of Grant's Gazelle—
notata and *Brighti*—Greyv's zebra, the reticulated giraffe,
a good bushbuck, a striped hyena, two buffalo bulls, and a
lot of Dik-diks (of two distinct species and, I think, possibly
three). I don't know whether you have seen two letters of
mine in the ' Field '[1] for June 8th and 15th, but if you have,
you will have read my account of a rather interesting experience I had with a lion. This was the only lion I actually

---

[1] Selous, like all other good sportsmen, cherished a warm appreciation
for the " Field " newspaper. Mr. J. E. Harting, the Natural History and
Shooting Editor, was an old and much valued friend.

fired at, though I saw four lionesses one day, and tracked a lion and lioness on another occasion for a long distance and got close to them, but, owing to the thickness of the bush, could not see them.   That was the trouble on the lower Gwas N'yiro river.   The bush was so frightfully thick along the river, and outside, too, very often, that it required great luck to get a lion in the daytime, and they would not come to baits at night.   The bush was simply awful for buffaloes.   Let me know what you are doing and I will try and come over to see you one of these days."

Selous seems to have been unusually unlucky on the few occasions he met with lions in the Gwas N'yiro bush.   On March 2nd, 1912, he suddenly came face to face with a big lion, but as soon as it saw him, it dived into the forest and was immediately lost to view.   On another occasion he wounded a pallah buck, which a lion then killed, and death was so recent that Selous sat over "the kill" and waited.   The lion came and stood within twenty-five yards of the hunter, who fired two shots at it, and although assured that it was severely wounded he never recovered the body.[1]

The most exciting incident, however, of this trip was the killing of what he calls " My Last Buffalo."   Near the river he found the tracks of two old buffalo bulls, which he followed industriously for six miles.   At last he obtained a snap shot and hit one of the bulls badly through the lungs. After following the wounded animal a short distance, he suddenly heard the unmistakable grunts which always precede a charge.   The next instant the buffalo was on us, coming over the edge of the gully with nose outstretched, half a ton of bone and muscle driven at tremendous speed by the very excusable rage and fury of a brave and determined animal. . . .   When I fired, the muzzle of my rifle must have been within three yards of the buffalo."   The buffalo fell to the shot, the vertebræ of the neck being struck, and as he fell struck Elani the Somali.

" He only received this one terrific blow, though he was pushed to the bottom of the gully—only a few yards—in front of the buffalo's knees and right under its nose, but

[1] See " The Field," June 8th, 1912.

my bullet had for a moment partially paralysed it. I got another cartridge into the chamber of my rifle as quickly as possible, and, turning to the buffalo, somehow got a second bullet into its hind-quarters, which brought it down altogether. When I was again ready to fire, the buffalo was on its knees, with its hind-legs doubled in under it, in the bed of the gully a few yards below me, and Elani was under its great neck between its nose and its chest, with one arm outstretched and his right hand on the buffalo's shoulder, so that I had to shoot carefully for fear of hitting it.

" Elani then pushed himself with his feet free of the buffalo, whilst I stood where I was, ready to put in another shot if necessary, and it was, for the brave and determined bull partially recovered from the shocks its nervous system had received, though the mists of death were already in its eyes." Another bullet finished this gallant old bull. Elani the Somali was little the worse for his severe handling.

Selous spent the autumn of 1912 quietly at home or shooting with friends.

Writing to Chapman, September 26th, 1912, he says : " Don't worry about our visit to Hexham the other day. We got through the time quite easily. I can always pass an hour or two reading, very comfortably, but what I dislike more than anything else in English life is the crowds of people everywhere. . . . The crowds spoil all the pleasure of going to a cricket- or football-match or a theatre. It is always such a trouble getting away. I am already longing to be in Africa again. If only Mrs. Selous would be happy there, I would rather live in East Africa than in this country."

His mother[1] was still alive at Longford House, Gloucester, but getting old and feeble. He visited her in December, 1912. On December 7th, 1912, he was in Devonshire, shooting pheasants at MacMillan's place. " We got two fine days' shooting," he writes to Chapman, " but at the best, pheasant shooting is a very inferior sport to the pursuit of the grouse and the blackcock on the wild free moors of Northumberland. May I live to renew my acquaintance with them next year."

[1] She died peacefully in 1913.

Never did the spring come round but it always filled Selous with new delight, and then he used to write me long letters of the arrival of the birds and the advent of the early flowers. His joy was great when the Wrynecks took to his nesting-boxes in the garden, the Long-eared Owls nested in the woods close by, or the rare Dartford Warbler was seen again in its old haunts. Thus, on April 15th, he says :—

" I was very disappointed not to see you yesterday, as I was looking forward to a good crack with you. I have not yet heard the cuckoo, but the cuckoo's mate has been here in the garden since April 2nd. There are several pairs of snipe on Whitmoor Common (just below Worplesdon village) this year. They are now in full ' bleat.' There are also a number of Redshanks, the first I have ever seen here."

We used often to go out and look for nests in the commons, hedgerows, and woods at Worplesdon, and it was now a sorrow to him that he could no longer, owing to a slight deafness, recognize the notes of birds at a distance. These nests, when found, he never touched, as he had already got specimens of the eggs of all common birds, but the joy of hunting was always present, and he never tired of watching the habits of birds, even though he knew them well.

In the early part of 1913, Selous made a little trip to Jersey and Normandy, to visit the home of his ancestors, in whose history he always showed a lively interest. He wrote a long account of this to President Roosevelt, who replied as follows (April 2nd, 1913) :—

" I was greatly interested in your account of your visit to the home of your people in the Channel Islands, and then to Normandy. Of course, the Channel Islands are the last little fragment of the old Duchy of Normandy. I was always pleased by the way in which their people, when they drink the health of the King, toast him as ' The Duke.' It is the one fragment of the gigantic British Empire which owes fealty to the Royal House of England primarily as the representative of the still older ducal line of Normandy. Moreover, the people of the Channel Islands have always seemed to me, like the French Huguenots, to combine the virile virtues of the northern races with that

quality of fineness and distinction which are far more apt
to be found in France—at least in old France—than among
our northern Teutonic peoples.

"Indeed, those cathedrals represent the greatest architecture this world ever saw, with the sole exception of
Greece at its best. All that you say about the Normans
is true. What they accomplished in government, in
war, in conquest, in architecture, was wonderful beyond
description. No adequate explanation of the Norman
achievements during the eleventh and twelfth centuries
has ever been or ever can be made. As you say,
it was their conquest of England and the Scotch low-
lands that gave to the English their great push forward ;
and they gave this push in many different lands. The
handful of Norman adventurers who went to Italy fifty
years before the conquest of England speedily conquered
South Italy and Sicily and part of Greece, and ruled over
Saracen, Italian and Byzantine alike. The handful of
Norman adventurers who conquered Ireland, thereby for
the first time brought that country into the current of
European affairs. It was the Normans to whom we owe
the great ' Song of Roland.' They formed principalities
and dukedoms in the Holy Land and the Balkan Peninsula.
They set their stamp on the whole contemporary culture of
Western Europe, just as their kinsfolk, who, as heathens,
conquered heathen Russia, were the first to organize the
Slav communities of Eastern Europe. In a way, the action
of the Normans in the eleventh and twelfth centuries (for
by the thirteenth century their importance had vanished)
represented the continuation, culmination, and vanishing
of the tremendous Norse or Scandinavian movement which
began about the year 800, and ended in the latter part of
the eleventh century, when its Norman offshoot was at the
zenith of its power and influence. There are many things
about these people and their movements which are hard to
explain. Wherever the Norsemen went, they became completely merged with the people they conquered, and although
they formed a ruling caste they lost all trace of their own
language and traditions. The Norse invaders became

Sicilians in Sicily, Russians in Russia, Frenchmen in Normandy, Irishmen in Ireland, English- and Scotchmen in Great Britain. They furnished kings to England, Scotland and Sicily, and rulers to a dozen other countries, but they always assimilated themselves to the conquered people, and their blood must always have been only a thin strain in the community as a whole. When the Normans came over to conquer England, I believe that they represented the fusion, not only of Scandinavians and Franks, but of the old Gallo-Romans, whose language they took. A great many of the adventurers were base-born. King William himself was the bastard son of a tanner's daughter. Cooks and varlets, if vigorous enough, founded noble families. Quantities of Bretons and Flemings accompanied the Normans to England. Their language was purely French, and their culture was the culture of Latin Europe. They had lost every trace of the Norse language, and every remembrance of Norse literature and history. In William's army there seems to be no question that any man of fighting ability came to the front without any regard to his ancestry, just as was true of the Vikings from whom the Normans were descended ; yet these people were certainly not only masters of war and government, but were more cultured, more imaginative, more civilized and also more enterprising and energetic, not only than the English but than any of the other peoples among whom they settled. In England two centuries and a half later, their tongue had practically been lost ; they had been completely absorbed, and were typical Englishmen, and their blood must have been but a thin thread in the veins of the conquerors of Cressy and Agincourt. Yet this thin thread made of the English something totally different from what they had been before, and from what their kinsmen, the low Dutch of the Continent, continued to be. It is all absorbingly interesting."

In the spring of 1913 Selous decided to take a hunt in Iceland to collect the eggs of the various northern species of birds, and in this I was fortunately able to be of some assistance to him, as I had ridden nearly 1000 miles there in 1899, to study the bird-life of the island. Wherefore I was

BULL MOOSE ABOUT TO LIE DOWN.

able to give him accurate information of the various nesting-localities, and where each species was to be found in the summer months. Of only one bird, the Grey Phalarope, I could tell him nothing, but he and his friend, Heatley Noble, were so industrious that they found it breeding on the south coast of the island and secured eggs.

Of this trip, Heatley Noble, an intimate and well-loved friend of Selous, kindly sends me the following notes :—

" Well do I remember our first meeting, which was destined to prove the beginning of a close friendship of more than twenty years—I was working on the lawn when I saw a picturesque figure dressed in shooting-clothes and the ever-present ' sombrero ' walking towards me. Off came the hat and ' Good morning, sir, my name is Selous. I am just beginning to arrange my collection of eggs and was advised at the Natural History Museum to call on you, as they say your method of keeping a collection was good.'

" How odd it seemed to me that this hero of a thousand hairbreadth escapes should start egg-collecting once more at his time of life (he was then about forty-five). I was soon to learn that the energy he has always thrown into his hunting-trips was to be given equally to this new pursuit —it was not really new, as he had collected as a boy at Rugby, and in Germany, but years spent away from home had seriously damaged the spoils of early days. I showed him my collection, and on hearing that he wanted to start with even the commonest species, we went off and collected what nests I knew. How interested I was to see the care with which this man, who could handle four-bore rifles as tooth-picks, yet retained the delicacy of touch which enabled him to wrap in cotton-wool such small eggs as those of Blue Tits and Chiffchaffs ! He told me he was off to Asia Minor for a few days, and then on to the plains of Hungary. This programme would have been sufficient for most men, but there were some days to spare, the season was short, so I recommended him to go to the Isles of Scilly ; the owner being an old friend, I was sure I could get him leave. He went, and subsequently wrote me a long letter mentioning

U

all the different species he had found, which fairly made my mouth water !

" Unlike some collectors, Fred Selous, if he knew where a good thing was to be found, made it his delight to share that knowledge. Perhaps to the detriment of the species, but greatly to the joy of his friends. Jealousy was unknown to him, his pleasure was always to help others, regardless of trouble ; had he been to any part of the world where you had not, he would make it his business to give you the minutest details so that you could go there almost blindfold ! I know this from personal experience, as it was thanks to him I went birds'-nesting into Andalusia and Hungary, besides many little trips in these Isles. If he had been lucky with some rare species in a foreign country, he would press his duplicates on anyone interested, and more than this, it was difficult to prevent him handing out eggs he really could not spare. His own large collection was purely personal. I believe there were only some Bearded Vultures' eggs in it that he did not take with his own hands. These came from Sardinia, where he had been after Mouflon—he had seen the birds, but was too soon for eggs. If I found a nest on this property which he wanted, he would never let me take the eggs and send them to him, he would bicycle over to lunch (twenty-three miles each way) and take them with his own hands !

" I had long wished to visit Iceland on a nesting-trip, and in the early spring of 1913, wrote asking Selous if he would come. To my great joy I found that he had already arranged to go there, and it was soon fixed up that we should go together. What a glorious time we had, and how much I owe to his companionship, invariable good temper and knowledge of travel ! The ship we went out in was a smelly beastly thing, the weather cold, sea rough and food vile. The latter bothered Fred not at all, he often said he could live on any food that would support a human being, and from subsequent experience I believe he was right. He liked some things better than others, but anything would do. I only saw him beaten once ; we had had an eight-hour ride in vile weather, at last we arrived at the farm where we were to spend the night. Fred loved meat, and our host produced a plate of stuff that might have been thin slices of mutton. Fred attacked it, and I watched developments ! In place of the Aldermanic smile I expected, the face contracted, the mouth opened, a sharp word escaped, and later on the first course of his dinner turned out to be pickled Guillemot of the previous season ! But to return to our ship. Fred didn't smoke, the rest of the company did to a man, rank Danish cigars, which made even a good sailor wish he had never left home. We were driven into the dining saloon, the only place where there was some peace, though the smell of ponies and cod took the place of vile cigars. Here Fred used to spend his day reading, his favourite book being ' Tess of the D'Urbervilles.' One day he complained bitterly of the light, and for the first time I noticed that this wonderful man was reading small print without glasses—aged, I think, sixty-three, and as long-sighted as anyone I ever met. All things come to an end in time, and after what seemed a month, and was really three days, we arrived at Reykjavik, starting the following day on our trip. The first trek was a short one, only twenty miles, but quite long enough for me, as next day I could hardly climb on the pony, whereas Selous jumped on like a boy, and during the whole of our journey, above 1000 miles on pony back, never once felt stiffness. We did well from an ornithological point of view, finding some forty-six different kinds of nests, and bringing home over 1000 eggs, *not one* of which was broken, thanks mostly to the careful packing of our friend. Selous had the greatest objection to getting his feet wet unnecessarily, and when crossing those rapid rough rivers would take his feet out of the stirrups and somehow curl them up behind him, it was a wonderful performance, and how he kept his balance with the pony stumbling and regaining his feet as only an Icelander can, fairly beat me. Once, when crossing an extra bad place, full of boulders and in a flooded condition, his pony got on the top of a flat rock under water ; when he went to crawl down on the other side, there was the inevitable hole from back-wash—down went the pony, the jerk pulling Fred over on to his ears—I thought he must have fallen into the boiling cauldron— No ; a short scramble, the pony righted himself and there was Fred as peaceful as ever, didn't even look round ! When we were safe on the far side, I said to him, ' If you had gone off then, you would not have stopped till you got to the sea.' His reply was, ' Yes, but I didn't.'

" I was very anxious to get on to the Island of Grimsey, one of the European breeding places of the Little Auk. It is situated some sixty-five miles from Akureyri, and I was told motor fishing-boats went there sometimes. I told our guide to telephone on and find out if such a boat could be hired, the reply came back that a small one would be available. The terms were settled, and the boat was to be ready the following evening, to start by 9 p.m. About 8 o'clock, we went to the quay to inspect our ship, when to my horror I was shown a single-cylinder thing not as large as a moderate Thames pleasure-launch, a free-board about 10 inches, no cabin, no deck. I'm bound to confess my heart failed me, it didn't seem quite good enough to trust ourselves to a sixty-five mile trip in a little tub with two youths (one of whom had a withered hand) and a very doubtful looking compass ! Not so Fred, he never raised the least objection to a North Sea trip in a ship dependent on a single plug, which might become sooty any moment ! In due time we started, and after watching the midnight sun, my shipmate remarked, ' I think I shall turn in.' ' Turn in where ? ' ' Oh, the cockpit will do.' It was full of rusty old chains, he could just get into it and lie curled up in a sort of knot on the rug, and here he passed a dreamless night, never moving until I called him as the boat touched land about 8.30 a.m. On landing, the first thing was to find out where the Little Auk might breed. The Parson told us he knew a man skilled in such matters. With a total population of 72 souls, 13 of which were belonging to the Parson, it ought not to be difficult to find the tastes of any unit of the congregation (especially after eighteen years' residence). In a short time a fisherman arrived with a coil of rope and a crowbar ; the latter he drove into the ground, tied the rope to it and heaved the end over the rock. Our friendly Parson then waved towards the sea, remarking, ' There you are, how do you like it ? The birds breed in the rocks at the bottom.' Honestly I did *not* like it, but Fred remarked, ' Thank you, that will do well,' and without another word seized the rope and was soon at the bottom. I *had* to follow, the Parson looking down from the top very much like the picture of Nebuchadnezzar looking down at Daniel in the lions' den. The Little Auk was not there, only Puffins inhabited that part of the island, and we had to regain the top as best we could. Later on we were shown a spot where the bird really did breed, and two eggs rewarded us for the long journey. We left again the same evening in a thick fog, Selous curling himself up once more on the rusty chains, and utterly oblivious to the fact that it was just a toss-up if our helmsman ever found the mainland again or not. A short time after this event we were resting at a farm-house, and as usual asked if the boys knew of any nests. One of them replied that there was a Merlin's nest with five eggs in some rocks a few miles from the farm. Off we started, and all went well until we came to the face of a nasty crumbling steep place. The farm-boy, with only a pair of shoes made from raw sheep-skin, made no bones about it and dashed up to the top. I was next, and after going up a certain distance could find no foothold and had to stop where I was. Selous was a little below me, and, when he reached my none too comfortable seat, I suggested that it was no place for me, and that the boy who was at the nest might as well bring down the eggs. This was not Fred's way of doing things, he simply remarked, ' I think I'll go a little further.' He did, right up into the nest, returning with the five eggs, and this too with a pair of long, heavy Norwegian field-boots on. I felt a proper weakling, but our friend never once rubbed it in by word or deed. Of side he had none, and the possibility of hurting anyone's feelings was absolutely repugnant to him *always*. During our long rides in Iceland, he told me many things about his life in Africa in the earlier days. How I wish I could have taken down the stories he related ! To hear him talk was like listening to someone reading a book. He was

never at a loss for a word or the name of a place. Perhaps
we would have been riding together in silence for some time,
then Fred would turn round with the remark, ' Do you
know,' he then would start and tell me something of his
early days in Africa, what may never have been published,
things *he* did for which *others* got the praise. I fear this
most unselfish of men was far too often made use of. Not
that Selous did not see through the schemes of various
impostors ; he did, but as he would never have done a dirty
trick to a living soul, he could not believe they would to
him. His fondness for tea was a fine advertisement for this
indigestible drink. He told me that in his early camping
days in Africa, he used to throw a handful of tea in the pot
before starting off to hunt, let it simmer all day, freshening
it with another handful in the evening. The tea-leaves were
never emptied ! The first time he stayed with me I saw him
making very bad weather of a glass of champagne ; on asking
if he would prefer something else, the prompt reply came—
' Tea.' Ever after that he was provided with his pet drink,
and it used to interest me to see how he invariably left the
spoon in the cup, a relic of old veldt days where manners
were unknown. Fred's ideas on food were different to most
people's. One evening after a wretched eight hours' ride
in pouring cold rain, just as we neared the farm where we
were to rest, I said, ' How would you like to dine with
me at the Ritz to-night ? A little clear soup, a grilled sole,
lamb cutlets and green peas, mushrooms on toast and a
bottle of Champagne 94 ? ' ' Thanks very much, but if I
had my choice of what I should like best, it would be good
fat moose and tea.'

" I think it was not generally known that Selous held
strong views about what he called Psychic Force, for during
the whole of our long friendship I only once heard him let
himself go on this subject, and I am bound to confess that
coming from a man like him whose every word was truth,
anyone who heard him relate what he had seen take place
in his own home with only his brothers and sisters present,
could not but help owning that he was in the presence of
something beyond his understanding. His conversation was

always worth listening to, but like all brave men, it was difficult to get him to talk. If he liked those present, he would often delight his audience and yarn on for hours, if he didn't, he was civility and politeness itself, but no yarns ! His little sayings, without *an atom* of side, always amused me. The last time but one that I saw him when on leave, I remarked on his close-cropped beard. ' Yes,' he said, ' it looked so white in the bush, they seemed as if they were always shooting at it.'

" When war broke out I had not seen him for some little time. I was killing rabbits in the park, and on looking up saw Fred. He was furious, he had hoped to be sent to France as a ' Guide,' but the scheme fell through, and he feared he would not get a job. How cross he was ! Shortly after I received a wire that he was coming over to lunch. He arrived radiant as a boy home from school, the reason being that he was to go to Africa with a contingent of 150 men with the rank of lieutenant, at the age of sixty-three ! And yet there are conscientious shirkers who *also* call themselves ' Englishmen.' The last time I saw him he lunched here on the way from Gloucester when he had been to say good-bye to his boy in the Flying Corps, and was just starting for his return to Africa. In the midst of all he had to do, and the rush of settling his affairs, he heard of our own trouble. Sitting down at once, he found time to write one of the most sympathetic, charming letters one pal may write to another. It came straight from that great heart which knew no fear, but loved his neighbour far better than himself."

Of the trip to Iceland Selous writes to Chapman (July 26th, 1913) :—

" Just a line to tell you that Heatley Noble and I got back from Iceland a few days ago. We had a lot of cold, disagreeable weather, but got a nice lot of eggs ; indeed, practically everything that one can get in Iceland, except the Purple Sandpiper. When we got to where they were, it was too late, and we only found a pair with young. We got some eggs which were taken a fortnight earlier. We found the Red-necked Pharalope breeding in hundreds at Myvatn

and other places, and we also took several clutches of Grey
Pharalope which we found breeding in some numbers in
two districts. We got all the Iceland ducks at and near
Myvatn, including the Harlequin, Barrow's Golden Eye,
Scaup, Long-tailed Duck, Scoter and several others.
Whooper Swans were plentiful in some parts of the south
and west, but not in the north, and we saw a good many
Great Northern Divers, and got several clutches of eggs.
We went out to the island of Grimsey, thirty miles north of
the north coast of Iceland and just within the Arctic circle,
and got the eggs of the Little Auk there ; and also Snow
Buntings, which were extraordinarily abundant on the
island. Redwings and Mealy Redpolls we got in the birch
scrub in the north. But I will tell you all about our trip
when we meet. The boys came home on Wednesday, and
we are all going to Scotland on August 9th. I don't yet
know when the show will come on at which I shall have to
speak, but I hope that it will not be before October. I found
the Sandpipers' and Wheatears' eggs on my arrival home."

In August and September he went to Scotland for the
grouse-shooting, which he enjoyed, but which never seemed
to fill the place in his mind of Africa. He was always
thinking of the land of sunshine, and says to Chapman
(September 9th, 1913) :—

" During the long waits at grouse-driving the other day,
I was always wishing myself in the forests on the slopes of
Mount Kenia, collecting butterflies, for there every moment
was full of excitement. I am sorry to tell you that my dear
old mother's health—she is now in her eighty-eighth year—
is such that it will henceforth be impossible for me to leave
England again on any long trip during her lifetime. She is
not ill, but she has lost strength terribly during the last
three months, and I do not think her life can be much
further prolonged. So now all hope of going to the Sudan
this winter is gone, and as at my age every year tells heavily
against me, I doubt whether I shall ever get a giant Eland
for the Natural History Museum."

Abel Chapman at this time asked Selous to go with him
to the Sudan, but Selous could not go then, as he had

business with his mother's will, but suggested he might possibly join him in February, 1914, down the Nile below the sudd.

In November, 1913, he went to Rugby to give a lecture, and to see his boy Freddy, of whom he was very proud. To Chapman he says :—

" I went there yesterday (Rugby) to see the football match against Cheltenham College. Freddy played for Rugby. He has played in every out match for the school this term, against the Old Guard, the Oxford A, the old Rugbeians, and Cheltenham College, so I think he is now definitely in the first fifteen. As he is now only fifteen years of age, and will not be sixteen till April 21st next, I think that is rather good ; indeed, I think he must be the youngest boy in the school fifteen, and so may some day be Captain of the Rugby fifteen. He plays forward, and weighed 11 stone 10 lbs."

Young Fred Selous was a true son of his father, and very like him in many ways. He had the same charm and modesty of manner, and had he lived would have gone far, and no doubt made his mark in the world. But it was not to be, for he gave his life for his country on January 4th, 1918, on the same day one year later than the death of his father. He was educated at Bilton Grange and Rugby, where he proved to be an excellent athlete, being in the Running VIII, and in 1915 Captain of the Rugby XV. He entered Sandhurst in September, 1915, and on leaving in April, 1916, was gazetted to the Royal East Surrey Regiment and attached to the R.F.C. Very soon he developed exceptional ability as a flying officer. In July, 1916, he went to the front and was awarded both the Military Cross and the Italian Silver Medal of Military Valour. My friend, Lieutenant Edward Thornton, was flying close to Freddy Selous on the fatal day, and states :—

" I was up at 15,000 ft. over the German lines, when I saw Captain Selous take a dive at a German machine some 2000 feet below. What actually happened I do not know, but all at once I saw both wings of the machine collapse, and he fell to the earth like a stone."

The major commanding Freddy's squadron thus wrote to his bereaved mother :—

" It is a severe blow to the squadron to lose him, for he was beloved by officers and men alike. In fact, his popularity extended to a much greater area than his own aerodrome. In the short time that I have known him I have been struck with the courage and keenness of your son— always ready for his jobs, and always going about his work with the cheeriest and happiest of smiles. He was the life and soul of the mess."

The second son of Selous and his wife is Harold Sherborne Selous, who will be nineteen in October, 1918. He was educated at Radley College, and is at present in the Officers' Cadet Battalion at Pirbright, and expects to take a commission shortly.

CHAPTER XIII

1914–1915

IN May, 1914, Selous went to Texel Island, on the coast of Holland, where he took a few eggs and enjoyed watching the Ruffs, Avocets, Godwits, Turnstones, and Spoonbills. In June and July he was making preparations for an expedition with his friend Abel Chapman to the Sudan and White Nile, with the object of collecting Gazelles and eventually, if possible, the Giant Eland. The plan was to enter via Port Sudan, shoot Ibex and Gazelles between that port and Khartoum and then go south in January, 1915, to Lake No, where Mrs. Gray's Lechwe could be found. Selous would then leave his friend and go to Wau for the Elands, and afterwards to the hinterland of the Bahr-el-Ghazal and search for the various local races of Uganda Kob found there and still imperfectly known.[1]

Other events of greater importance, however, put an end to this proposed trip. In August commenced the Great War, in which Selous at first had no thought of taking part, but as a succession of adverse circumstances multiplied, he felt that interest and responsibility in the conflict of nations that true men of whatever rank or station must experience. Foresight, common sense, and a knowledge of the great power of the Central Empires soon convinced him that in order to beat them, sooner or later we should have to enrol every fit man in the United Kingdom. He was not a man to delay once his mind was made up. The question was only how and where his services could be of most use. He understood " the bush " and " bush fighting " better

---

[1] The Kob of Western Bahr-el-Ghazal has whitish ears and a white area round the eye, which is not found in the Uganda Kob. It has been named by Dr. Heller, Vaughan's Kob, from a single specimen.

than most men and he resolved to try and join the forces fighting in East Africa.

Soon he learned that it was probable that his friend Colonel Driscoll was about to organize a force, perhaps for service in East Africa, or even for the front in France.

Writing to Abel Chapman on August 12th, 1914, he says :—

" Before seeking enrolment in the Legion of Frontiersmen, I went to one of the biggest Life Insurance Companies in London and was examined by their chief medical officer, and I have got a splendid certificate of health. After saying that he found all my organs perfectly sound he goes on, ' his heart in particular, considering the active life he has led, is in excellent condition. He is also remarkably active and muscular and in my opinion fit for service anywhere.' I may say that Colonel Driscoll has not yet got his authority from the Government to get his men together, though he has enrolled several thousand and is prepared to come forward at a moment's notice. I fear that there will be frightful delay, as I have good reason to believe that none of our troops have yet left England and the Government will attend to nothing until they have got all their regular forces to the front. However, if the war goes on for any time they will want all the men they can get, and I fully expect that the Legion of Frontiersmen will get to the front sooner or later, but perhaps not till the Colonial forces arrive in England."

Writing on August 14th, 1914, he says :—

" I believe this war will be a terrific business, and that we shall have to send something like a million of men out of the country before it is over, so that sooner or later I think I shall get into the fighting line. Freddy will not be old enough to volunteer until April 21st next, when he will be seventeen, and I fully expect that he will be wanted. *If I should be eliminated it would not matter a bit as I have had my day*, but it would be a pity if so promising a boy got scuppered at the outset of his life."

All this time he was fretting at official delays, for writing to Chapman, September 22nd, 1914, he betrays his impatience.

" It passes my understanding why the War Office will not give the order to Colonel Driscoll to take some of his men, who are all well disciplined and can shoot, to the front at once. . . . I am afraid that Lord Kitchener has no intention of employing anything in this war but regular troops. . . . Driscoll offered to take 1000 men to British East Africa to invade and take German East Africa,[1] but this offer was also refused."

In October, Colonel Driscoll thought there was no chance of being employed. " I personally," writes Selous to Chapman, October 23rd, 1914, " do not think he will ever be employed at all, so I determined to make an application direct to the War Office for service at the front with the Army Service Corps, or as an interpreter, or for any kind of work in which a good knowledge of French and some German might be useful. I got two letters of introduction to two members of Parliament who are working at the War Office and was sympathetically received by them. I took my health certificate with me. My application for service was submitted straight to Lord Kitchener, and I have got his reply from H. J. Tennant, M.P. : ' I spoke to Lord Kitchener to-day about you and he thought that *your age was prohibitive against your employment* here or at the seat of war in Europe.' Well, I suppose that is the end of it, for I put no faith in Driscoll's belief that sooner or later his services will be required, so I suppose that neither you nor I will be allowed to serve our country in this war. We are looked upon as useless old buffers."

In November, 1914, he was doing special constable at Pirbright and was rather depressed that he could get nothing better to do, and that his boy Freddy would soon have to go into training as a soldier. He hoped his son would be able to join the Egyptian Army and have " a good time in the Sudan or the King's African Rifles. As I can do nothing that really matters, I often feel that I should like to go right away—say to the Belgian Congo—hunting

---

[1] As a matter of fact his proposition was a heavier one than the authorities imagined. It took a large army, working hard over a period of four years, before the Germans were driven out of British and German East Africa.

and collecting for a year. But until the war is over, or nearly over, I am afraid I shall not be able to leave here, as besides being enrolled myself as a special constable, I have now undertaken to do a lot of work under the ' Defence of the Realm ' Act. I feel it is all unnecessary fuss and bother, as even if a raid could be made on the East coast of England, no invasion could take place south of the Thames until the French are conquered and crushed, and the Germans take possession of all the Channel ports opposite our south-eastern shores, and further until our Navy has lost command of the seas. Personally I don't believe that either of these disasters can ever happen, so I must do what the Government requires. Anyhow I feel that it is a waste of energy." (Letter to Chapman, November 11th, 1914.)

In February, 1915, he still had hopes of going to East Africa with Colonel Driscoll's force, and speaks of the difficulties he had encountered in obtaining his commission in a letter to my wife. (February 18th, 1915.)

" I know absolutely nothing about the ' Legion of Frontiersmen ' as far as service is concerned, but Colonel Driscoll has always promised me that if he was sent abroad, he would take me with him as ' Intelligence Officer.' After last September, when he offered to take 1000 or 2000 men to East Africa and his services were declined by the War Office and the Colonial Office, I tried to get a job myself with the Army Service Corps in France. I went to the War Office and saw Mr. Tennant and said that I could speak French, a good deal of German and make the Flemish people understand my South African Dutch. Mr. Tennant laid my application and my very excellent bill of health before Lord Kitchener, who wrote me the next day simply saying that ' my age was prohibitive against giving me any employment either here or at the seat of war in Europe.' After that I gave up all hope of being able to do anything and settled down as leader of the special constables of Pirbright, and also did work for the ' Defence of the Realm ' Act. In December, however, I got a letter from Colonel Driscoll saying, ' If I am ordered out—as is very probable—to East Africa, will you come with me ? ' I wired at once to say I would be ready at very short notice, and went to see him. I found that the War Office had sent for him and asked him how long it would take him to get together 1000 men for service in East Africa. He said that the War Office had already got 3000 men, originally enrolled in the Legion, who when they found that they could not be employed in a body had enlisted in the new army. However, he undertook to get 1000 men by the end of January, and I can vouch that he was working very hard to accomplish this, when he got a letter from the W. O. (who had told him to get on with the enlistment of the men) saying that for the present his services would not be required, as they were in communication with the Government of India as to getting more troops for East Africa from there. Everything seemed over again, but about three weeks ago, I got another letter from Driscoll saying, ' Are you available for service at once ? ' The W. O. had come to him again and asked *him* to get 1000 men together by February 10th. I have been helping him since then in getting notices in the papers, and receiving the names of men willing to serve in East Africa. Colonel Driscoll wanted and still wants to take me with him as Intelligence Officer, so I went last Monday to the War Office and saw Major Guest (who was with Major-General Lloyd the other day when he inspected Driscoll's men) and asked him about maps of German East Africa, and Major Guest then told me that they were not going to give Driscoll an Intelligence Officer. He told me that Driscoll would just have to put down the names of his officers and submit them to the W. O. for acceptance or rejection. As I told Major Guest, this would mean that my name would certainly be rejected on account of my age. I then saw Driscoll again, and found him very much discouraged, as he said that not only had the W. O. refused to allow either a signalling officer, a transport, or an intelligence officer[1] on his strength, but they also wanted to impose some men of their own choosing on him as officers, whom he does not know, thereby obliging him to dismiss some of his company officers,

---

[1] This was hardly the fault of the War Office, who had already organized their local intelligence officers in East Africa.

who have served with him, and whom he does know. I think it quite possible that Driscoll may resign, but he will not do so until he has got the men the War Office want. As far as I am concerned I now think my chances of going to Africa with this force are small, although Major Guest told me that General Lloyd was in favour of letting me go. I know absolutely nothing about the Legion of Frontiersmen in this country, nor do I believe that there is the slightest chance of the Germans landing any force in this country, as long as our Navy remains in being."

On February 4th, 1915, he went to see Colonel Driscoll, who said the War Office had stretched the age-limit in his case, that he would take him to East Africa as Intelligence Officer. " I hope I shall not prove too old for the job and break down," he writes. Colonel Driscoll expected to have two or three months' training and leave for East Africa in April. On March 7th, Mrs. Selous went to Havre to work in the Y.M.C.A. hut there. Selous then left for London. " It was thought that I would start for East Africa with an advance contingent before she left for France," but he was delayed, waiting for the whole regiment to go together. Writing to Chapman, March 21st, 1915, he says : " I understand that we are to start for East Africa next Saturday, or very soon afterwards. Well, good-bye, old friend. These troublous times will be over some day and then if we are still both alive and have any vitality left, we must do that Nile trip."

Selous landed with his battalion at Mombasa on May 4th, 1915. Colonel R. Meinertzhagen gives a few particulars of the strange assortment of men comprising the force :—

" The battalion (25th Royal Fusiliers) concentrated at Kajiado soon after landing at Mombasa, when it was inspected by General Tighe, then Commanding in East Africa. I accompanied Tighe on this inspection, and we formed a very high opinion of the officers and men. They were an unpolished lot but real good business-like men who meant fighting.

" Selous was then in front of his platoon, looking very serious and standing strictly to attention. We recognized

MT. KILIMANJARO FROM THE NORTH.

each other at once and were soon deep in the question of the validity of the Nakuru Hartebeest and the breeding of the Harlequin Duck in Iceland. We both forgot we were on parade, much to the amusement of Selous' platoon, who still stood rigidly to attention throughout the discussion.

" Selous' company was indeed a mixed lot and contained men from the French Foreign Legion, ex-Metropolitan policemen, a general of the Honduras Army, lighthouse keepers, keepers from the Zoo, Park Lane plutocrats, music-hall acrobats, but none the less excellent stuff and devoted to their officers."

After some delays the regiment was sent up by the Uganda railway to the Victoria Nyanza, where they went by steamer to attack the German forces on the Western bank of the Great Lake at Bukoba. The following notes are Selous' own account of these operations.

Personal Experiences, during the Attack on and Capture of the Town and Wireless Installation at Bukoba, on the Western side of Lake Victoria Nyanza.

It was about midnight on June 21st, 1915, or very early on the morning of June 22nd, that we approached an island in the bay of Bukoba, which, as the captain of our ship no doubt knew very well, and as we were to find out on the following day, was only about half a mile from the town, and the fine wireless installation close to the Lake shore. We had been going very slowly and quietly for some time before nearing the island, and the intention of our com-mander-in-chief may have been to land his forces in the dark, without the knowledge of the Germans. But the guard on the island were wide awake, and either heard or saw our steamer approaching, as they immediately sent up six blue lights, one after the other, which illuminated the whole island, and of course, warned the Germans in Bukoba that a hostile British force was about to attack the town. They no doubt thought that this attack would be made in the bay itself, under cover of the ships' guns, as we found later that all their trenches and block-houses along the shores of the bay had been manned. After the flashlights

x

had gone up, and it was evident that a surprise attack on the town was no longer possible, all our ships retired in the darkness for some little distance, but before daylight again approached the coast, at a point some three miles to the north of Bukoba, from which they were hidden by a point of land. We all stood to arms on the crowded decks at 4 a.m., and silently waited for daylight. At the first streak of dawn, about 5.30, the disembarkation of our men (400 of the 25th Battalion Royal Fusiliers) commenced. My Company, A, was the first to land, a somewhat slow process, as the heavy row-boats only travelled very slowly and our ship was further than it looked from the shore. From within a few yards of the water's edge to the base of a precipitous slope, some 200 yards distant, which in places was a sheer cliff, some 300 or 400 feet high, the ground was covered with bush and large banana-plantations, amongst which were scattered a few large and comfortable-looking native huts. Had the Germans only known that we were going to attempt a landing at this spot and brought a machine-gun to the top of the cliff, or had they even lined the top of the cliff with riflemen, they would probably have been able to kill every man in the closely packed boats, and sunk the latter before they reached the shore. Luckily they did not know where we were going to land, until too late, for once on shore, we worked our way as quickly as possible through the banana-plantations, and gained the top of the cliff unopposed. We were only just in time, however, as we were soon engaged with the enemy's forces, which, having now become aware of our intentions, were rapidly advancing to meet us. The disembarkation of B, C, and D Companies (100 men each) of our battalion was now proceeding rapidly, and the advance towards the town commenced.[1]

---

[1] Note by Col. R. Meinertzhagen, Chief of Intelligence Department :—
" This landing was really a very fine piece of work for troops who had had no previous experience. The Germans themselves, which we learnt later, thought that a landing at that particular spot was an impossible operation, and therefore failed to guard against it. The rapidity with which the Fusiliers got ashore and up a steep bush-clad escarpment gave the enemy no time to meet it. This initial success, which was intended as a covering movement for the main landing, was largely responsible for the capture of Bukoba."

It is impossible for me to attempt to give any general idea of the whole engagement, which lasted for two days, and I can only tell you some of my own experiences and impressions. We fought in a long thin skirmishing line, which extended from the sea to over a mile inland, and slowly and gradually pushed our opponents back towards Bukoba. On the right of our frontiersmen were 300 men of the Loyal North Lancashire regiment, and somewhere—I believe near the sea-shore, though I must confess that I never saw them—was a contingent of the King's African Rifles—native African troops, commanded by white officers. Our whole force was supported by four guns of an Indian Mountain Battery (the 28th) and four machine-guns. The forces opposed to us were undoubtedly very inferior to ours numerically, and consisted, I think, entirely of well-trained and well-armed native and Arab troops, commanded by German commissioned and non-commissioned officers, and a number of German civilian sharpshooters (men who no doubt have done a lot of big game hunting) armed with sporting rifles, fitted with hair-triggers and telescopic sights. With these rifles they used soft-nosed expanding bullets.[1] They had two cannons, I do not know of what calibre,[2] but of quite a considerable range and two machine-guns. But in another way our opponents had a very great advantage over us, as they had the benefit of the most splendid cover, banana-plantations, patches of thick bush, and bits of ground strewn with rocks, against which we had to advance in the open. Many bullets seemed to pass very close to me, whilst others were much too high. Several times, too, a machine-gun was turned on my platoon, but the range was quite 2000 yards and my men were very scattered, and the rocks and stones gave us good cover between our advances. Presently two of our own machine-guns came up, and searched the hill-side for the enemy's gun, firing all along the crest of the hill. I do not know if they actually put any of the German machine-gun con-

---

[1] In two authenticated cases a ·600 Rigby cordite rifle and a Holland ·375 were used in each case with sporting ammunition.
[2] 75 millimetres or 3 inch (R. Meinertzhagen).

tingent out of action, but they certainly caused them to withdraw their gun.

In the course of the day I had a rather curious experience. I was expecting to see the men of C Company on my right, when I suddenly saw two men dressed in khaki and wearing helmets amongst the rocks, less than 200 yards away from me on my right. There were also two or three natives in khaki with them. I said to Corporal Jenner, who was close to me, "Those must be two of our men with some of the native carriers," and we stepped out into the open. We were immediately fired on, but still I could not bring myself to fire back at them, and thinking that they were our own men and that seeing us suddenly, where they did not expect any of our men to be, they had mistaken us for Germans, I took off my helmet and waved it to them. One of them at once removed his helmet and waved it back to me. I was just putting on my helmet again, when the Germans— for they were Germans—fired at me again, and then dived in amongst the rocks. Their bullets appeared to whistle very close past me, though they may not have been as near as they seemed. At one point a lot of the enemy whom my platoon had gradually forced out of the rocks had to cross the open valley below, but they were then a long way off, and though we expended a lot of ammunition on them I only saw one drop. We also killed one black soldier at close quarters in the rocks, and I have his rifle, which I shall keep as a souvenir.

About 5 o'clock our whole force advanced across the open valley below the ridges we had taken nearly the whole day to clear. To do this we had to get through a swamp, intersected by a small river, which was much more than waist deep. Having negotiated this, we then took possession of two rocks, hills from which we drove the enemy just before it got dark. I was standing beside a stone on the top of the first hill, when a bullet struck a small dead stump just in front of and within a yard of me. Where the bullet afterwards went I don't know, but it sent a large chunk of dead wood against my chest, and another against a man just behind me, which hit him in the groin. He evidently thought he was hit and fell to the ground with a groan. But he was no more hit or hurt than I was, and soon recovered his composure. We had had a very hard day, having had nothing to eat, and not even a cup of coffee before leaving the ship. Provisions were to have been sent on shore for us, but if they were, we never got them. I had a hard biscuit and a lump of cheese in my pocket, but these were ruined in the swamp. General Stewart and his Staff joined us in the evening, and one of his staff gave Major Webb, Lieutenant Hargraves and myself each a small sausage. Colonel Kitchener (Lord Kitchener's brother) was with General Stewart's Staff, and he introduced himself to me, and was as nice as possible. He insisted on giving me a few thin biscuits which I shared with my two company officers. The day had been intensely hot and muggy, but the night was clear and there was a good moon. Colonel Driscoll wanted to go on and take the town by storm in the night ; but General Stewart thought it better to wait until the morning. Most of our men were, I think, very much exhausted, but I, I think, was in as good shape as any of them. I really was not tired at all. We passed a most uncomfortable night.[1] As soon as the dew began to fall it got very cold, so cold that we could not sleep at all. We were wet through too up to our chests. During the night someone set light to some native huts in the banana-plantation below our hill, so I took advantage of the blaze and went down there, and stripping stark naked dried all my things before going up the hill again. Whilst I was doing this our dead were taken past on stretchers. The wounded had been taken on to our hospital-ship in the afternoon.

Before dawn on the morning of June 23rd, we all stood to arms again on the top of the hills we had occupied the previous evening, and very glad we all were when at last day broke and the long, cold, dreary, sleepless night was past. We had nothing to eat, and nothing to drink but the

---

[1] " I slept under a rock near Selous that night. He was full of enthusiasm, and we discussed ' birds ' till far into the night, getting drenched through with the dew and badly bitten by mosquitoes " (R. Meinertzhagen).

water in our water-bottles, and again commenced the day's work on empty stomachs. Soon after daybreak, our signaller brought a message to Colonel Driscoll from General Stewart, telling him to send an officer and twenty men through the bush and banana-plantations below the hill, in order to find out the line taken by the road (which we could plainly see passing below our hill and entering the plantations) through the swamps which lay between us and the town of Bukoba, and then to approach as near the town as possible in order to ascertain what forces were defending it. Colonel Driscoll and Major Webb did me the honour to select me to lead this patrol, and I lost no time in selecting twenty good men of my own platoon to accompany me. After getting off the hill we advanced in single file along the road, I leading, and my men following, with intervals of about six paces between them. We followed the road, and it was somewhat jumpy work, passing along the edge of several banana-plantations, and patches of bush, as they afforded such ideal cover for sharpshooters of the type we had encountered on the previous day. However, there were none there, and we presently emerged on to an open plain covered with grass about two or two and a half feet high, and saw the road running through it straight in to the town. All along the road were posts at intervals of fifty yards or so supporting a telegraph or telephone wire which was probably connected up with some fort from which we had compelled the enemy to retire on the previous day.

On emerging into the open beyond the plantations at the foot of the hill, we were perhaps twelve or fifteen hundred yards from the wireless installation and the nearest houses. The sea-shore was perhaps half a mile to our left, and between us and the lake ran a reedy swamp, which we could see ran to within some 500 yards of the wireless installation and then curved to the right, the straight road we were on going right across it over a bridge. I now followed the road across the open ground, searching both to right and left and straight in front for any signs of the enemy. But we could see nothing and hear nothing, and I began to think that possibly Bukoba had been deserted during the night, and that I and my patrol might walk right into it unopposed. But as we approached the bridge over the swamp, I saw the opportunities it offered for an ambush, and so passed the word down my line of men telling them to leave the road, and keeping their relative positions, edge off to the left, in the direction of the swamp. We had hardly commenced this movement, when we were fired on from somewhere near the bridge. " Down," I shouted, and my command was obeyed with the utmost alacrity. The bullets whistled past us, but no one was hit, and we then crawled through the grass to the swamp, and then again advanced along its edge until we were within about 600 yards of the wireless installation. Along the swamp we usually had good cover, but whenever I tried to reconnoitre and raised myself above the grass to get a good look round I was fired on, I could not tell exactly from where. Two or three times a machine-gun was turned on us, but except when trying to reconnoitre we were pretty safe, and the bullets really whizzed over us. I expected that our whole battalion would have received orders to advance on the town shortly after my patrol had shown that there were no enemy forces on this side of where the road crossed the swamp. But before this happened the enemy's gun positions were shelled both by the Indian Mounted Battery on the hill, and by the guns on our ships, which were now closing in on the Bay of Bukoba. The Germans returned the fire of the Mountain Battery most pluckily with two guns mounted on the hill behind the town, but did not reply to the fire of the ships' guns. This artillery duel had gone on for some time when about 9 o'clock a terrific storm burst over the area of the fighting, accompanied by torrential rain and partial darkness. In a few minutes my men and I, and all who were exposed to its violence, were soaked to the skin. The rain, however, was luckily, if not exactly warm, not cold and gave us no sense of chill.

When the storm was over, the big guns again opened fire. Several hours had now passed since I left the hill on which our battalion had passed the night, and I wondered why no general advance had been made on the town. I did not think that it would be either wise or right to advance any further with only twenty men, as I knew there was a machine-gun in front of us, somewhere near the wireless installation, and it was impossible to tell what forces were still holding Bukoba and waiting to open fire from the shelter of the houses on any men advancing against it. So I sent one of the men with me—a South African named Budler—and my native boy Ramazani, with a note to Colonel Driscoll that there was a good line of advance towards Bukoba, along the edge of the swamp where my men were lying. My men met Colonel Driscoll and learnt from him that a general advance was in fact then taking place. C Company soon came up and took up their position a little beyond me along the reed-bed, and I learnt that Major Webb with the rest of A Company was advancing on our right, and then B and D Companies were still further to the right. The Adjutant, Captain White, then came along and thought that some of us ought to cross to the further side of the swamp. This was at once done by the men of C Company, some of my men with myself as their leader, and Captain White himself. The stream in the middle of the swamp was quite deep and we all got wet up to our breasts. Just before we crossed the swamp Lieutenant Miles of the King's African Rifles came up with a machine-gun, with which he opened fire on one of the houses near the wireless installation, from which we thought that a German machine-gun had been firing at us. This proved to be right, but unfortunately the German gun got the range of our gun first, and when three of his men had been wounded, one very severely, Lieutenant Miles had to withdraw his gun into the shelter of the hollow formed by the reed-bed. German sharpshooters, firing from we could not tell exactly where, were now sending some bullets disagreeably close to us as we lay flat just beyond the swamp. These bullets, fortunately in no great number, seemed to ping past us only a few inches above our bodies. Presently Sergeant-Major Bottomly of C Company came across the swamp, and lay down alongside of me, or at least separated from me by just a yard, my black boy Ramazani lying between us,

but a little lower down, so that his head was on a line with
my hips. I just said a word to Bottomly, and then turned
my head away from him again to look in the direction from
which the bullets were coming. Almost immediately my black
boy Ramazani touched me, and said : " Master, soldier hit,
dead." I had never heard a sound, but turning my head
I saw poor Bottomly lying on his back, stone dead, with a
bullet through his head. I noticed a large signet ring on his
right hand, as his arm hung limp across his body. His
head and face were nearly covered by his helmet, but the
blood was trickling down over his throat, and I knew that
he must have been shot through the brain and killed instantaneously.

Our ships had now crept right into the Bay of Bukoba,
and as they fired on the town, or the enemy's gun positions,
their shells came screaming and whistling over us. The
machine-guns were going too with their wicked rattle, and
bullets from snipers' rifles came with an unpleasant sound,
sometimes apparently within a few inches of our bodies,
which were just then pressed as close to the ground as
possible. I thought, as I lay there only a yard away from
the blood-stained corpse of poor Sergeant-Major Bottomly,
listening to the peculiar noise of each kind of projectile as
it found its invisible course through the air above and around
me, that I could recall various half-hours of my life passed
amidst much pleasanter surroundings. And yet what a
small and miserable thing this was, after all, in the way of a
battle compared with the titanic combats which have been
taking place in Europe ever since the greatest war in history
commenced last August. I can well understand how the
nerves of any man, however strong, may be shaken to
pieces, by the awful clamour of the giant shells and the
concentrated fire of many machine-guns, and countless
numbers of rifles, and the terrible havoc wrought by
these fearful weapons of destruction.

As the advance of the companies of our battalion on the
right seemed to be very slow, and we did not know exactly
what opposition lay in front of us, Colonel Driscoll asked
me to call for three or four volunteers, and crawl forwards

in order to make a reconnaissance. I took four men of my own platoon who were close to me. We had not proceeded far when a shot was fired at us from somewhere to our right. This bullet seemed just to skim over us. We immediately lay flat, and wriggling to the left got shelter in a slight hollow of the ground. Along this hollow we advanced to within some three hundred yards of the house nearest to the wireless installation, when several shots were fired at us, and we could also hear talking beyond the rising ground to our left. We could see no sign of the enemy near the wireless installation, nor anywhere down the main street of the town, and I think that Bukoba was at that time already deserted, except for a few sharpshooters who were covering the evacuation, so I at once crawled back to make my report to Colonel Driscoll. On our way we passed some of Major Leitch's men (C Company) and on my reaching Colonel Driscoll and making my report, he asked me to collect the rest of my own men, and then took one of the four men with me to guide him to where Major Leitch was, as he wanted to speak to him. Almost immediately after I had parted from him, my man, Private Mucklow (from Worcestershire), was shot dead alongside of Colonel Driscoll, as he had incautiously stood up. This, I think, was almost if not absolutely the last shot fired by the enemy, and no opposition whatever was made to the advance upon, and occupation of the town by our battalion. I think that both their machine-guns had been put out of action by shells from the Indian Mounted Battery, but they were carried away. They abandoned one of their pieces of artillery, however. We found it with four oxen ready yoked to drag it away, but a shell from our battery had killed one of the oxen and so in their hurry the Germans abandoned the gun. The sappers destroyed most completely the wonderful structure of the wireless installation, which was something like a small Eiffel Tower, and nearly if not quite 200 feet high, with immensely strong concrete foundations. It must have cost a great deal of money to construct in Germany and then convey over so many thousands of miles of land and sea to the very heart of Africa all the component parts of this wonderful example of material civilization, but I suppose the destruction of this wireless installation was the chief object of this expedition to Bukoba.

Immediately upon entering the town my company was sent on to the hill behind it to guard against any attack, and the men of the Loyal North Lancashire regiment presently worked round along the ridge of the higher hills beyond, and posted pickets on all points of vantage. I therefore did not actually witness the destruction of the wireless installation. Neither I nor my men had had anything to eat since the previous evening and very little since the evening before we left the ship, but we got some bananas in the plantations on the hillsides below us, though only a few of them were ripe. My men, however, brought me two fine large ones quite ripe and of a most delicious flavour.

There was a sort of arsenal on the hill we were guarding, and this was blown up about 5 o'clock, an immense amount of ammunition being destroyed. The houses of the German residents, probably Government officials for the most part, were very well and comfortably built and furnished. The arsenal in the town was set alight and great quantities of ammunition and some dynamite destroyed. A good deal of beer and wine and provisions of various kinds was discovered in Bukoba, but I saw no drunkenness amongst our men.

Just at sundown the order came from General Stewart that our battalion was to parade and march to the jetty and re-embark at once. But at first we had to bury our dead. A great grave was dug in the sandy soil, between the burning arsenal and the Governor's house, and in it were laid three deep the bodies of six Britons, still swathed in their blood-stained clothes, who had given their lives for King and Country, far, far away from their native land and all who held them dear. These men had all been killed outright, but two more who had died of their wounds after being taken to the hospital-ship were brought ashore and buried within sound of the murmuring waters of the great inland lake. Altogether our casualties amounted to twenty ; 8 killed and 12 wounded. The re-embarkation of our battalion took a very long time, and it was not till 2 a.m.

on the morning of June 24th that my company, A, at last got on board. Until then we had been sitting and lying about on the jetty in our wet clothes, without food, fire, or warm tea or coffee.

Before midday on the 24th our flotilla started back across the lake for Kisumu, which we reached on the evening of the 25th. The authorities had made our men intensely uncomfortable on board the steamer by putting a lot of mules on the crowded decks with them. They were able to rest and get food at Kisumu, and about six o'clock on the evening of the 26th we started by train for Nairobi. Again the authorities packed our men like sardines into miserable third-class carriages made for natives. They could surely have given us two trains and so allowed our tired men a little space to stretch themselves. We arrived at Nairobi at 6.30 on the evening of the 27th, and were packed off again at 7 o'clock for Kajiado. One would have thought that as our men had come out from England to fight for East Africa, and that as we had just returned from a success-ful attack on an enemy's stronghold, and as our time of arrival in Nairobi had been telegraphed on ahead, that something might have been done by the townspeople on behalf of our tired and hungry men ; or that even some kind of official welcome might have been accorded them. But not a bite of food for man or officer was to be had on our arrival at Nairobi, and not even hot water could be obtained to make tea with.

Leaving Nairobi on the evening of June 27th, we reached our camp at Kajiado early the following morning, and our first expedition against the Germans was at an end.

F. C. SELOUS,

Lieutenant 25th Battalion
Royal Fusiliers.

In a letter to his friend Heatley Noble (July 26th, 1915), Selous, who was then with his battalion guarding the Uganda railway near Voi, speaks of the difficulties lying ahead of our people and the efforts, only partially successful, to hold our territory against the splendidly organized German forces.

" Since our fight at Bukoba we have made an attack on a German post in British territory on the road from Voi to Taveta. Our attack in this case failed, as our information seems to have been all wrong, and the Germans were found to be more strongly posted than had been supposed. An Indian Punjabi regiment was badly cut up, the Colonel killed and the Adjutant wounded and taken prisoner. The native porters, carrying ammunition and equipment of all kinds, threw down everything and cleared as soon as the first shots were fired, and the Germans took possession of everything, including the dead and wounded. They buried the Colonel with full military honours, and allowed the Adjutant to send word that he was being well looked after. There were several other units engaged in this affair, 500 Rhodesians, some of the Loyal North Lancs, and three companies of the K.A.R. ; but the casualties in all these contingents were very small, only the Indian regiment apparently having got up against the machine-guns. Things are now at a standstill out here, and when there will be another move it is impossible to say. Botha had 50,000 men, and equipment of all kinds to conquer the Germans in South-West Africa, and he did his job splendidly. Here we have under 2000 white troops, some 2000 African blacks and a considerable number of Indians, most of them very much demoralized as they caught it badly at Tanga and Jasin. The Germans are said to have 4000 or 5000 white men in G.E.A. and nearly 20,000 very well trained black troops under German officers.[1] They are, too, splendidly equipped in every way, and have no end of machine-guns and ammunition. Even if we had a large army here, we could not move it across country to the vital points in G.E.A., as the difficulties of transport would be insurmountable. The only way would be to take Dar-es-Salaam and Tanga, and then advance

[1] On the best authority the Germans had 2500 white troops and 4200 askaris at the beginning of the War. During the War they raised their black troops and police to from 12,000 to 18,000.

methodically up their railways, as Botha did in S.W. Africa. For this we should require at least 20,000 or 30,000 men, and as we are not likely to get them, in my opinion we shall be stuck out here until peace is made in Europe. I hope to God that will be before many months are over, or all our young men will be killed. I hope and trust your sons are still alive. I often think of them and of your and Mrs. Noble's terrible anxiety. There has been a lot of sickness—fever and dysentery—both amongst the officers and men of this battalion, but only two deaths—two privates died of dysentery. I think that I am the only one of our officers who has not suffered at all from either bad diarrhœa, dysentery or fever. I have been quite well all the time, and have never been an hour off duty. Bukoba was rather hard, scarcely any food for two days and nights, up to our chests in the swamps, and then lying out in our wet clothes without fire or blanket. I did not suffer any after-effects at all, I am glad to say, and have now got into very good condition. The long marches do not tire me at all, and the men now say that when I fall out no one will be left standing in the battalion. This is, of course, nonsense, but as far as standing fatigue, sun, thirst, etc., I think that I am really better than most of them. Three of our officers have been found unfit for further service, and there are some others who are weak constitutionally, and will never be able to stand any really hard work. So we are very short of officers, and whether Colonel Driscoll's recommendation in my favour for good conduct in the field is attended to or not, I shall very likely get to be a captain before long, as I am the senior subaltern in the battalion. I don't know my drill very well, but my men, I hear, say they have great confidence in me, and will go anywhere with me ; but once I am through with this job, no more military duty for me. I hate all the drill and routine-work, and I shall be far too old to take part in any other war after this one."

In a letter to me, written from Voi (December 8th, 1915), Selous gives a short general survey of the operations since he landed.

" MY DEAR JOHNNY,

"Your letter of October 31st reached me here three days ago, and I was very pleased to get it and to hear all your news. It is now more than seven months since we landed at Mombasa, on May 4th, and we have had a wearing, trying time ever since. Only one of our officers has been killed, but there has been much sickness both in our battalion and the Loyal North Lancs regiment, which came here from India, and several of our men have died from dysentery or fever, and several of our officers have been invalided home. I think that I am the only officer who has not been in hospital. So far I have not been ill at all and I have never yet been a day off duty or had a day's leave. I have never applied for leave, but if I can last out for a few months longer, and during that time we are able to push the Germans back over their own frontier, and are then able to force them to give in, I want to get a couple of months' leave, and go to Uganda, after those fine water-bucks on the Semliki river. We were first of all on the high veldt in the game reserve on the Magadi railway, and there the climate was very fine, but for the last four months we have been in this comparatively low hot country, protecting the Voi-Maktau railway, and hunting German patrols and dynamiting parties, in the most frightful bush. I was out in command of 30 rifles to the west of the Teita Hills towards the Tsavo river, and tracked a German dynamiting party for two days, and at one time was very close to them, but the bush was simply awful and they got off (without bombing the Uganda line) by moonlight, when we could no longer follow their tracks. The day after I got back from this 11 days' patrol, I was sent out again with 70 rifles and 120 porters to examine the courses of the Mwatate and Bura rivers, and see how far they carried water, and if there were any German patrols about. I was out 7 days on this patrol. These patrols are not all pure joy, as the heat of the sun is now very great, and heavy rain falls almost every night. We can carry no tents or any kind of protection against the weather, and we had three very bad nights during the two patrols, lying in the soaking rain and mud all night. Every night heavy thunder-storms break all round about, but they are very local and we have been lucky in not getting into the middle of more of them at nights. We often get soaked in the daytime, but dry again as soon as the storm is over. This bush-work is very trying, as the German black askaris are very much better at it than heavily equipped white men, many of whom have always lived in towns before coming out here. They are recruited from fighting tribes—mostly Manyamwesi—and are not only very brave, but very well armed. We have met with some nasty knocks in this district, but have also ambushed the enemy now and again, and inflicted heavy punishment on them. A party of the Lancs were ambushed and badly cut up 6 miles from here not long ago, losing 2 officers and nearly 20 men killed, and when Lieutenant Dartnell of ours was killed,[1] the mounted infantry to which he was attached were ambushed and suffered severely. On the other hand, the mounted infantry with two companies of Baluchis not long afterwards waylaid a party of the enemy, and killed over 30 of them, and one German officer. Only yesterday, the Boer force from the Uas n'gishu (Belfield's Scouts) 100 men under Major Arnoldi, went out from Maktau, and meeting a German force coming towards Maktau from their strongly fortified position at M'buyuni, 13 miles away, attacked them, and killed two white Germans and over 20 askaris, and took prisoners 4 white Germans (2 wounded). The Boers had only one casualty, which was unfortunately their leader Major Arnoldi. He was only wounded in the shoulder, but fell from his saddle, and his foot unfortunately catching in his stirrup had his brains knocked out against a tree. In all the time I have been out here I have only taken part in one incident of interest. That was the journey up to

---

[1] " Dartnell was awarded the V.C. posthumously for gallantry, when wounded preferring to stop behind with his men, when he could have been evacuated. The enemy on returning to the scene of the fight where Dartnell had been left with the wounded, commenced to kill them, and Dartnell fought to the last, trying to protect his men " (R. Meinertzhagen, Col.).

A Shot on the Plains, British East Africa.

and across the Victoria Nyanza, and the attack on and capture of Bukoba on the western side of the lake. 400 of our men took part in this adventure, and it was we men of the 25th Fusiliers who did everything that was done. I was then a lieutenant in A Company, and led my platoon on the first day, and conducted a very risky patrol of 20 men early on the second day, and a reconnaissance later—more risky still—with four men who volunteered for the job. We had two days' fighting, and, as I was always in front, I had personally some very narrow escapes. I may tell you privately, but keep it to yourself, that Colonel Driscoll was very pleased with my conduct at Bukoba, and told me that he had recommended me for promotion and something more, but as I have never heard anything more about it, no notice was taken, I suppose, of Colonel Driscoll's recommendation. I should certainly have liked my name to have been mentioned in despatches. However, it can't be helped, and I may get another chance. I have got my promotion to captain, but that came to me in the natural course of events, as a Captain Williams was invalided home, and I was the senior subaltern. You may possibly have heard that there have been disasters out here, but if the whole truth about everything out here is ever known it will be a revelation to most people. It was certainly an evil day for British East Africa *when the Indian Government took over the defence of this country.*[1] With the exception of the Baluchis and the Cashmiris all the other Indian troops have failed badly out here, and have proved very inferior to either our own K.A.R.'s or the German native askaris. The attack on, and capture of Bukoba by our men is the only success on any considerable scale yet scored by the British out here. I do not say it was much, but at any rate we carried out what we were set to do, and captured the town of Bukoba and destroyed the very fine wireless installation. We hear that a British general from France is on his way out here as G.O.C., and that large numbers of troops

---

[1] The Indian Government were not to blame. They had sent all their best troops to France and had to keep large reserves in India for possible contingencies, so that the troops they sent to East Africa were not of the best quality.

Y

are coming here both from South Africa and other parts. Something is undoubtedly in preparation, but I suppose it will be another two months before everything is in readiness for a big advance. And the Germans may move first, as they have four times as many men as we have, and many more guns and machine-guns. We are now in a camp built by the North Lancs and some Indian troops, or rather two camps a mile apart. Sickness has reduced our battalion to about 700 men, and of these many are weak and ill, and I don't think we have more than 400 men who are really strong and capable of marching 20 miles in the hot sun, with their heavy equipment. Our whole battalion, after having been continually split up and sent in batches all over the country, were at last brought all together again here under Colonel Driscoll ; three companies in the one camp and one in the smaller camp a mile away. But last week the Colonel in command at Maktau got nervous and ordered Colonel Driscoll to send half his battalion there. Now we are left in this very large camp with under 200 rifles—counting all our black scouts—and all the tailors, cobblers, barbers, commissariat and orderly-room people. We haven't a gun of any kind, nor even a single machine-gun, and the camp itself is in a hollow commanded by higher ground on all sides. We have another 100 or 150 rifles in the smaller camp a mile away. Well, news came a few days ago that a large enemy force with several Hotchkiss guns and many Maxims was advancing on Kisigau, from which an Indian garrison was driven some time ago. We had another small garrison at Kisigau of 50 K.A.R.'s. The Germans have again captured the place after killing or wounding 40 of the garrison. The remainder made their escape. When the G.O.C. and the other generals at Nairobi and Voi heard of this advance on Kisigau, they thought the Germans intended making a determined attack on the railway line, and sent 1500 troops— Rhodesians, North Lancs, K.A.R.'s, and Indians—down to Voi to march from Maungu to Kisigau, leaving Maktau very short of men, though they there have plenty of guns, a mountain battery and machine-guns, and the place is very strongly fortified. At the new station Mashoti, between here and Maktau, only 100 men have been left, but they have guns and machine-guns, and are in a very well constructed camp in a very good position. If we are attacked here by any considerable force with guns and machine-guns we can do nothing, and shall probably all get scuppered. We were fully expecting an attack yesterday, last night, or this morning, as we got a message from Maktau that a large force was approaching. The last rumour is that 10,000 men are advancing on Maktau. At the same time, if the Germans are going to do anything worth while, now is their chance, before the new troops get here. They know everything about us from their Arab and native spies. Well! if the Germans know the state of this place and do not attack it, they will be great fools. The whole position is farcical. This is a very important point, as if it is taken, the water supply to Maktau and Mashoti will be cut off, and yet we have been left with only a few rifles and not a single gun or machine-gun to defend an immense perimeter. Well! all we can do is to ' wait and see,' as Mr. Asquith would say. I am afraid that the war will go on for some time yet, and thousands more of our men will be killed before it is over. I have two young nephews at the Front in France now and I think a third has gone to Serbia with the Motor Transport. My eldest son Freddy will not be eighteen till next April, but I expect he will be sent out soon after then, as he is big and strong for his age. If he goes out and gets killed[1] it will break his mother's heart and mine too, if I should live to come home, and it will be the same for you and your wife if you lose Geoff ;[2] but I pray God he will be spared to outlive this terrible war. I suppose the Germans cannot now possiby win the war ; but can the Allies absolutely crush them before their finances are exhausted ? The war will soon probably be

[1] Capt. Freddy Selous, m.c., R.A.F.C., killed in action, January 6th, 1918.
[2] Capt. G. de C. Millais, Bedfordshire Regiment, killed in action, August 22nd, 1918.

costing us £6,000,000 a day instead of £5,000,000.   How long can we stand that ?   We seem to have made some terrible mistakes and miscalculations, especially in the Dardanelles and the Balkans.   However, like everyone else out here, I suppose I am despondent.   Perhaps the heat down here is depressing.   This place has the reputation of being very unhealthy in the rainy season, and I fear our men will suffer very much during the next two months. Your naval work must be very interesting, and you must tell me all about it, if we ever meet again.   I was very sorry to hear that poor Gerald Legge[1] had been killed. But who is going to be left alive when this war is over ?

" Well ! good-bye, old friend, and with very kind regards to Mrs. Millais and all your family and wishing Geoff the best of good luck, yours ever,   FRED.

" P.S.—I have not seen Judd yet.   He was scouting down on the German border for some months after the war broke out, but has been on his farm near Nairobi for the last six months."

The following letters from Ex-President Roosevelt in reply to letters from Selous, describing local conditions in B.E. Africa, give some of his views on Germany prior to the entry of America in the Great War :—

"OYSTER BAY,
            " LONG ISLAND, N.Y.,
                              " April 2nd, 1915.

" MY DEAR SELOUS,

        " I have received your letter of February 23rd and send this to Nairobi.   I am exceedingly glad you have gone to British East Africa.   I am sorry to say that very reluctantly I have come to the same conclusion that you have about the purposes and conduct of Germany.   The

---

[1] Capt. the Hon. Gerald Legge, second son of the Earl of Dartmouth, killed in action in Gallipoli, August, 1915 ; an excellent naturalist and a great friend of ours.

behaviour of her armies in Belgium and in the North of France was, I think, the inevitable result of the kind of doctrine that has been preached by those high in authority in Germany and which was typified by the Emperor's famous advice to his troops in China to ' behave like Huns.' A man cannot direct soldiers to behave like Huns and then escape responsibility for the swinish horrors that follow. From my book you have already seen how strongly I have spoken as to the failure of the United States and other neutrals to do their duty when the Hague Conventions were violated. You cannot speak any more strongly than I have spoken.

" One genuine surprise to me was the strength that the Germans have shown in their colonies.[1] I agree with you that the attitude of the Boers has been one of the finest tributes imaginable to the justice with which England has behaved in South Africa. I have sent your letter to Kermit. It will make him eager to be beside you under Driscoll. I most earnestly hope that you won't be used as a transport officer. Tarlton writes me that he was not allowed to go to the front either. I would a good deal rather trust Tarlton and you in a fight than most of the men who are technically entirely fit because of their youth and physical soundness.

" I have not the heart to write to you about ordinary things while you are in the midst of this terrible struggle. As I have said in an article I recently wrote, I do not believe in neutrality between right and wrong ; and I am very sorry that the United States is not in the struggle. If there were a war, my four boys would go, although I suppose that the two younger ones would have to go as enlisted men ; and I should ask permission to raise a division of nine regiments of the same type as the regiment I commanded in Cuba. They were men in whom your soul would have delighted. They were much of the stamp of the Hills of

[1] " The German strength was not so much (at any rate in East Africa) their numbers, but their efficiency, and the fact that they were prepared and we were not. They also scored heavily by being able to draft into their black ranks ten per cent of trained white soldiers who were settlers and business men in peace time. We had no such asset. Moreover, the German superiority of machine-guns, 2 to every 100 men, outweighed our 2 to 800 men ! " (R. Meinertzhagen, Col.)

British East Africa—by the way, if you see them give them my warm regards, as also to Newland and any other friends you meet. I am delighted to hear about your son.

" With hearty good wishes,

" Faithfully yours,

" THEODORE ROOSEVELT."

" *August 26th,* 1915.

" DEAR SELOUS,

" Your letter of July 11th has just come. I congratulate you with all my heart. It is simply first-class to have you a fighting officer in the fighting line, leading your men in the very work that you are particularly and peculiarly fitted to do. I was wholly unable to understand Lord Kitchener refusing you a commission. It seemed to me to be an instance of following the letter that kills instead of the spirit that gives life. The Germans have used Von Hindenburg,[1] who was away over the legal age-limit for generals ; and he has been their best general. There is undoubtedly a certain type of bureaucrat who would have thought it more important to observe the rule by keeping him at home than to have secured his leadership in victory. Of course, I personally believe in universal military service, and in the most rigorous application of military law during a war. If I had control in East Africa—or in Great Britain or the United States, for that matter !—I would make every man do whatever was best for the nation, whether this meant that he was to fight or to produce ammunition or to produce coal, and I would treat the man who sought to make a profit out of the war or who went on a strike so as to avoid doing his duty in the war just as summarily as I would treat the soldier who flinched in a fight.

" I am so pleased that MacMillan is with you and is doing so well with the commissariat. Give him my heartiest regards. I wish to heaven Kermit and I were with you,

---

[1] " Hindenburg has been a mere figure-head and idol of the people. Ludendorff is the brain of the German Army and real conducting head " (R. Meinertzhagen, Col.).

or at least that Kermit[1] was with you, and that I was helping in the trenches in Flanders, where I would be of more service.

"I send you herewith two articles I have just written in reference to what I regard as the frightful misconduct of my own country. The trouble is that the men at the head of our Government are doing just exactly what the men at the head of your Government did up to a year and a quarter ago ; and they treat the words of men like myself precisely as your men treated Lord Roberts—I do not mean to compare myself to Lord Roberts in this matter, but the attitude of the governmental authorities toward him and toward me has been the same.

"That was a first-class little fight at Bukoba. If the Germans keep sinking boats with our citizens on them, sooner or later I cannot help thinking our citizens as a whole will themselves insist on fighting. The professional pacifists have done this country a damage that cannot be overstated. If you come through all right and if, in the event of war, I come through all right, I shall look forward eagerly to seeing you when the war is over and asking for more details about what you tell me concerning the attitude of so many people in British East Africa and in Nairobi, for I am immensely puzzled over it. Pray present my warmest regards to MacMillan and my hearty congratulations as well, and also present my respects and congratulations to Colonel Driscoll."

Writing at an earlier date (December 4th, 1914), Roosevelt in his usual vigorous style thus expresses his estimate of German policy :—

"I don't wonder that you feel a little bit concerned about the war. Moreover, I am not certain that the theory that France and England are to act as anvil and Russia as hammer will work out. It looks to me as if, unit for unit, the Russians had shown a marked inferiority to the Germans,

[1] In 1917, Kermit Roosevelt joined our forces in Mesopotamia. Since this date Roosevelt's three other sons have joined the American troops, and two have distinguished themselves as soldiers. Lieut. Quentin Roosevelt was killed in action in France in July, 1918.

French, and English. They have enormous numbers and great endurance, and these may become decisive factors in the end. I do hope that your army will increase in numbers, however, to the point of being able to become formidable as an offensive factor.

" I have a great admiration and respect for the Germans. I wish to heavens that this country would wake up to the hideous damage, moral and physical, caused by the deification of mere industrialism, of softness and of self-indulgence. National acceptance of the need of hard labour, of facing risk, and of the exercise of foresight is necessary to national greatness. If I must choose between a policy of blood and iron and one of milk and water—especially of skimmed milk and dishwater—why I am for the policy of blood and iron. It is better not only for the nation, but in the end for the world. But my admiration for the Germans does not blind me to the fact that for the last fifty years their development along the lines of policy advocated by Frederick the Great and Bismarck, and so enthusiastically championed by Carlyle, has resulted in their becoming a very grave menace to every nation with which they are brought in contact. I immensely admire German industrial, social, and military efficiency ; but I abhor the kind of militarism which has resulted in such cynical contempt for international morality and such appalling ruthlessness in war. I think it folly for a man not to admire the German efficiency ; and utter weakness for him not to realize that that efficiency may be used against his own nation and take steps accordingly. I wish I were in the war myself ! "

The authorities at home at last resolved to take the East African campaign into their own hands, and in January appointed General Smuts to the command and gave him adequate forces with which to make an advance into German East Africa. Selous' letter to me, February 25th, 1916, brings his narrative up to date.

" MY DEAR JOHNNY,

" After a long interval we got a mail here yesterday, and it brought me your letter of January 5th. This is the second letter I have received from you, so I think I must have missed one, and it may have gone down in the ill-fated 'Persia,' which had mails for East Africa on board. I have not much news to give you, nor much time to write it, as we are now just getting ready for a move forward. After over five months of hard grinding work in the very hot sun, guarding the line from Voi to near Mombasa, and from Voi to Maktau, on the way to Taveta, and many patrols without any kind of shelter all through the heavy rains of December and January, we were sent up to Kajiado on the Magadi railway, and then on here about a fortnight ago. We are now camped just over the German border, and go on to Longido, 18 miles ahead, very shortly. You will have seen in the papers that General Smith-Dorrien was taken ill in South Africa, and that General Smuts has taken his place as G.O.C. out here. He will, I think, commence the offensive against the Germans immediately, but *if* the Germans have the forces they are said to have, and *if* all their native troops remain loyal to them, we shall have a devil of a job. I hear that General Smuts, who arrived in the country a week ago, and has already been to Longido by motor-car, fully realizes that this affair will be a much more difficult business than the South-West Africa campaign. There the Germans had no native troops, and Botha had ten men for every man the Germans could muster. Then the country in German S.W. Africa was much easier to work in than this dense tropical bush, which lends itself at every yard to ambushes and is everywhere very much in favour of the defending forces. Water is a great difficulty here, too, and the greater part of German East Africa between our border and the Dar-es-Salaam, Tanganyika railway, except round Kilimanjaro and other high mountains, seems to be very waterless. There is only one permanent water between Kajiado and this camp, over 50 miles, and the transport animals have to do a trek of over 30 miles without water. However, we have this year had no dry season, for since it commenced to rain in November, it has been raining off and on ever since, not sufficiently to fill the water-holes, but quite enough to make things very uncomfortable, and to keep the grass growing, which I am afraid is all in favour of the Germans, as it makes good cover for their ambushes everywhere. The German officers out here seem to be very fine soldiers, and what people do not realize, their black troops are not only as brave as any Zulus, but splendidly led and well armed and supported with any number of machine-guns. No better men could be found in the whole world, and personally, in this bush-covered, overgrown, but still hot and waterless country, I would much sooner have to fight against Germans from the Fatherland than these well-trained and elusive blacks. If we could only gain some success a lot of them might desert. But all the successes have been on their side up to now (except at Bukoba), and they must be full of confidence. A fortnight ago, just before General Smuts reached this country, an attack was launched against a German position not far from Taveta, by three regiments of South Africans, supported by a regiment of Baluchis and some Rhodesians. The situation was only saved from complete disaster by the Baluchis and the Rhodesians. I enclose a reference to the affair in the Nairobi paper, but it has been very unfortunate, and is a very bad beginning to the new campaign now opening, as it will keep the German black troops loyal to their masters, and fill them with renewed confidence. Smuts' generalship may prove superior to all the difficulties he will have to contend with, but I expect he now realizes that he is up against a much more difficult proposition than he had expected. When we advance from our most forward base—Longido—we are not to carry any kind of tents or shelter from the weather, and as the heavy rains now seem to be setting in (we are having heavy thunder-storms with soaking rain now every day or night) we are likely to have a very bad time, and most of us who are still fit will be sure to go down with fever or dysentery, as the heavy rains may last all through March, April, May, and June. Well! the future is on the knees of the gods, and we must take the luck they send us. Lately we have been practising attacks on positions, advancing in bush formation under General Sheppard, an awfully nice man, who I think will command the brigade to which we are attached. I am now in command of A Company of the 25th Fusiliers, and in all our manœuvres A and B Companies have to lead the advance, so I expect we shall have to do the same when it comes to actually attacking any German position. When we landed at Mombasa on May 4th last our battalion was nearly 1100 strong and there were 273 men in A Company. Now we have lost more than half our officers, and have not more than 400 men fit to march and fight. This is the effect of the climate. In A Company we can muster about 100 fit men, and three officers (myself and two men raised from the ranks). Well! I hope that this accursed war will be over by next August, and I think it will, as by that time Germany will surely be exhausted, as well as some of the Allies. By April, I see it is stated, that the war will be costing us £6,000,000 a day. How long can we stand that? What I cannot understand is, where are our armies of millions of men, and all the stores of munitions we are making and buying from America. We are said to have now 5,000,000 of men well armed and equipped, and yet we do not appear to have more than 1,000,000 in France and Flanders, nor more than 500,000 in Salonika and Egypt together. In Mesopotamia and East Africa, we have only a few hundreds of British troops, all the rest being Indians and South Africans. Well! I hope I shall live through this show, and come home again, as I want to see my wife again, and watch my boys' careers. I believe that Freddy will pass out of Sandhurst this month. I was very pleased to hear that all is so far going well with you and yours. May your boys be spared to you and their mother whatever happens. With very kind regards to all of you."

"OLD MOSCHI,
"ON THE SLOPES OF KILIMANJARO,
"May 2nd, 1916.

"MY DEAR JOHNNY,
"It is a long time now since I last heard from you, but I trust that all is still going well with you and yours. On the day after to-morrow we shall have been a whole solid year

out here, as we landed at Mombasa on May 4th, 1915. Of that year we have been over six months in the low unhealthy bush-country, doing heavy marches in the hottest hours of the day, and lying out on patrols with no shelter or protection whatever from the weather, all through the heavy rains of December and January last. As I never had any fever, diarrhœa or dysentery, but was always well, I did more of this patrol work than any other officer in our battalion, and it meant long marches too, sometimes following small parties of Germans trying to blow up the Uganda railway. In common with all the other white troops serving on foot out here, our battalion has suffered terribly from the climate, and is now almost quite used up. The Loyal North Lancs regiment has been out here eighteen months ; but they have had two strong drafts from home to make good their losses. However, they have now been sent or are just about to go to Wynberg, near Cape Town, to recruit, and from there will probably be sent home. Four of our officers and a lot of our men have also been sent there. The Rhodesian regiment which first came out here has also suffered very badly from the climate, and has now been sent to the escarpment near Nairobi to recruit. The South African troops which have only just come out here are also suffering a lot from fever and dysentery, and Van Deventer is said to have lost about 1400 horses (from horse-sickness) out of the 2000 he had six weeks ago. The condition of our battalion is simply lamentable. When we came up from the low country at the end of February to Kajiado (5800 feet above sea-level) Colonel Driscoll tried to collect all his men from the various hospitals and convalescent homes in the country. We had landed at Mombasa on May 4th, 1915, with 1127 rifles, and we mustered at Kajiado about 700 on February 1st, 1916 ; but of these many were no longer of any use for marching in the hot sun. From Kajiado we went to Longido, and were incorporated with Colonel Stewart's Brigade, which had to march right round Kilimanjaro, and meet General Smuts' much larger force at Moschi. As far as our Brigade was concerned only 449 of the 691 who had left Kajiado were found to be fit enough for the heavy marching in front of us. Starting from Longido late in the morning of March 5th, we marched 9 miles under a very hot sun to Sheep Hill. There was there no shelter from the sun, and we passed a very unpleasant day. We were told to rest and sleep, as we had a long night-march of 20 miles before us. We marched all night long except from 12 to 2 a.m., and did not get to the water until after midday the next day, and the distance registered in General Stewart's motor-car was 30 miles instead of 20. We had other very long marches in the very hot sun, in choking clouds of fine lava-dust, churned up by the heavy transport. The Germans had prepared to dispute our advance along the main road from Longido to New Moschi, which passes N'gara Nairobi. But under the guidance of a Boer settler in German East Africa, named Pretorius, we left the road soon after leaving Sheep Hill and travelled across country to Boma N'gombi, 15 miles from New Moschi (the railway terminus), on the road to Aruscha. The Germans, whose main forces were trying to hold back Smuts' big columns advancing on Taveta, apparently had not sufficient forces to come out and attack General Stewart's column, so we got through with nothing more than a little sniping. Arrived at Boma N'gombi, we got into communication with General Smuts through our wireless, and General Stewart was ordered to send a picked force by a forced march to join up with one of his forces at Masai Kraal, and then advance together to New Moschi. About half of our 449 men (many of whom were now badly knocked up) were considered fit for this advance and I led 55 men of my A Company, the 55 fittest men of the 282 of A Company who had stepped ashore at Mombasa less than a year before. The night we left Boma N'gombi heavy rain came on and we marched in rain and mud and pitch darkness for many miles along an old abandoned waggon-road. Before daylight we joined up with some mounted scouts, who informed us that the Germans had evacuated New Moschi and gone off down the railway, and that South African troops had occupied both New Moschi and Old Moschi (where I am now writing on the slopes of Kilimanjaro and six miles by road from New Moschi in the plain below us). The day after we got to New Moschi, we were sent off with part of General Stewart's Brigade, under Colonel (now Brigadier-General Sheppard) to co-operate with the S. African forces against the Germans, who had retired from Taveta towards the Ruwu river. A night march of 16 miles brought us to Newi Hill on the road to Taveta, and after a march of a few miles the next afternoon we got in touch with the E.A.M.R., and shortly afterwards a few German snipers. We pushed them back and then entrenched as well as we could. That night they sniped us a bit, but did no harm. The bush was very thick all round our camp, but it was nearly full moon. We heard the attack on one of the S.A. Brigades to our left, and also the heavy German gun (a 4.1 naval gun from the ' Königsberg ') firing both at this brigade and at Van Deventer's Brigade, which had advanced down the railway line from New Moschi to Kahi station. These brigades, I believe, ought to have got in touch with us, but they did not do so. During March 20th we improved our trenches and prepared for a night attack, which in fact started at 8.45 and was kept up till 1 a.m. The black troops, under German officers, behaved very pluckily, and time after time answered the bugle call to advance on our camp. Our Maxims kept them off. Fortunately they had no machine-guns with them, and though they fired thousands of shots at our camp they did very little damage, as almost all the bullets went pinging over us. Soon after 1 a.m. we heard their bugle sounding the ' assemble ' and they drew off. In the morning the dead just in front of our machine-gun commanding the road were collected and laid out in a row—like pheasants or hares after a drive—but the bush was not searched for the rest of the dead, as we had to push on and attack the Germans who were entrenched across the road a few miles on ahead on the Soko river. They held us off all day, and we had about 200 casualties, as the South African Brigades on our right and left which were to have enveloped them could not or did not come up. The men of our battalion (about 50 of each of our 4 companies) were in reserve, but late in the afternoon A, C, and D Companies had to go forward to support an Indian regiment. I was in command of my 50 men of A Company. We really could do nothing but lie very flat, trying to dig ourselves in with bayonets and fingers, being under the sweeping fire of three or four machine-guns. The lie of the ground just saved us when lying flat, and the bullets just swept over us in bouquets. We only had 17 casualties, and only 2 men killed dead. So far our battalion has not had much fighting, but we have gone through much hardship, fatigue, and exposure. You will wonder how I have stood it all at my age. But the fact remains that from May 4th, 1915, to February 6th, 1916, I never took leave or a day's rest, and was never a single day off duty or away from my company. From February 6th to the 12th I had to lie up, as I had jiggers in one of my toes, and the inflammation went to my groin. Since then I have never been a day away from my company again up till to-day, and have never put my leg over a horse, but done all the marching with the men, carrying my rifle, 50 or 60 rounds of ammunition, water-bottle, glasses and haversack with food—at least 20 lbs. altogether. But the men have usually had to carry 150 rounds of ammunition. Still, considering that I shall be sixty-five at the end of this year I have stuck it out remarkably well, and am one of the very few in the battalion who has never yet had a day's illness, for inflammation caused by jiggers cannot be called illness. But now I am beginning to be troubled with hæmorrhoids and another trouble. I have kept this in check out here for a whole year with astringent ointment, but during the last month it has got much worse and it may oblige me to come home on leave for an operation. The wet and damp of the last month here may have had something to do with the aggravation of my trouble.

" General Smuts was very lucky. He was just given time to carry out his operations round Kilimanjaro and drove the Germans down the line towards Tanga before the rain set in. We have been up here (about 300 men, of whom 100 have been in hospital and a lot more ill in camp, as the hospital is full) for nearly a month and it has rained almost day and night all the time, and we have lived in a sea of vile sticky mud. One of our officers as near as possible died of dysentery, but he is now much better. We—both officers and men—have had nothing but bare army rations since leaving Longido on March 5th last. However, we are now leaving this place, and going to M'buyuni, near Maktau, on the Voi-Taveta Railway, as the railway is now through to New Moschi—but from Taveta to Moschi it is very uncertain, as the heavy rains keep washing parts of the line away. The Germans blew up their naval 4.1 gun at the Ruwu river after firing all the 70 rounds at our camp and the two S.A. Brigades. They put the shells very close to our camp but did not hit it, but they dropped one amongst Van Deventer's men and killed five or six men and horses. After the fighting at the Soko and round Kahe on March 20th and 21st, the Germans retired down the Tanga Railway, and are said to be entrenching at various places. Nothing further can be done on our side until the rains are over, as all transport of a railway line is now almost impossible. Horses, mules, and men are all suffering terribly from the climate, and diseases of man and beast, and the frightful thick bush will help the Germans very much if they intend to fight on till the bitter end. Van Deventer has had a fresh lot of horses sent to him, and is now near the main German Railway from Dar-es-Salaam to Lake Tanganyika. The Belgians ought, too, soon to be co-operating from the Congo. We have just got the terribly bad news of General Townshend's surrender to the Turks in Mesopotamia, and the outbreak in Ireland. My son Freddy passed out of Sandhurst on April 6th and is, I expect, now attached to the Royal West Surrey regiment. The Commandant at Sandhurst has written to my wife speaking in very high terms of praise about him ; but, alas, I may never see him alive again if this accursed war goes on much longer. And you and poor Mrs. Millais must now be most anxious about your eldest boy too. Well ! of course their country comes first for them and for us, and we must all try and do our duty, but it will break our wives' hearts if either of them loses her boy, and it will take all the joy of life out of us

FARU! FARU!

too. Well! I have written you an unconscionably long letter, but it has hardly ever stopped raining now for more than an hour or so at a time for two days and nights, and we are enveloped in thick mist, and there is nothing to do but read and write. The weather gets worse and worse, that is the rain gets more incessant. Everything is saturated with moisture, and my blankets seem quite wet when I get into them at night. It is the constant unending wet and damp I think that gets to the men's stomachs and bowels and gives them dysentery. The slopes of Kilimanjaro may be a health resort in the dry season, but they are not much of a place to live in during the heavy rains. And the natives say that the rains will go on until the middle or end of June. Well! once more good-bye, old fellow, and with very kind regards to Mrs. Millais and your children, and trusting that all is well with all of them."

" *May 4th*, 1916.

" To-day is the anniversary of our landing at Mombasa on May 4th, 1915. Since writing to you two days ago I have seen a good doctor, as my trouble with piles is getting bad. He says I must have an operation soon, as if I went on long hard marches now I might get into a state which would require an immediate operation or serious consequences to me might happen. He advises me strongly to go home and have the operation there, as he does not think there is a really skilful surgeon out here. In all probability, therefore, as soon as I get to the big camp at M'buyuni, I shall be again examined, and a board of medical men will recommend that I shall be given three months' leave of absence to go home and have this operation, so I may be home almost as soon as this letter. Really it does not much matter, as our battalion is played out, used up, and they will probably not find more than 300 men fit for duty, and these only fit for garrison-duty on the lines of communication. The forward movements to the Dar-es-Salaam line will I think be carried out by Smuts' mounted forces and his 1000 motor bicyclists and armoured motors, as soon as

z

the rains are over and the country becomes possible for transport. During the rains I believe the railway will be pushed on from New Moschi towards the main German railway line. Well! good-bye again."

In June, 1916, after an examination by a medical board, Selous came home to undergo an operation which was completely successful. He was only ill for twelve days and then went to his home for a short rest. In August he went out again with a draft to East Africa, going via the Cape.

Both at the time Selous served with them and during his short absence, the sufferings and difficulties of our troops in this bush fighting under tropical rains and intense heat were such as to try the nerves of the strongest troops. Colonel Driscoll, who commanded the battalion of Frontiersmen, gives a vivid picture (" The Weekly Dispatch," July 21st, 1918) of the sufferings endured by the men who were so unfortunate as to be wounded.

" It's very different when you get down to the plains and the bush. I don't think any words could describe that. A vast and almost impenetrable forest so thick that when an aeroplane goes up the observer sees nothing but a great green carpet below him. And wild animals, mind you, as well as wild devils to fight ; the sun burning your very flesh ; the flies intolerable.

" Imagine a camp at night under these conditions. Round and about the lions are roaring from hunger. Hyenas prowl in the hope of snapping up a sentry or leaping in and carrying off a wounded man. I have known a man with a temperature of 105 Fahrenheit stagger up in the morning and insist upon continuing the march. It was the old spirit of my Scouts ever unquenchable.

" The natives—the old natives, as I have said—were always on our side. What would have happened to us if they had not hated the German like the devil I cannot tell you. But they followed us through the bush, often for miles, brought us food and attached themselves to us as servants, who were quite ready to carry rifles upon occasion. This was very helpful, for sometimes at night, when the force was absolutely without provisions, we had to send men scouting in native villages, and they could easily have been betrayed. Nothing would have been easier for a treacherous native than to have sneaked out while two or three of our men were in his hut and to have warned the nearest camp of Askaris. It never happened. The loathing of the Blonde Beast was too universal.

" All this sounds bad enough, but believe me, it gives you but a poor account of what it cost us to win ' German East.' "

CHAPTER XIV

SEPTEMBER, 1916–1917

SELOUS left England on his last journey on August 10th, 1916, and landed at Mombasa (via the Cape) in September with a draft of 400 new recruits for the 25th Royal Fusiliers. First he went up the Uganda railway to Nairobi, and later to Korogwe in the Usambara valley, and after resting here a week or two brought his detachment on to Tanga in September, where he was detained for nearly eight weeks. He remained at Tanga until December 2nd, until his force moved up to Dar-es-Salaam to take part in a fresh movement against the Germans.

The campaign in German East Africa had now entered on its most difficult period. Owing to the enormous wastage in men and horses, transport of all kinds was most difficult and in some cases impossible during the rainy season. Writing from Tanga on November 11th, 1916, to Chapman, he says :—

" The war has now entered upon a very difficult phase. As von Lettow-Vorbeck—a very able and determined man —the German commander, has been allowed to escape with considerable forces well equipped with machine-guns, into the wilderness towards the Portuguese border. We hold all the ports, all the towns, plantations, etc., and both the railway lines—but von Lettow still commands a force, it is thought, of over 1000 whites and several thousand trained black troops, well found in arms and ammunition. The wastage from fever and dysentery has been terrible, and, as the heavy rains will come on, where the Germans are, very shortly now, if Smuts cannot round them up quickly it will be impossible to continue this campaign for months. He is busy repairing roads and railways and getting up supplies to near the Front, and we are expecting to get forward again at any moment. With the latest drafts our battalion has had 1400 men out here. All we have left of them are 149 at Kijabe (but these must mostly be unfit for further hard service) and 394 here, of which latter number 101 are sick. Two have died in hospital this week. Of the two fine Rhodesian regiments, it is said that only 68 are fit. The North Lancs Regt. has wasted to nothing, in spite of many drafts. The position is now most difficult, and unless a decision can quickly be arrived at, this campaign may drag on for months and have to be finished by black troops, as another month in a heavy rainy season, without shelter and short rations, will lay out all the white troops still left.

"F. C. S."

During the period March–September, 1916, General Smuts captured the region from Kilimanjaro to Dar-es-Salaam, whilst the Belgians gradually occupied the western part of German East Africa, from the Great Lakes to Tabora, and General Northey the south-west part of the country. The Germans were thus restricted to the south, the south-centre and south-eastern regions, except the actual coast-line.

" After evacuating Tabora the German troops in that region, who were under General Wahle, retired south-east towards Mahenge, a government station on a high plateau centrally situated between the northern end of Lake Nyasa and the sea at Kilwa. Part of the enemy force which had opposed General Smuts also retreated to Mahenge, its commanding officer being Major Kraut. In its retreat General Wahle's force harried, and was harried by, General Northey's columns. Wahle broke through the British lines and joined Kraut, who was being threatened from the north by General Van Deventer, the commander of General Smuts' Second Division. In the closing days of 1916 and the beginning of 1917 a combined effort was made by Generals Van Deventer and Northey to ' round up ' the Germans holding the Mahenge plateau. The movement promised success, but, in the words of General Smuts, the enemy ' eventually escaped through the dense bush and forest under cover of darkness, and eluded pursuit.'

" Meantime the main enemy force, under Colonel von Lettow-Vorbeck, upon whom the Kaiser in November, 1916, conferred the Ordre Pour le Merite, had been driven by General Smuts to the region of the Rufigi, south of Dar-es-Salaam. At this period General Smuts reorganized his forces, and, in view of the extremely unhealthy character of the country in which further operations were to be conducted, as many as possible of the white troops from South Africa were sent home, over 12,000 leaving East Africa between the middle of October and the end of December, 1916. They were replaced by newly raised battalions of King's African Rifles and by a Nigerian Brigade under General Cunliffe. On January 1, 1917, General Smuts began a new offensive in the Rufigi area, his object being to cut all connection between the enemy in the Rufigi and Mahenge regions and either to envelop the enemy on the Rufigi or to deal a heavy blow as he escaped south. The last object was accomplished ; a heavy blow was inflicted upon von Lettow-Vorbeck's force, but it was not brought to a decisive engagement. This brief campaign was ended in March by the advent of the rainy season. While it was in progress General Smuts was summoned to England to represent South Africa in the special sittings of the War Cabinet. He relinquished his command on January 20, 1917, being succeeded by Major-General A. R. Hoskins, C.M.G., D.S.O., who had previously commanded the First Division."— " The Times History and Encyclopædia of the War," the campaign in German East Africa (III), pp. 397–398.

On December 8th, the Royal Fusiliers went in open trucks by rail to Mikesse, near Morogoro, and from thence had a very trying eight days' march to Kissaki. During this and previous marches Selous never rode a yard of the way, but marched like his men, living on their rough fare and enduring the constant rain and soaking bivouacs with stoical indifference. On December 15th he writes to his wife from Tulo :—

" We are now marching to Kissaki, and from there will

probably advance and attack the Germans on the Rufigi river. Very heavy rains have now set in, and we have had rather a bad time of it, and our detachment has shrunk from 384 to 170, with which we march to-day. We hear the bridge over the Rufigi river has been washed away by the floods and the German forces cut in two."

One of his last letters, written on Christmas Day, 1916, from Kissaki, states :—

" We are on the eve of an attack on the Germans out here. Their lines here are quite close to ours, our forces are gathering, and we shall now attack their lines in several places simultaneously in a few days. Our forces are terribly depleted principally from sickness. The German forces are sure to be entrenching, and as they still have a number of machine-guns, it may be no child's play attacking their positions, and we may meet with heavy losses."

During the last three weeks of 1916, General Smuts (except for Van Deventer's Division) had not been engaged in important operations but was busy reorganizing his columns. Von Lettow-Vorbeck was, however, forced out of Kissaki on September 15th, by the brigade under Brits and Nussey. He then took up his position between the Ingeta and Rufigi rivers, where he remained until January 1st, when General Smuts began another offensive from Kissaki.

An attack was made on the German positions by General Smuts on December 2nd, but the enemy again escaped and took up a fresh position in dense bush on the Beho-Beho ridge. All January 2nd and 3rd General Smuts spent in developing a new encircling movement of which the following is the " Times " History account :—

" The troops, which had to march through most difficult country, got in touch with the enemy again on the afternoon of the 3rd, and at 10.30 a.m. on January 4th Sheppard's Brigade caught up the chief enemy force as it was retiring from Beho-Beho. A sharp engagement followed, but though severely handled the enemy ' again slipped past,' to use General Smuts' phrase. The brunt of the action was borne by the 25th Royal Fusiliers (the Legion of

Frontiersmen). During the fight Captain F. C. Selous fell at the head of his company. He was buried under the shadow of a tamarind tree, beside the graves of members of his company who fell at the same time. Thus ended the life of the most distinguished of the hunter-naturalists of recent years, the man who had opened up thousands of miles of South Central Africa. Throughout the campaign, though well over sixty, he had set an example of endurance and devotion to duty unexcelled by any member of the force. As stated in Chapter CLXXXIII, he had already been given the D.S.O. in recognition of his services. None knew better than Selous the dangers and difficulties of the campaign. Writing home from Tanga in November, 1916, he set forth some of these difficulties, adding : ' I shall try and hold out to the end, if possible, or, at any rate, as long as my health and strength last. General Smuts is now working . . . for the next forward movement, and when he is ready the remnants of my battalion will join him.' "

General J. Smuts, who was in command of the British Forces in German East Africa, has kindly given me the following account of the fight at Beho-Beho, Sugar Mountain, on January 4th, 1917, when Selous met his death. General Smuts, with the aid of a large-scale map, personally explained to me the feature of the operations on that day, and though it was instrumental in driving the enemy from their positions, causing them to retreat to the Rufigi river, it did not result in the capture of the enemy's force, which it was hoped would be the case.

" Our force moved out from Kissaki early on the morning of January 4th, 1917, with the object of attacking and surrounding a considerable number of German troops which was encamped along the low hills east of Beho-Beho (Sugar Mountain) N.E. of the road that led from Kissaki S.E. to the Rufigi river, distant some 13 miles from the enemy's position. The low hills occupied by the Germans were densely covered with thorn-bush and the visibility to the west was not good. Nevertheless, they soon realized the danger of their position when they detected a circling movement on the part of the 25th Royal Fusiliers, which had

been detailed to stop them on the road leading S.E., the
only road, in fact, by which they could retreat. They
must have retired early, for their forces came to this point
at the exact moment when the leading company of Fusiliers, under Captain Selous, reached the same point. Heavy
firing on both sides then commenced, and Selous at once
deployed his company, attacked the Germans, which
greatly outnumbered him, and drove them back into the
bush. It was at this moment that Selous was struck dead
by a shot in the head. The Germans retreated in the dense
bush again, and the Fusiliers failed to come to close quarters,
or the enemy then made a circuit through the bush and
reached the road lower down, eventually crossing the
Rufigi."

When he came to the road, Selous and his company met
the German advanced guard, which probably outnumbered
his force five to one. He had, however, received his orders
to prevent, if possible, the enemy from reaching the road
and retreating, so he immediately extended his company
and himself went forward to reconnoitre. It was whilst
using his glasses to ascertain the position of the enemy's
advance guard that Selous received a bullet in his head and
was killed instantly.[1]

Thus died Frederick Selous of the Great Heart, a splendid
Englishman, who in spite of age and love of life, gave up all
pleasant things to follow the iron path of duty. To him
his country's needs were ever before his private interests.
Like the voyageurs of old he was ever looking for some
far-off country where his restless soul could sleep in peace.
Let us hope that he found his Valhalla on that day.

He sleeps with other gallant comrades who fell beside
him in the heart of Africa, far from home and loved ones.
Yet it seems fitting that he should lie at last in the land
of his dreams, where he laboured so much, and where his

[1] Colonel Driscoll, who commanded the 25th Royal Fusiliers, writes :
" Captain Selous, the great hunter, was one of the hardest men in the
battalion, in spite of his 65 years. He was shot dead while leading his
company through the bush against an enemy four times their strength.
Lieutenant Dutch, another very gallant man, took his place and received
a mortal wound immediately afterwards."

name will never be forgotten. No sculptured mausoleum
records his prowess, but only a simple wooden cross bearing
his name and that of his good comrades stands beneath the
shade of a tamarind tree in the woody forest, where the bush-
cuckoo heralds the dawn and the lion roars his requiem to
the night.

> "Under the wide and starry sky,
>   Dig the grave and let me lie.
> Glad did I live and gladly die,
>   And I laid me down with a will.
> This be the verse you grave for me :
> *Here he lies where he longed to be.*
> Home is the sailor, home from the sea,
>   And the hunter home from the hill."

I am indebted to Captain R. M. Haines of the South
African Forces for the following account of Selous' life from
the time he landed at Mombasa till his death :—

" I did not actually bury Captain Selous, but I was present
at his funeral. I think I had better give you his doings
from about the end of August. He came out for the second
time about the end of August, 1916, and landed at Mombasa
(via the Cape) with a draft of about 400 new men for the
25th R. Fusiliers. He took these up the Uganda Railway
to a small detail camp called Korogwe, in the Usambara
Valley. After waiting there for a week or two, he brought
the draft to Tanga, when to his intense disgust he was
held up for nearly eight weeks. In the meantime the original
part of the regiment was trekking down the centre of the
country towards the German Central Railway. Whilst at
Tanga, he lived in a house with Captain MacMillan, whom
you probably know. It was here that he heard he had been
awarded the D.S.O. Whilst we were waiting here, he
frequently gave the men lectures on his early life in South
Africa, to their intense delight. Here I first met him.
He was literally adored by the men. From a boy he had
always been a hero of mine, and to my great joy I actually
met him. He wore a double Terai grey slouch hat, slightly
on the back of his head. Khaki knickerbockers, with no
puttees, bare legs, except for his socks, and shirt open at
the neck, with a knotted handkerchief round the neck to

keep the sun off, with a long native stick in his hand. He
had a rooted objection to wearing a cork helmet. It is
impossible to forget the impression he made. He was as
straight as a guardsman, with a broad deep chest, with a
beautiful healthy look in his face.

"We left Tanga, on board an armed merchantman,
at the end of November, and after calling in at Zanzibar
for a few hours, arrived at Dar-es-Salaam. At Zanzibar
I went ashore with him and had breakfast at the
English club. We were landed at Dar-es-Salaam at about
10.30 at night and went into the local detail camp. He
remained there about a week and was then sent up to take
up the draft he had brought out to Kissaki, which is about
100 miles south of the German Central Railway, where the
rest of the regiment was waiting.

(Here I went down with fever, and so had to stay behind
for two weeks.)

"He went by train to Mikessi, about 150 miles up the
Central Railway, and from there started with his draft of
400 men to reach the regiment. He reached Kissaki in a
fortnight. This is practically the last point where any life
exists, except game, in this part of the country. In many
ways it is terrible country; there are no names, save such
names as we gave it, no roads. It is covered with thick
elephant-grass, six to eight feet high, and very thick thorn-
bush and swamp. Although I was one of them, I honestly
think that the sufferings of the troops in this horrible trek
have hardly been exceeded by any in the war. There was
only filthy water, we marched on half-rations, with no
bread at all, only flour being issued and occasionally biscuit.
The whole country was poisonous with fever and ' blackwater '; hardly any natives live here, as it is too poisonous.
Most of the men went sick and died like flies. It was just
south of Kissaki he caught the regiment up. He was just
as cheerful as a schoolboy.

"The day he was killed, I passed him in the morning
with his company, I was driving an armoured machine-gun,
as the driver was ill. As I passed him, I shouted out, ' I
shall be back and have *tea* with you to-day, sir,' for we

used to joke him about his habit of drinking tea with every meal.

"That was the last I saw of him. There was some fighting in the bush during the day, and when I came back in the afternoon I was greeted with the news of his death. I was just in time to see him buried. He was sewn up in a blanket, and buried with five other men of the R. Fusiliers. I was told he was first wounded in the right arm, which was broken, but was bandaged up, and he remained with his company.[1]

"A little later he was again hit in the mouth and was killed instantaneously and apparently painlessly.

"A little space was cleared in the bush and he was buried, at one of the most impressive services I have ever attended, the same day in the afternoon. I intended to photograph the spot, but next day I went down with a bad attack of blackwater fever, and the next few weeks are a complete blank to me. My memory is still somewhat out of gear. My diary and camera were missing when I came round, and so all my exact records are going to some scamp. He is buried about 60 miles south of Kissaki, in a nameless spot, but if you will wait a month or two I may yet be able to get you some photographs and further details.

"As I said before, he was always my hero as a boy in books, and he remains so now. He had all that simplicity and modesty of great men. He was the easiest of all men to cheat, but yet no one ever dared to do it. He was a moral antiseptic in a country where men are not saints. Anything mean or sordid literally shrivelled up in his presence.

[1] Mr. Lamb also mentions that Selous was wounded before he was killed, but this is contradicted by others who were present. Mr. Denis Lyell, writing in the "Field," August 17th, 1918, says: "Details of his death were given to Mr. W. Watmough by a friend in his regiment who was present. He says: 'Capt. Selous was shot through the head and right side. We were on a crest line at the time with the Germans in front and on both flanks. We were subjected to very heavy enfilade fire, and could not locate the enemy properly owing to the wooded nature of their positions. At this stage Selous went forward down the slope about fifteen yards, and was just raising his glasses in order to see (more particularly) where certain snipers were when he received his first wound in the side. He was half-turning towards us when he was shot through the side of the head. He died immediately.'"

" Although I am a young man, my fate has led me to travel in all our white colonies, and I can honestly say that of all the men I have met, good or bad (and they have been mostly good), no one has ever left me with the impression of being a ' whiter ' man, or who was a more perfect English gentleman.
" R. M. HAINES, S.A.F."

Mr. P. H. Lamb, writing in " The Field," June 18th, 1918, gives some details of the actual position of Selous' grave, of which he furnishes a photograph.

" The geographical position of his grave is approximately lat. 7 deg. S., long. 38 deg. E. It is not near any village but lies only a few yards to the east of the main road leading south from Mikesse, on the Central Railway to the Rufigi river, from which it is about 10 miles distant. There is a stream crossing the road at this point. It was here that the gallant 25th Royal Fusiliers were camped on the day (January 4, 1917) when Selous was killed. It was to this spot that the fallen hero was carried.

" The graveyard is situated close by the old camp, and contained at the time of my visit seven simple wooden crosses. Besides the one in memory of Captain Selous are those of Sergeant Knight, Lance-Corporal Evans, and Privates Taylor and Evans, all of the Royal Fusiliers, who were killed on the same day. The other two graves are those of privates of the British West Indies Regiment who died at the same place months later. The precise spot where Selous was fighting when he was first wounded was pointed out to me. It was among some small knolls which lie about a mile to the north, on which the present camp, known as Chogawali, has since been built. . . .

" The stream running by the spot where Captain Selous' remains are laid to rest is the last fresh water met with along the road before reaching the Rufigi. It is for the most part a wild inhospitable district—the haunt of a great variety of big game, including elephants, giraffes, and rhinos. Not more than four miles away is a warm salt spring running down into a salt lake, where hippos, wild ducks, egrets, and numerous other wild fowl abound. But despite these alleviations it can hardly be called a fascinating part of the country, and the object of most people who have seen it will be to avoid it carefully in the future."

The war in German East Africa dragged its slow length along throughout 1917, in November of which year it may be said to have terminated, when the remnant of the German forces under Colonel von Lettow-Vorbeck were driven right across the borders into Portuguese territory. There, owing to the rainy season in the early part of 1918, they split up into small parties and searched the country for native supplies, being finally (September, 1918) forced into the low-lying country between the north of the Zambesi and the coast.

Since then they have attacked various Portuguese stations and encampments and taken fresh supplies of provisions, medical necessaries and ammunition and are still (September, 1918) causing much trouble to trace, British forces relentlessly pursuing them. Colonel R. Meinertzhagen, who is well acquainted with the local conditions, writes :—

" The campaign is not over to-day (August 1st, 1918), and it is by no means impossible that Von Lettow breaks north again into his old colony.[1] He is an exceptional man of iron will and great personality. I met him in Tanga in November, 1914, and he then declared that even though we might drive him from his colony he would fight to the last, and that he would never be taken alive."

Commenting on the great difficulties of the campaign, General Smuts, at a meeting of the Royal Geographical Society (January 28th, 1918), designated the travels of Livingstone and Selous as mere " joy rides " compared to what had been done by Empire troops in East Africa.

" The Germans," he remarked, " are not in search of colonies after the English model. Not colonies, but military power and strategic positions for a great Central African Empire, comprising not only her colonies before the war,

[1] This view has proved to be correct.

but also all the English, French, Belgian, and Portuguese possessions south of the Sahara and Lake Chad, and north of the Zambesi river in South Africa.

" Towards this objective she was steadily marching even before the war broke out, and she claims the return of her lost African colonies at the end of the war as a starting-point from which to resume the interrupted march. This Central African block was intended in the first place to supply the economic requirements and raw materials of German industry, and in the second and far more important place to become the recruiting ground of vast armies. The natural harbours on the Atlantic and Indian Oceans were to supply the naval and submarine bases from which both ocean routes would be dominated and British and American sea-power be brought to naught.

" No fresh extension of Prussian militarism to other continents and seas should be tolerated, and the conquered German colonies can only be regarded as guarantees for the security of the future peace of the world. The premature or unwise restoration of German East Africa to its former owners might have consequences reaching far beyond the confines of the African continent. Perhaps I may be allowed to express the fervent hope that a land where so many of our heroes lost their lives may never be allowed to become a menace to the future peaceful development of the world."

All of which is very true, for after the war, if German East Africa is restored to Germany, as some of our socialists, like Mr Wells, seem to desire, it is a certainty that in time we shall lose all our South African possessions as well as those in the north.

CHAPTER XV

PERHAPS Selous' chief success as a hunter lay in his untiring energy and fearless intention to gain some desired object. He brought the same force into play in pursuit of a bull elephant as of a small butterfly, and allowed nothing to stand in his way to achieve success. Time, distance, difficulty, or danger were all things that could be conquered by a man of strong will, and his bodily strength was such that even to the end he almost achieved the virility of perfect youth. He would come back from the early morning hunt, the best time of all for pursuing big game, and have some breakfast. Then, when others were tired and glad of some hours' sleep in the camp or waggon, he would call a native boy to carry his rifle and a few cartridges—in case of an unexpected meeting with some rare animal—take his butterfly-net and collecting-box, to spend the hot hours of the day in search of Lepidoptera. Few men, even young men in the prime of life, are capable of pursuing insects under a tropical sun after the fatigue of the early morning hunt, but Selous not only did this almost to the day of his death, but also went out again in search of big game in the hours between three o'clock and sunset.

It was his untiring love of Nature and the possible capture of some victim new to science that always drove him on and banished fatigue. His whipcord frame responded readily to all the calls he made upon it, for from his youth he had inured himself to strain and privation, and was extremely moderate in any indulgence. He ate less than most men, and never drank anything but tea, which he enjoyed at every meal. Sometimes he drank champagne at big dinners, but rich wines and high feeding had no attractions for him.

He always rated himself as a very moderate shot, and doubtless, in the early days, when he was only armed with clumsy and indifferent weapons, his success was not always of a high order, but with the advent of rifles of greater precision he was certainly a good shot, and he killed a large proportion of the game he fired at. This was especially so when he got what he described as his first first-class rifle, a ·450 single shot, made by Gibbs, of Bristol, and with this he killed a large quantity of game. All of us who are big game hunters, however, know how greatly the average of hits has advanced since the introduction of the small-bore high-velocity rifles. In 1895 came the British ·303, the German ·275 Mauser, and the Roumanian ·256 Mannlicher, and these weapons possess such accuracy and flatness of trajectory that a poor shot becomes a moderate one, a good shot a first-class one, and a first-class performer something remarkable. Since 1900 some firms, notably John Rigby, have utilized the best points of these smaller weapons to make them successful on the largest and most dangerous game in the hands of experienced men, and have invented weapons of tremendous hitting power with magazine rapidity of fire.

London gunmakers were so anxious for Selous to use every new weapon they put on the market that he was bombarded with gifts of new weapons, in the hope that he would use them and advertise their wares. In many cases he did accept them, and between 1896 and 1915 he tried, on his numerous trips, perhaps a dozen different rifles. In this he admitted that he made a great mistake, for he would have done much better if he had adhered to one rifle for small game, such as the common ·256 Mannlicher, and one large one, such as the ·450 Rigby for heavy or dangerous animals. Many of these new rifles, though they nearly all shot well *when they worked*, developed glaring faults in magazine construction or defective bullets. What does well enough on the target at home is often quite a failure in the wear and tear of the African wilderness. A bullet that " mushrooms "

2 A

nicely on the carcase of a horse may completely fail to stop a tough African antelope, and so on. Thus Selous lost his faith in specious promises, and often wished he had stuck to his old ·450 single-shot Gibbs, which always gave good results on all medium-sized game, and even on the few occasions when he met elephants.

As an example of Selous' practical nature with regard to rifles, and the absolute necessity of testing them thoroughly before field-use, he told me one day the following story :—

At a leading London gunmaker's he had ordered a heavy high-velocity rifle, which he intended to use on large game in one of his more recent expeditions. As so often happens, the gunmaker in question delayed the delivery of the weapon till the very last moment, and one hour before he was to depart for Africa, Selous found himself in possession of a new weapon whose sighting and cartridges he had not tested. Now, to a man of his experience, such a thing as taking a rifle to Africa without first shooting it carefully was unheard of. The cartridges might not fit, or the sights might be set too high or too low. There was only one thing to be done, he must test the rifle somehow, even though located as he was in a house in Regent's Park. Calling the servant he asked her to get a cab and put all his kit therein and to place his hat and coat ready in the hall. When the maid announced that this had been done, he then opened his bedroom-window, and selecting a neighbouring chimney-stack, at about 100 yards distance, he fired five shots in quick succession.

The effect in the densely populated neighbourhood may be more easily imagined than described. Heads appeared at every window and knots of people began to assemble in the streets below. What on earth was happening ? Had someone suddenly gone mad ? Was a murder being perpetrated, or had the Germans landed ? Selous quickly got out his field-glasses, and noticed that the pattern on the brick chimney was distinctly good. He then carefully cleaned the rifle and put it in its case, donned his hat and coat, and opened the front door. Here was assembled a group of scared people, whilst a policeman was seen hastily crossing the road. Someone asked him as he entered the cab if he had heard the shots, and the old hunter replied that he had, and that the sounds seemed to have come from one of the rooms above. So Selous tried his rifle and went on his way rejoicing.

Speaking of him as a hunter, Sir Alfred Pease, himself one of our best performers in the field, writes :—

" It would be easier to write more fully of Selous, if he had occasionally ' broken out ' and ' bucked ' a bit—his very modesty and reserve and his care about what he said and his delightful simple-heartedness concerning his own achievements[1] were something difficult to cope with— much as they added to the charm and attractiveness of the man and fortified one's confidence in him. To me that he was absolutely true and the pure stuff was what made him stand out. Personally I never saw him do anything brilliant—I have seen many men shoot better, quicker, and so on, but no man who got so much or at any rate any more interest out of all that pertains to a hunter's and naturalist's life. He was a rather deliberate than quick observer, as far as I can judge, but when he had reached a conclusion you might lay your money he was right. I re- member one day being rather inclined (being myself of an eager, quick, and perhaps impatient nature) to think him tiresome. He was with me at Kilanga (my B.E.A. farm), and said, ' Now I want to get a good Kongoni ' (Coke's Hartebeest)—we were standing where there were always hundreds, and often thousands, in sight. We regarded Kongoni like the flocks on a hundred mountains. The old bulls' heads were much alike ; in early days I had measured perhaps a dozen, and did not find that any one was much more interesting than another. I said I didn't know that I could help him, ' they were much of a muchness.' He asked me questions about measurements and weights and so on, most of which I could not answer. I told him there were

---

[1] Writing to H. F. Wallace in 1911 Selous speaks of his own capacity in characteristic style : " That quotation (in your article) from Roosevelt's book as to my being ' the greatest of the world's big game hunters ' is all bunkum. Because I have hunted a lot, that is not to say I am a specially good hunter."

plenty to choose from, and off he went and spent the whole of a hot day trying to find a ' specimen ' worth having. He returned at night with a head and neck, and then the inquisition began again after measuring and remeasuring, and after a time (perhaps he was two hours messing about with his Kongoni head in the evening, after a tiring day, when I wanted him to come in and sit down) he came to the conclusion that there was not much difference between his head and the horns lying about of those we had shot for meat. He went to Juja (MacMillan's), and a few days after showed me two other heads he had got there, and no doubt had given the same exertion and examination to get, and with not much different result. It is well for science that there are such men, and some of my neighbours were amazed at this man, whose great reputation had reached them, and had expected to see him galloping after lions and shooting them from the saddle, etc., bothering himself over Kongoni heads, but I must say I admired immensely this persistence to get at a definite knowledge about a common beast."

It is a little difficult to gauge the shooting quality of a man by reading published works, because rifle-shooting at big game in various countries involves such various conditions. In Scotland, Norway, and the high grounds of Europe, Asia, and America, a good shot would probably kill ten beasts out of every fifteen or twenty cartridges expended, or even less. Many men do not take "all chances," moving or otherwise, whilst the best hunters *do* take all targets offered at a good head and at all ranges up to 350 yards, but in the plains and forests of Africa the average of shots fired is far higher, because the conditions are more difficult, and, broadly speaking, from three to six shots[1] are required in the course of a trip to every animal brought to bag. In Africa visibility, except in the early morning and late evening, is curtailed by refraction from the earth of the sun's rays, and animals are much shyer ; on the plains and in the bush it is difficult to pick out the best head or to see it clearly. Often too, especially in bush, the shot is hurried, and has to be taken when the shooter

[1] According to the quality of the shooter.

is standing in a bad position. There is always too the nervous tension on the part of the hunter when pursuing dangerous game, a nervousness not necessarily fear, which makes him ever on the alert for danger or alarm caused by some other animal of the same herd. All these circumstances create other conditions unfavourable to good shooting, although they undoubtedly add to the charm of African sport. In earlier days too in South Africa (and more recently sometimes in East Africa) most of the game killed was shot after riding down the animal or quickly galloping after it and jumping off for the shot as soon as the beast came to a standstill and was not greatly alarmed. At this form of sport Selous was, when once well armed, a very skilful performer. His excellent horsemanship, fearless dash through " wait-a-bit " thorns, and keen eye enabled him almost invariably to run to a standstill almost any animal he had set out to chase, and though he admitted he frequently used many cartridges before he achieved success, I think he was a much better shot than he professed to be. In later years, when he hunted the beasts of the plain, forests, and mountains in Europe, Asia Minor, and North America, his expenditure of cartridges (if we read his books carefully) certainly proves him to have been a very good performer with the rifle.

After his marriage, in 1895, he spent much of his time in England and took " seriously " to the shot-gun. I say " seriously," because everything he did was adopted with the same whole-heartedness that he brought to other things. At first it must be admitted he was a very poor performer, and did not kill any except the ordinary rising bird ; but, as time went on, he practised so assiduously that he was soon able to kill a few driven grouse and part-ridges. After twenty years he became quite a good shot, certainly above the average, but was always depressed that he could not master the slowness which is ever the lot of a man who takes up the shot-gun after middle age. Such, how-ever, was his persistence and determination to excel that on occasion he performed so well that his hosts thought he had been shooting with the smooth-bore all his life, and complimented him on his skill. I remember one day in particular at Tatton Park, Lord Egerton's beautiful seat in Cheshire, when Selous really shot brilliantly and quite as well as any of the other guns, who were accounted first-class shots. We killed over one thousand pheasants that day, and Selous took down the high birds with a speed and accuracy that I think even astonished himself. He was like a schoolboy in his joy that day at shooting so well, and as usual said it was a " fluke " and he could never do it again. Another day at Swythamley, where, at the invitation of our old friend, Sir Philip Brocklehurst, we drove the moor for grouse, Selous killed for the first time twenty birds at one stand. He was in the seventh heaven of delight, nearly walked us off our legs, and told us " lion " stories till far into the night. We had many happy days at Swythamley between the years 1896–1914, and Selous was always at his best there under the rain of " chaff " and practical jokes of our host. Sir Philip's two sons, the present Sir Philip, who accompanied Shackleton to the Antarctic, and Courtenay, a captain in the 10th Hussars, and at present " flying " in East Africa, were boys after Selous' own heart, and have since become keen and successful big game hunters, whose youthful imagination Selous did so much to fire. At Swythamley we were all a happy party with congenial tastes and full of fun, and I always look back on the many delightful days we spent there as some of the best of life.

He liked nearly all outdoor sports at different times. He played an energetic game of tennis and was a really good croquet-player. Most of all he loved cricket, and played regularly for his local club at Worplesdon, taking part in all their matches until 1915. When any great game was fought at Lord's, such as England v. Australia, he was generally there before the game began in the members' enclosure, and, much as he detested crowds, he with his wife would sit out the whole three days and watch every ball that went down. On such occasions he seldom spoke, but kept his eyes firmly fixed upon the players, noting the skill displayed on both sides. At Worplesdon he put such life into the local club that they were soon able to leave the rough common where former matches were played and take and keep in order an excellent cricket-field. I played in some of these matches, which were rather of the " Dingley-Dell " type, and it was always a treat to see Fred standing so close " in " at " point " that he looked as if he would catch the batsman before he hit the ball. " Big Game Hunters v. Worplesdon " was always a great and solemn occasion.

In his later years he was a most indefatigable cyclist, and thought nothing of riding over to see his friends thirty and forty miles away and back, even when he was over sixty years of age. When at home he never rode in a car if he could avoid it, as his policy was ever to keep fit by physical exercise.

The following is an example of his energy as a cyclist (September 5th, 1909) :—

" I got home yesterday evening, having bicycled all the way from Gloucester—about 100 miles—in pouring rain most of the way, and over heavy, muddy roads, in just twelve hours, including stoppages for breakfast and lunch. I am not at all tired to-day, and next year, if I can get a fine day, I shall see if I cannot do 120 miles between day-light and dusk." Not bad for fifty-seven years of age.

With regard to the personal appearance and character of the man, his hard, gruelling life had left him straight and well-conditioned at the age of sixty. Few men interested others so much. He stood for all that was best in romance and high adventure. His life was of the hardest, for he loved to pit his strength against the forces of Nature. From childhood he only knew physical discipline as a virtue and battle as a self-enforced necessity. In appearance he was deep-chested, straight as an arrow, and with immensely powerful muscles on his arms and legs. Latterly he was inclined to stoutness, but this was kept in check by con-stant exercise. If there was one striking feature in his physiognomy it was his wonderful eyes, as clear and blue as a summer sea. Nearly every one who came in contact with him noticed his eyes. They were the eyes of the man who looks into the beyond over vast spaces. Instinctively one saw in them the hunter and the man of wide views. Their clarity of expression was so intense that any observer could see at a glance the whole nature of the mind that lay behind.

In social intercourse Selous had a presence that was apt to make other people look insignificant. He was adored by all his friends, and even perfect strangers seemed to come under his magnetism at the first introduction. It was not only the interesting things he had to tell, and the way he told them, but the kindness of heart and modesty that forced their way through any narrative, and which seemed to grow upon him with the years. Often was he the most sympathetic of listeners, but as a rule he was a great talker and an unrivalled story-teller. His memory was marvellous. Never halting for a word, his tales would flow on for hours without a check, and he was so skilful in the art of telling a tale that he seldom repeated stories with which he knew his audience were familiar. Well as I knew him for twenty years, I have rarely heard him repeat himself. Great as he was in this character, as powerful as any professional who holds his audience entranced in the courtyards of the Eastern cities, it was not a sense of vanity that inspired his volubility. It was always others who drew him on to talk, and he was so good-natured that he hated to leave his friends disappointed when he felt that stories were expected from him. Life was to him an endless adventure, and the freshness of his curiosity, the tireless spring of youth and romance, and the eagerness with which he attacked any subject, were such as to cause delight in the minds of all men who love to hear of high adventure and are yet debarred from playing their part. Nothing could quench his ardour when once his mind was set upon a thing. To hear him was to experience some fresh breeze blowing off the shores of youth. He possessed charm in the highest degree because he always seemed to like best the people he was with. He led his audience along pleasant ways and knew the secret of raising others to the plane of his own intellectual level. Alternately he was romantic, brilliant, fiery, brave, or kind, and thus ran through the gamut of human emotions.

Yet with all his high enthusiasm he always displayed a

curious diffidence as regards his own exploits—a modesty that perhaps endeared him best to those who loved him, for he was like all big men—a man who had no illusions. In all success he was ever alive to his own limitations, and none was more severe than he upon himself when he felt he had done some foolish thing or failed in some achievement from want of knowledge or skill. Few people knew how hardly he judged himself, or what anxieties he passed through before attacking some new problem. But the mental drag was there nevertheless, and though he may have laughed at it afterwards, there was something curiously feminine and introspective in his dual nature.

In many of the letters written during his early life in Africa, there is a certain strain of melancholy which seemed to overwhelm him when he found that after all his efforts to " make good," the results had not been a financial success. But these times of sadness were for the most part only temporary, and soon gave way under the influence of fresh enterprise.

" It was curious," writes his sister, Mrs. A. Jones, " that for all my brother's splendid health, great and varied interests, and good spirits—though not of the wildly elated kind—there was a strain of sadness in his nature, and he had not the love of life that would have seemed so natural— though there seemed to be so much in his life to live for. I have often heard him say that he would not mind dying at all, or would as soon die as live, or some expression to that effect. He was very philanthropic, and accepted any reverse of fortune or disappointment with calmness and fortitude. He suffered much, I think, through his views on the Boer War, but he was steadfast and true to his beliefs and principles always, and in this he showed a fine and noble spirit. This high sense of honour and integrity shone out like a bright star from a very feebly lit world in this respect. To me he was ever the most loving and tender brother, and his loss I shall ever lament."

All men and women have a real age which never leaves them from the cradle to the grave. Some are always twenty, and others drag through life with the soul of sixty. Fred

Selous was one of those happy creatures who die young, for he never resigned his youthful ideals.

He had a great sympathy with emotional people. Good acting or the " French temperament " appealed to him. Though slow to anger as a rule, it was not rare to see him spring from his chair and jerk his head fiercely from side to side at any story of injustice. The Norman blood in his veins caused him to like the French and to appreciate their " bonhomie " and excitability. With him too it was always near the surface—ready to sympathize, swift to resent—but over it all was the iron check of Scottish caution.

One night in Vienna, in 1910, Prince Henry Liechtenstein gave a little dinner party at " Sacher's." Slatin Pasha was there, and told us some interesting stories of his adventures as a captive of the Mahdi. Then came what I thought to be a somewhat garbled version of the Fashoda incident. Finally he made certain remarks, in very bad taste, of the leave-taking of Marchand with the French colony at the Cairo railway station. To him it was exceedingly " funny " that Marchand should burst into tears and kiss his friends. I got angry at this, and we had a somewhat heated passage of words. " Why," he sneered in conclusion, " what had Marchand to complain of—he was only a miserable Captain before, and was now made a Colonel." Such a gross mis-understanding of a man's temperament and ideals and am-bitions seemed deplorable indeed. It was quite German in its total failure to appreciate national psychology. In those two years of trial, privation and danger which Marchand had to face what must his thoughts have been. Twice on the road his expedition met with disaster from sickness, desertion and other causes. Yet he had re-formed it and marched successfully across unknown Africa from West to East with a handful of Senegalese sharpshooters, courting almost certain death at the end at the hands of the Mahdists. Only our expedition to Khartoum had saved him, by destroying the power of the Khalifa at the eleventh hour. What did such a man as he care for a trumpery military advancement ? He was out to do his duty for France, and he did it where nine hundred and ninety-nine men out of a thousand would have failed. He achieved his end, but owing to our policy—for once strong—his Government failed him. Marchand was truly a great man. When I told this trifling incident to Selous he seemed to be thrown into a frenzy of rage, for I did not then know his views on Marchand. " Why," he shouted, " Marchand did the biggest thing any man has ever done in Africa, and of course no one knows it— I should like to kiss him myself ! "

In speaking his voice possessed a singularly rich tone and resonance, and with all it carried a sympathetic quality that seemed to play directly on the heartstrings of his audience. Such gestures as he used were purely natural and necessary, and though possessing the volubility and excitable temperament of the southern races, the northern strain kept in check any excessive gesticulation. Although latterly his hearing was poor, he possessed a wonderful discrimination in shades of pronunciation when making use of native or foreign languages. Ever alive to the picturesque or the romantic, he clothed his stories in the language of which the true story-teller has the key, whilst over all hung the indelible stamp of truth and accuracy that characterized the man himself. His thoughts ranged over a wide field of emotions and ideas, in which chivalry perhaps played the most important part. It was always present in all his thoughts and acts. This with the intense energy or " fury of play," backed by the vehemence of emotion, carried him far in the higher flights both of act and imagination. " It is easy to be an ass and to follow the multitude like a blind besotted bull in a stampede," says Stevenson. Selous followed no leader but himself. Success left him humble, and the sharp ferule of calamity only crushed him for the moment. As he hated conventionality, so he loathed respectability—" that deadliest gag and wet blanket that can be laid on men." It meant nothing to him but the crystallized demeanour of spineless invertebrates. Thus when he spoke either in public or private life, he spoke direct from his heart and experience, and Men recognized the Man. He had a few mannerisms, and all have that—but was never the victim of stereotyped phrase or trite quotation. He took infinite care in his composition, but seldom altered, once the written thought was on paper. Unlike most authors he did not prune the " flesh " off his " bones " until the residue was satisfactory. Every line was complete when once he had set it down, and his manuscripts are as unaltered as at the moment they were written. In his lectures, as in his writings, he seemed to complete his thoughts before they were transferred to speech or writing. Having made up his mind what to say he just delivered himself over, as it were, to the absorbing interest or ruling passion of the moment. All his written work cannot be said to be of equal merit. Perhaps his best efforts are to be found in " African Nature Notes and Reminiscences," in which his command of English reaches a high level, yet in all circumstances, especially when narrating his own adventures in simple style such as in " A Hunter's Wanderings," or his escape from the Mushukulumbwe, he enjoyed " the happy privilege of making lovers among his readers." He possessed a certain quiet gift of humour, which he seldom indulged in except in such quaint instances as the remarks he makes on the vicious horse he gave to Lobengula in the hope that he would give it to one of his chiefs whom Selous particularly detested.

Pathos too, to the man who so frequently met with it was something too terrible for soul disintegration. He often told me he simply could not speak of the circumstances of poor French's death in the bush in 1879. It hurt him so much. But romance, tragedy, the beautiful, the picturesque, or the noble deeds of unpretentious men all fell into their natural places in his scheme of colour and formed a completed whole that was the outcome of perfect spontaneity and natural utterance. Thus he saw life in a vision as wide and untrammelled as the desolate plains he loved. He seemed to divine from his own experience how other men felt, and with the intensity of human sympathy knew how to encourage and console others in times of difficulty. To him no man was so poor that he was not ready to give him a " lift " on his waggon or through his purse. Sternness and tenderness were nearly matched in his conduct, the former for himself and the latter for the failings of others. In spite of his knowledge of the world he had no cynicism, his motto being to make things easier to those who were less fortunate than himself. He bore no grudge, nor did he feel sore at ingratitude, and might truly have said, " There is no man born with so little animosity as I."

In later years Selous often confessed to an enduring restlessness. There was always so much to be done and so little time to do it. Even when at home, where he was perfectly happy and always immersed in some form of brain work or outdoor activity, this restlessness never left him. He felt it ever in his blood, and it would act like some violent force—most violent when the turmoil and pettiness of human life or the futile presence of crowds jarred upon him. Life in cities was to him so infinitely inferior to the grandeur of nature and interest of the unknown. Having tasted of the best it is hard after a life spent amid romance and adventure to settle down comfortably amidst the tiny affairs and tittle-tattle of everyday things at home. He hated intensely lawyers, politicians, theorists and men who daily live in the public eye without knowing anything of the great world in its wide sense. This spirit of restlessness seems to have been ever present in his later life. He confessed that he found it difficult to stay in England for more than six months at a time. There was always some new country and the pursuit of some new animals which he wished to add to his unique collection. Africa seemed to draw him like a loadstone, as it had always done, and its never-ceasing call was ever sounding in his ears. Even when on service in 1916 he talked with William Judd in Nairobi of a trip he wished to make with him, after the war had ended, to the Amala to get a really good black-maned lion. Yet when he was on board ship he confessed that he was overcome with such home-sickness that he felt inclined to "throw himself overboard and swim ashore." It must be admitted that he suffered to some extent in his later days from a disease which for want of a better word we must call the Nostalgia of Travel—a disease which attacks many old

Big Game hunters—for often there comes a time when weariness of actual travelling creates depression, but in his subsequent letters from the actual hunting-grounds these adverse conditions disappear and he is once more keen and happy in the fascination of the chase and the clean conditions of a hunter's life. If we read carefully the classics in hunting and travel such as Baldwin, Neumann, Livingstone, etc., we constantly come across records of depression on the part of the writers. Were all the hardship, toil, dangers and the eternal difficulties of keeping an outfit in order and even temper good enough ? Was not all the money so hardly won to gain this trip not thrown away ? Would the elephants (it was generally elephants) or the rare horns ever be sighted ? Would the horses or oxen that were left be sufficient to carry the expedition through after the best had been killed or died of sickness ? And yet there was always an answer to these questions when the leaders were men of grit. Clouds pass away, men recover their spirits, and we find them writing, it may be a few weeks or even days afterwards, as if " all was lovely in the garden."

All his life he was a great reader, and rather preferred the old "classics" of English literature to modern books, except those on travel and big game hunting, of which he had an extensive library. He would read again and again and enjoy the works of Thackeray and Dickens, and amongst poets Byron was his favourite. Of modern writers no one appealed to him so much as Thomas Hardy, all of whose works found great favour, and especially "Tess of the D'Urbervilles," which he rightly esteemed as perhaps the greatest modern novel in the English language. Of writers on Big Game he esteemed highly Baldwin, Roosevelt, Charles Sheldon, Stewart Edward White, and Arthur Neumann. If he was bored in a crowd or had to wait at a railway station, he generally had a book in his pocket, and passed the hours happily in complete absorption of the author's descriptions. His tastes were wide, as we should expect, ranging from Tom Hood's humorous poems and such modern imaginative adventures as " Raffles " and " Stingaree " to Gibbon's " Decline and Fall of the Roman

Empire." He considered "Robbery under Arms" the most delightful modern romance, with a substratum of fact, he had ever read, but it always held second place to "Tess." He loved novels about imaginary people leading heroic lives, suffering, loving, hating, adventuring and fighting—all on some high level above the petty joys and sorrows of a work-a-day world.

Of his personal friends it is somewhat difficult to speak, as he knew so many in so many different lands. His circle of acquaintances was immense, though it was natural that his intimates should be men of similar tastes. In England we have a very excellent institution known as the "Shikari Club," an association of Big Game hunters founded by Captain C. E. Radclyffe, Captain P. B. Vanderbyl and Selous himself under the presidency of the Earl of Lonsdale. This club meets but once a year on the night of the Oaks, and members dine together at the Savoy Hotel. Here all matters relating to hunting throughout the world are discussed, plans are made for the future, and it is, as it were, a general meeting round the camp fire of brothers of the rifle. The camaraderie is excellent, and we all know and help each other with information as to future travels. Admission to its ranks is somewhat severe, for no man, unless he has proved himself to be a sportsman of the best type, is ever elected. Amongst these men, who have probably travelled and hunted more extensively than any other community in the world, Selous counted many close friends whose names are too numerous to mention, and from them he got the latest information for some projected trip just as he on his part helped many of them. Another club which at one time he constantly visited to hear discussions on the subject of birds was the British Ornithologists', a dining branch of the British Ornithologists' Union, where after dinner specimens of interest were exhibited, and discussions took place. Most of the principal members were his friends, as well as leading Zoologists in the Zoological Society and the British Museum (Natural History), whom it was always his pleasure to serve and help with new specimens. In later years nearly all his old South African friends were dead or had retired, so he saw little of them, but in England, after his return from South Africa, he made many new friends whose homes he constantly visited. From 1896 till the time of his death he often stayed with Lord Egerton of Tatton, whose son, the Hon. Maurice Egerton, whom he had first met in Alaska, was a great friend of his ; with Abel Chapman, with whom he had been at school at Rugby, and who had many kindred tastes ; with Heatley Noble, to whom he was much attached ; with Sir Philip Brocklehurst and his family, for whom he entertained a warm affection ; and with Mr. MacMillan, in Devonshire. These are only a few of the friends who were in intimate sympathy with him, and to whom he constantly wrote accounts of his more recent travels. I met him first in 1897, and from then until his death he wrote to me constantly, and never did either of us go on an expedition without his coming to see me or my going to Worplesdon to discuss the matter in the smallest detail. In those twenty years we both hunted or wandered in other lands every year, and I cannot adequately express what his warm friendship and help was to me, for when Selous opened his soul to anyone he did it with a whole-heartedness and an abandonment of all reserve that are rare in these days. In our lives there come only a few fellow-creatures to whom we can say anything that comes into our minds without being misinterpreted. Even in absence we think about them as they about us, and we know how they will rejoice at our successes and sympathize with our failures, because they know and understand. When such a man as Selous passes away, and we have enjoyed that intimacy, the world indeed seems desolate, even though we have the poor consolation that what has been was very good.

In his own home Selous was hospitality itself, and loved to entertain visitors from all parts of the world who came to see him or his museum. Complete strangers were received with the same courtesy as intimate friends, and Selous would spend hours showing his trophies to anyone who exhibited the smallest interest in the subject. Officers from Aldershot or Naval men were always welcome, and I

THEY CANNOT BREAK HIS SLEEP.

should think that a large portion of the British Army and Navy had at one time or another enjoyed the pleasure of seeing his trophies under his personal supervision, and it was this abandonment of self and personal interest in his fellow-creatures that made him so popular.

One day I found him in fits of laughter over one of his visitors. A telegram had been received in the morning stating that Lewanika, chief of the Barotsi, whom he had known in old days, would visit him. His dusky majesty, attended by a cicerone, arrived in a very perturbed state of mind. It appeared that in the morning he had been received by His Majesty the King at Buckingham Palace, and when he left he was under the impression that he had not behaved properly in the royal presence. These fears were confirmed when the train which bore the party to Worplesdon entered the long tunnel just before reaching Guildford. The absence of lights, and the darkness of the surroundings, seemed to have been the climax, for the dusky monarch dived under the seat of the carriage, and was with difficulty removed when the train reached Guildford. Never before having experienced such a horrible thing as a tunnel, Lewanika considered that the English King was taking this new method to destroy him.[1]

As a man of such breadth of mind his friendships were cosmopolitan rather than insular. He had many friends in Austria, such as the three Counts Hoyos; in America, such as President Roosevelt, Charles Sheldon, and the members of the Boone and Crockett Club; in Asia Minor and Transylvania, such as Sir William Whittall and Consul Danford; whilst in South Africa he knew everyone in all grades of politics or outdoor life. To enumerate the men he knew well would fill a volume.

One of Fred's missionary friends in the pioneer days was the Rev. Isaac Shimmin, a type of those hard-working, unassuming men who go out into the wilderness to do good to

---

[1] Tunnels seem to have some terrifying effect on the mind of the black man. I travelled to Africa in 1913 with the King of Uganda and used to play at draughts with him nearly every day. He expressed great pleasure at his recent visit to England and the hospitality he had received there, but said he could not forget the horror of the tunnels on the railways.

2 B

others. He is kind enough to send me a few lines denoting Selous' attitude towards the spread of religion in the new country and his broad-minded tolerance of various creeds.

" It is now nearly thirty years since I first met my old friend, Fred Selous. At that time I was living at Klerksdorp, in the Transvaal, and among my friends were some who in former years had lived in the interior ; such as Mr. Thomas Leask, Mr. Alec Brown, and several others. I was therefore in the right atmosphere for hearing thrilling stories of African adventure, in which men like Hartley the hunter and Westbeech the trader had played a prominent part. For this little town had for years been the refitting station for men from the north, and because of this we always seemed in close touch with the regions beyond. One day I met Mr. H. C. Collison, and soon after I heard Mr. G. A. Phillips (' Elephant Phil ') describe realistically an encounter with a lion. But there was one name around which a halo of peculiar distinction had already gathered, for I noticed that when these men spoke of Selous it was always with a note of personal affection ; they not only admired him as a successful hunter, but they evidently loved him as a well-tried friend. And when I actually met him I soon recognized the charm of his simple and winning personality. The friendship which was then begun quickly ripened into an intimacy which lasted until the day of his death. I was only a young Wesleyan minister, and he was the famous hunter, and yet we had many things in common, and what attracted me most was his unaffected manner and genuine honesty of thought and conduct. How well I remember his first visit to my little parsonage, his stories of travel and adventure told with such quiet and characteristic modesty, and our long talk on Spiritualism and kindred subjects. He was one of the best conversationalists I have ever met, he could listen as well as speak, he had kept up his reading all through his wanderings, and his lonely life in the African veldt had given him many opportunities for keen and original reflection.

" About the date to which I refer he was making preparations for leading the pioneers of the Chartered Company into Mashunaland, and he kindly invited me to accompany him, offering me the use of one of his own waggons. To my great regret I had to decline, but the following year (1891) I was appointed to represent the Wesleyan Church in the new Colony, and by the end of September I found myself established in the small town of Salisbury. One of the first to give me a welcome was Fred Selous, who was then employed by the Government in making roads and helping to open out and settle the country.

"It is impossible in these few lines to say very much about my friend, but by giving two or three simple incidents I may help the reader to see Selous as I saw him. His hatred of boasting and exaggeration was very marked. One day he called on me in Salisbury and asked me to go to his house, as he had something to show me. He had just returned from Hartley Hills, and whilst there had shot his largest lion. How modestly he told the story, and with what interest I looked upon the skin of the huge beast (now mounted at Worplesdon). His humility was always as conspicuous as his bravery. Nor would he condone any false pretensions in others. He was once having breakfast in my waggon, and a gentleman who was outspanned near by asked me to introduce him to the great hunter. I did so, and immediately Selous began to ask him about certain incidents in a book he had published some time before. The replies, I could see, were not satisfactory and the subject was dropped. What amused me later was the surprise of the visitor that such a quiet and unassuming man should be the famous personage whose name was revered by every man who carried a gun. But such a person could not possibly understand Selous, who, neither in speech nor in print, would ever make a statement which he could not verify. His veracity was unimpeachable, and his ' Hunter's Wanderings ' was the favourite text-book of every amateur. His word could be taken for every trivial detail ; as I once heard an old hunter remark, ' Whatever Fred Selous says is absolutely true.' This was not a cheap testimony in a country where the imagination so often colours the records of personal adventure.

" He was never afraid to express his opinions, however unpopular they might be at the time. We were both in Bulawayo when word came from the south that Dr. Jameson had invaded the Transvaal with a few hundred men. An open-air meeting was held in the town, and Selous was one of the speakers. There was great excitement and we hardly knew what to believe. In the afternoon I rode out with him to his farm (Essexvale), about twenty miles from Bulawayo, and spent a few pleasant days in his home, but I remember how strongly he expressed his doubts as to the genuineness of the message of distress from Johannesburg. When I got back to town I heard of the capture of Jameson by Cronje, and later events proved that the doubts of my friend were amply justified.

" Selous was thought by some to have been rather critical as regards the work of the missionaries, but from various conversations I had with him I am convinced that his criticsms applied only to those whose methods were more idealistic than practical. Among his warmest friends were those devoted men who had toiled for years in Matabeleland, and who had succeeded in raising the physical and moral status of the natives. That he was always in sympathy with all good work was evident. Soon after going to Salisbury I was engaged in building a small church and the other denominations were also doing their best for the new community, all of us working together in the most friendly spirit. One day Selous said to me, with a touch of hesitation, ' By the way, Shimmin, I wish you would do me a favour. Would you give this small donation to Canon Balfour, of the Church of England, and this to Major Pascoe, of the Salvation Army, and keep the other for your own building-fund. You are all doing good work, and I want to help you.' And he handed me three five-pound notes. It was a good proof of his broad and liberal outlook and of his recognition of the practical benefits of the Christian Church.

" This sketch is necessarily very brief and imperfect, and, as I write, my memory brings before me many scenes which are associated with my old friend. I think of the fashionable crowd in the Imperial Institute, with the Duke of Fife in the chair, and Selous giving a lecture in his own inimitable style. I was very proud of him, but that evening, as I sat with Mrs. Selous and Miss Rhodes, I somehow felt that the speaker was closer to me than to any of that admiring audience, for he and I had been together in the African wilds.

" And now he sleeps in the land he loved so well. At an age when most men would seek retirement and rest, he went forth to fight for justice and righteousness, and in that cause he made the supreme sacrifice of his life. Fred Selous was one of God's true and valiant gentlemen.

' One who never turned his back but marched breast forward,
  Never doubted clouds would break,
Never dreamed, though right were worsted, wrong would triumph,
Held we fall to rise, are baffled to fight better,
  Sleep to wake.'

" He lived the simple creed of sincerity and trust. Fearless for the right and dauntless in the face of danger, he won the hearts of men, and by the influence of his strong and genuine character he gave to us all a higher and purer conception of the inherent nobility of our common humanity.

" ISAAC SHIMMIN."

Colonel Roosevelt, who knew Selous well and understood his character, kindly sends me the following note :—

" There was never a more welcome guest at the White House than Selous. He spent several days there. One afternoon we went walking and rock climbing alongside the Potomac ; I think we swam the Potomac, but I am not sure. Another afternoon we rode, going over some of the jumps in Rock Creek Park, as well as those rail-fences that we were sure were not wired, in striking across country.

" What made Selous so charming a companion was his entire naturalness and lack of self-consciousness. There are persons who pride themselves on a kind of ingrowing modesty which forbids them to speak of anything they have themselves done, or else causes them to speak of it in such a bald fashion that they might as well keep silent. This really represents extreme self-consciousness, and it is only one degree less obnoxious than the self-consciousness which shows itself in boasting and bragging. Yet, rather curiously, the exhibition of this particular kind of morbid self-consciousness is a source of intense pride to many otherwise intelligent persons.

" Selous was as free from this vice as from its opposite. He never boasted. He was transparently truthful. But it never occurred to him not to tell of his experiences, and he related them very simply but very vividly, and with the attention to minute details which marks the born observer and narrator. When my children were little I had now and then read to them aloud some of the more exciting extracts from Selous' hunting adventures. At the time that he visited me at the White House they were older, and I got him to tell them two or three of the adventures himself. He made us actually see everything that had happened. He not only spoke simply and naturally, but he acted the part, first of himself, and then of the game, until the whole scene was vivid before our eyes. He would stand and bend forward, and then he would instantly identify himself with the lion or buffalo or elephant, and show what it did in its turn.

" It was on this visit that he promised me that he would write out some of his observations on the life histories of African big game. I felt that it would be a real misfortune if this record were not preserved in permanent form ; for Selous had the eye of a faunal naturalist of the highest type.

" But our conversation was far from being confined to natural history and hunting. His reading had been done rather late in life, and only along certain lines, but he had the same unerring eye in history and literature that he had in the hunting-field. Naturally he liked what was simple and straightforward, and the old Scotch and English ballads appealed very strongly to him. His people had originally come from that last fragment of the old-time Norman Duchy, the Channel Islands ; and he was keenly interested in the extraordinary deeds of the Normans.

" It was through Selous and Edward North Buxton that

I made my arrangements for my African hunting-trip. Much to my delight, Selous went on the ship with us from Naples to Mombasa. He was, of course, a delightful travelling companion. He was very much interested in the way in which the naturalists who were with me did their collecting, being much impressed by the scientific efficiency they showed. Whenever possible I would get him talking about some of his past experiences ; and then gradually other acquaintances would stroll up and sit in an absorbed circle, while he not only told but acted the story, his keen, simple, fearless blue eyes looking up at us from time to time, while his hands moved with a vivacity we are accustomed to think of as French rather than English.

" After landing in Africa I saw him but once or twice. Of course my hunting was that of a tyro compared to his, and he took a kind of elder brother's interest in what I did and in my unimportant successes.

" Later I spent a night with him at his house in Surrey, going through his museum of hunting-trophies. What interested me almost as much was being shown the various birds' nests in his garden. He also went to the British Museum with me to look into various matters, including the question of protective coloration. I greatly valued his friendship ; I mourn his loss ; and yet I feel that in death as in life he was to be envied.

" It is well for any country to produce men of such a type ; and if there are enough of them the nation need fear no decadence. He led a singularly adventurous and fascinating life, with just the right alternations between the wilderness and civilization. He helped spread the borders of his people's land. He added much to the sum of human knowledge and interest. He closed his life exactly as such a life ought to be closed, by dying in battle for his country while rendering her valiant and effective service. Who could wish a better life or a better death, or desire to leave a more honourable heritage to his family and his nation ?

" THEODORE ROOSEVELT."

The best work that Selous did and the qualities for which the British Nation should be grateful to him are those which he displayed as a Pioneer. Where Selous went any Englishman could follow and hold up his head. Selous set up a standard of conduct which people of our own, as well as those of other nations, might be proud to follow. He, as it were, stamped his personality on the wilderness, where life is hard and man easily loses his grip. He never shot a native except purely in self-defence, and established a reputation for square dealing and indomitable courage that made the pathway easy for all those who came after. He never made a sixpence for himself when gains, if he had been the least unscrupulous, would have been easy, but set up wherever he went a certain ideal, especially in dealing with natives, that made the road of colonization easy for tens of thousands. After all, in the life of any man it is character and example that count, and if Selous did nothing else, and had, in fact, never killed a single wild animal in his life, his name would still be one to conjure with in South Africa or wherever he wandered.

> " Summers shall be forgotten with the rose,
> Yea, winters fall from memory like quenchéd fire,
> Loves shall depart unseen, and the voice of desire
> Be hushed and stilled in the garden close,
> Yet you they shall remember in the land."

INDEX

Printed in Great Britain by
Amazon.co.uk, Ltd.,
Marston Gate.